PARIS ACCESS

Orientation

At first glance, Paris' broad expanse looks like one great tangle of medieval streets. Don't be dismayed, however, for there's logic in the layout that, once grasped, makes Paris as easy to navigate as your average college campus. Tall buildings are forbidden (the **Montparnasse Tower** was a temporary aesthetic lapse on the part of former president **Georges Pompidou**), and the reference points provided by the major monuments (**Eiffel Tower, Panthéon, Arc de Triomphe**, etc.) and the Seine river make locating yourself and your destination reassuringly easy. Part of the logic is that the city is subdivided into 20 numbered *arrondissements* (quarters). Starting from the first arrondissement (the area around the **Louvre**), they spiral outward like the compartments of a snail's shell to the city limits.

Since each arrondissement has its own distinct class and character, Paris feels less like a monstrous metropolis than a score of small towns. The itineraries presented in this book offer you a diverse array of Parisian neighborhoods to explore. As you take in the sights, the distinct flavor of each district will reveal itself. The system of axes that cuts through the city, connecting landmarks and generally giving the city shape, is also a splendid means of orientation. The most obvious axis runs in a straight line from **La Défense** in the west, eastward through the Arc de Triomphe, down the **Champs-Elysées** to the Louvre, continuing all the way to the **Bastille.**

On roads perpendicular to the Seine, the street addresses begin at the river and increase as you move inland. With your back to the Seine (on either bank), the even numbers will be on the right, the odds on the left. Streets running parallel to the Seine are numbered from east to west, the direction the river flows. If the street is on an island, with the Seine all around, a No. 1 address is to the south, closest to Rome. Be aware that even and odd street addresses often don't correspond; No. 42 may be across the street from No. 85, not No. 43 as you might expect.

While this overall understanding of Paris is helpful, it won't change the fact that the streets are labyrinthine. The basic—and essential—tool for threading your way through this maze is the *Paris par Arrondissement,* a pocket-size book of maps sold at newsstands and bookstores throughout Paris and at some specialty travel bookstores in the United States. It contains a map of each arrondissement, as well as métro and bus-route maps. Every thoroughfare in the city, from Rue de l'Abbaye to the Boulevard de la Zone, is listed alphabetically in the front of the book, with its arrondissement, letter/number map coordinates, and the nearest métro station. Be sure to check carefully whether the street you need is designated *rue* (street), *boulevard,* or *avenue.*

Notre-Dame

Getting to Paris
Airports

There are two main airports in Paris: **Roissy-Charles de Gaulle** (16 miles or 25.75 kilometers to the north) and **Orly** (about the same distance to the south). They can be reached from the center of the city by bus or taxi in about 45 minutes, barring any major traffic snarls. Trains and the métro also provide 45-minute service, except during peak commute hours when there may be significant delays. Play it safe by allowing about an hour and a half to reach your destination. The buses and trains leave approximately every 15 minutes.

From **Roissy-Charles de Gaulle Airport,** a shuttle bus will take you to the **RER** (Réseau Express Régional) train, which runs south through the **Gare du Nord** and the **Luxembourg** métro stations. There is also a bus that takes passengers to the **Porte Maillot** (on the métro line **Pont-de-Neuilly/ Château-de-Vincennes**).

From **Orly Airport,** the **Orly Rail** will take you to the **Gare d'Orsay, Gare St.-Michel,** and **Gare d'Austerlitz** stations. The bus from Orly will take you to the **Invalides Air Terminal** located in the center of Paris. From there, you can take the métro or bus to your destination.

Roissy-Charles de Gaulle Airport **48.62.12.12**
Airlines
Air France .... 800/237.2747 (US); 44.08.24.24 (Paris)

Lufthansa ... 800/645.3880; 42.65.37.35, 48.62.59.60

Northwest ... 800/225.2525; 42.66.90.00, 48.62.97.13

TWA 800/221.2000; 40.69.70.00, 49.19.20.00

United 800/241.6522; 48.97.82.82, 48.62.96.50

General Information
Airport Information 48.62.22.80, 48.62.12.12

Airport Security 48.62.31.22

Customs and Immigration 48.62.35.35

Damaged Baggage 48.62.52.89

Lost and Found 48.62.20.85

Medical Emergencies 48.62.28.00, 48.62.53.32

Parking 49.75.56.50

Rental Cars
Avis 48.62.34.34, 48.62.59.59

Eurorent 48.62.40.77, 48.62.57.66

Hertz 48.62.58.58, 48.62.29.00

Orly Airport **49.75.52.52**
Airlines
American 800/433.7300; 42.89.05.22

Continental 800/525.0280; 49.75.10.86

Delta 800/221.1212; 49.75.52.05

US Air 800/428.4322; 49.75.40.31

General Information
Airport Information 49.75.52.52

Airport Security 49.75.43.04

Customs 49.75.78.60

Lost and Found 49.75.34.10, 49.75.42.34

Parking 49.75.56.50

Rental Cars
Avis 49.75.44.92, 49.75.44.97

Budget 49.75.56.00, 49.75.56.05

Eurorent 49.75.47.48, 49.75.47.45

Getting around Paris
Autos

If you have a suicide wish, hire a car and drive around the Arc de Triomphe a few times. But be forewarned: the most civilized Parisian becomes a homicidal maniac on the road—stoplights are ignored and one-way streets simply imply a challenge. Any vehicle entering from the right has the right of way. And if you think driving is tough, wait until you try to park the car (your best bet is to find an underground parking lot). *Bonne chance.*

Bicycles

Two wheels can be more fun—not to mention more hazardous—than four. The energetic and adventurous can rent bicycles from **Paris Vélo** (2 Rue du Fer-à-Moulin, 43.37.59.22) or **La Maison du Vélo** (8 Rue de Belzunce, 42.81.24.72).

If you're planning day trips outside Paris, however, you may want to wait until you get to Chantilly, Fontainebleau, Versailles, or other destinations and rent a bike for the day at the local train station. You can rent a bike from the RER stations in Noisiel-le-Luzard, Vincennes, St.-Germain-en-Laye, Courcelle Vallée de Chevreuse, or Vallée de la Marne. Paris is surrounded with beautiful, flat countryside that's perfect for bicycling. During the summer, cycling trips outside Paris are sponsored by the **Bicy-Club de France** (8 Place-Porte-de-Champerret, 47.66.55.92). For general cycling information, contact the **Fédération Française de Cyclotourisme** (8 Rue Jean-Marie-Jégo, 44.16.48.48).

Boat Tours

On a late summer afternoon, nothing surpasses an hour touring the Seine river in a *bateau mouche* (a small passenger steamer), especially if you take along some creamy goat cheese, a fresh baguette, and a bottle of cool St.-Joseph. Take a seat at the rear of the boat out of range of the irritating tape-recorded commentary, then put your feet up and watch the sun set over the City of Light. Or try a more luxurious option—booking one of the expensive candlelit dinner cruises. Rides lasting between one and three hours (the lunch and illuminated dinner cruises) are available from **Bateaux Mouches** (Embarcadère du Pont de l'Alma, Rive Droite, 42.25.96.10); **Bateaux Parisiens** (Port de La Bourdonnais, 44.11.33.44); and **Vedettes du Pont-Neuf** (Square du Vert-Galant, 46.33.98.38).

Buses

Riding the métro may be the quickest and easiest way to get around town, but buses are a far more pleasant means of transportation in Paris. The tourist office on the Champs-Elysées has selected more than a dozen get-acquainted bus routes for tourists, and it provides maps and trilingual commentary on the sights along the way. The **No. 24** bus, for example, makes a marvelous circuit of Paris. It crosses the Seine four times and passes Place de la Concorde, the National Assembly, the Louvre, Pont-Neuf, Notre-Dame, Ile St.-Louis, Place St.-Michel, goes down Boulevard St.-Germain, then turns back past the Jardin des Plantes and the Musée d'Orsay—all for just a few francs. The **No. 30, 48, 82,** and **95** routes are equally enjoyable.

Maps of the bus system are usually pasted on the walls of bus shelters. When planning a sight-seeing excursion, remember that bus service is limited in the evenings and on Sundays. Bus tickets may be purchased from all métro stations, or you may buy a single ticket on the bus. You must punch in your ticket in the machine beside the driver when you board. Bus rides of more than four or five stops may cost extra unless you have a pass. (For discount ticket information, see "Métro" below.)

If observing the city through the windows of a climate-controlled, double-deck tour bus is your idea of an ultimate sight-seeing experience, climb aboard one of the coaches at **Cityrama** (4 Place des Pyramides, 44.55.61.00) or **Paris Vision** (214 Rue de Rivoli, 42.60.31.25). They both offer tours (in several languages) past all the main attractions, as well as separate tours to **Versailles, Malmaison, Chantilly, Chartres, Fontainebleau, Mont St.-Michel,** the **Loire Valley,** and **Barbizon.** Night tours journey to the **Moulin Rouge, Lido,** and **Folies Bergère.**

Car Rental Agencies

If you dare to drive, the main car rental agencies are: **Avis** (5 Rue Bixio, 45.50.32.31, or 60 Rue de Ponthieu, 43.59.03.83); **Hertz** (92 Rue St.-Lazare, 42.80.35.45, or Air France Terminal at Invalides, 45.51.20.37); and **Europcar** (48 Rue de Berri, 45.63.04.27). Europcar offers a nonresident discount, but you must make your reservations 24 hours before arriving in France, and there is a minimum rental period of three days and a maximum of 99 days. Be sure to take out car insurance if you aren't covered by your own auto insurance agency.

Maps

For navigating the city's streets, Parisians carry a map of the métro in their heads and a *Paris par Arrondissement* guide in their pockets. Sold at most newsstands and bookshops, this little book lists every street in Paris, with indexed references to maps of each of the city's 20 arrondissements. Don't leave home without it.

Métro

It's one of the oldest—and best—subway systems in Europe. The first line, designed by engineer Fulgence Bienvenue, opened on 19 July 1900 between Maillot and Vincennes. In the early 1900s the station

entrances were covered with exotic Art Nouveau masterpieces designed by Hector Guimard. These days, the motif of the system is the aqua- and brown-striped ticket of the **RATP** (Réseau Autonome du Transport Parisien).

Nearly 120 miles of rail snake beneath the streets of Paris, connecting about 300 stations. Aboveground, you're never too far away from a métro stop, and for the cost of a single ticket you can ride all day anywhere within the system, which operates from 5AM to about 12:45AM (each train pulls into its final destination at 1:15AM). Hang onto your ticket: occasionally a *contrôleur* in a blue uniform boards the train to check tickets.

Getting lost in Paris takes some effort. Métro maps are everywhere—inside and outside the stations. And the métro lines are named for the stations at which they end. Simply follow the signs for the terminus in the direction you are headed. If, for example, you want to go from the Louvre to Concorde, take the line marked *Direction Neuilly*. To transfer from one line to another, look for an orange-and-white *correspondence* sign on the station platform. Each station has a map of the neighborhood surrounding it, so you can get your bearings before you emerge aboveground.

When purchasing tickets, it's cheaper to buy a *carnet* (a book of tickets) of 10, which cuts the price of a single ticket in half. Also available are tourist passes, which are valid for both the métro and the bus. A *Formule 1* pass is valid for one day, a *Le Paris Visite* pass is good for two, three, or five days, and a *carte orange* offers a month of travel privileges and requires a photograph.

Slip the magnetized ticket into the slot by the turnstile, retrieve it when it pops up, and pass through. Remember that when getting on and off the métro you must open the car door yourself; it closes automatically behind you.

A métro ticket also allows you to use the RER rail system (an express métro) within Paris, but study its route before you board because it is primarily for the suburbs, and the stops within the city are few and far between. Always hang onto your tickets; you may need them to get in and out of the station.

Taxis

Most of the time, the city's 15,000 taxis are clustered at *tête de stations* (taxi stations)—except, of course, when you really need one. While it may be more convenient to just hail a cab, it is not an acceptable practice in Paris, and the taxis will not stop in the middle of the street to accept passengers. Your best bet is to locate a *tête de station* and wait for the next taxi with its roof light on bright (a dim light means the cab is occupied). Even then drivers may not pick you up, because if you're not going in their direction, *tant pis* (tough luck). Bluff some understanding of the city and tell drivers the main street or métro station closest to your destination; given that guidance, they are less likely to take you out of your way. Taxis aren't usually expensive, but the rates increase at night (between 10PM and 6:30AM), on Sundays, and if you're picked up at a train station, hotel, or outside the city. If you need to be somewhere at a specific time (including the airport), phone ahead for a cab; the meter starts running the moment the cabdriver receives the call, but the dispatcher will tell you how long it will take for a cab to arrive (it's usually less than ten minutes). Tip the driver 10 to 15 percent. For a taxi, call 49.36.10.10; 47.46.11.11; 47.39.47.39; or 49.00.05.55.

Trains

In Paris you can't simply jump into a taxi and cry *"A la gare!"* (To the station!). It may be a dramatic gesture, but it would be incomplete. Paris has six train stations, each one serving different regions of France. The destinations available at the stations are as follows: **Gare d'Austerlitz** for southwest France, Spain, and Portugal; **Gare de l'Est** for eastern France, Luxembourg, Switzerland, southern Germany, Austria, and Hungary; **Gare de Lyon** for south and southeastern France, Switzerland, Italy, and Greece; **Gare Montparnasse** for western France (including Versailles), Chartres, and Brittany; **Gare du Nord** for northern France, Belgium, the Netherlands, Scandinavia, the former Soviet Union, northern Germany, and Britain; and **Gare St.-Lazare** for northwestern France, Normandy, and Le Havre, a port city where ships depart for Britain and the Americas. Within each station, there are two types of trains: *banlieue*, for riding to the suburbs, and *grandes lignes* for long distances. Before boarding either train, you must punch *(compostez)* your ticket in one of the orange machines in the station or else the conductor might charge you the price of another ticket. For general train information for all stations, call 45.82.50.50.

Walking in Paris

Whether promenading along the broad boulevards or threading through intimate medieval neighborhoods, the best way to discover Paris and its environs is on your own two feet. As you will learn on the itineraries outlined in this book, strolling yields the joy of discovering the little things—the grace notes, embellishments, and architectural details that define the feel and texture of Paris. But walking can be a somewhat perilous proposition: on the street you're fair game for distracted drivers, and on the sidewalk you're likely to tread on what dogs have left behind (every third Parisian owns a dog, and someone in city hall has calculated that the average pedestrian sets foot in canine droppings every 286th step. As a result, ever-vigilant squads of sanitation workers on motorcycles sweep and vacuum the sidewalks of Paris constantly).

FYI

Banks

Banks are generally open from 9AM to 4:30PM, but they close at midday the day before a holiday. They will display a sign reading CHANGE if they exchange foreign currency. For the best exchange rates, try **American Express** (11 Rue Scribe), which is open on Saturday. If you're stuck with a fistful of dollars and the banks are closed, you can also change money at these train stations: **Gare d'Austerlitz** (until 5PM), **Gare de l'Est** (until 7PM), **Gare St.-Lazare** (until 8PM), and **Gare de Lyon** (until 11PM).

Cafés

As noble a French institution as the Académie Française, cafés serve light meals and a variety of beverages throughout the day. Try a *crème* (strong coffee with hot, frothy milk) in the morning, and in the afternoon you might switch to *vin rouge, un demi* (a 25-centiliter draft beer), or a *citron pressé* (fresh lemonade). Drinks are cheaper at the *zinc* (bar), and coffee is more expensive after 10PM, but by then you'll probably have moved on to cognac, Armagnac, brandy, or perhaps *eau de vie.*

Cinema

Parisians are film fanatics. Each week more than 300 films are shown in the city and are all listed along with their show times in the weekly publications *Pariscope* and *L'Officiel des Spectacles.*

The *v.o. (version originale)* after a film title means it's in its original language, with French subtitles, while *v.f. (version française)* means it's dubbed in French. If you arrive in time for the *séance* (cinema previews), you'll see the ads, which are sometimes risqué, usually silly, and often themselves worth the price of admission. Once in the movie theater, be prepared to surrender a franc to the usher, who may do no more than tear your ticket and gesture toward an empty seat. If you resent this practice, go to the movies on Monday, when ticket prices are uniformly reduced by 30 percent.

Climate

Chances are that fabled Paris in the springtime will be soggy. The city logs more rainy days a year than London, so equip yourself with an umbrella or trench coat. Winters are cold and damp, and summers can be as cool and dry as the martinis at the Ritz bar. The average temperature ranges from 38°F in January to 75°F in July. May and September are the best times for finding decent weather and fewer tourists. August, when many Parisians leave the city, can be quite hot.

Embassies and Consulates

American Embassy
2 Avenue Gabriel 42.96.12.02

American Consulate
2 Rue St.-Florentine 42.96.14.88

British Embassy
35 Rue du Faubourg St.-Honoré 42.66.91.42

British Consulate
9 Avenue Hoche 42.66.38.10

Canadian Embassy/Consulate
35 Avenue Montaigne 44.43.32.00

Emergencies

For round-the-clock medical house calls, call **SOS Médecins,** 43.37.77.77. The **American Hospital** is just outside Paris (63 Ave Victor-Hugo, Neuilly-sur-Seine, 46.41.25.25), and most of the physicians speak English.

Entertainment

"Everything that exists elsewhere exists in Paris," said Victor Hugo in *Les Misérables*. So it goes for the array of entertainment options available—as a spectator or a participant. For a daily recording (in English) of exhibitions and concerts, call 49.52.53.56.

There are two kiosks that sell half-price tickets to about 120 events in Paris, including plays, concerts, ballets, and operas on the day of the performance. One is in the **Châtelet-Les Halles** métro station and the other is at the **Place de la Madeleine.**

Hotels

Hotel reservations are essential in Paris not only in the summer months but also during the heavy convention and trade-show months of March and October. A free brochure from the tourist office charting room availability throughout the year is available through the Office du Tourisme de Paris, 127 Avenue des Champs-Elysées, 75008 Paris; 49.52.53.54.

Museums

Most Parisian museums tend to stay open late one night a week and are open on Sunday, but many are *fermé* (closed) on Tuesday. If you're planning on some serious museum-hopping, buy a *carte* pass, which gains you reduced admission to more than 65 Parisian museums and monuments. You can buy a pass that's valid for one, three, or five days. They are sold in major métro stations and at most of the participating attractions.

Pharmacies

In Paris, all pharmacies are marked by a neon green cross on the front of the building. When the cross is lit, it means the pharmacy is open for business. Although many pharmacists speak English, at the following places you will be certain to get English prescriptions translated and filled with equivalent medicines: **British and American Pharmacy** (1 Rue Auber, 47.42.49.40); **Pharmacie Anglaise** (62 Ave des Champs-Elysées, 43.59.22.52); and **Pharmacie Swann** (6 Rue de Castiglione, 42.60.72.96).

Phone Book

Ambulance 71

Burn Center 42.34.17.58

Fire Department 18

Poison Center 40.37.04.04

Police Department 17

Speaking Clock 36.99

Tourist Information 47.23.61.72

Weather 36.68.00.00

Post Offices

Post offices are marked **PTT** and are open from 8AM to 7PM on weekdays and 8AM to noon on Saturdays. The main post office at 52 Rue du Louvre

is open 24 hours a day. If you want to buy stamps, make sure you're in the correct line and not wasting your time queuing up at the window where Parisians pay their gas and telephone bills. Stamps are also sold at *tabacs* (tobacco shops), hotels, and some newsstands.

Publications

The International Herald Tribune (a felicitous child of the *Washington Post* and *The New York Times*) will keep you abreast of world events and Parisian happenings. It appears at newsstands every morning except Sunday. The French dailies in Paris are *Le Monde, Le Figaro,* and *Libération.*

For weekly listings of exhibitions, movies, concerts, plays, discos, and restaurants, pick up a copy of *Pariscope* or *L'Officiel des Spectacles,* which both come out on Wednesday. They are on sale for a few francs at newsstands, and although they're written in French, they are not impossible to decipher if you do not speak the language.

Radio Stations

The only English-language radio station in Paris is the European News Service (ENS), a cable station that broadcasts into 30 major hotels. If you have a very strong receiver, however, you may be able to pick up the BBC or even Voice of America.

Restaurants

To dine at a particularly popular restaurant such as Taillevent or Lucas-Carton, you might have to book reservations months in advance, but in most cases advance notice of one week, or even a day or two, should suffice. In many restaurants you can order à la carte or choose a less expensive fixed-priced menu, which often includes the day's special. The fancier restaurants usually offer a *dégustation* (sampler) of the chef's specialities. If the wine list puzzles you, ask the waiter or the sommelier for advice; and remember, the quality of the wine does not necessarily increase with the price. Cleverly, a 15-percent service charge is almost always included in the bill, so, even if you are served shoddily, the server gets a tip. Therefore, in Paris and throughout France, a supplementary tip is not necessary, though you may leave an additional five percent for *service extraordinaire.*

Shopping

When the going gets tough, the tough go shopping in Paris. Perhaps no other city in the world enjoys such a reputation as a shoppers' mecca. Haute couture, jewelry, perfume, and gourmet delights are all here. The smaller shops are likely to be closed Monday and don't open their doors the rest of the week until 10AM. Most stay open until 6:30PM. While August is still the *fermeture annuelle,* when many Parisians flee the city on holiday and leave countless shops and restaurants closed in their wake, more and more stores and restaurants are staying open. Also, annual closing times may vary from one year to the next.

For those indefatigable shoppers interested in tours, bilingual guides offer four shopping tours (each about four hours long) weekday afternoons and

Saturday mornings. Stroll the Left Bank or the Marais, peruse the flea markets, or go whole hog with the VIP Tour—a private tour in a chauffeur-driven limousine for you and a few of your closest friends. For more information, contact **Chic Promenade** at 7 Rue Le Châtelier, 43.80.35.35.

Street Smarts

Pickpockets flock to tourists like fruitflies to bananas, and the busy métro lines, such as Grande Arche de La Défense to Château-de-Vincennes, are their natural habitat. In crowds, watch your money pouch, keep the clasp of your purse against your body, and don't put your wallet in your back pocket, especially if it bulges. Beware of bands of children—sometimes they possess a sleight of hand Fagin would have envied. Don't wear the right jewelry in the wrong places (like on the métro or at Montmartre), don't leave possessions unattended, and if you see trouble coming, try to avoid it.

Telephones

Phone booths adorn half the street corners in Paris, but it's a minor miracle to find one that works. Most operate only with *télécartes,* special phone cards, which are sold at post offices and *tabacs.* For phones in cafés, you may have to purchase a *jeton* (phone token) at the bar. Save your international calls for the post office or your hotel. For calls outside Paris, dial 16 for the provinces, 19-1 for the United States and Canada, and 19-44 for the United Kingdom. For fast access to an English-speaking AT&T operator, dial 19-00-11. From a public phone no coins or *télécartes* are required.

Toilets

You can usually walk into any café and use the toilet, though in some cases you must tip the *gardienne* (keeper) a couple of francs. Such a facility may be a hole or a throne, with or without toilet paper. Your alternative is using the beige automatic toilets in the streets. For a couple of francs, these clever contraptions automatically let you in and out and disinfect themselves between visits. Warning: don't let young children into the automatic toilets alone; they may not be strong enough to push open the doors to get out.

VAT Refunds

Included in the purchase price of many items is a VAT (value-added tax) that may be around 20 percent of the price. To reclaim it, ask for the VAT refund forms when you make your purchase and be prepared to produce the item and the forms at the airport *détaxe* (refund) desk.

Visas/Passports

In 1989 France and the United States reached a bilateral accord removing tourist visa requirements between the two countries. Passports are always required when traveling abroad.

How To Read This Guide

PARIS ACCESS® is arranged by neighborhood so you can see at a glance where you are and what is around you. The numbers next to the entries in the following chapters correspond to the numbers on the maps. The text is color-coded according to the kind of place described:

Restaurants/Clubs: Red   Hotels: Blue

Shops/ 🌳 Outdoors: Green   **Sights/Culture:** Black

Rating the Restaurants and Hotels

The restaurant star ratings take into account the quality, service, atmosphere, and uniqueness of the restaurant. An expensive restaurant doesn't necessarily ensure an enjoyable evening; however, a small, relatively unknown spot could have good food, professional service, and a lively atmosphere. Therefore, on a purely subjective basis, stars are used to judge the overall dining value (see the star ratings above at right). Keep in mind that chefs and owners often change, which sometimes drastically affects the quality of a restaurant. The ratings in this guidebook are based on information available at press time.

The price ratings, as categorized above at right, apply to restaurants and hotels. These figures describe general price-range relationships among other restaurants and hotels in the area. The restaurant price ratings are based on the average cost of a dinner entrée for one person, excluding tax and tip. Hotel price ratings reflect the base price of a standard room for two people for one night during the peak season.

Restaurants

★	Good	
★★	Very Good	
★★★	Excellent	
★★★★	An Extraordinary Experience	
$	The Price Is Right	(less than $10)
$$	Reasonable	($10-$25)
$$$	Expensive	($25-$40)
$$$$	Big Bucks	($40 and up)

Hotels

$	The Price Is Right	(less than $75)
$$	Reasonable	($75-$150)
$$$	Expensive	($150-$225)
$$$$	Big Bucks	($225 and up)

Map Key

(M) **Pont-Neuf** •

Flower market held
daily and bird market
open on Sundays

In 1985, Christo wrapped
Paris' oldest bridge in beige
canvas and seven miles of rope

Paris' first public clock
(1334)—and it still works

(M) **Cité** •

Seine boat tours leave
the **Square du Vert-Galant**
daily every 30 minutes

Stop by the law courts
and watch French
Perry Masons in action

Pet stores galore with
everything from parakeets to
boa constrictors

Tour de Bonbec (**Babble Tower**)
—used as a torture chamber
during the Revolution

Square du Vert-Galant
—best fish-eye view of
Paris and a haunt of
anglers and lovers

Place Dauphine—actor
Yves Montand once lived here

(M) **St.-Michel** •

Breakfast on croissants and
café au lait in any of a half-dozen
cafés on **Place St.-Michel**

Marie Antoinette, Danton, and
Robespierre were all imprisoned in the
notorious **Conciergerie** before they were
carted off to the guillotine

Ste.-Chapelle's windows (1245-48)
are older than Notre-Dame's and comprise the
largest stained-glass surface in the world. Don't
miss the candlelit concerts in the summer

Pilgrims wearing scallop shells on
the one-hundred-mile trek to
Santiago de Compostela
in Spain began their voyage on
the **Rue St.-Jacques**

Archaeological Crypt •

(M) **Maubert-Mutualité** •

(M) = Métro

The Islands:
Ile de la Cité & Ile St.-Louis

At the heart of Paris are two islands: the sloop-shaped **Ile de la Cité,** which cradles **Notre-Dame** in its stern, and the **Ile St.-Louis,** which follows in the wake. Although the islands have no grand hotels, banks, major restaurants, theaters, or designer shops, they do possess two gems of Gothic architecture (Notre-Dame and **Ste.-Chapelle**), a world-famous prison, an elegant 17th-century subdivision, some of the city's most beautiful private mansions, the nation's law courts and police headquarters, an Art Nouveau métro station, a flower and bird market, 15 bridges, and one too many souvenir shops selling miniature Napoléon busts and "I Love Paris" bumper stickers.

Point Zéro—all distances in France are measured from this point

Climb 225 steps to the top of **Notre-Dame's** north tower for a close-up look at the gargoyles and a magnificent 360-degree view of Paris

Ⓜ Hôtel-de-Ville

Memorial to 200,000 French, most of them Jews, deported to Nazi death camps

Step lightly: This is the ninth bridge on this site. The first collapsed opening day in 1634 and 20 Parisians drowned

Berthillon—best ice cream in Paris—and perhaps the world

Ⓜ Pont-Marie

In 1860, architect Viollet-le-Duc added a statue of himself among the 12 apostles surrounding **Notre-Dame's** spire. Free Sunday afternoon organ concerts are held in the cathedral

The following sites serve as an introduction to the islands. If you happen to tour this area on a Sunday, the added attractions include **Notre-Dame's** morning Mass (10:30AM) and late-afternoon organ concerts, and the bird market at **Place Louis-Lépine.** If visiting the Ile St.-Louis galleries and boutiques and the **Palais de Justice** is more your style, a weekday would be a better time to drop by. You might begin with a stop at a pastry shop to purchase croissants and brioches in time for a boat tour up the Seine (tour boats leave from the Pont-Neuf). Then, after stopping at the flower market and Notre-Dame, have lunch at a tea salon on Ile St.-Louis before strolling down to the **Hôtel Lauzun.** Top off your day with a candlelit concert in **Ste.-Chapelle,** followed by dinner at the exceedingly fancy **L'Orangerie** or the more plebian, all-you-can-eat **Nos Ancêtres Les Gaulois.**

Ile de la Cité

The Cité, the birthplace of Paris founded by the Parisii in the third century BC and overtaken by the Romans in 52 BC, survived attacks by Germans, barbarians, flood, and famine, but succumbed to a Frenchman, **Baron Georges-Eugène Haussmann,** Napoléon III's prefect (1853-1870), who ordered the Cité's *hygienizing.* Haussmann destroyed 90 streets and most of the medieval and Louis XIII homes. In their place, he constructed four architecturally dull buildings (Hôtel-Dieu Hospital, Préfecture de Police, Tribunal of Commerce, and Palais de Justice) and increased by six times the size of the square in front of Notre-Dame.

1 Pont-Neuf Despite its name (New Bridge), the Pont-Neuf was completed in 1607 and is the city's oldest and most famous bridge, and the first in Paris to be constructed without houses on top of it. Crossing the Seine with 12 broad arches at the river's widest point, the city's grandest bridge incorporates a series of turrets for street vendors, jugglers, and acrobats. The bridge became such a well-traveled thoroughfare that, legend held, it was impossible to cross without encountering a monk, a prostitute, and a white horse. One of the most notorious Pont-Neuf charlatans was the **Great Jean Thomas,** who in 1715 set up a stall on the bridge to peddle bottles of an odorous elixir called Solar Balm. As part of an inventive advertising campaign, he hawked his wares dressed in a scarlet suit, a hat of peacock feathers, and a string of human teeth hung around his neck.

The Pont-Neuf was completed under **Henri IV.** The popular Henri of Navarre, who is remembered best for promising the peasants in his kingdom "a chicken in every pot," inaugurated the city's first pedestrian bridge by galloping his charger across it. The bronze equestrian statue of **Henrici Magni** at the bridge's center is an 1818 replacement; the original, erected two centuries earlier by the king's wife, **Marie de Médici,** was melted down to make cannons during the Revolution. The cornices overlooking the river have a carved frieze of grimacing caricatures, perhaps of King Henri's ministers and courtiers. Designed by **Androuet du Cerceau,** the bridge was painted by **Turner,** rhapsodized by poets, and, in 1985, wrapped by Bulgarian artist **Christo** in acres of beige canvas and more than seven miles of rope. ♦ Métro: Pont-Neuf

2 Square du Vert-Galant Borrowing **Henri IV's** nickname ("Merry Monarch" and "Gay Old Dog"), this cobblestoned spit of land lush with chestnut trees may be reached by steps behind the king's statue. A haunt of anglers by day and of lovers on warm summer nights, the

Pont-Neuf

square affords the best fish-eye view of Paris. Departing from here are one-hour boat tours of the Seine offered by **Les Vedettes du Pont-Neuf.**♦ Tours: daily every 30 minutes 10AM-noon, 1:30-6:30PM; F-Su only 9-10:30PM. May-15 Oct: "Lights of Paris" boat tours begin departing at 9PM. Métro: Pont-Neuf. 46.33.98.38, 43.29.86.19

3 Rue Dauphine The construction of the Pont-Neuf channeled traffic over to the Left Bank. When **Henri IV's** request to put a highway through a monastery's vegetable gardens was denied, he snapped: "I will open the new road with cannonballs!" Rue Dauphine was built and named after his son. ♦ Métro: Pont-Neuf

4 Taverne Henri IV ★★$ Named after the king in bronze across the street, this reasonably priced bistro serves delicious charcuterie, regional cheeses, and goose rillettes and is well stocked with Bordeaux and Burgundy. ♦ Lunch, afternoon snacks, and dinner. Closed Saturday, Sunday, and from 15 Aug to 15 Sept. 13 Place du Pont-Neuf (at Rue Henri-Robert). No credit cards. Métro: Pont-Neuf. 43.54.27.90

5 Place Dauphine Once the royal garden, this tranquil triangle of stone and redbrick town houses dates from 1607 and takes its name from **Henri IV's** son, the princely Dauphin who became **Louis XIII.** The square was one of Henri IV's first city-planning projects in the 16th century and regrettably lost its third side with the expansion of the Palais de Justice. Surrealist poet **André Breton** (1896-1966) called it "one of the most secluded places I know." ♦ Métro: Pont-Neuf

5 Hôtel Henri IV $ The wallpaper is peeling, the rooms are tiny, and the showers and bathrooms are in the hall, but that's a minor price for a room with a view of one of the prettiest squares in Paris and a daily rate that costs less than a decent bottle of wine. Very popular and only 22 rooms, so reserve well in advance. ♦ 25 Place Dauphine. Métro: Pont-Neuf. 43.54.44.53

5 La Rose de France ★★$$ This tiny restaurant with an outdoor terrace specializes in tasty *côtelettes d'agneau,* (lamb chops with *herbes de Provence*), mussels in vermouth, and *filet de boeuf en croûte.* ♦ Lunch and dinner. Closed Saturday and Sunday, the last three weeks of August, and Christmas through New Year's Day. 24 Place Dauphine. Métro: Pont-Neuf. 43.54.10.12

5 Laine en Couleur Vegétale True to its name, richly colored wool yarns, hand-dyed with natural vegetable substances, are the specialty here. The delightful owner **Anne Rieger** derives her reds from red cabbage, her blues from indigo, and her yellows from the leaves of the chestnut trees right outside her door. ♦ M-F 3-7PM. Closed in August. 18 Place Dauphine. Métro: Pont-Neuf. 40.51.72.65

5 Le Caveau du Palais ★★$$ A comfortable restaurant (illustrated above) wedged between the Quai des Orfèvres and the Place Dauphine. Sample the salad of lamb sweetbreads in a raspberry vinegar, *filet de boeuf à la moutarde de Meaux,* grilled grouper with basil, and *fondant au chocolat.* ♦ Lunch and dinner. Closed Saturday and Sunday. 19 Place Dauphine. Métro: Pont-Neuf. 43.26.04.28, 43.26.81.84

5 Le Bar du Caveau ★$ Managed by Le Caveau du Palais next door, this wine bar serves light lunches: charcuterie, country cheese, and a variety of Bordeaux and Beaujolais. ♦ Breakfast, lunch, afternoon and evening snacks. 19 Place Dauphine. Métro: Pont-Neuf. 43.54.45.95

6 Chez Paul ★★$$ Long marble tables and cloth napkins as big as dish towels dominate this spot. Try the lobster salad with honey vinegar, the *mignon de veau en papillote,* and, for dessert, the baba rhum flambé with red currant jam. During the summer months don't miss the wild strawberries. ♦ Lunch and dinner. Closed Monday and in August. 15 Place Dauphine (52 Quai des Orfèvres). Métro: Pont-Neuf. 43.54.21.48

7 Quai des Orfèvres The **Goldsmiths Quay** is the Scotland Yard of Paris. PJ stands for "police judiciare" or detective force. The famous member of the PJ in the detective stories of the late **Georges Simenon** is, incidentally, not Parisian; Inspector Maigret comes from Belgium. ♦ Métros: Pont-Neuf, St.-Michel.

8 Palais de la Cité This massive interlocking structure has been occupied by the French government since 52 BC, first as the palace of Roman prefects, later as the Gothic palace of the first 12 kings of France. In the 13th century it was the residence of **Saint Louis** (Louis IX), who lived in the upper chambers (now the First Civil Court). The king meted out justice beneath a tree in the courtyard. All that remains of the original palace is the breathtaking **Ste.-Chapelle** and the gloomy **Conciergerie,** one of history's most hideous and brutal prisons. Most of the site was covered by the **Palais de Justice,** built after the great fire of 1776. ♦ Métros: Pont-Neuf, St.-Michel

9 Tours de Bonbec, d'Argent, and de César Along the Quai de l'Horloge side of the old palace is a set of round, imposing towers. The first is Tour de Bonbec, nicknamed the "babbler" because it was used as a torture chamber during the Reign of Terror, a period of brutal purges following the Revolution. Next are the Tour d'Argent, where the royal treasure was once kept and where the famous restaurant across the river got its name; and the Tour de César, two steepled gate towers beside the entrance to the Conciergerie.

♦ Métros: Cité, Pont-Neuf

10 La Conciergerie Following the bloody mob revolt led by **Etienne Marcel** in 1358, young **King Charles V** moved the royal residence to the Marais but left behind the royal dungeon and supreme court in the charge of the concierge (*Comte des Cierges* or Count of Candles), the king's caretaker. The guest list included distinguished criminals such as **Ravaillac,** the fanatic who murdered popular **Henri IV** and was imprisoned and tortured here before his execution.

During the Revolution, the Tribunal commandeered the palace and administered its own ruthless form of justice. The Conciergerie became the antechamber to the guillotine during the Reign of Terror between January 1793 and July 1794. About 2,600 Parisians were condemned to death, among them **Charlotte Corday,** who had stabbed **Marat** in his bath, and, perhaps the best remembered inmate, **Marie Antoinette,** the Austrian queen who had reputedly scoffed at the starving French masses with the phrase "Let them eat cake." Shortly after the Tribunal executed her husband, **King Louis XVI,** she was held here in a tiny cell from August until October 1793, when the tumbrils delivered her to the guillotine. Royalty were not the only victims; no one in a position of authority was safe. Revolutionary **Danton,** who had ordered the execution of 22 people, was in turn condemned to death by citizen **Robespierre,** who later was sent to the guillotine by a panel of judges, the Thermidor Convention. At the end of the Terror, the Tribunal's own public prosecutor, **Fouquier-Tinville,** was dragged off to the gallows shouting "I am the ax! You don't execute the ax!"

Put yourself in the shoes of Marie Antoinette as she walked down Rue de Paris (which once led to the quarters of an executioner during the Terror known as **Monsieur de Paris**) with footsteps echoing off the vaulted ceiling. She was jailed in dank cell number VI; in the cell next door, both Danton and Robespierre were held on death row, and, in the adjoining chapel, the 22 condemned Girondins heard Mass before their execution. All these rooms, as well as the *salle de la dernière toilette,* from which prisoners were led to the block, have recently been restored.

On your way out, duck into the magnificent medieval vaults of the four-aisled **Salle des Gens d'Armes** (Hall of the Men-at-Arms), frequently used these days for classical concerts, theater, and wine tastings. The spiral staircase at the far end of the hall is worth a peek. Waltz through the 14th-century kitchen that served some 3,000 guests and had walk-in ovens large enough to roast a pair of oxen. The souvenir shop near the exit sells replicas of Revolutionary playing cards that replace kings, queens, and jacks with humbly clothed men and women personifying common virtues such as Industry and Justice. The original deck (1793) by **Jaume** and **Dugorc** is kept in the Bibliothèque Nationale. ♦ Daily 9:30AM-6PM Apr-Sept; M-Sa 10AM-4:30PM Oct-Mar. Closed holidays. Guided tours available in the Conciergerie. 1 Quai de l'Horloge. Métro: Cité. 43.54.30.06

11 Tour de l'Horloge This tower was the site of the city's first public clock (1334). Today's more baroque version is set in a constellation of golden *fleurs-de-lis* and flanked by angels, rams, and royal shields. Until the French Revolution, the clock signaled royal births and deaths by pealing nonstop for three days. ♦ Quai de l'Horloge (at Blvd du Palais). Métro: Cité

12 Palais de Justice (Law Courts) Behind the lusciously gilded Louis XVI railing and portal gates on the Boulevard du Palais is the main entrance to the Palais de Justice and the **Cour du Mai.** This courtyard was the last stop for the condemned before leaving by wooden carts, or tumbrils, for the gallows in the **Place de la Concorde.** Look above the door at the top of the grand marble steps for the words *Liberté, Egalité, Fraternité.*

Inside and to the right in the lobby (**Salle des Pas-Perdus,** literally "The Room of the Wasted Steps") is the amusing statue of **Berryer,** a 19th-century barrister. To his right sits a sculpted muse with her foot on a turtle, a candid jab at the speed of the legal process. Behind the door to the left is the gorgeous blue-and-gold **Première Chambre** (also known as Chambre Dorée, or Gilded Chamber), where the Revolutionary Tribunal sat on 6 April 1793 and sentenced **Queen Marie Antoinette** to death.

In the "cathedral of chicanery," as **Balzac** called the **Law Courts,** a thicket of police, public *écrivains* (letter writers), and prisoners used to gather while hawkers sold newspapers and rented black judicial robes. Today, the lobby is still a chaos of black-robed barristers, plaintiffs, and judges dashing about. If you'd like to see a French Perry Mason putting *liberté, egalité,* and *fraternité* into action during the week, you may visit the courtroom proceedings (except the juvenile court). ♦ Tours M-Sa 1:30-4PM. 2 Blvd du Palais. Métro: Cité. 44.32.50.00

Restaurants/Clubs: Red
Shops/ 🌳 Outdoors: Green
Hotels: Blue
Sights/Culture: Black

Jeremiah
Tobias
Judith
Job
Esther
Kings: Samuel, David, Solomon
St. Helena
True Cross
St. Louis relics of passion
Ezekiel
John the Baptist
Daniel
15th-century rose window:
The Apocalypse
Christ's Passion
St. John
The Virgin
Christ's Childhood
Isaiah
The Tree of Jesse
Judges
Gideon
Samson
Deuter-onomy
Joshua
Ruth & Boaz
Exodus
The Law of Moses
Exodus
Moses on Mt. Sinai
Genesis
Adam & Eve
Noah
Jacob

13 Ste.-Chapelle After Notre-Dame, this is the city's most significant medieval monument. **Saint Louis** (Louis IX, 1214-1270), France's only canonized king, erected this Gothic jewel of a chapel in 1248 to enshrine the relics he bought from Venetian merchants during his first crusade. His purchases included Christ's Crown of Thorns, two pieces of the True Cross, a nail from the cross, the Roman soldier's lance that pierced Christ's side, and several drops of Christ's blood. For the relics, he paid 35,000 livres in gold, a sum far in excess of what it cost to construct Ste.-Chapelle.

Ste.-Chapelle was built in less than five years and is thought to have been designed by **Pierre de Montreuil**. It soars 67 feet without the aid of flying buttresses, a daring architectural accomplishment. In medieval times it was connected to the palace of St.-Louis, but today is hidden away in a side courtyard of the 19th-century **Palais de Justice.** Ste.-Chapelle is a two-tiered chapel;

Ste.-Chapelle

sequestered from view, the royal family worshiped upstairs in the light and airy **Chapelle Haute,** while members of the court prayed on the somber ground floor.

The chapel suffered considerable damage during the Revolution, when the gold reliquary was melted down and the structure was put to use as a flour warehouse. In the 19th century the chapel was thoroughly made over by **Eugène-Emmanuel Viollet-le-Duc** (1814-1879), one of the **Baron Haussmann** architects who also restored Notre-Dame and cathedrals at Amiens and St.-Denis. **Steinheil,** a compatriot of Balzac and Baudelaire, restored the windows. Of the 12 apostle statues, only one (the bearded apostle fifth down on the left side) is original. Portions of the damaged originals are on exhibit in the Cluny Museum.

The chapel's spectacular windows are older than Notre-Dame's and comprise the largest expanse of stained glass in the world—1,500 square yards, enough to cover three basketball courts. Created in an age of mass illiteracy, this illustrated Bible consists of 1,134 scenes. The windows (diagram above) read chronologically beginning on the left near the entrance and progressing clockwise. Start with the lower left panel and read from left to right, row by row from bottom to top. The narrative begins with Genesis and the Old Testament, continues through the Crucifixion (illustrated in the choir apse), the acquisition of the relics, the construction of the chapel Ste.-Chapelle, and, finally, the Apocalypse. Notice that a liberated Saint Louis devoted entire windows to two women of the Old Testament, **Judith** and **Esther.** The thick, predominantly red-and-blue dyed glass of the 15 main windows contrasts sharply with the green-and-yellow hues of the flamboyant rose window (restored by **Charles VIII** in 1485) illustrating the Apocalypse. Because the windows are backlit by the sun, you must read along with the sun's rising and setting. Thus, you have to get up early to catch the Battle of Jericho and must come after lunch for David and Goliath. And, if the flies on Pharaoh's face interest you, bring your opera glasses, because many of the panels, particularly the highest ones, are nearly impossible to decipher. Anyone who identifies even a few Bible characters in a short visit is doing well. Not long ago a Belgian Benedictine monk arrived at Ste.-Chapelle with his Bible and a pair of binoculars; it took him two full weeks, gazing every day from dawn to dusk, to complete the cycle.

For an initial visit, the best approach is to set aside your guidebook, gaze upward, and imagine yourself among the royal family in the 13th century watching as Saint Louis mounted the stairs to the gold reliquary to display the sacred Crown of Thorns. The crown now resides in Notre-Dame and is exhibited only on Good Friday. In addition to its visual splendors, the acoustics of Ste.-Chapelle are renowned; **Couperin** played the organ here in the 17th century. Nowadays, rather expensive evening concerts of classical music are held here several times a week between March and November. ♦ Admission. Daily 9:30AM-6PM Apr-Sept; daily 10AM-4:30PM Oct-Mar. 2 Blvd du Palais. Métro: Cité. 43.54.30.09

14 Les Deux Palais $ This corner café with Roaring Twenties mirrored columns serves omelets, good coffee, and hot lunch specials. ♦ Breakfast, lunch, afternoon snacks, and dinner. 3 Blvd du Palais (at Rue de Lutèce). No credit cards. Métro: Cité. 43.54.20.86

15 Cité Métro One of the original 141 Art Nouveau "dragonfly" métro station entrances designed by **Hector Guimard** in 1900.

15 Place Louis-Lépine Named after a Belle Epoque police chief remembered for having armed Parisian *gendarmes* with whistles and truncheons, this square is a charming urban Eden surrounded by the grim walls of **Hôtel-Dieu Hospital,** the **Préfecture de Police,** and the **Commercial Tribunal.** One of the largest flower markets in Paris blooms here year-round with everything from chrysanthemums to lemon trees. On Sunday, the square is

transformed into a bird market selling fresh seed, cages, and a palette of colorful canaries, finches, and parrots. ♦ Métro: Cité

16 Préfecture de Police This bunker of a building is the headquarters of the fictional Inspector Clouseau of *Pink Panther* fame and the very real Paris police. On 19 August 1944, during the liberation of Paris, about a thousand Paris police officers revolted against the German occupation, barricaded themselves in the préfecture, hoisted the tricolor to a rousing chorus of the *Marseillaise,* and held off Nazi tanks and artillery for four days until the Allies arrived. In the ensuing battle, 280 died, and buildings around Notre-Dame's parvis are still pockmarked with bullet holes. ♦ Place Louis-Lépine. Métro: Cité

17 Petit Pont The *Little Bridge* on this site was first built in 1185 by **Bishop Maurice de Sully,** who also oversaw the construction of Notre-Dame. A 19th-century version now stands where, in the Middle Ages, minstrels used to cross toll-free. ♦ Métros: Cité, St.-Michel

18 Rue St.-Jacques The city's oldest street, which begins at the Petit Pont, originated as a Roman road. A thousand years later, it was named after the crusading **Saint Jacques,** whose body miraculously washed up on the Spanish coast in the ninth century. Paris was the principal starting point of a one-thousand-mile pilgrimage to the Shrine of St. Jacques in Santiago de Compostela in Spain. In medieval times, pilgrims wearing scallop shells (the symbol of Saint Jacques) would set off down this street. The delicious contents of such shells are served throughout Paris as *Coquilles St.-Jacques.* ♦ Métros: Cité, St.-Michel

Strolling on the Seine

Rhapsodically portrayed by such painters as **Turner, Monet,** and **Sisley,** the seven-mile stretch of the Seine that passes through Paris is the most famous and beautiful length of urban riverfront in the world. Within the city, the river is spanned by 33 bridges, and from the oldest (Pont-Neuf) to the dandiest (Pont Alexandre III) to the most humble and delicate (Pont des Arts), there is nary an ugly one among them. The Pont de Grenelle is of special interest to Americans; beside it is a replica of the Statue of Liberty. And along the banks of the gentle, green river is a panoply of famous monuments: the Eiffel Tower, the Grand Palais, the Musée d'Orsay, the Louvre, the Institute of France, the Conciergerie, Notre-Dame, and the famous penthouse restaurant Tour D'Argent, plus the former homes of **Baudelaire, Voltaire, Rilke, Daumier, Balzac,** and **Corot,** and the stately islands Ile de la Cité and Ile St.-Louis. Strolling along the tree-lined quays, one encounters lovers hand-in-hand; anglers casting their lines; clochards making their digs under the bridges; flower and bird markets; and, of course, *bouquinistes* peddling postcards, 19th-century pornography, and an occasional rare first-edition book from their zinc-topped boxes.

19 Archaeological Crypt In 1965, while excavating for an underground parking lot, the city of Paris unearthed Gallo-Roman and medieval ruins, now preserved in this slightly eerie but intelligent archaeological site/ museum beneath the parvis of Notre-Dame. Designed by **André Hermant,** the crypt is worth a quick visit, if only to see the scale models of Paris, which show its evolution from a Celtic settlement during the Second Iron Age to a Roman city in 500 BC. Notice that the Romans, in anticipation of another barbarian invasion, reinforced the original ramparts with a second wall. This is one of the city's most accessible museums (commentary is in English and French). And if you're lucky, you may see a few trowel-and-toothbrush archaeologists still digging. ♦ Admission. Daily 10AM-6PM Apr-Sept; 10AM-4:30PM Oct-Mar. Enter at the west end of the Parvis. Métros: Cité, St.-Michel

20 Hôtel-Dieu Hospital Behind the double row of chestnut trees is **God's Hostel,** founded in AD 651 by **Saint Landry,** Bishop of Paris. The hospital was an important training facility for American doctors in the 19th century. The oldest known cabaret in Paris, **La Pomme de Pin,** stood on this site in 1400. It was frequented by **Rabelais, Villon, Molière,** and **Racine.** ♦ Parvis Notre-Dame. Métros: Cité, St.-Michel

21 Parvis of Notre-Dame In the Middle Ages, when miracle plays were performed, the square in front of Notre-Dame represented *paradis,* or paradise, a name contracted over the centuries to *parvis.* Critics of **Baron Haussmann,** who enlarged the parvis sixfold in the 19th century, called it the "paved prairie." ♦ Métros: Cité, St.-Michel

21 Rue de Venise Paris in the Middle Ages was a snarl of narrow horse paths. Marked in the pavement of the parvis in front of the cathedral is the former position of this one-yard-wide medieval alley, no doubt once the narrowest street in Paris. ♦ Métros: Cité, St.-Michel

22 Charlemagne and His Vassals On the south side of the parvis rests a bronze statue created in 1882 of **Charlemagne,** the Frank who was crowned the first Holy Roman Emperor in AD 800. Under Charlemagne and his successors, Paris was merely a provincial town. The center of Charlemagne's empire was at Aix-la-Chapelle. (If you happen to be looking for public toilets, follow the tail of Charlemagne's prancing horse; it points west to nearby stairs leading underground.) ♦ Parvis of Notre-Dame. Métros: Cité, St.-Michel

23 Point Zéro All distances in France are measured from this brass compass star *(Point Zéro des Routes de France)* fixed in the pavement in front of the cathedral. Throughout France, highway signs tell you how far away you are (in kilometers) from *Paris Notre-Dame.* ♦ Métros: Cité, St.-Michel

Notre-Dame

24 Notre-Dame The cathedral of Notre-Dame, wrote **e.e. cummings,** does not budge an inch for all the idiocies of this world. For six centuries, this world-famous masterpiece of the Middle Ages has endured as a sonnet in stone, harmonizing mass and elegance, asymmetry, and perfection. Among its architectural triumphs are the Gothic ribbed vaulting and the flying buttresses, which opened up the church by permitting the erection of higher, more slender walls pierced by glories of stained glass.

In 1163 no less a personage than **Pope Alexander III** laid Notre-Dame's foundation stone, and the final masterful touches were not completed until 1345—more than two centuries later. (Ste.-Chapelle, by comparison, was erected in five years.) The design followed the sketches executed in 1159 by **Bishop Maurice de Sully** and was implemented by architects **Pierre de Montereau,** who was responsible for Notre-Dame's south transept, and **Jean de Chelles,** and by generations of anonymous workers.

To tour Notre-Dame is to stroll through French history. On this site the Romans built a temple in antiquity to **Jupiter** and the **Emperor Tiberius.** In the cathedral, during the Middle Ages, the homeless slept and were fed; trade unions met; passion plays were performed; and merchants from the Orient sold everything from ostrich eggs to elephant tusks. During the 12th century Notre-Dame's adjoining cathedral school became an intellectual center known throughout Europe and eventually gave birth to the Sorbonne. During the Revolution the cathedral was rechristened the "Temple of Reason," with the dancer **Mademoiselle Maillard** chosen as Goddess of Reason; shortly thereafter, the cathedral was actually auctioned off to a demolition contractor for scrap building material. Though never actually demolished, Notre-Dame was in shambles in 1804 when **Napoléon Bonaparte** called **Pope Pius VII** from Rome to officiate at his coronation, which was held before the cathedral's high altar. After the anointing, Napoléon defiantly snatched the crown from the pontiff and crowned himself emperor, a dramatic scene captured by **Jacques-Louis David** in his famous painting that hangs in the Louvre.

West Facade At the base of the west facade, which is topped by two 69-meter (226-foot) towers, are three famous portals devoted to (from left to right) the Virgin Mary, the Last Judgement, and Sainte Anne, the Virgin's mother. Royalty couldn't stay out of the act; in the tympanum of the portal to Sainte Anne, a kneeling **King Louis VII** (far right) dedicates the cathedral with Bishop Sully (on the left with a crook in his hand), as the bishop's faithful secretary takes notes straddling a Gothic stool. The presence of **Barbedor,** the scribe, represents one of the first times an intellectual was honored in a cathedral facade.

Above the three portals is the **Gallery of Kings, Viollet-le-Duc's** 19th-century replicas of medieval masterpieces, which were once painted in vibrant yellow, cobalt, and scarlet. The 28 kings represent the kings of Judea and Israel, thought in the Catholic Church to be the ancestors of Christ. In 1793 Revolutionaries mistook them for the kings of France and toppled and decapitated them. Fortunately, at the time, an educator spirited away the sculpted heads and buried them in his yard at 20 Chaussée

d'Antin, near the present site of the Paris Opéra. They languished there until 1977, when they were unearthed in the course of excavations for a bank vault and put on exhibit at the Cluny Museum. The facade will be partially obscured by scaffolding for the remainder of the decade as, section by section, it is carefully cleaned. This delicate process, which requires using only warm water (no soap, solvent, or sandblasting is allowed), won't be completed until the year 2000.

Gargoyles

North and South Towers At the top of a spiraling 255-step climb up the north tower you will find not Victor Hugo's *Quasimodo,* the tormented hunchback of Notre-Dame's belfry, but an equally unsettling sight: **Viollet-le-Duc's** stone bestiary of gargoyles, gremlins, and demons. It was believed that the gargoyles kept evil spirits from the cathedral (a number of them serve as downspouts, squirting rain from their mouths—sheer entertainment in spring showers). The 90-meter spire was added during the heavy-handed Gothic Revival restoration of 1860. In addition, architect Viollet-le-Duc placed a statue of himself alongside the copper apostles and evangelists. The apostles stand on the cathedral roof looking outward,

Notre-Dame, East Facade

blessing the city, but the architect looks upward, admiring his work. (For a bird's-eye view of Viollet-le-Duc, the celebrated flying buttresses, and a splendid chain of bridges over the Atlantic-bound Seine, climb the last 125 steps to the top of the south tower. You won't regret it.)

Interior As you enter Notre-Dame, the nave appears more somber than the transept and altar. This is due, in part, to your eyes adjusting to the darkness, but the difference in hue is mostly a matter of dirt. The same cleanup process now being used on the west facade was brought to a halt in the early 1990s, when it was found that even warm water sponge baths would be harmful to the western-most portion of the nave. The remaining bays have suffered more pollution damage than the rest of the interior, and unlike the facade had not been protected for centuries by decorative paint. Restorers will continue with the cleaning only after they have developed a suitably safe technique.

The massive organ is France's largest, a masterwork installed in 1730 by **Aristide Cavaillé-Col.** A century later, the organ was restored. And now, following in the tradition of **Couperin, Franck,** and **Messiaen,** all of whom performed here, some of Europe's greatest organists offer free recitals here every Sunday in the late afternoon. These, as well as the candlelit Easter vigil and Christmas Eve Mass, draw ample crowds. The cathedral's seating capacity for Mass and organ concerts is nearly 10,000.

Each 11 November, in a deeply moving cathedral service, the Royal British Legion honors British and Commonwealth soldiers who died on French soil during World War I.

Mays Paintings Every year in May during the Middle Ages, paintings called *Mays* were given by the Orfèvrerie, the gold workers' union. The paintings (among them a **Le Brun** and a **Le Sueur**) were originally hung between the church pillars; today, they are displayed in the side chapels.

Windows New windows were installed in Notre-Dame's clerestory after World War II, but not because of damage caused by the

Germans. In the 18th century **Louis XV** declared stained glass *déclassé,* destroyed the Gothic glass in the upper-level nave windows, and replaced it with clear glass, to give the cathedral interior a bright Protestant appearance. It was not until after the war that contemporary glass replicas of the original Gothic windows were installed. Of Notre-Dame's three famous rose windows (north, south, and west), only the north has the original 13th-century glass. The south and west rose windows glow most brilliantly at twilight, while the north window is best viewed in morning light. The stained glass windows of the 13th and 14th century are thick, with small images predominantly portrayed in deep reds, blues, and purples (they're actually dyed into the glass). Over the centuries, it became possible to make thinner glass. Images became larger and were handpainted on the surface, and ways of making brighter greens and yellows were discovered. These developments are evident in the differences between the original windows and the modern replicas.

Wood Sculpture One of the cathedral's most charming decorations is the 14th-century Gothic relief on the north side of the chancel that depicts the life of Christ from the Nativity to the Last Supper.

The new altar (in front of the old altar) betokens the liturgical changes in the 1960s that allowed the priest to say Mass facing the congregation instead of turning his back. In addition, Mass is now said in French, instead of the original Latin, but even so, given the cathedral's echoing acoustics, sometimes it sounds as if it could be Greek to most listeners. ◆ Daily 8AM-6:45PM. Rue d'Arcole (at Rue du Cloître-Notre-Dame). Métros: Cité, Maubert-Mutualité

25 La Colombe ★★$$ Originally a 13th-century tavern and later a famous cabaret in the 1950s, The Dove restaurant is classified as a French historic landmark and, according to *Le Figaro* magazine, is the most photographed house in Paris. The sagging beamed ceilings, cages of cooing doves, and the profusion of fresh flowers complement the home-style menu of seasonal specialties such as filet of veal in a mushroom and carrot cream sauce, *confit de canard,* an excellent foie gras de maison, and a rich chocolate mousse. The concierges at the Crillon and Plaza Athenée hotels have this on their list of American favorites. Dining on the arbored terrace is available in the summer. ◆ Lunch and dinner; dinner only on Monday. Closed Sunday. 4 Rue de la Colombe (between Quai aux Fleurs and Rue Chanoinesse). Métros: Cité, Hôtel-de-Ville. 46.33.37.08

25 Rue de la Colombe This medieval street is cut where the old Roman wall once ran to protect Paris against barbarian invasions.
♦ Métros: Cité, Hôtel-de-Ville

26 La Lieutenance ★★$$$ Housed in a 16th-century building that once belonged to the canons of Notre-Dame, this fashionable restaurant caters at night to the show-biz crowd but is less frantic during lunch. Chef **Daniel Lemounier** serves his *magret de canard* with sauce Perigordine and *feuilleté de trois poissons.* ♦ Lunch and dinner; dinner only on Saturday. Closed Monday. 24 Rue Chanoinesse (between Rues de la Colombe and des Chantres). Métros: Cité, Hôtel-de-Ville. 43.54.91.36

27 9-11 Quai aux Fleurs The sculpted heads on the face of this 19th-century building on the Quai aux Fleurs (which, by the way, sells no flowers) commemorates two of history's most famous lovers, **Héloïse** and **Abélard,** who today cast plaintive glances at couples strolling arm-in-arm along the Seine. In 1118 Pierre Abélard (1079-1142), an iconoclastic theologian who helped found the University of Paris, fell in love with one of his students. She was Héloïse (1101-1164), the brilliant niece of **Fulbert,** the foul-tempered canon of Notre-Dame. "Under the guise of study, we gave ourselves to love," wrote Abélard. . . . "We exchanged more kisses than sentences." Their passionate affair was brought to an abrupt, brutal, and tragic end by her uncle, whose thugs emasculated Abélard. Héloïse and Abélard lived on, cloistered separately for many years, but were buried side-by-side in Père-Lachaise Cemetery. ♦ At Rue des Chantres. Métros: Cité, Hôtel-de-Ville

28 Le Vieux Bistro ★★$$ Far removed from the traffic and crush of tourists is this quiet, charming restaurant featuring the cuisine of Lyon. The roast quail in gin and cream sauce is delicious. ♦ Lunch and dinner. 14 Rue du Cloître-Notre-Dame (between Rues d'Arcole and Massillon). Reservations recommended. Métro: Cité. 43.54.18.95

29 Square Jean XXIII Cherry trees blossom here in the spring, lime trees shade in the summer, and the chestnut leaves are heaped ankle-deep in autumn. Notre-Dame's west face tower is above but it looks flat compared to its south and east sides shored by dramatic flying buttresses. Here is a place to pause and feed the birds or to perch on a wooden bench during an occasional outdoor concert given by a local police officers' orchestra. ♦ Métros: Cité, Maubert-Mutualité

30 Mémorial de la Déportation The Deportation Museum, designed by **G.H. Pingusson** in 1962, commemorates the 200,000 French, most of them Jews, who died during the Holocaust. Some 30,000 people from Paris alone were deported to Nazi death camps during World War II. Reflecting the Jewish tradition of paying homage to the dead by placing a stone on the grave, the memorial is constructed around a tunnel of 200,000 quartz pebbles. It also contains small tombs with earth from each of the concentration camps. The visitor here feels trapped visually and psychologically by the low ceiling and iron bars. Stark and simple, the memorial in the Square de l'Ile-de-France is one of city's most moving monuments. ♦ Daily 10AM-noon, 2-7PM Apr-Sep; daily 10AM-noon, 2-5PM Oct-Mar. Quai l'Archevêché. Métros: Cité, Maubert-Mutualité

31 Pont St-Louis Step lightly; this pedestrian bridge is the ninth on a site that has had a shaky, if not disastrous, history. The first bridge linking the two islands was erected in 1634 by developer **Jean-Christophe Marie;** it crumbled on opening day, drowning 20 people. And this wasn't the worst of Marie's bridge disasters; his **Pont Marie,** built the following year, later collapsed during a flood, killing 121 people. ♦ Métros: Cité, Pont-Marie

Ile St.-Louis

A world apart from the rest of Paris, this once-bucolic cow pasture and site of sword duels is jammed today with grand 17th-century town houses (which with few exceptions are closed to the public) and fashionable shops. Somehow it remains a peaceful oasis in the heart of a bustling city. Ile St.-Louis is named after **Louis IX,** the saintly French king who recited his breviary here among the cows. **Voltaire** considered this island the "second best" location in the world (his first choice was the straits of the Bosporus separating Europe from Asia).

Communities have only lived here for 300 years, yet the island is the oldest preserved section of the French capital, bisected by a single commercial street. When **Henri IV** decided to "urbanize" the pastoral Ile St.-Louis for his courtiers as an extension of Place des Vosges, he hired **Jean-Christophe Marie.** Between 1614 and 1630, Marie laid out one of the city's first real estate developments with straight streets on a grid, an avant-garde idea in an age when streets followed meandering medieval cow paths.

Only six blocks long and two blocks wide, Ile St.-Louis is an isolated village with no subway stop, four small hotels, and a baker whose ovens are fueled with wood. The 6,000 *Louisiens* (as island residents are called) are a proud, independent breed who don't always take kindly to interlopers (Ile St.-Louis was the first quarter in Paris to chase out the Nazis during the Liberation). When Louisiens leave the island, they say they are going "to Paris" or "to the continent" or "to the mainland," a voyage that's less than the length of a football field. Many of the elder residents have not been off the island in years, and less than 25 years ago there was so little traffic on Sunday, the islanders played *boules* in the streets.

Soon after **Berthillon** opened its doors for business, ice cream became the rage of Paris, the island was rediscovered, and along with the notoriety came the inevitable chic tea salons and hordes of tourists. Among the island's better known residents: **Apollinaire, Balzac, Voltaire, Zola, Baudelaire, Cézanne, Courbet, Daumier, Delacroix, Colette, George Sand,** and **Georges Pompidou.**

32 Brasserie de Isle St.-Louis ★★$$ This Alsatian brasserie/tavern comes complete with the regional mascot—a stork perched on the old wooden bar. The bird, of course, is stuffed, and soon so are the neighborhood habitués who sit elbow-to-elbow dining on sausage, sauerkraut, ham knuckles, blueberry tarts, and *chopes* (steins) of Mutzig beer served by gruff waiters. The 1913 silver-plated espresso machine is a museum piece, as is the bartender, **Yvon Cottet.** This feisty Breton, who has worked for **Brigitte Bardot, Charles de Gaulle,** and **François Mitterrand,** has served in this noisy brasserie for the last 40 years. He is even immortalized by a statue in New York's Museum of Modern Art. Ask him for that story and you'll be his friend for life. ♦ Lunch, dinner, and late-night. Closed Wednesday, Thursday, and in August. 55 Quai de Bourbon (at Rue Jean-du-Bellay). No credit cards. Métro: Pont-Marie. 43.54.02.59

33 Le Flore en l'Ile ★★$ This recently renovated Viennese-style tearoom boasts a three-star view of the Panthéon on the Left Bank and the flying buttresses of Notre-Dame. It still offers music by Mozart and a good pot-au-feu, hearty breakfasts, and chocolate cake. ♦ Breakfast, lunch, snacks, dinner, and late-night. 42 Quai d'Orléans (between Rues Jean-du-Bellay and Boutarel). Métros: Maubert-Mutualité, Pont-Marie. 43.29.88.27

33 La Chaumière en l'Ile ★★$$ Enjoy the white tablecloths, fresh-cut flowers, and traditional French cuisine of **Gilles Ferron.** ♦ Lunch and dinner. 4 Rue Jean-du-Bellay (at Rue St.-Louis-en-l'Ile). Métros: Maubert-Mutualité, Pont-Marie. 43.54.27.34

34 18-20 Quai d'Orléans Columnist **Walter Lippmann** lived here in 1938. ♦ Between Rues le Regrattier and Budé. Métro: Pont-Marie

34 10 Quai d'Orléans The author of *From Here to Eternity,* **James Jones,** resided here with his family from 1958 to 1975 and entertained the likes of **Henry Miller, Alexander Calder, William Styron, Sylvia Beach,** and **James Baldwin.** ♦ At Rue Budé. Métro: Pont-Marie

35 Adam Mickiewicz Museum The life and times of exiled Mickiewicz, the "Byron of Poland," as well as the poet's relationships with the great Romantic French authors and musicians, are brought to life on the second floor of this library and museum. The private library, established in 1852, contains some 200,000 volumes, as well as copies of nearly every Polish newspaper published in the 19th century. In the Chopin Room on the first floor

are the composer's frayed armchair, his hand-penned mazurka scores, a death mask, and the world's only daguerreotype of the young pianist. ♦ Guided tours: Tu, Th-F 2-6PM. Call for summer hours. 6 Quai d'Orléans (between Rues des Deux-Ponts and le Regrattier). Métro: Pont-Marie. 43.54.35.61

36 Alain Carion A rock collector's paradise. You'll find minerals, geodes, meteorites, and minuscule fossilized black nautiluses fashioned into earrings. ♦ Tu-Sa 10:30AM-1PM, 2PM-7:30PM. 92 Rue St.-Louis-en-l'Ile (between Rues Jean-du-Bellay and le Regrattier). Métro: Pont-Marie. 43.26.01.16

36 La Crêpe St.-Louis ★$ A Breton crêperie offering 40 varieties of paper-thin pancakes filled with Roquefort, andouillette, curry, and spinach. For dessert try the flambé Irish Mist or the Amandine (vanilla ice cream, almonds, and chocolate). ♦ Lunch and dinner. 86 Rue St.-Louis-en-l'Ile (between Rues Jean-du-Bellay and le Regrattier). No credit cards. Métro: Pont-Marie. 43.26.34.21

37 Hôtel St.-Louis $$$ The cousin of the Lutèce and the Deux Iles, this modest hotel has exposed wooden beams, Louis XIII furniture, thick carpeting, and modern bathrooms, but *petits* bedrooms. Fifth-floor rooms have a view. ♦ 75 Rue St.-Louis-en-l'Ile (corner of Rue Boutarel). Métro: Pont-Marie. 46.34.02.13

37 Le Monde des Chimères ★★$$ This stone-and-beam bistro is a strong favorite of Ile St.-Louis natives. Among the specialties of chef **Cécille Ibane** are her 40-garlic chicken, *la brandade de morue,* and wild duck with apples. ♦ Lunch and dinner. Closed two weeks in February. 69 Rue St.-Louis-en-l'Ile (between Rues Boutarel and le Regrattier). Métro: Pont-Marie. 43.54.45.27

37 Hôtel de Lutèce $$$ Named after the first Roman settlement in Paris, this restored 17th-century town house is now a three-star hotel. Ask for one of the brighter rooms on the top floor; they offer exquisite views of the island's rooftops and the dome of the Panthéon across the river. ♦ 65 Rue St.-Louis-en-l'Ile (between Rues Boutarel and le Regrattier). Métro: Pont-Marie. 43.26.23.52

Believe it or not, the home of the Gauloise is exhibiting signs of a no-smoking consciousness. A law was recently passed in France outlawing (in theory) smoking in public places. Although posted signs say one thing—*Ne Pas Fumer*—smokers continue to light up, as the law is considered more a formality than an actual mandate. Some restaurateurs even gather up all the ashtrays from the tables—only to leave them conspicuously piled on a nearby sideboard for the asking.

38 Aux Anysetiers du Roy ★$$ Originally called *Au Petit Bacchus* (the scorched remains of a 300-year-old effigy of the God of drink and revelry slouch above the entrance), this tavern used to serve the gamblers and jocks who frequented the ancient *jeu de paume* (tennis) court across the street at No. 54. The chef recommends the *moules marinières* and the *profitéroles au chocolat*. Don't leave without washing your hands in the 17th-century pewter bathroom sink upstairs. ◆ Dinner. Closed Wednesday. 61 Rue St.-Louis-en-l'Ile (at Rue le Regrattier). Reservations required. Métro: Pont-Marie. 43.54.02.70

38 Hôtel des Deux-Iles $$$ A 17th-century mansion-turned-hotel with an abundance of fresh flowers. The hotel bar with a fireplace in the cellar and the Renaissance-style ceramic tiles in the bathrooms are adequate compensation for the smallish pastel rooms. ◆ Bar: M-Sa 6:30PM-midnight. 59 Rue St.-Louis-en-l'Ile (between Rues le Regrattier and Budé). Métro: Pont-Marie. 43.26.13.35

38 Pylones The place where whimsical rubber jewelry and accessories sell as briskly as hot chestnuts on a winter afternoon. In lieu of that Boucheron diamond bracelet, wouldn't you rather be wearing a fanciful cactus, fish skeleton, monkey, or maybe the Pyramids of Giza on your wrist? Other novelties include children's bibs and rubber padded overalls, plus whimsical alligator knives, Flintstone chess sets, and New Wave egg cups. ◆ Daily 11AM-7PM. 57 Rue St.-Louis-en-l'Ile (between Rues le Regrattier and Budé). Métro: Pont-Marie. 46.34.05.02

38 Hôtel Chenizot This former residence of the city's archbishops was also the home of **Theresia Cabarrus,** a noblewoman of insatiable sexual appetite. She offered herself to drawing-room Revolutionaries in 1789 and as a result of this gesture was dubbed *Notre-Dame de Thermidor*. While the plaster cornucopia and ferns in the first courtyard date from an 18th-century restoration, the mythological sea god over the front door and the sundial in the clammy rear courtyard are original 17th-century decorations. ◆ 51 Rue St.-Louis-en-l'Ile (between Rues le Regrattier and Budé). Métro: Pont-Marie

38 Rue de la Femme Sans Teste (Street of the Headless Woman) Shortly after the Revolution, the Rue Le Regrattier (named in the 17th century for an entrepreneur in the island development consortium) was dubbed the "Street of the Headless Woman" (in old French, *tête* was spelled with an *s*) after a decapitated statue at the corner of Rue Le Regrattier and Quai de Bourbon. "Headless woman," however, is a misnomer; the robed stone figure, severed at the torso, is believed to be Saint Nicholas, the patron saint of boatmen. His statue stands at the top of the stairs that once led down to the ferry. ◆ Métro: Pont-Marie

38 L'Insulaire ★★$$ In this 17th-century vaulted stone *cave*, used as a prison during the Revolution, owner and former Shakespearean actor **Jean-Baptiste Aubertin** entertains a late-night theater and nightclub crowd—until 4AM—with such delights as swordfish carpaccio, *magret de canard entier* with peaches, and *tagliatelles fraîches aux Saint Jacques et saumon*. For dessert, the *millefeuilles aux poires caramélisées* always gets rave reviews. ◆ Dinner and late-night. Closed Sunday. 8 Rue le Regrattier (between Rue St.-Louis-en-l'Ile and Quai d'Orléans). Reservations recommended. Métro: Pont Marie. 43.25.70.43

38 Galerie Robert Burawoy Specializing in ancient Japanese armor, this gallery feels like the battlefield locker room for filmmaker Akira Kurosawa's next samurai epic. You will find a $15,000 coat of 19th-century mail (complete with a mustachioed mask), ceremonial stirrups, lacquered wooden saddles, and sabers sharp enough to carve sushi. Burawoy exhibits and sells museum-quality Japanese weaponry to collectors and Walter Mitty shoguns. ◆ W-Sa 2-7PM. 12 Rue Le Regrattier (between Rue St.-Louis-en-l'Ile and Quai d'Orléans). Métro: Pont-Marie. 43.54.67.36

38 6 Rue Le Regrattier The voluptuous West Indian mistress of **Baudelaire, Jeanne Duval,** who was known as the "Black Venus," lived here (between Rue St.-Louis-en-l'Ile and Quai d'Orléans). ◆ Métro: Pont-Marie

38 La Castafiore ★★★$$ Five years ago the Anglo-American owners **Gerard** and **Ed** left the advertising business to open the Island's only Italian restaurant. The terracotta walls and white tablecloths create a warm ambience in which to enjoy *tagliatelles aux cèpes* or *poulet Bolognaise*. Don't pass up the homemade *tiramisù* or the naughty *Coupe Amarena* for dessert. ◆ Lunch and dinner. 51 Rue St.-Louis-en-l'Ile (between Rues le Regrattier and Budé). Reservations recommended. Métro: Pont Marie. 43.54.78.62

38 L'Epicerie French gourmands will feel right at home in this tiny shop packed to the rafters with delicacies to do penance for. Champagne mustard, *terrine de lapin*, foie gras, homemade wild strawberry jam, and beautifully wrapped bonbons are but a few of the treats. ◆ M-Sa 10:30AM-9PM; Su 1-7PM. 51 Rue St.-Louis-en-l'Ile (between Rues le Regrattier and Budé). Métro: Pont Marie. 43.25.20.14

"If you are lucky enough to have lived in Paris as a young man, then wherever you go for the rest of your life, it stays with you, for Paris is a moveable feast."

Ernest Hemingway, *A Moveable Feast*

39 Hôtel du Jeu de Paume $$$ Deftly fashioned around a royal tennis court dating from 1624 (*jeu de paume* is the medieval precursor of the game now played at Wimbledon and Flushing Meadow), this refined 32-room hotel is the first new hostelry on the islands in two decades. Room No. 4 overlooks the garden, and No. 7 features a terrace. ♦ 54 Rue St.-Louis-en-l'Ile (between Rues le Regrattier and des Deux-Ponts). Métro: Pont-Marie. 43.26.14.18

40 Les Fous de l'Ile ★★★$ Fresh-cut flowers on the bar and brass candlesticks on old wooden bistro tables, coupled with wacky monthly art exhibitions, surrealist postcards, and music from Telemann to Talking Heads make this converted *épicerie* the island's most relaxing and hip restaurant/café. At lunch, famished drama students arrive for the warm goat cheese salad, *tagliatelles au saumon fumé* with caviar, steak with Roquefort sauce, and all-American brownies and carrot cake. ♦ Lunch, dinner, and snacks. 33 Rue des Deux-Ponts (between Rue St.-Louis-en-l'Ile and Quai de Bourbon). Métro: Pont-Marie. 43.25.76.67

40 Marcel Haupois The home of old-fashioned bakery bread cooked in wood-burning ovens (*four chauffé au bois*). ♦ M-W, Sa-Su 6:45AM-1:30PM, 3-8:30PM. 35 Rue des Deux-Ponts (between Rue St.-Louis-en-l'Ile and Quai de Bourbon). Métro: Pont-Marie. 43.54.57.59

40 Au Franc Pinot ★★$$ One of the last of the island's original 92 taverns, this 350-year-old watering hole originally catered to sailors who anchored cargo ships next to the Pont-Marie. The metal grape cluster over the door dates from 1637. Not as old but agelessly satisfying are the Loire Valley reds served with homemade minced goose *rillettes* in the upstairs wine bar. For dinner, venture downstairs into the 17th-century vaulted wine cellar/restaurant where you may enjoy, among other specialties, the roast pigeon in cereal. ♦ Lunch and dinner. Closed Monday and Sunday. 1 Quai de Bourbon (at Rue des Deux-Ponts). Métro: Pont-Marie. 43.29.46.98

40 Au Pont Marie ★★$ Run by the Griffoul family from southwest France, *Rouergue* specialties are the highlight at this small rustic restaurant. Deserving of hearty appetites are the cabbage stuffed with beef and herbs and the cassoulet. ♦ Lunch and dinner. Closed Saturday and Sunday, and one week in August. 7 Quai de Bourbon (between Rues des Deux-Ponts and le Regrattier). Métro: Pont Marie. 43.54.79.62

40 3 Quai de Bourbon Explaining the plainness of the facade of this real-estate agency is a story in itself. The sumptuous Empire-style windows and storefront you don't see at **No. 3** were purchased by **J. Pierpont Morgan** and moved in 1926 to the Metropolitan Museum of Art in New York. They now serve as the entrance to the museum's Wrightsman Galleries, which house a superb collection of Louis XVI furniture and porcelain. ♦ Between Pont Marie and Pont Louis-Philippe. Métro: Pont-Marie

41 Post Office Cabins are available for making international phone calls. ♦ M-F 8AM-7PM; Sa 8AM-noon. 16 Rue des Deux-Ponts. Métro: Pont-Marie

42 Librairie Ulysse I In 1971 the free-spirited **Catherine Domain** opened this vest-pocket shop specializing in travel books. She has crammed in, higgledy-piggledy, 20,000 French and English titles on everything from trekking in the Himalayas to canoeing in South America. Domain recently opened a second bookshop, **Ulysse II** (26 Rue St.-Louis-en-l'Ile, 43.29.52.10), specializing in books on France, maps, and travel magazines. It's worth a special trip. ♦ Tu-Sa 2-8PM. 35 Rue St.-Louis-en-l'Ile (between Rues des Deux-Ponts and Budé). Métro: Pont-Marie. 43.25.17.35

42 Nos Ancêtres les Gaulois ★$$ A cavernous 240-person all-you-can-eat establishment tackily decorated with sheepskins, battered shields, and wild boars' heads (in sunglasses) to loosely evoke the Middle Ages. Earthy do-it-yourself salads, greasy sausage platters, grilled meat, chocolate mousse, and barely drinkable red wine are perennial hits with starving students and rowdy German tour groups. Always crowded. Arrive early and avoid Saturday nights, when the ambience is raucous, bordering on neanderthal. ♦ Dinner; Sunday lunch. 39 Rue St.-Louis-en-l'Ile (between Rues des Deux-Ponts and Budé). Reservations required. Métro: Pont-Marie. 46.33.66.07, 46.33.66.12

When one of the 170 big clocks found on Paris' public buildings and lampposts breaks down, the city's clock services, by tradition, place the hands at 12 o'clock until repairs can be made.

Restaurants/Clubs: Red   **Hotels:** Blue
Shops/ 🌳Outdoors: Green   **Sights/Culture:** Black

𝕭erthillon

GLACES	SORBETS	Pamplemousse rose
Agenaise	Abricot	Pêche
Cacahuète	Airelles	Poire
Caramel	Ananas	Quetsche
Chocolat	Cacao	Reine Claude
Chocolat au nougat	Cassis	Rhubarbe
Créole	Cerise	Thé
Dauphinois	Citron vert	**FRUITS**
Feuille de Menthe	Fraise	**EXOTIQUES**
Gianduja	Framboise	Banane
Grand-Marnier	Figue	Corossol
Marron glacé	Fraise de bois	Fruit de la Passion
Moka	Groseille	Goyave
Noisette	Mandarine	Kiwi
Noix	Melon	Kumquat
Nougat au miel	Menthe	Litchees
Pistache	Mirabelle	Mangue
Plombières	Mure	Noix de coco
Praliné aux pignons	Myrtille	Papaye
Vanille		

43 Berthillon ★★★$ This Ile St.-Louis landmark is so popular that around Christmastime the police show up to direct the flow of Parisians queuing around the block for what is undeniably the best ice cream and sorbet in Paris. Berthillon enjoys the luxury (or chutzpa) of closing two days a week and going on vacation at the height of the ice cream-eating season. Surly women in pink aprons scoop up more than 50 flavors made without an ounce of artificial ingredients. Sample the exotic fruit flavors in season: rhubarb, black currant, fig, kumquat, and fresh melon. ♦ W-Su 10AM-8PM. Closed the last half of July, August, and during all school holidays. 31 Rue St.-Louis-en-l'Ile (between Rues des Deux-Ponts and Poulletier). Métro: Pont-Marie. 43.54.31.61

44 Au Gourmet de l'Isle ★★$$ A bustling bargain bistro famous for its andouillette (sausage with tripe)—a nice dish if you can stomach it. Other less challenging specialties: artichoke hearts and pork in red wine sauce, strawberry tarts, and Auvergne wines. ♦ Lunch and dinner. Closed Monday and Tuesday. 42 Rue St.-Louis-en-l'Ile (between Rues des Deux-Ponts and Poulletier). Dinner reservations recommended. Métro: Pont-Marie. 43.26.79.27

44 L'Auberge de la Reine Blanche ★$ Named for the mother of the Island's patron Saint Louis, this restaurant, with its pretty, pink interior, offers dependable French classics: *canard à la orange, coq au vin,* and *boeuf Bourguignon.* Catch the cute dollhouse furniture displayed on the walls. ♦ Lunch and dinner. 30 Rue St.-Louis-en-l'Ile (between Rues des Deux-Ponts and Poulletier). Reservations recommended. Métros: Pont Marie, Sully-Morland. 46.33.07.87

44 L'Orangerie ★$$$ A mini Maxim's with 18th-century decor and background harpsichord music that specializes in elegant late suppers. The ribs of beef and leg of lamb (cooked over a wood fire) and rich Bordeaux reds cause Rolls-Royce traffic jams out front. ♦ Dinner. Closed August. 28 Rue St.-Louis-en-l'Ile (between Rues des Deux-Ponts and Poulletier). Reservations required. Métro: Pont-Marie. 46.33.93.98

44 La Charlotte de l'Isle ★★$ At this little-known tea salon try the *gâteau du diable,* the half-moon cookies, or a wickedly delicious witch's broom (chocolate-dipped orange rinds). Sound diabolical? Charlotte, the hospitable kimono-clad owner, appears strangely obsessed with Halloween but swears she has yet to turn a customer into a toad. In the back room near the kitchen, you may sip freshly brewed Chinese tea at one of three tiny tables nestled among the clutter of puppets, dried-flower bouquets, and an old stereo playing Poulenc, while under Charlotte's spell. ♦ Afternoon and evening tea. Poetry readings Tu 8:30PM; puppet shows W at 2:30PM and 4PM; piano concert and tea F 6-8PM. Closed July and August. 24 Rue St.-Louis-en-l'Ile (between Rues des Deux-Ponts and Poulletier). Métro: Pont-Marie. 43.54.25.83

45 St.-Louis-en-l'Ile Church Popular for weddings and candlelit concerts, this Jesuit baroque edifice was built in 1726 after the plans of island resident **Louis Le Vau,** the great French architect who designed portions of the Louvre and Versailles. Inside is a statue of Saint Louis in chain mail and crusader's sword, and next to the tomb of a Polish freedom fighter with a daunting name (**Damaiowicestrzembosz**) is a 1926 plaque that bears the inscription: "In grateful memory of St. Louis in whose honor the City of Saint Louis, Missouri, USA, is named." The church was heavily vandalized during the Revolution, as you can see by the carved cherubs over the massive wooden west portal who look strangely empty-handed; they once held the king's *fleur-de-lis.* The only reason the church statues of Sainte Geneviève and the Virgin Mary survived the Revolution is because they were disguised as the goddesses of Reason and Freedom. Evening concerts are held here frequently. ♦ Daily 9AM-noon, 3-7PM. Mass: M-F 8AM; Sa 6:30PM; Su 11AM. 3 Rue Poulletier (19bis Rue St.-Louis-en-l'Ile). Métro: Pont-Marie

46 24 Quai de Bethune In 1935 **Helena Rubinstein** demolished one of the island's finest town houses (constructed in 1642) and built an Art Deco structure in its place, over which she reigned from the rooftop apartment. ♦ At Rue de Bretonvilliers. Métro: Pont-Marie

47 Square Barye At the eastern tip of the island, this pocket park is all that remains of the terraced gardens of **Duc de Bretonvillier.** You might glimpse sunbathers or witness a schoolboys' fishing competition here on the cobblestone *quai.* ♦ Métros: Pont-Marie, Sully-Morland

Renderings of Hôtel Lambert

48 Hôtel Lambert Probably the most opulent of 17th-century private residences in Paris, this frescoed and pilastered *hôtel particulier* was designed by **Louis Le Vau** in 1640 for **Lambert the Rich.** Its lavish gilded ceilings by **Charles Le Brun** predate and rival his Great Hall of Mirrors at Versailles. After the 1830-31 insurrection, Polish **Prince Adam Czartoryski** fled to France, married **King Louis-Phillipe's** granddaughter, and bought the Hôtel Lambert for his digs. Over the years, Czartoryski's residence served as a salon for expatriate Polish royalty and intelligentsia and as a rehearsal hall for **Frédéric Chopin.** Later it functioned as a girls finishing school and a safe house for Allied fighter pilots shot down in France. **Voltaire** briefly nested here with his lover, the **Marquise de Châtelet,** while writing the **Henriade.** Since 1972 the house has belonged to the **Rothschilds.** Behind the locked gate is a horseshoe-shaped courtyard and the famous **Galerie d'Hercule,** containing the **Le Sueur** frescoes and **Jacques Rousseau** trompe l'oeil landscape paintings. Open to the public on rare occasions. ♦ 2 Rue St.-Louis-en-l'Ile (between Pont de Sully and Rue Poulletier). Métros: Pont-Marie, Sully-Morland

48 Librairie Libella This dissident Polish bookstore and small press smuggled out the sermons of priest **Jerzy Popieluszko** in 1984 and published them shortly before his murder. Libella stocks everything from Polish fairy tales to Solidarity literature in French and English. The Lambert Gallery next door exhibits the works of contemporary Polish and Eastern European painters. ♦ Bookstore and gallery: Tu-Sa 9AM-noon, 3-7PM. 12 Rue St.-Louis-en-l'Ile (between Pont de Sully and Rue Poulletier). Métros: Pont-Marie, Sully-Morland. 43.26.51.09

48 5 Rue St.-Louis-en-l'Ile The expatriate literary agent **William Aspenwall Bradley,** who represented **Thornton Wilder, Edith Wharton, Katherine Anne Porter,** and **John Dos Passos,** lived here. Bradley was the one who closed the deal for publication of the *Autobiography of Alice B. Toklas* by **Gertrude Stein.** ♦ Between Pont de Sully and Rue de Bretonvilliers. Métro: Pont-Marie

49 9 Quai d'Anjou The 19th-century illustrator and satirist, **Honoré Daumier,** lived here off and on for 17 years in the company of distinguished islanders such as poet **Baudelaire** and fellow artist **Delacroix.** It was on the Ile St.-Louis that Daumier sketched his mordant portrayals of life and politics and painted masterpieces such as *La Blanchisseuse* (The Washer Woman), which hangs in the Louvre. ♦ Between Pont de Sully and Rue Poulletier. Métros: Pont-Marie, Sully-Morland

50 Hôtel Lauzun **Louis Le Vau** built a mansion in 1656 for a corrupt French army caterer, **Charles Gruyn des Bordes,** who was arrested soon afterward. That is why the building is named for its second tenant, **Saint Simon's** brother-in-law, the dandy **Duke of Lauzun.** The roll call of residents and visitors to the Hôtel Lauzun includes **Rilke, Wagner, Daumier, Delacroix,** and **Steinheil** (who restored the Ste.-Chapelle windows). In 1834 **Baudelaire** gathered his bohemian "hashish club" in an upstairs room and conducted the hallucinatory research for his book *Les Paradis Artificiels.* Some of the gaudiest suites in all of Paris are the *chambres de parade* (parade rooms), which are cluttered with golden nymphs, cut-velvet walls, trompe l'oeil murals, and allegorical figures. In 1928 the city bought and restored it as a residence for visiting heads of state. ♦ Currently under renovation with no plans to open to the public. For information, call the Centre d'Accueil de la Ville de Paris. 17 Quai d'Anjou (between Pont de Sully and Rue Poulletier). Métros: Pont-Marie, Sully-Morland. 42.76.54.04

51 29 Quai d'Anjou In 1922, with a hand-printing press, American **William Bird** established his **Three Mountains Press** here. Under the editorial aegis of **Ezra Pound,** it published **Ernest Hemingway** and **Ford Madox Ford.** ♦ Between Rues Poulletier and des Deux-Ponts. Métros: Pont-Marie, Sully-Morland

51 37 Quai d'Anjou When he arrived in France in 1921 after the acceptance of his first major novel, *Three Soldiers,* **John Dos Passos** rented a room in this building. ♦ Between Rues Poulletier and des Deux-Ponts. Métros: Pont-Marie, Sully-Morland

52 Pont Marie King Louis XIII laid the first stone of this bridge, which was completed in 1635 and partially destroyed by the 1658 spring thaw. The thaw caused a flood that dumped 22 of the bridge's four-story houses into the Seine, drowning 121 residents and shopkeepers. The bridge is not named after **Marie de Médici, Henri IV's** widow, who commissioned the work, but after **Jean-Christophe Marie,** the contractor hired to develop Ile St.-Louis and the *quais.* ♦ Métro: Pont-Marie

53 Le Trumilou ★★$ The perfect way to enjoy this authentic Parisian bistro is at a window table overlooking the Seine and Notre-Dame. **Jean-Claude Dumond** and his family prepare home-cooked food at sensible prices. Favorites include duck with prunes, lamb with white beans, *sole meunière,* and *poulet provençal* (chicken in tomato sauce with *herbes de Provence*). For dessert, try the *oeufs à la neige* (meringue floating in *crème anglaise*). ♦ Lunch and dinner. Closed Monday. 84 Quai de l'Hôtel-de-Ville (between Pont d'Arcole and Pont Louis-Philippe). Métro: Hôtel-de-Ville. 42.77.63.98

53 Miravile ★★★$$$ The word is out: Gilles Epié, the highly regarded young chef, is expected to achieve *grand chef* status by the end of the decade. His elegant restaurant is appropriately named after the word for marvelous in Old French. Epié's imaginative takes on French cuisine include Italian and provençal accents. Among his celebrated creations are *beignet de foie gras caramélisé au porto,* prawns marinated in balsamic vinegar with a *tapenade tomatée,* lobster tail grilled with *jus gras de jambon* served with white beans, and garlic-roasted lamb served with *foie gras.* For dessert, the *chaudcocolat mousse,* a warm, chewy chocolate mousse cake served with coconut sorbet, is as divine as it sounds. ♦ Lunch and dinner; dinner only on Saturday. Closed Sunday. 72 Quai de l'Hôtel-de-Ville (between Pont d'Arcole and Pont Louis-Philippe). Reservations recommended. Métro: Hôtel-de-Ville. 42.74.72.22

> "Paris is the greatest temple ever built to material joys and the lust of the eyes."
>
> **Henry James**

Bests

Gonzague Saint Bris
Author

Paris is the world's best city for a love affair. It is like the compartmentalized shell of a snail, or the plan of a brothel that Leonardo da Vinci once drew, where the clients never run into each other. You move to another quarter and you're unrecognized. Thus some people can carry on several love affairs at the same time, as long as they don't have two mistresses in one neighborhood.

The most cinematic place to take a girl is the **Château Raray,** where **Jean Cocteau** made the film *Beauty and the Beast.*

The best secret place in Paris is the varnished wooden cabin in the sky that **Gustave Eiffel** built at the top of the tower that bears his name; it was for seducing adventurous visitors.

Best place to break up: **Françoise Sagan** says there is no better spot than the table near the door of the **Brasserie Lipp**—you know so many people coming in that you have to greet them endlessly, never allowing time to try to explain your questionable conduct to your companion. Thus one avoids long, sad justifications.

Best hotels: For a night of love, a room at the **Hôtel Bristol.** For writing, **Oscar Wilde's** room at **L'Hôtel** on the Rue des Beaux-Arts. For dreaming, the roof of the **Crillon Hôtel** in the golden dawn, from which you can contemplate the **Place de la Concorde** (**Curzio Malaparte** said, "The Place de la Concorde isn't a place, it's an idea").

My favorite place: the **Palais Royal,** where I can sing under the window of **Inès de la Fressange,** the most beautiful woman in Paris and a former top model for Chanel.

My favorite museum: **Le Musée Carnavalet.**

My favorite restaurant: **Le Grand Véfour.**

My favorite garden: the one on the **Champs-Elysées,** where the infant **Proust** played with my great-grandmother in the sandpile. I also like the public gardens, where, in summer, without asking permission, I give rustic dinner parties (particularly in the **Place du Canada,** which is hidden from view with its woods and romantic rocks).

My favorite rendezvous spot: on **Rue de Rivoli,** across from the **Louvre,** under the statue of my ancestor, **General Desaix,** a rival and friend of **Bonaparte.** He was killed in civilian costume because he arrived late to the Battle of Marengo. He had superb long hair.

My simplest pleasure: walking my dog, Byron, through any street in Paris.

Régine
Owner of Régine's restaurant and nightclub

Lunch at the **Relais Plaza, Stresa, Le Pré Carré,** or the **Bar des Théâtres.**

The **Louvre** and **Georges Pompidou** museums.

Clothes from **Alaïa, Ungaro,** and **Jean Claude.**

Peter Dawson
Author

My favorite places for a rendezvous:

The summer house in the **Parc de Bagatelle** that dominates the prettiest rose garden in Paris—enchanting in any season.

At the counter of **Ma Bourgogne,** in the **Place des Vosges,** sipping a simple wine and nibbling a *croque monsieur.*

In the main salon at **Angélina,** eating a ruinous **Mont Blanc** and drinking the richest hot chocolate in the world, protected by the last vestiges of old Europe.

The **Espadon** bar of the **Ritz** for a cocktail at 6PM and maybe an impromptu performance by Gainsbourg on the piano.

The top-floor bar of the **Concorde Lafayette** at the Porte Maillot with a glass of champagne at sundown.

The **Ste.-Chapelle** on the night of a candlelit concert.

Le Vivarois for whatever brilliant entrée **Claude Peyrot** may recommend that day.

The **Bistro 121** for their *poireaux vinaigrette,* which you must order when you make your reservations (it raises the humble leek to an art form), and the *poule-au-pot.*

The **Cochon d'Or** for the best grilled *pied de cochon* in the world and the finest piece of grilled French beef.

Chez Allard for the *pâté de foie de volaille* and the *canard aux olives.*

Chez Georges at Porte Maillot for the perfectly cooked *train de côtes de boeuf.*

The **Train Bleu** for a *saucisson chaud de Lyon* and the illusion of travel in the most stunning fin-de-siècle decor.

Gerri Gallagher
Managing Editor, W Fashion Europe magazine

Breakfast at **La Palette** on weekdays: This is regarded as one of the greatest watering holes in Paris, and **Jean-François** (one of the owners but better known as a waiter to the clientele) has a reputation as the gruffest waiter in Paris (not true!). Breakfast is my favorite time because all the people who live in the neighborhood stop for coffee and croissants and to catch up with each other. It's ideal in the spring and summer when you can sit on the terrace, soaking up the early morning sun and the truly Parisian atmosphere.

Les Puces at **Porte de Clignancourt** on Sundays: It's in a distant arrondissement (the 18th), but this flea market is well worth the trip. Some think it's too expensive, but for quality and interesting antiques, I think it's the best. Go early (but not before 9AM) and stay for lunch. There's lots to see. My favorite arcade is **Serpette.**

Au Sauvignon in the afternoon: The perfect wine bar to stop by after work for delicious wine and a ham sandwich, cut into little pieces. Nobody pressures you about leaving, so it's perfect for watching the world go by.

Philippe Uzzan
Gallery Owner

Late-night supper at **Le Val d'Isère,** a rare touristless French restaurant near the Champs-Elysées.

Luxembourg Gardens—in December at 5PM, in April at 10AM.

La Hune's bookshelves.

Paris Store in the Chinese district—the only food market where you can find grapefruit over 10 inches in diameter.

Being stuck in front of the **Bonpoint** children's store display.

Going to the street market on Avenue du Président Wilson, in front of the **Musée d'Art Moderne de la Ville de Paris ("l'Arc")** on Saturday morning: it's a unique mixture of the 16th-district Parisian way of life and the culture of cutting-edge art.

A view of the **Grande Arche de la Défense** from behind at night.

Any kind of terrace of any apartment in any district.

Doing the **Rue du Pré-aux-Clercs** stores—except on Saturday.

Eggs at **Coffee Parisien,** duck at **Poule au Pot,** salad at **Stella,** Italian entrées at **Cherche Midi.**

And all that I can discover without a tourist guide.

Jane Ailsa Wrightson
Architect

To visit the bustling market street of Rue Montorgueil in the early morning and have coffee in the **Sega Fredo** café.

To lunch at **Le Reveil du 10e** with a fine wine and simple plate of charcuterie.

To relax and read beside the Italian fountain in the **Luxembourg Gardens,** to contemplate in the tiny Japanese garden behind **Musée Guimet,** and to stroll through the **Palais Royal,** which changes mood with every passing hour and season.

To visit the terrace of **L'Institut du Monde Arabe** and enjoy the light and movement of its design; the ground floor and bookshop of the **Centre Georges Pompidou;** and the **Pont des Arts,** the beautiful wood-and-iron bridge across the Seine.

To attend a ballet at the **Paris Opéra;** to admire the Grand Staircase and circular anterooms at intermission.

To stand underneath the **Tour Eiffel.**

To have a cocktail at the **Montparnasse Tower** for the view or at **La Chope des Artistes** for the piano music and artistic clientele. To hear jazz at the **China Club** near Place de la Bastille.

Finally, to drive at night around **Place de la Concorde** and then across the Seine toward the golden dome of **Hôtel des Invalides.**

Restaurants/Clubs: Red	Hotels: Blue
Shops/ Outdoors: Green	Sights/Culture: Black

The Latin Quarter

This section of the city is Roman Paris, the university, and the bohemian quarter. The **Henri Burger** novel *La Vie Bohème*, which became the **Puccini** opera *La Bohème*, was set here. The Latin Quarter was once the home of **Verlaine** and **Descartes**, and is still the home of the **Sorbonne**, old bookshops, student cafés, publishing houses, jazz clubs, and, more recently, expensive boutiques. For seven centuries, this was a city within a city, where scholars had a tongue of their own (Latin), were exempt from the civil law, and recognized no authority except for the Pope. Latin, which hasn't been spoken here since the Revolution, was replaced on the streets of the Left Bank by the Moroccan, Greek, and Vietnamese of immigrant families selling couscous, souvlaki, and Imperial rolls to supplement the basic bohemian diet of coffee and cheap cigarettes.

Ⓜ = *Métro*

Dodin-Bouffant—look for François Mitterrand at the next table. This is one of his favorite neighborhood restaurants

Old Roman Arena—the benches make this a good picnic spot

France's oldest mosque features minarets, pink marble fountains, Turkish baths, and sweet mint tea

Ⓜ **Monge**

In 1938, workers found 3,351 22-karat gold coins hidden in the wall at Nos. 51 to 55 Rue Mouffetard

Ⓜ **Censier-Daubenton**

The colorful, open-air **Mouffetard Market** (a shopping site since 1350) begins here next to the street's best café, **Brasserie Mouffetard**, where the Chartrain family bakes croissants, brioches, and fruit tarts daily

On weekend afternoons, an old organ grinder cranks out traditional French chansons

Ⓜ **Gobelins**

Gobelins Tapestry Factory—visit the weavers at work during tours Tuesday through Thursday between 2:00 and 3:00PM

Ⓜ **Gare d'Austerlitz**

Ⓜ **Jussieu**

This itinerary begins at the **Pont de la Tournelle**, in front of the famed penthouse restaurant, **La Tour d'Argent,** and takes in the booksellers along the Seine and a splendid view of **Notre-Dame's** flying buttresses. Next comes **François Mitterrand's** house, two funny, offbeat museums—the **Musée des Hôpitaux de Paris-Assistance Publique** (Museum of Public Health and Welfare) and the **Musée des Collections Historiques de la Préfecture de Police** (Police Museum)—and then the **Rue des Ecoles** to the Sorbonne and the **Collège de France,** which for centuries have been the most celebrated seats of learning in Europe. At the end of the street are the Roman baths adjoining the extraordinary medieval **Cluny Museum.** Climbing **Montagne Ste.-Geneviève,** named after the patron saint of Paris, you pass **King Philippe Auguste's** 13th-century city wall; **Le Raccard,** a landmark for fondue lovers; and the **Panthéon,** a classical monument in whose crypt lie **Voltaire, Rousseau,** and **Victor Hugo.**

At the **Place de la Contrescarpe,** the more adventuresome may peel off for a detour past a Roman arena and a Turkish mosque complete with minarets, arriving at the zoo and botanical gardens—a nice spot for a picnic lunch purchased in the **Place-Monge** or **Mouffetard Market.** On the **Rue Mouffetard,** a medieval market street frequented this century by the likes of **Ernest Hemingway** and **Josephine Baker,** you might meander past stalls selling everything from tropical mangoes to African monkey bread and end up at **Gobelins,** the old royal weaving mills, for a possible afternoon tour. If you hunger for a meal, you will find inexpensive Vietnamese and Greek shish-kebab restaurants abounding along Mouffetard around Gobelins. For the more pricey establishments, including **Dodin-Bouffant, Auberge des Deux Signes,** or **La Tour d'Argent,** and the nightspots in this vicinity, such as the **Paradis Latin** or **Les Trois Maillets,** head toward the Rue des Ecoles and the Seine.

Pont de la Tournelle

1 Sainte Geneviève On the **Pont de la Tournelle** (illustrated above), one of the Seine's newest bridges (1928) and the fifth in a long line that dates back to 1369, is a missilelike statue of the city's patron. Apparently ready for a heavenly liftoff, the angular obelisk of Sainte Geneviève by **Landowski** turns her back on Notre-Dame and faces upriver, guarding the city as her spirit has done since 450. In that year, the prayers of the then 27-year-old nun were credited with halting **Attila the Hun's** advance on Paris, after his army of barbarians had just sacked Cologne and brutalized 10,000 of its maidens.

In 473, while the city was under siege by the Franks, Geneviève courageously smuggled 11 boatloads of food to starving Parisians through enemy lines. She lived on this Left Bank mountain until the ripe age of 89 and, like France's other virgin saint, **Jeanne d'Arc,** was consigned to flames, but not until 1,281 years after her death. The fanatic anticlerics of the Revolution burned her remains and cast the ashes into the river. ♦ Métros: Cardinal-Lemoine, Pont-Marie

Restaurants/Clubs: Red   **Hotels:** Blue
Shops/ 🌳 Outdoors: Green   **Sights/Culture:** Black

2 La Tour d'Argent ★★★★$$$$ This may no longer be the best restaurant in Paris, but its penthouse panorama of Notre-Dame's flying buttresses and the barges passing on the Seine has helped make it the city's most famous, expensive, and spectacular eating establishment. Tour d'Argent is successor to an earlier *auberge* that occupied the same site, the **Café Anglais**, which was founded in 1582. The Café Anglais was mentioned by **Madame de Sévigné** in her famous letters and provided the setting for a **Dumas** novel. It is said that this is also where the fork was first used in Paris. On the ground floor of the restaurant is a table set with the original silver, crystal, and china that were used on 7 June 1867 to serve a dinner at the Café Anglais attended by **Czar Alexander II**, the **Czarevitch**, **Wilhelm I**, and **Bismarck.**

The touch of class is evident throughout the Tour d'Argent, from the Grand Siècle-style elevator to the traditional blue cornflower in the jacket lapel of restaurant owner and dandy **Claude Terrail**. The Tour d'Argent's pièce de résistance is its pressed duck flambé, first served in 1890 to **Edward VII**, then Prince of Wales. More than 600,000 ducklings later, the dish is still a hit. The kitchen keeps a running tally of the number of ducklings pressed, and each order arrives at the table with a numbered card. Other recommended dishes include cold Lagardère lobster, flambéed peaches, and bittersweet chocolate cake. The wine list draws from the 300,000 bottles in the vaulted cellars underground. You can tour the cellars after dessert and watch Terrail's little sound-and-light show while sipping a vintage liqueur. In the rooftop restaurant you must reserve your table far in advance; ask for one by the picture window. Bear in mind, however, that lunch is just half the price of dinner and midday is when Parisians eat out. The Tour d'Argent is popular with Americans and Japanese, and the only French speakers in the place at dinner may be the waiters. ♦ Lunch and dinner. Closed Monday. 15 Quai de la Tournelle (at Rue du Cardinal Lemoine). Reservations required. Métro: Maubert-Mutalité. 43.54.23.31

3 Les Comptoirs de la Tour d'Argent If you want to take one of the Tour d'Argent's trademark blue-and-white Limoges plates home as a souvenir, walk across the street to the gourmet boutique of **Claude Terrail**, the enterprising restaurateur who has become the Pierre Cardin of French cuisine. Here, instead of dinner for $180, you can buy a menu for $18, fresh *foie gras de canard* to go, or an entire Tour d'Argent place setting, including fluted champagne glass, coffee spoon, and ashtray. Prices start at $4 for 140 grams of Dijon mustard and escalate to more than $2,000 for a bottle of Fine Clos du Griffier 1788. ♦ Tu-Sa 10AM-midnight; Su noon-midnight. 2 Rue du Cardinal-Lemoine (at Quai de la Tournelle). Métros: Cardinal-Lemoine, Maubert-Mutalité. 46.33.45.58

4 Le Rallye ★★$ Locals lunch here during the day, but when an earthy crowd takes over at night, the café comes to resemble an Amsterdam bar. It's just down the street from **La Tour d'Argent** but it's a world away in spirit, with *Tintin* cartoon memorabilia on display, a friendly boxer named Figaro underfoot, and music ranging from opera to Jimi Hendrix. Avoid the bathroom. ♦ Breakfast, lunch, and snacks. 11 Quai de la Tournelle (between Rue du Cardinal-Lemoine and Blvd St.-Germain). Métros: Cardinal-Lemoine, Maubert-Mutalité. 43.54.29.65

5 L'Atlas ★★$$ Chef **El Jaziri Bijamin** likens himself to a culinary ambassador promoting unique dishes from his native Morocco. The *tagines* include a lustily spiced fish stew with saffron and a lamb stew with forest mushrooms. The elegant couscous *de L'Atlas*, which includes veal, meatballs, and lamb, is another fine main course. A sweet mint tea with orange blossom nectar will end the meal soothingly. ♦ Lunch and dinner. 12 Blvd St.-Germain (at Rue du Cardinal-Lemoine). Métros: Cardinal-Lemoine, Maubert-Mutalité. 46.33.86.98, 44.07.23.66

6 Chez René ★★$$ An authentic bistro with amusing waiters, Chez René offers tasty daily specials that range from Monday's pot-au-feu to Friday's *blanquette de veau* (veal in white sauce). Also on the menu are cucumbers and cream, country sausages, mutton with white beans, *entrecôte Bercy*, and in the autumn, *pleurotes provençales* (fresh wild mushrooms baked with garlic). ♦ Lunch and dinner. Closed Saturday, Sunday, August, and two weeks at Christmas. 14 Blvd St.-Germain (at Rue du Cardinal-Lemoine). Reservations recommended. Métros: Cardinal-Lemoine, Maubert-Mutalité. 43.54.30.23

7 Campagne et Provence ★★★$$ Gilles Epié's classy new restaurant is simpler and less expensive than his marvelous **Miravile** across the river. Here chef **Alain Gerard** prepares a palette of provençal dishes whose tastes range from soothing to robust. Choose from such specialties as vegetables stuffed with ground beef à la provençale, fresh cod with aioli, and lamb with wild herbs. Those who habitually abstain from dessert may be tempted by the blueberry tart with *sorbet fromage blanc* or the superb *tiramisù*. ◆ Lunch and dinner; dinner only on Monday. Closed Sunday. 25 Quai de la Tournelle (between Rues du Cardinal-Lemoine and de Poissy). Métro: Maubert-Mutualité. 43.54.05.17

8 Vivario ★★$$ **Michel Hilaire,** the owner of this small neighborhood restaurant, is serious about the quality of the Italian and Corsican meals he serves. The menu changes every day to make the most of what's fresh, but it always includes some delicious pasta. ◆ Lunch and dinner; dinner only on Sunday. Closed Monday, Saturday, from mid-Aug to mid-Sept, and one week at Christmas. 6 Rue Cochin (between Rues de Pontoise and de Poissy). Métro: Maubert-Mutualité. 43.25.08.19

9 Boulangerie Beauvallet Julien Modesty may prevent **Monsieur Ousbih** and his family from putting their bakery's name in the window, but they won't divulge the recipe that results in the best baguettes in the Latin Quarter. Thin, crusty, with the tang of sourdough, one of these baguettes is the perfect base for building a picnic to take down to the *quai*. ◆ M-Tu, Th-Su 7AM-8PM. Baking times: 7AM, 11AM, 1PM. Closed in August. 6 Rue de Poissy (at Rue Cochin). Métro: Maubert-Mutualité. 43.26.94.24

10 Chez Toutoune ★★$$$ **Colette Toutoune Dejean** offers traditional home-style meals at old-fashioned prices. The five-course menu chalked on the blackboard changes daily, but you can count on the pot-au-feu, braised guinea hen with cabbage, mussels with endive, grilled leg of lamb, currant tarts, and creamy Brie. ◆ Lunch and dinner; dinner only on Monday. Closed Sunday, and in August. 5 Rue de Pontoise (at Rue Cochin). Dinner reservations recommended. Métro: Maubert-Mutualité. 43.26.56.81

10 La Marée Verte ★★$$ This bargain seafood restaurant is known for its hearty fisherman's plate, turbot soufflé (which rivals the one served around the corner in the chic Dodin-Bouffant), and delicious meringue tarts. ◆ Lunch and dinner. Closed Monday. 9 Rue de Pontoise (between Rue Cochin and Blvd St.-Germain). Reservations recommended. Métro: Maubert-Mutualité. 43.25.89.41

10 Le Bistro d'Hannah ★$ At this unassuming bistro, restaurateurs **Eric** and **Sonia Marcyz** serve four flavorful cuts of Aberdeen Angus beef from the sole supplier in France, accompanied by refreshing Beaujolais *crus.* ◆ Lunch and dinner; lunch only on Monday. Closed Tuesday. 9 Rue de Pontoise (between Rue Cochin and Blvd St.-Germain). Métro: Maubert-Mutualité. 43.54.68.23

11 Pontoise Swimming Pool and Club Quartier Latin Squash Club Surrounded by rows of old lockers and changing rooms, this pretty indoor pool is one of the few in Paris where lap swimming is the norm and lane markers are respected. Downstairs is an athletic club with four squash courts, Jacuzzi, sauna, dance classes, lounge, and a snack bar where salads, steaks, and fruit juices are served. Day passes to the pool and squash club are available. ◆ Gym and squash club: M-F 10AM-10PM; Sa-Su 9:30AM-7PM. 43.54.82.45 (call for summer hours). Pool: M, F 7-8:45AM, noon-1:45PM, 5-9PM; Tu noon-1:45PM, 5-9PM; W 7-8:45AM, 11:15AM-9PM; Th noon-1:45PM, 5-7:30PM; Sa 10AM-7:30PM; Su 8AM-6PM. 43.54.06.23 (call for summer hours). 19 Rue de Pontoise (between Blvd St.-Germain and Rue St.-Victor). Métros: Cardinal-Lemoine, Maubert-Mutualité. 43.54.06.23

12 St.-Nicolas-du-Chardonnet Built in 1709, this sanctuary was originally a 13th-century chapel standing in a field of *chardons* (thistles). Later redesigned by **Charles Le Brun**, it now houses the Le Brun family chapel, along with Charles Le Brun's *The Martyrdom of Saint John.* The beautiful wood carving over the side door on the Rue des Bernadins is also his work. St.-Nicolas-du-Chardonnet happens to be one of the most liturgically conservative churches in Paris: Mass is said entirely in Latin. ◆ Blvd St.-Germain (at Rue des Bernardins). Métros: Cardinal-Lemoine, Maubert-Mutualité

13 Diptyque Run by English and French artists who met while studying at the Ecole des Beaux-Arts after World War II, this tiny corner shop specializes in elegant antique bead necklaces, rose-petal sachets, Welsh bedspreads, Shetland plaids, and candles scented like the forest floor on a damp May morning. ◆ Tu-Sa 10AM-7PM. 34 Blvd St.-Germain (at Rue de Pontoise). Métros: Cardinal-Lemoine, Maubert-Mutualité. 43.26.45.27

13 HG Thomas The boutique of **Hervé Gerald Thomas** offers the *très chic* gifts that are Italian luggage, *double* umbrellas, hunting knives,

Braun clocks, and whiskey flasks. The inventory ranges from designer ballpoints to Weber barbecues. Most everything at HG Thomas comes in black. ♦ Tu-Sa 10:30AM-8PM. 36 Blvd St.-Germain (between Rues de Pontoise and des Bernardins). Métro: Maubert-Mutualité. 46.33.57.50

13 Au Pactole ★★$$$ François Mitterrand favors this seafood restaurant. The delicacies of chef **Roland Magne** encompass *marbre de poissons aux algues*, lobster sautéed in ginger, and Argentine steak with a red wine sauce. ♦ Lunch and dinner; dinner only on Saturday. Closed Sunday and Christmas Day. 44 Blvd St.-Germain (between Rues de Pontoise and des Bernardins). Reservations recommended. Métro: Maubert-Mutualité. 43.26.92.28, 46.33.31.31

14 Musée des Hôpitaux de Paris—Assistance Publique (Museum of Public Health and Welfare) Tucked away in this 17th-century mansion, which was converted into the central pharmacy for the city's hospitals after the Revolution, is one of Paris' most offbeat yet entertaining museums. Unknown to most Parisians, this museum of French medicine contains an extraordinary collection of old ceramic apothecary jars, Roman medicine vials, hospital rosters, pewter syringes, copper basins, blocks of marble that were pulverized to powder baby bottoms, and a mechanical model of a quasi-night deposit box that 19th-century nuns invented for abandoned babies. ♦ Admission. Tu-Sa 10AM-5PM. Closed August and holidays. 47 Quai de la Tournelle (between Rues de Pontoise and des Bernardins). Métro: Maubert-Mutualité. 46.33.01.43

14 45 Quai de la Tournelle After being discharged from the American Ambulance Corps in the spring of 1919, **John Dos Passos** sublet a playwright's apartment here and began what would become his first successful novel, *Three Soldiers*. ♦ Between Rues de Pontoise and des Bernardins. Métro: Maubert-Mutualité

15 Jean-Pierre Stella Legions of lead soldiers stand at attention and ready to serve. Stella's little shop on the quay also deals in military medals, samurai armor, Napoleonic helmets, and vintage weaponry. ♦ M-Sa 2-7PM or by appointment. Closed in August. 67 Quai de la Tournelle (between Rues Maître Albert and de Bièvre). Métro: Maubert-Mutualité. 46.33.40.50

15 Rue de Bièvre This unpretentious street of abandoned shops and couscous restaurants is barricaded at both ends and guarded round the clock. That's because French **President François Mitterrand** lives at **No. 22.** Though the Elysée Palace is the official presidential residence, Mitterrand, a socialist, has departed from tradition and returns here to sleep as often as possible. A blue police van parked on the *quai* is the tip-off that the president is at

home. At **No. 12,** a statue of Saint Michael slaying the dragon marks the former site of **Collège St.-Michel.** ♦ Métro: Maubert-Mutualité

16 Galerie Urubamba Traditional Indian art from the Americas is the specialty of this gallery/folk-art shop: Guatemalan weaving, handpainted Mexican masks, feathered Brazilian headdresses, and Panamanian shirt panels. You could spend hours perusing the ethnographic books and curios here. ♦ Tu-Sa 2-7:30PM. 4 Rue de la Bûcherie (at Rue du Haut Pavé). Métro: Maubert-Mutualité. 43.54.08.24

16 Patchworks du Rouvray Like the Galerie Urubamba across the square, this quilt emporium is run by an American woman. **Diane de Obaldia's** shop is named after a 14th-century farmhouse near Chartres, where she started her business. Today she sells the traditional American Midwest patchwork quilts of the 1930s. She offers about 40 quilting classes (in French and English) and 700 varieties of cotton fabric for inspired quilters. ♦ M 2-6:30PM; Tu-Sa 10:30AM-6:30PM. 1 Rue Frédéric-Sauton (at Impasse Maubert). Métro: Maubert-Mutualité. 43.25.00.45

17 Chieng-Mai ★★$$ An excellent Thai restaurant, Chieng-Mai serves beef *satay*, squid and mint salad, spicy pork brochette, and, for dessert, grilled flan with coconut milk. The pineapple salad is divine. ♦ Lunch and dinner. Closed Sunday. 12 Rue Frédéric-Sauton (at Rue des Trois-Portes). Reservations required. Métro: Maubert-Mutualité. 43.25.45.45

18 Dodin-Bouffant ★★$$$ One of the best seafood restaurants in Paris, Dodin-Bouffant (named after a character in a **Marcel Rouff** novel who's an extravagant gourmet) orders 500 pounds of fish daily, smokes its own herring and salmon, and has oysters delivered every day from Brittany and Ireland. Order the steamed scallops with fresh pasta or the curried sole with squash fondue and discover why this warm, casual bistro is one of François Mitterrand's favorite neighborhood restaurants. ♦ Lunch and dinner. Closed Sunday, August, and two weeks at Christmas. 25 Rue Frédéric-Sauton (at Rue Maître Albert). Reservations required. Métro: Maubert-Mutualité. 43.25.25.14

19 Than Binh This little Vietnamese grocery store supplies the many Southeast Asian restaurants and families clustered around Place Maubert. The exotic spices and bewildering assortment of food (rice steamed in banana leaves, tapioca in grape leaves, shrimp muffins) will transport your imagination to the Mekong Delta. ♦ Tu-Su 9AM-7:30PM. 29 Place Maubert (at Blvd St.-Germain). Métro: Maubert-Mutualité. 43.54.03.34

20 Place Maubert The name *Maubert* is probably a contraction of **Maître Albert,** who was a Dominican teacher at the University of Paris in the Middle Ages. For centuries, this wide spot in the road was a crime-ridden skid row, a resort for tramps drinking *gros rouge* (cheap red wine), and the site of public executions. Here, in 1546, during the reign of **François I,** printer and humanist philosopher **Etienne Dolet** was burned at the stake as a heretic; his own books were used to kindle the fire. In addition to serving as an execution ground, from the Middle Ages hence this crossroads has been a bustling open-air market. ◆ Market: Tu, Th, Sa 7AM-1PM. Métro: Maubert-Mutualité

21 Colbert $$$ From many of the 16 rooms in this former 18th-century residence (parts of the building date back to 1500), you can contemplate Notre-Dame while having breakfast in bed. The decor is a bit grim, but the rooms are quiet and simply furnished, and the beds have luxuriously smooth sheets (No. 41 is a studio with an especially fine view). The **Duke of Windsor** once sponsored an animal hospital on the site of the present courtyard garden. ◆ 7 Rue de l'Hôtel-Colbert (at Rue de la Bûcherie). Métro: Maubert-Mutualité. 43.25.85.65

22 Quai de Montebello Booksellers The *bouquinistes* who work in the shadow of Notre-Dame practice one of the city's oldest trades, selling old Daumier prints, volumes on everything from Balzac to bebop, and the occasional naughty postcard out of their green boxes on the quay (see illustration below). These famous, free-spirited cowboys of the book business open and close their sidewalk stalls when they please and sell only what interests them. ◆ Daily 11AM-7PM, depending on the weather. Located on the Quai de Montebello from the Petit Pont to the Pont de l'Archevêché. Métro: St.-Michel

22 Pont au Double The only bridge in Paris whose toll was double—two sous instead of one. ◆ Métro: St.-Michel

23 St.-Julien-le-Pauvre This odd, ungraceful amalgam of Romanesque and Gothic church architecture has no bell tower, transepts, or organ, and squats on a small square lined with acacia trees. With its iron-caged well in front, it looks more like a humble country church than a Parisian monument. Started in 1165 (and restored in 1250 and 1651), St.-Julian-the-Poor (named after a martyred third-century bishop who gave all his money to the penniless) claims to be the oldest church in Paris. (Construction began two years after Notre-Dame's started, but St.-Julien-le-Pauvre was completed first. Furthermore, purists point out that when St.-Germain-des-Prés was built, it stood outside the city walls and therefore was not, strictly speaking, a Parisian sanctuary.)

In the 12th century, when renegade theologian **Pierre Abélard** quit Notre-Dame, he took more than 3,000 students along with him and established a new university at St.-Julien. The church thus became the seat and meeting place of the new University of Paris. In 1524 students critical of a new rector ransacked and nearly destroyed the church. After the Revolution, St.-Julien-le-Pauvre was used variously as a salt storehouse, a wool market, and a flour granary. Since 1889 it has belonged to the Greek Orthodox church. The enormous stone slab beside the well came from the fourth-century Roman highway that became the Rue St.-Jacques. ◆ Daily 9AM-1PM, 2:30-6:30PM. 1 Rue St.-Julien-le-Pauvre. Métro: St.-Michel

23 Square René-Viviani In this lovely little park stands what is reputed to be the oldest tree in Paris. This false acacia *(Robinia pseudoacacia)* leans on concrete crutches, infirm but erect, and blooms every spring.

Quai de Montebello

Not bad for a sprout that crossed the ocean from Guyana to be planted in 1680 by **Jean Robin.** Sit for a moment on one of the park benches and notice the pieces of worn and broken statuary surrounding you; they were once part of Notre-Dame. ♦ Métros: Maubert-Mutualité, St.-Michel

23 Les Trois Maillets The Three Mallets began in the 13th century as a tavern to serve the stonemasons constructing Notre-Dame. Some 700 years later it was transformed into a postwar jazz club first frequented by American GIs. It has one of the best piano bars in Paris. ♦ Admission. W-Su 7PM-3AM. Dim sum and music: 10:30PM-2:30AM. 56 Rue Galande (at Rue St.-Julien-le-Pauvre). Métros: Maubert-Mutualité, St.-Michel. 43.54.00.79

24 Rue du Fouarre Seated on *fouarres* (bundles of straw), undergraduates in the Middle Ages attended open-air lectures along this alley of rowdy intellectuals, notorious throughout Europe. In an attempt to ease tensions in 1358, **Charles V** chained the street at both ends and closed it at night. During his visit to Paris in 1304, even **Dante** harkened to the scholars here and later made reference in his writing to this *vico degli strami* (the road of straws). ♦ Métro: Maubert-Mutualité

24 La Fourmi Ailée ★★$ This women's bookstore has a tearoom in the rear, where on a chilly day you can order a hot goat cheese salad, sit back in a caned bentwood chair by the fireplace, and peruse a book by Simone de Beauvoir. ♦ Lunch and afternoon snacks. Closed Tuesday. 8 Rue du Fouarre (between Rue Galande and Quai de Montebello). Métro: Maubert-Mutualité. 43.29.40.99

24 Rue Galande The beginning of the old Roman road to Lyon, this meandering street was named in 1202 after a family who lived nearby. It was one of the fancier neighborhoods in 17th-century Paris. ♦ Métro: Maubert-Mutualité

24 Studio Galande Catch one of the cinema's nightly showings of *The Rocky Horror Picture Show.* Being surrounded by funkily costumed French college students enjoying their umpteenth viewing of this crazy cult film, singing and miming the lines, is 90 minutes of guaranteed belly laughs. Outside the theater, glance up at the 14th-century stone relief of **Saint Julien** crossing the Seine, which originally stood over the portal of nearby **St.-Julien-le-Pauvre** church. ♦ 42 Rue Galande (between Rues Dante and St.-Julien-le-Pauvre). Métro: Maubert-Mutualité. 43.54.72.71

25 Rue des Anglais In medieval times this street was a favorite haunt of English students attending the Sorbonne. ♦ Métro: Maubert-Mutualité

26 Librairie Gourmande The celebrated *bouquiniste,* **Madame Baudon,** has graduated from her stall on the quay to a shop where she sells books on food and wine from the 17th century to the present. ♦ M-Sa 10AM-7PM; Su 3-7PM. 4 Rue Dante (between Blvd St.-Germain and Rue Galande). Métros: Maubert-Mutualité, St.-Michel. 43.54.37.27

26 Album From *Action* comics to *Zot,* and Donald Duck to Dick Tracy, this *bande dessinée* shop specializes in new and vintage American comic books. For the seriocomic art collector, there are oil paintings of Batman and portraits and statues of Mr. Spock. ♦ M 2-7PM; Tu-Sa 10AM-1PM, 2-7PM. Closed Sunday and Monday in August. 6 Rue Dante (between Blvd St.-Germain and Rue Galande). Métros: Maubert-Mutualité, St.-Michel. 43.54.67.09

26 A l'Imagerie The largest old print and poster shop in Paris specializes in Art Deco, Art Nouveau, and late 19th-century Japanese prints and stamps. ♦ Tu-Sa 10:30AM-1PM, 2-7PM July-Aug; M 2-7PM, Tu-Sa 10:30AM-1PM, 2-7PM Sept-June. 9 Rue Dante (at Rue Domat). Métros: Cluny-La Sorbonne, Maubert-Mutualité. 43.25.18.66

27 Auberge des Deux Signes ★$$$ Restaurant owner **Monsieur Dhulster** shops every day before dawn at the Rungis market for the raw materials that his chef, **Nicolas Cano,** transforms into a sublime array of dishes, such as soufflé de sole with prawn raviolis and *foie gras d'oie en brioche.* The inn's setting, which includes a stone spiral staircase, a vista of Notre-Dame (splendid at night), and St.-Julien-le-Pauvre's gardens, could not be more medieval. ♦ Lunch and dinner; dinner only on Saturday. Closed Sunday. 46 Rue Galande (between Rues Dante and St.-Julien-le-Pauvre). Reservations recommended. Métro: Maubert-Mutualité. 43.25.46.56, 43.25.00.46

28 Rue St.-Julien-le-Pauvre The magnificent gate at **No. 14** marks the 17th-century home of the governor of the old Petit-Châtelet prison. Also, don't miss the house of the dwindling windows at **No. 10;** they start with the largest ones on the ground floor and shrink all the way up to the maids' rooms in the attic. ♦ Métros: Maubert-Mutualité, St.-Michel, Cité

Restaurants/Clubs: Red   **Hotels:** Blue
Shops/ 🌳Outdoors: Green   **Sights/Culture:** Black

28 The Tea Caddy ★$ Looking like your prim and proper English great-aunt's library, with dark wood paneling and thick-paned windows, this is the place for afternoon tea and crumpets. Light meals of quiche, salads, and omelets are also served. ♦ Snacks, lunch, and dinner. Closed Tuesday. 14 Rue St.-Julien-le-Pauvre (between Rue Galande and Quai de Montebello). Métros: Maubert-Mutualité, St.-Michel, Cité. 43.54.15.56

28 Caveau des Oubliettes A cabaret that looks like what it used to be: the dungeons of the old **Petit-Châtelet** prison. Be ready for such amusements as waiters in minstrel garb, bawdy songs, a guillotine, ancient torture instruments, and chastity belts on the walls. Inquire about the late-night tour of the *oubliettes* (dungeons) below the stairs. ♦ M-Th 9PM-1AM; F-Sa 9PM-2AM. 1bis Rue St.-Julien-le-Pauvre (at Rue Galande). Métros: Maubert-Mutualité, St.-Michel, Cité. 43.54.94.97

28 Esmeralda $$ This popular small hotel is a favorite of traveling actors and artists. Rooms with views of Notre-Dame are subjected to the midnight noise of *The Rocky Horror Picture Show* crowd exiting the Studio Galande cinema. ♦ 4 Rue St.-Julien-le-Pauvre (between Rue Galande and Quai de Montebello). Reservations required. Métros: Maubert-Mutualité, St.-Michel, Cité. 43.54.19.20

29 Rue de la Bûcherie A *bûcherie* is a woodshed, and this part of the *quai* is where firewood-laden barges dropped their cargo. ♦ Métros: Maubert-Mutualité, St.-Michel, Cité

29 Shakespeare and Company Septuagenarian **George Bates Whitman**—who was raised in China, speaks five languages (including Russian), and claims the poet **Walt** as a distant forebear—has for the last 45 years run this charitable bookstore/inn for authors, vagabond intellectuals, and literature professors. Spiritual heir to **Sylvia Beach** (whose famous Paris bookstore of the same name on the Rue de l'Odéon supplied **Hemingway** with free reading material and was the only house that would publish **Joyce's** *Ulysses*), Whitman bought part of her collection and borrowed the name Shakespeare and Company. In his late sixties he fathered a daughter whom he named **Sylvia Beach Whitman**. Throughout the years, Whitman's chaotic stacks, which defy the Dewey decimal or any other system of categorization, have been frequented by the likes of **Lawrence Durrell, Henry Miller, J.P. Donleavy,** and beat poet **Lawrence Ferlinghetti.**

Although Whitman is rarely in the bookstore, if he appears while you're browsing he may offer you a cup of tea and, if you happen to be penniless and show promise as a writer, may invite you to spend a night in the **Writer's Room** or to bed down on the floor of his upstairs library. To the left of the bookshop, which has one of the world's most eclectic bulletin boards, Whitman keeps his own private collection and his motor scooter. Any book purchased in the shop is stamped with an inscription that reads: *Shakespeare and Co. Kilometer Zero Paris.* ♦ Daily noon-midnight. 37 Rue de la Bûcherie (between Rues de Petit Pont and St.-Julien-le-Pauvre). Métro: Maubert-Mutualité, St.-Michel, Cité. 43.26.96.50

29 La Bûcherie ★★$$$ Bernard Bosque's menu, featuring stuffed cabbage with crayfish, ocean salmon with chives, and wild duck and oysters in champagne, hasn't changed in years and neither has the popularity of this restaurant (illustrated above). Expect a crowd, and try to get a table near the crackling fireplace. At all costs avoid sitting behind the chimney, where famished customers can go unnoticed for days. ♦ Lunch and dinner. 41 Rue de la Bûcherie (between Rues de Petit Pont and St.-Julien-le-Pauvre). Reservations recommended. Métros: Maubert-Mutualité, St.-Michel, Cité. 43.54.78.06

30 Petit Pont Bishop **Maurice de Sully** was responsible for the construction of both majestic Notre-Dame and this little bridge, which was in earlier days animated by jugglers, sharpers, and dog trainers. Formerly located at the end of the bridge was the **Petit Châtelet** fortress and prison, a more diminutive version of the **Grand Châtelet** on the Right Bank. ♦ Métro: St.-Michel, Cité

31 Mirama ★★$ With glazed, roasted ducks hanging in the window and a cauldron whose contents bubble mysteriously just inside the door, this Chinese restaurant at first seems suspect. Yet it's crowded all day long, and deservedly so: the ingredients are fresh and the price is right. Try the king prawns with cashews, the crispy mixed vegetables, the pork ribs in black bean sauce, and, of course, the *canard laqué* you saw on the way in. ♦ Lunch and dinner. 17 Rue St.-Jacques (between Blvd St.-Germain and Rue Galande). Métros: Maubert-Mutualité, St.-Michel. 43.29.66.58

31 Rue St.-Jacques More than a hundred sundials can be found in Paris, but few were created by artists of worldwide repute. Surrealist **Salvador Dalí** designed this *cadran solaire* for friends whose furniture store was located here. The timepiece's completion in 1968 was televised, with Dali mounting a cherry picker to carve his signature into the still-wet cement. Set on the south face of the building, the sundial depicts a female face done in the form of a *coquilles St. Jacques* (a scalloped shell). ♦ Between Blvd St.-Germain and Rue Galande. Métros: Maubert-Mutualité, St.-Michel

31 Le Bar à Huitres ★★$$ This seafood restaurant has the best and least expensive shellfish in the city. Fresh oysters and scallops arrive daily from the Normandy and Brittany coasts to become components in sumptuous platters of mollusks and crustaceans. Cooked fish specialties include monkfish curry in winter and roast turbot with wine and butter sauce during the summertime. Served with velvety beurre blanc for dipping, the grilled lobster is heavenly. Making this place truly a paradise for shellfish lovers, the bar outside sells oysters and such for take-out. ♦ Lunch, dinner, and late-night. 33 Rue St.-Jacques. Métros: Maubert-Mutualité, St.-Michel. 44.07.27.37. Also at: 112 Blvd du Montparnasse. 43.20.71.01; 33 Blvd Beaumarchais. 48.87.98.92

31 Mexi & Co It's possible to find good Mexican restaurants in Paris, but amateur cooks can have a tough time procuring the ingredients to make their own Mexican meals and snacks. This store, however, stocks corn and flour tortillas, nacho chips, salsa, jalapeño peppers, refried beans, Dos Equis beer, and seven varieties of tequila. Savory burritos, tacos, and quesadillas are also available for those who can't wait until they get home. ♦ M-Sa 11AM-9PM. 10 Rue Dante (between Blvd St.-Germain and Rue Galande). Métros: Maubert-Mutualité, St.-Michel. 46.34.14.12

32 Café de Cluny ★$ Set at one of the Latin Quarter's busiest corners, this sprawling cafe commands a front-row seat on the boulevards St.-Michel and St.-Germain. Upstairs in the quiet plush booths, Sorbonne professors take their morning coffee or have a dish of ice cream with their graduate students in the afternoon. ♦ Breakfast, lunch, dinner, and late-night. 102 Blvd St.-Germain (at Blvd St.-Michel). Métro: St.-Michel. 43.26.68.24

33 Hôtel de Cluny, Museum, and Palais des Thermes This magnificent mansion (see below), built by the abbots of Cluny in 1330 and rebuilt in 1510, is one of the oldest private residences in Paris. It straddles the ruins of second-century Roman baths and contains one of the world's finest collections of French medieval art, including the beautiful *Lady and the Unicorn* tapestries.

The baths date from **Marcus Aurelius** (161-180); **Julian the Apostate,** proclaimed Roman Emperor in 360, lived in the adjoining palace. The baths and palace were sacked during numerous barbarian invasions, and in 1340, **Pierre de Châlus,** abbot of Cluny, the wealthy Benedictine abbey in Burgundy, bought the ruins and erected the Hôtel de Cluny as a pied-à-terre to lodge the abbots when they visited Paris. Shortly after the Revolution, the Cluny was occupied by a cooper, a laundress, French Navy astronomers, and a surgeon who used the chapel for his dissections. Among the mansion's tenants in 1833 was **Alexandre du Sommerard,** an art collector who had specialized in Gothic and Renaissance art for decades. When he died in 1842, the state bought the building as well as du Sommerard's collection and appointed his son **Edmond** as the museum's first curator.

As you enter the museum courtyard by the Rue du Sommerard, notice the polygonal stair tower sprinkled with carved shells *(coquilles St.-Jacques),* the symbol of the patron saint of **Jacques d'Amboise,** the abbot of Jumiéges, who between 1485 and 1510 rebuilt the hotel in its present flamboyantly Gothic style. The first rooms of the museum are replete with delicate ivory carvings, embroidered Egyptian silks, and Flemish tapestries of gentlemen setting off for the hunt.

Hôtel de Cluny

Within Hôtel de Cluny, Museum, and Palais des Thermes:

Notre-Dame Gallery In this stark white room are the sculpted stone heads (1210-30) of 21 noseless but nevertheless majestic kings. They represent the kings of Judea and Israel, who, according to Saint Matthew's genealogy, were ancestors of Christ. Like most men too closely associated with religion and royalty at the time of the Revolution, they lost their heads. But theirs is a case of mistaken identity. Originally enshrined in the **Gallery of Kings** on **Notre-Dame's** west facade, they were toppled in 1793 by an angry mob who assumed they were the kings of France. In 1977, during excavations for a new bank in the Hôtel Moreau near the Opéra, these heads were unearthed; the discovery is considered one of the 20th century's major archaeological finds.

Roman Baths The towering roof of the *frigidarium* (cold bath) is the largest Roman vault in all of France. The ceiling has survived 18 centuries of wear and tear, not the least of which was the eight feet of topsoil heaped on it by an abbot who rooted his apple orchard and kitchen garden on the roof. The ship prows decorating the base of the groined vaulting are the building signatures of the powerful Boatmen's Guild of Paris. Nearby is the *Boatmen's Pillar,* one of the oldest pieces of sculpture in Paris. It was supposed to be a column from Jupiter's Temple, which stood, during the reign of Roman emperor **Tiberius** (AD 14-37), where Notre-Dame is today.

Treasury Upstairs is a dazzling display of Gallic, Barbarian, and Merovingian jewelry, including six gold Visigoth crowns, two 13th-century gold double crosses, and the sublimely delicate 14th-century *Golden Rose* that was presented to the Bishop of Basel by **Pope Clement V.** The designs are so modern, so elegant, you get the impression that you're not admiring jewelry from the Middle Ages, but rather window-shopping around the Place Vendôme.

Stained Glass Among the medieval stained-glass windows in the upstairs corridor are religious scenes from the Ste.-Chapelle and the St.-Denis cathedrals. Take a close look; in the actual churches—even with a strong pair of opera glasses and a craned neck—you won't get this good a view. Three large windows and the surrounding stonework come from the church of St.-Jean-de-Latran, demolished in 1859 to make way for the Rue des Ecoles built between the Cluny and the Sorbonne.

Abbots' Chapel One of the few surviving interior details of the original mansion, this chapel was used as the ancient oratory of the abbots and is an architectural masterpiece. The elaborate vaulting sprouts palmlike from a single slender pillar. In a room near the chapel is a 1383 eagle lectern and a 12th-century gilt copper altar table.

Tapestries Saving the best for last, enter the rotunda on the top floor, dimly lit to protect the world-famous *Lady and the Unicorn* tapestry series. In 1844, quite by accident, writer **George Sand** discovered the tapestries hanging at the **Château de Boussac;** supposedly they were a wedding present in the 15th century from magistrate **Jean Le Viste** to his bride (the Le Viste coat of arms appears in each panel). The artist, who remains unknown, is thought to have designed the similar set of six tapestries that is now hanging in the Cloisters museum in New York City. The delicate tapestries allegorically depict the five senses. In *Sight,* for instance, the noble unicorn gazes into the mirror of a bejeweled blond woman. In the mysterious sixth tapestry, the woman's tent is emblazoned with the words *A Mon Seul Désir* (To My Only Desire), thought to represent mastery of all five senses. Notice that the woman on the red *millefleur* (literally *one thousand flowers*) background changes from one sumptuous gown to another in a veritable fashion show as you progess around the room. ♦ Admission. M, W-Su 9:15AM-5:45PM. 6 Place Paul-Painlevé (between Blvd St.-Michel and Rue de Cluny). Métros: Cluny-La Sorbonne, Maubert-Mutualité, St.-Michel. 43.25.62.00

34 **Au Vieux Campeur** France's best mountain-climbing outfitters this side of Chamonix carry pitons, ice axes, alpine sleeping bags, and giant spools of brightly colored climbing rope for your next ascent of Everest or the Eiffel Tower. If a bivouac at a wine bar atop the Montagne Ste.-Geneviève's slopes is more your aim, pause on the sidewalk and watch France's next generation of rock climbers testing new equipment, rappelling down an indoor version of what looks like the Eiger's North Face. This is one of the Vieux Campeur's nine stores on the Left Bank. ♦ M 2-7PM; Tu, Th-F 10:30AM-7:30PM; W 10:30AM-10PM; Sa 9:30AM-7:30PM. 48 Rue des Ecoles (between Rues St.-Jacques and Thénard). Métros: Maubert-Mutualité, St.-Michel. 43.29.12.32

35 **Hôtel Collège de France** $$ Some of the sixth-floor rooms of this quiet bed-and-breakfast hotel offer a glimpse of the Notre-Dame towers. ♦ 7 Rue Thénard (between Rues du Sommerard and de Latran). Métros: Maubert-Mutualité, St.-Michel. 43.26.78.36

35 **Prosciences** This store stocks supplies for high school biology classes and all the Collège de France research laboratories. Amid the test tubes and life-size plastic skeletons (shrouded in tinsel at Christmas) are glass beakers and white porcelain pitchers that French householders love to buy, not for their children's chemistry experiments but as measuring cups for the kitchen. Also, the 125-centiliter pitchers make dandy creamers. ♦ M-F 10AM-12:30PM, 1:30-7PM. Closed in

August. 44 Rue des Ecoles (at Rue Thénard). Métro: Maubert-Mutualité. 46.34.56.56

36 Attica This English-language bookstore, run by the knowledgeable **David Chardin,** specializes in classical English literature and English history. With the best prices in town, it caters to French and American students as well as to the British Consulate. Readings by English and American poets usually take place on Tuesdays and Fridays at 8PM (call to verify). ♦ M-Sa 10AM-7PM; Su 4-8PM. 23 Rue Jean-de-Beauvais (between Rues des Ecoles and de Lanneau). Métro: Maubert-Mutualité. 46.34.62.03

37 Beauvais College Chapel One of the Sorbonne's first college chapels, it was built in 1380 and is now restored. This tiny sanctuary has been used since 1882 by the Romanian Orthodox church. ♦ Services: M-Th 11:30AM-12:30PM; F 11:30AM-12:30PM, 6-7PM; Su 10AM-12:30PM. 9bis Rue Jean-de-Beauvais (between Rues des Ecoles and du Sommerard). Métro: Maubert-Mutualité. 43.54.67.47

38 Musée des Collections Historiques de la Préfecture de Police (Police Museum) This fascinating, often grisly, little collection surveys the city's most notorious crimes, from the 16th century to the present. Exhibits include a graphic representation of the 1563 punishment accorded the **Duc de Guise's** murderer (quartering by four horses); orders for the arrest of **Dr. Guillotin** in 1795; an account of **Charlotte Corday's** murder of **Marat** in his bath; a book stained with blood from the 1932 assassination of French **President Paul Doumer;** and **Verlaine's** statement of his attempted murder of fellow poet **Rimbaud.** Among the more ingenious weapons on display are a strangling cord made of twisted paper, a knife concealed in a lady's fan, and a guillotine blade used during the Revolution. This petit Guignol requires Holmesian perspicacity to find. Enter the lobby of the fifth arrondissement police head-quarters, gumshoe your way up the stairs, and knock on the door marked Musée. ♦ Free. M-F 9AM-5PM; Sa 10AM-5PM. 1bis Rue des Carmes (between Blvd St.-Germain and Rue des Ecoles). Métro: Maubert-Mutualité. 43.29.21.57

39 Montagne Ste.-Geneviève This French Parnassus, the central point of the old University of Paris, is named after the city's sanctified patroness (**Saint Denis** is the male patron saint). It is admittedly steep, but to call any of the city's seven hills a mountain must certainly have been Roman grandiloquence. The summit of Ste.-Geneviève is gracefully crowned with the **Panthéon,** whose columned dome dominates the Left Bank. Here was the convent where **Saint Thomas Aquinas** wrote his *Summa Theologica,* upon which the orthodox philosophy of Catholicism is based. It is a vicinity rich in intellectual history:

Ignatius Loyola and **Calvin** studied here; **Marat** drew up his pamphlets; and **Pascal** died a stone's throw from the place where **Verlaine** was to pass away many generations later. The hill counts among its educational institutions the world-famous **Sorbonne,** the **Collège de France,** prestigious medical and law schools, and three large secondary schools, and was at one time the site of the **Ecole Polytechnique,** the French equivalent of MIT. In 1804 the Rue de la Montagne-Ste.-Geneviève was the scene of a plot to murder **Napoléon Bonaparte.**
♦ Métro: Maubert-Mutualité

40 Rue des Ecoles This street name celebrates the presence of all the academic institutions and university establishments hereabouts.
♦ Métro: Maubert-Mutualité

40 Librairie Presence Africaine Need a few *Wolof* lessons before visiting Gambia? Looking for a Senegalese cookbook? Want to hear a black gospel concert on the Left Bank? This African bookstore includes a Third World periodical section and a bulletin board. ♦ M-Sa 10AM-7PM. 25bis Rue des Ecoles (between Rues de la Montagne-Ste.-Geneviève and des Bernardins). Métro: Cardinal-Lemoine. 43.54.15.88

40 Da Capo Charles Recht runs this postage stamp-size shop dealing in 78-rpm records, old sheet music, and opera programs. ♦ M-Sa 1-7PM. Closed in August. 14 Rue des Ecoles (between Rues de la Montagne-Ste.-Geneviève and Monge). Métro: Cardinal-Lemoine. 43.54.75.47

41 Le Paradis Latin Jean Kriegel's glittering nightclub has one of the top 10 dinner-floor shows. ♦ Dinner: M, W-Su starting at 8PM. Shows start at 10PM, but you must be there 30 minutes in advance. 28 Rue du Cardinal-Lemoine (between Rue des Ecoles and Blvd St.-Germain). Métro: Cardinal-Lemoine. 43.25.28.28

PARADIS LATIN

42 Moissonnier ★★★$$ Earthenware bowls spilling over with Lyonnais salads, friendly waiters, generous charcuterie, and a homey setting have earned this Left Bank establishment a loyal clientele. Specialties include roast kidneys, duck with turnips, tripe baked with onions and white wine, creamy au gratin potatoes, and delicious Bordeaux. ♦ Lunch and dinner; lunch only on Sunday. Closed Monday and in August. 28 Rue des Fossés-St.-Bernard (between Rues des Chantiers and Jussieu). Métros: Jussieu, Cardinal-Lemoine. 43.29.87.65

Restaurants/Clubs: Red		**Hotels:** Blue
Shops/ Outdoors: Green		**Sights/Culture:** Black

43 Jean-Baptiste Besse How affable **Papa Besse** (one of the most respected wine merchants in Paris since 1932) manages to find what he's looking for in his helter-skelter corner store is anybody's guess. A little man who sports a beret and a peasant's guileless smile, Besse has a story and a vintage for every occasion. If a customer is unpleasant, Besse will let him or her leave with run-of-the-mill wine, but he'll invite those he likes into his cobweb-covered cellars for a serious consultation. ◆ Tu-Sa 1-8:30PM. Closed in August. 48 Rue de la Montagne-Ste.-Geneviève (between Rues des Ecoles and de l'Ecole Polytechnique). Métro: Maubert-Mutualité. 43.25.35.80

43 Shobudo International A building on this tranquil 17th-century courtyard houses Europe's oldest judo school. If you don't have time for a self-defense class and would like to fake it in hopes of intimidating those muggers back home, you can buy a black belt and the latest kung fu paraphernalia in the **Budo Store** on the second floor. Or walk to the end of the courtyard, turn left, and squeeze into the spectators' gallery for a few bouts of *ken-jitsu*, a Japanese martial art predating the shoguns. The judo school is in a building that was once part of the **Hostel of the 33** (named for the number of years Christ lived), established by monk **Claude Bernard** as a dormitory for theology students. ◆ M-Sa 9AM-7:30PM. 34 Rue de la Montagne-Ste.-Geneviève (between Rues des Ecoles and de l'Ecole Polytechnique). Métro: Maubert-Mutualité. 43.29.00.41

44 La Nef Parisienne Affixed on this small square, as on city schools and other public structures throughout Paris, is a sailing vessel (*la nef* is the nave of a ship), which has been the city's coat of arms (see above illustration) since 1260, when Saint Louis appointed the Boatmen's Guild to administer the affairs of the city. *Fluctuat nec mergitur* (float never sink) is the city motto. In addition to adorning buildings, *La Nef Parisienne* is embossed on everything from the mayor's stationery to police officers' badges. ◆ Métros: Cardinal-Lemoine, Maubert-Mutualité

45 Ecole Polytechnique These massive buildings once housed the French MIT. Founded as an Army-run engineering school by **Gaspard Monge,** the mathematician who accompanied **Napoléon** to Egypt, the Ecole Polytechnique's best known graduates are car designer **André Citroën** and former French President **Valéry Giscard d'Estaing.** Its annual grand ball at the Opéra is pretty famous, too. Several years ago the prestigious university moved to the suburbs. ◆ Rue de l'Ecole Polytechnique (between Rues Valette and de la Montagne-Ste.-Geneviève). Métros: Cardinal-Lemoine, Maubert-Mutualité

45 Crocojazz This cubbyhole of a record shop resounds with the music of **Art Blakey, Miles Davis, Louis Armstrong**, and **Coleman Hawkins.** Jack Daniels whiskey bottles on the wall, the occasional country twang of **Hank Thompson** and **Ricky Skaggs,** and the worn Levis and ersatz cowboy boots of the French clientele round out the ambience at this treasure chest of American LPs. ◆ Tu-Sa 11AM-1PM, 2-7PM. 64 Rue de la Montagne-Ste.-Geneviève (between Rue Laplace and Place du Panthéon). Métro: Maubert-Mutualité. 46.34.78.38

45 Au Vieux Paris ★$$ In the shadow of the St.-Etienne-du-Mont church, **Jean Vergez's** restaurant of wooden beams and stone pillars serves rich food from France's southwest: foie gras, *confit de canard,* blood sausage, and its special tournedos Rossini. Dessert might be a pleasing *charlotte aux poires.* ◆ Lunch and dinner. Closed Sunday. 2 Place du Panthéon (at Rue de la Montagne-Ste.-Geneviève). Reservations recommended. Métros: Cardinal-Lemoine, Luxembourg (RER). 43.54.79.22

45 51 Rue de la Montagne-Ste.-Geneviève **James Joyce** shared a flat here with French writer **Valéry Larbaud.** ◆ Métro: Cardinal-Lemoine

45 Le Raccard ★★$$ The Swiss chalet decor may be heavy-handed, but the all-you-can-eat raclette is as authentic and delicious as it comes. In winter, fondues made with Gruyère or Vacharin are served. ◆ Dinner. Closed Monday and in August. 19 Rue Laplace (between Rues Valette and de la Montagne-Ste.-Geneviève). Reservations recommended. Métro: Cardinal-Lemoine. 43.25.27.27, 43.54.83.75

46 Le Coupe-Chou ★$$ This seductive inn occupies the site of a famous Parisian barbershop whose proprietor slit the throats of his customers, whom his neighbor the butcher then made into pâté. If you can cast that grisly chapter from your mind, you will probably enjoy this attractive restaurant serving salmon ravioli, lamb with mint, magret of duck with peaches, and hot homemade puff pastries, although you may opt to stay away from the pâté. ◆ Lunch and dinner. Closed Sundays in August. 11 Rue de Lanneau (at Impasse Chartière). Métro: Maubert-Mutualité. 46.33.68.69

47 Collège de France First called the Three-Language College because Hebrew and Greek were taught here as well as Latin, this institution, founded by **François I** in 1529, counts among its famous faculty **Frédéric Joliot-Curie,** who split a uranium particle; the physicist **André-Marie Ampère,** after whom a unit measuring electric current is named; poet **Paul Valéry;** and the more contemporary scholars **Roland Barthes, Michel Foucault,** and **Claude Lévi-Strauss.** ◆ 11 Place Marcelin-Berthelot (at Rue St.-Jacques). Métro: Maubert-Mutualité. 44.27.12.11

BRASSERIE BALZAR

48 Brasserie Balzar ★★$$ **Camus** and **Sartre** had their last argument at the Balzar, and **James Thurber, Elliot Paul, William Shirer,** and the old *Chicago Tribune* crowd gathered here for the beer and *choucroute* (sauerkraut) *garni.* The Balzar's literary clientele, its old wood paneling and mirrors, and its waiters in long white aprons create an ambience that makes it one of the best brasseries in Paris. Getting a table for lunch is not difficult; dinner, however, is a different story. At night, especially after the theater, the vinyl banquettes are jammed with university professors, actors, editors, journalists, and aspiring poets dining on hearty fare such as the pig's feet Sainte-Memehould, *cervelas rémoulade,* cassoulet, and calf's liver *niçoise* washed down with a bottle of Bordeaux.

This restaurant is worth a visit even if you only stop for a Kir or coffee on the terrace. Conveniently, when the Balzar is closed, the **Lipp,** another literary shrine (on the Boulevard St.-Germain) stays open, an arrangement dating from the days when they were under the same management. Another attractive quality of the Balzar is its refusal to admit customers accompanied by poodles or Doberman pinschers. ◆ Breakfast, lunch, dinner, and snacks. Closed August and Christmas through New Year's Day. 49 Rue des Ecoles (at Rue de la Sorbonne). Reservations recommended. Métro: Maubert-Mutualité. 43.54.13.67

49 Place de la Sorbonne This square, lined with cafés and lime trees, was a focal point for the student-worker protest of 1968. That year, on 10 and 11 May, police and students clashed violently, resulting in the injury of 400 participants and the arrest of hundreds of others. Today you will find a graffiti-marred statue of **Auguste Comte** (1798-1857), who was fired from his job as examiner in mathematics at the prestigious Ecole Polytechnique for his revolutionary ideas. Comte is best remembered as the founder of Positivism, a philosophy that strongly influenced John Stuart Mill. ◆ Métros: Cluny-La Sorbonne, Luxembourg (RER)

49 Hôtel Select $$ Located on the Place de la Sorbonne, this quiet 70-room hotel is an ideal location for exploring the Latin Quarter. In 1937, 25-year-old **Eric Sevareid** checked into a 50-cents-a-night room here on the square and headed off to work for the *Paris Herald,* soon accomplishing feats such as an interview with **Gertrude Stein.** ◆ 1 Place de la Sorbonne (at Rue Victor Cousin). Métros: Luxembourg (RER), St.-Michel. 46.34.14.80

50 Sorbonne France's most famous university began in 1253 as humble lodgings for 16 theology students. In medieval times, the university was not a mass of edifices, pedants, and bureaucrats; it was a loose assembly of soapbox academics giving street-corner lectures to students who boarded at inns throughout Paris. However, by the end of the 13th century, when the Sorbonne became the administrative headquarters for the University of Paris, there were 15,000 undergraduates studying in the city. **Saint Thomas Aquinas** and **Roger Bacon** were among the Sorbonne's great teachers; **Saint Ignatius Loyola, Dante, Erasmus,** and **John Calvin** were students here. The Sorbonne grew in size and power and frequently contradicted the authority of the French throne. During the Hundred Years' War (1337-1453), the Sorbonne had the audacity to side with England against France. It recognized **Henri V** as king of France and cravenly sent one of its best prosecutors to Rouen to try **Jeanne d'Arc.**

In 1642 **Cardinal Richelieu** (pictured above) was elected grand master of the Sorbonne; he commissioned architect **Jacques Lemercier** to restore the dilapidated college buildings and erect a Jesuit-style church. During the Revolution the Sorbonne closed down and remained empty until 1806, when **Napoléon** headquartered his **Académie de Paris** there. Following the May 1968 student-worker demonstration, the state unceremoniously rechristened the Sorbonne as "Paris University IV," nominally tossing it into the archipelago of institutions of higher learning scattered about the city.

Don't be shy about wandering down the long stone corridors of the Sorbonne and visiting the university's lecture halls, such as the **Amphithéâtre Descartes** or **Salle Doctorat.** (Unfortunately, the ornate **Grand Amphithéâtre** with its famous *Puvis de Chavannes* fresco is strictly reserved for ceremonies of state.) In the event that you enroll for a four-month crash course in French (as hundreds of Americans do every year), you may come to know the dusty domed ceiling and stiff wooden benches of the **Richelieu Amphithéâtre** intimately. ♦ M-Sa 8AM-10PM. For an admission application, contact the Cours de Civilisation Française de la Sorbonne. Galerie Richelieu. 45-47 Rue des Ecoles (between Rues St.-Jacques and de la Sorbonne). Métro: Cluny-La Sorbonne. 40.46.26.64, 40.46.26.75

50 Ste.-Ursule-de-la-Sorbonne Nothing of **Richelieu's** Sorbonne remains save **Jacques Lemercier's** chapel (1642), which was the first completely Roman-style building in 17th-century Paris (shown above). Richelieu is buried here. Above **François Girardon's** beautiful white marble tomb (1694), which depicts a half-recumbent Richelieu, his red cardinal's hat still hangs by a few slender threads from the ceiling. According to tradition, the hat will remain there until Richelieu's soul is freed from Purgatory, at which time the threads will rot and the hat will drop. The chapel is closed to the public except during its special exhibitions of stained glass, tapestry, and old manuscripts. ♦ Church services are held in the chapel on 21 October (the feast day of Sainte Ursule) and 4 December (the anniversary of Richelieu's death). Place de la Sorbonne. Métros: Cluny-La Sorbonne, Luxembourg (RER)

51 Lycée Louis Le Grand Founded in 1550, this 1,500-student state-run high school

numbers among its former pupils **Molière, Voltaire, Robespierre, Hugo, Baudelaire, Pompidou, Giscard d'Estaing, Chirac,** and **Senghor** (the former president of Senegal). For information on touring the building, contact the lycée's secretary on the second floor. ♦ M-F 9AM-noon, 2-5PM. 123 Rue St.-Jacques (between Rues Cujas and des Ecoles). Métros: Luxembourg (RER), St.-Michel. 43.29.12.06

52 Chez Pento ★★$$ Professors from the Sorbonne and nearby lycées frequent this 1930s-style bistro at midday, drawn by its reasonably priced lunch menu. At dinnertime, a less homogeneous crowd of Parisians settles into the faux leather banquettes, choosing among such entrées as *roulé de canard rôti,* quail with grapes in rum sauce, and guinea hen marinated in lime. The *délice aux trois chocolats*—shaved white, milk, and dark chocolate on a bed of *crème anglaise*—is a divine dessert. ♦ Lunch and dinner; dinner only on Saturday. Closed Sunday. 9 Rue Cujas (at Rue Toullier). Métro: Luxembourg (RER). 43.26.81.54

53 Bibliothèque Ste.-Geneviève This library, constructed in 1850 on the Place du Panthéon, occupies the site of the old **Collège Montaigu** where **Erasmus, Calvin,** and **Loyola** studied. Architect **Henri Labrouste's** revolutionary use of steel frame and masonry construction (further elaborated in his other library, the Bibliothèque Nationale, which was finished in 1868) makes this building one of the most important 19th-century forerunners of modern architecture. While you may peek inside, the library itself is restricted to visitors with a valid reader's card. ♦ Place du Panthéon (at Rue Valette). Métro: Cardinal-Lemoine

54 Rue Soufflot Looking down the Rue Soufflot (named for the architect of the Panthéon), you will see two matching buildings, the **City Hall** of the fifth arrondissement and the **University of Paris Faculty of Law** building with the **Luxembourg Gardens** and **Eiffel Tower** in the distance. Eighteen feet below the Rue Soufflot lie the remains of a Roman forum, discovered by 19th-century archaeologists; however, the ruins are not open to the public. ♦ Métros: St.-Michel, Odéon

55 Perraudin ★★★$ Popular among Sorbonne students and their profs, this bargain canteen with archetypal bistro decor (lace curtains, red-and-white checked tablecloths, and tiled Deco floors) offers a panoply of *cuisine bourgeoise:* lamb and kidney beans, beef stew, au gratin potatoes, and rough red wines. ♦ Lunch and dinner; dinner only on Saturday. Closed Monday, Sunday, and last two weeks in August. 157 Rue St.-Jacques (between Rues Soufflot and Fossés-St.-Jacques). Métro: Luxembourg (RER). 46.33.15.75

56 Les Fontaines ★★$$ This bistro may look like it lost its soul somewhere in all the cigarette smoke, but it serves surprisingly good hearty fare for quite reasonable prices. Co-owner **Roger Lacipière**, once a butcher, still roams the markets at Rungis during the pre-dawn hours two or three times a week to purchase rib steaks for the menu that are as thick as a Gideon Bible, and he offers a superlative *gigot* and *fricassée de volaille de Bresse aux girolles*. ◆ Lunch and dinner. Closed Sunday and in August. 9 Rue Soufflot (at Rue Paillet). Métros: Maubert-Mutualité, Odeon. 43.26.42.80

57 Hôtel des Grands Hommes $$$
Comfortable and right in the heart of the Latin Quarter, this is a fine place to stay if you can hack the lobby with its plastic plants and disco music. The apartment of **Laurent Fabius**, former prime minister under **François Mitterrand**, is next door at **15 Place du Panthéon**. ◆ 17 Place du Panthéon (between Rues d'Ulm and Clotaire). Métro: Luxembourg (RER). 46.34.19.60

58 Panthéon When **Louis XV** recovered from gout at Metz in 1744, he vowed, in gratitude, to build a great temple honoring **Sainte Geneviève**. The architect, **Jacques-Germain Soufflot**, chose to construct a classical edifice based on the form of a Greek cross (339 feet long and 253 feet wide). Soufflot, who had been inspired by his trips to Italy, intended his building to resemble the Panthéon of Agrippa in Rome (however, the Paris Panthéon's lofty 52-pillar dome and handsome Corinthian colonnade—see picture above—wound up being much more suggestive of St. Paul's Cathedral in London). Finished in 1850 by **Guillaume Rondelet**, one of Soufflot's students, the Panthéon was secularized into the Temple of Fame, a necropolis for the distinguished atheists of France. In its rather depressing crypt lie the likes of **Voltaire,**

Rousseau, Victor Hugo (whose coffin passed a ceremonial night under the Arc de Triomphe and was carried to the Panthéon in the hearse of the poor), **Gambetta, Emile Zola, Louis Braille** (the 19th-century Frenchman who, blinded at age three, went on to invent the system of embossed dots that enables the sightless to read), **Jean Jaurès** (the celebrated leftist politician and orator who was assassinated in 1914), and **Jean Moulin** (the Resistance leader in World War II who was tortured to death during the Occupation). After the Revolution, the Panthéon's 42 tall windows were walled up, and today the monument looms over the square like a prison, grandiose and austere. ◆ Admission. Daily 10AM-12:30PM, 4-5:30PM. Place du Panthéon. Métros: Cardinal-Lemoine, Luxembourg (RER). 43.54.34.51

59 Lycée Henri IV Dating from Napoleonic times, the Lycée Henri IV is one of the city's most prestigious high schools; **Jean-Paul Sartre,** the French novelist and playwright who refused the Nobel Prize for Literature in 1964, taught here. The school's most notable architectural feature is the **Tour de Clovis,** a Gothic belfry. The tower is all that remains of the **Abbaye Ste.-Geneviève,** built by **King Clovis** after he was converted to Christianity by his wife, **Clotilde of Burgundy,** and Sainte Geneviève herself. **Saint Thomas Aquinas** (1225-74) taught at the abbey. ◆ Closed to the public. 23 Rue Clovis (at Rue Clotilde). Métro: Luxembourg (RER)

60 St.-Etienne-du-Mont (St.-Stephen-of-the-Mount) Its mélange of triple classical pediments, Gothic rose window, medieval-style belfry, and Renaissance dome defy the laws of architectural purity (see picture above). Its low-hanging chandeliers are a menace to anyone over six feet tall. It must be the only church in Paris that closes for lunch. But, *mon Dieu!*, it's beautiful. Completed in 1626, St.-Etienne-du-Mont is home to two graceful 16th-century spiral staircases, an extraordinary wooden pulpit (1650) shouldered by a grimacing Samson, and the only rood screen left in Paris, as well as the tombs of **Pascal, Racine,** and **Marat.** The church surrounds a shrine to Sainte Geneviève, which Paris fathers have visited the first Sunday of each year for centuries. During the annual pilgrimage on 3 January 1857, while bowing to bless a child, **Monseigneur Sibour,** Archbishop of Paris, was stabbed to death by an unfrocked priest named **Verger,** who apparently objected to the ban on marriage that compelled priestly celibacy. A marker at the rear of the center aisle indicates the spot where the murder was committed. ♦ M-Sa 7:30AM-noon, 2:30-7:15PM; Su 7:30AM-12:30PM, 4-7:30PM. Place Ste.-Geneviève. Métro: Cardinal-Lemoine. 43.54.11.79

61 La Truffière ★$$ The antithesis of nouvelle cuisine, rich specialties from Périgord are served here: black truffles, foie gras, and generous portions of goose and duck prepared in every conceivable fashion. Have an aperitif near the fireplace in the sitting room before proceeding to dinner. ♦ Lunch and dinner; dinner only on Saturday. Closed Monday and the first two weeks of August. 4 Rue Blainville (between Rues Mouffetard and Tournefort). Reservations required. Métros: Cardinal-Lemoine, Place-Monge. 46.33.29.82, 46.33.64.74

61 9 Rue Blainville The site of the first public library in Paris. ♦ Between Rues Mouffetard and Tournefort. Métros: Cardinal-Lemoine, Place-Monge

61 The Rib Joint ★★$$ Randy and Tony are American and Pascal is French; together they brew up the best barbecue sauce in town. Decorated with checked tablecloths and homey Americana, this hole-in-the-wall also serves corn on the cob, red beans and rice, potato salad, coleslaw, homemade pies (pecan, apple, blueberry, and sweet potato), and special house cocktails such as *Lemon Boogie, Blue Troubles,* and *Monkey Business.* There's no charge for Randy's extemporaneous stand-up comedy. ♦ Dinner. 14 Rue Thouin (between Rues Descartes and de l'Estrapade). Métro: Cardinal-Lemoine. 43.26.37.09

62 Rue Descartes This street carries the name of French mathematician and philosopher **René** "I-think-therefore-I-am" **Descartes** (1596-1650). He lived on Montagne Ste.-Geneviève from 1613 to 1619 and again in 1625, but it is doubtful he ever lived on this street, which was then known as **la Rue des Bordels** (the street of brothels). Descartes emigrated to Sweden, where he died in the arms of **Queen Christina.** ♦ Métro: Cardinal-Lemoine

62 39 Rue Descartes A plaque below the awning marks the house where poet **Paul Verlaine** (1844-96) died. Later there was a hotel at the same address, where in 1922 **Ernest Hemingway** rented a room which he later described in *A Moveable Feast.* ♦ Between Rues Thouin and Clovis. Métro: Cardinal-Lemoine

62 47 Rue Descartes At the end of the passageway in this historic 17th-century, half-timbered Norman-style house is another section of **King Philippe Auguste's** medieval city wall. ♦ Between Rues Thouin and Clovis. Métro: Cardinal-Lemoine

63 Rue Clovis This short street is named after **Clovis** (AD 466-511), king of the Franks, who defeated the Romans at Soissons, consequently ending the Roman Empire's dominion of Gaul and founding France. The narrow sidewalk on the south side of the street (near No. 5) is practically blocked by the ivy-draped ruins of **King Philippe Auguste's** fortified wall. It was originally 33 feet high, with a pathway on top, and was patrolled by the city sentries (during the 19th century, a bronze regiment of these sentries was enshrined on the roof of the City Hall in the Place de l'Hôtel de Ville). Construction of the wall started in 1190, and it marked the city limits of Paris until the 17th century. The wall was pulled down when **Louis XIV** left Paris for Versailles. At the bottom of the hill at **No. 67 Rue du Cardinal-Lemoine** is the house where **Pascal** died in 1662. ♦ Métro: Cardinal-Lemoine

64 Hôtel des Grandes Ecoles $$ Entering the hotel's courtyard is like stepping into an Impressionist painting. This homey, family-run establishment comprises two ivy-covered houses set in a lush garden. Each of the delightful rooms is decorated differently; ask for one with a garden view. On cool mornings, enjoy your croissants and café au lait in the charming lace-curtained breakfast room; in summer, you can eat amid the trees and flowers. Guests return year after year, so make reservations well in advance. ♦ Reservations taken 2-6PM only. 75 Rue du Cardinal-Lemoine (between Rues Monge and Rollin). Métro: Cardinal-Lemoine. 43.26.79.23

65 Place de la Contrescarpe In the Middle Ages, this dark, dangerous neighborhood lay outside **King Philippe Auguste's** city wall, beyond the moat, on the counter-escarpment. Since the days of Hemingway's *A Moveable Feast,* the public urinals and bus stop have disappeared, but a certain seediness remains. In winter, the local *clochards* (street people) still huddle over the heating duct and live off spoils from the markets and spare change from tourists. On summer weekends, harmless bikers in black leather congregate here. ♦ Métros: Cardinal-Lemoine, Place-Monge

65 1 Place de la Contrescarpe The name **Maison de la Pomme de Pin** (Pine Cone Cabaret) is carved into the wall above the *boucherie* at this address. It marks the site of an old café frequented by satirist **François Rabelais** (1494-1553), author of *Pantagruel* and *Gargantua.* ♦ Métros: Cardinal-Lemoine, Place-Monge

65 La Chope ★$ Once a **Hemingway** haunt, this café is crowded with stout butchers drinking Calvados and students from the Lycée Henri IV playing pinball. You will also find chef's salads and banana splits. ♦ Breakfast, lunch, dinner, and late-night. 2 Place de la Contrescarpe. Métros: Cardinal-Lemoine, Place-Monge. 43.26.51.26

66 Rue Mouffetard Leading out of the **Place de la Contrescarpe** is the 13th-century Rue Mouffetard. As you descend the narrow street, let your imagination take you back to the time when it was the main Roman road to the southeast, Lyon, and Italy. During the 12th century the area near the **Bièvre River** was filled with the country homes of rich Parisians. Within four centuries the Bièvre became a foul-smelling stream polluted by the animal wastes and dyes flushed by tanners, skinners, and the Flemish tapestry weavers from the Gobelins factory. In 1910 the river was covered over and incorporated into the sewer system.

Some guess the name Mouffetard comes from *mouffette,* French for skunk; more likely it is a corruption of the Roman name of the hill it traverses, **Mont Cétar.** Prior to the Revolution the poor of Paris lived here in utter wretchedness. The unadorned mansard-roofed 17th-century houses that still line the Rue Mouffetard were built for ordinary folk. In the 1600s one French writer said more money could be found in one single house of the Faubourg St.-Honoré than in all of those combined on the Rue Mouffetard. ♦ Métros: Censier-Daubenton, Place-Monge

66 12 Rue Mouffetard Façade Above this charcuterie is an astounding painting that looks more suited to early Atlanta than Paris. *Le Nègre Joyeux* (The Happy Negro) portrays a stereotyped grinning black servant in striped pants serving tea to his mistress. ♦ At Rue Blainville. Métro: Place-Monge

66 51 to 55 Rue Mouffetard In 1938 workers discovered 3,351 coins of 22-karat gold weighing 16.3 grams each and bearing the image of **Louis XV** hidden inside the wall here. The buried treasure, according to an accompanying note, belonged to **Louis Nivelle,** the royal counselor who mysteriously disappeared in 1757. ♦ At Rue Ortolan. Métros: Censier-Daubenton, Place-Monge

66 Pot-de-Fer Fountain What appears to be an Italianate roadside dungeon is actually a restored historic monument. Behind this wall is one of the 14 fountains constructed in 1624 at the behest of **Marie de Médici.** The fountain was designed to handle the overflow from the Gallo-Roman aqueduct that she had refurbished to supply water for her new palace in the Luxembourg Gardens. What a sprinkler system it must have been! ♦ 60 Rue Mouffetard (at Rue Pot-de-Fer). Métro: Place-Monge

Keeping Fit in France

Although it may seem as if Parisians do most of their huffing and puffing on cigarettes, there are a variety of athletic centers in Paris, and it is possible to maintain your exercise regime while you're away from home. Municipal tennis courts abound, and some of the larger hotels have health clubs that are amenable (in varying degrees) to offering one-day or monthly passes to nonguests for reasonable fees.

Health Clubs and Gyms:

Club Jean-de-Beauvais 15 Rue Jean-de-Beauvais, 46.33.16.80

Espace Vit'Halles 48 Rue Rambuteau, 42.77.21.71

Hôtel Méridien 81 Boulevard Gouvion-St.-Cyr, 40.68.34.34

Samourai 26 Rue de Berri, 43.59.04.58

Horseback Riding:

Manège de Neuilly 19bis Rue d'Orléans, 45.01.20.06

Poney-Club de la Cartoucherie Bois de Vincennes, 43.74.61.25

Swimming Pools:

Henry-de-Montherlant 32 Boulevard Lannes, 45.03.03.28

Jean-Taris 16 Rue Thouin, 43.25.54.03

Piscine de la Porte de la Plaine 13 Rue du Général-Guillaumat, 45.32.34.00

Piscine Georges Vellerey 148 Avenue Gambetta, 40.31.15.20

Tennis Courts:

Centre de Tennis du Jardin du Luxembourg Luxembourg Gardens, 43.20.67.64

Centre Sportif d'Orléans 14 Avenue Paul-Appell, 45.40.55.88

Cours du Polygone de Vincennes Avenue du Tremblay, 43.74.78.70

Mondial Tennis Country Club 58 Avenue du Président Wilson, 46.07.62.69

There is no food in Paris, only cuisine.

Anonymous

Restaurants/Clubs: Red   Hotels: Blue
Shops/ ⛺Outdoors: Green   **Sights/Culture:** Black

67 Chaussures Georges This dinky one-hundred-year-old shoe store run by a garrulous Armenian named **Georges** supplies the neighborhood butchers, fishmongers, and masons with their rubber boots and wool-lined French *sabots* (wooden shoes). These are shoes for function, not fantasy, proclaims Georges, who keeps all his footwear in 19th-century boxes with pewter handles. He also sells plain espadrilles—the *real* ones from Spain, not Chinese imitations. ♦ Tu-Sa 9:30AM-12:30PM, 2:15-7:30PM; Su 9:30AM-12:30PM. 64 Rue Mouffetard (between Rues Pot-de-Fer and Jean-Calvin). Métro: Place-Monge. 47.07.16.66

68 10 Rue Vauquelin On 26 December 1898, working in a ramshackle ground-floor laboratory here at the **Sorbonne School of Physics and Chemistry** (which is now housed in a shiny new redbrick-and-glass building), **Marie Curie** and her husband, **Pierre,** discovered radium. The discovery of radioactivity not only earned them a Nobel prize in 1903 (the first of two for Marie) but triggered a fundamental rethinking of theoretical physics. A few months after their achievements, the quantum theory was published. ♦ Between Rues Lhomond and Claude Bernard. Métro: Censier-Daubenton

69 Mouffetard Market A bustling pedestrian street market has convened at the bottom of the hill ever since 1350. It begins at the Rue de l'Epée-de-Bois. Among the gastronomical items purveyed here are mangoes, blood oranges, horse meat, wild boar, sea urchins, Colombian coffee, and hundreds of marvelously smelly cheeses. Take a self-guided tour: just follow your nose. Be sure to go down the Rue Daubenton and Passage Passé Simple to visit the flower shops and the stalls specializing in Auvergnat sausage. As you wander, remember the two cardinal rules of marketing in Paris: first, *don't touch the produce;* and second, *the vendor, not the customer, is always right.* ♦ Tu-Sa 9AM-1PM, 4-7PM; Su 9AM-1PM. At Rue Censier. Métro: Place-Monge

69 Brasserie Mouffetard ★★$ The croissants, brioches, and fruit tarts are made fresh daily by the friendly **Chartrain** family, owners of the best café on the street. It's noisy, always crowded with vendors and students, and in winter the windows steam up with animated conversation. ♦ Breakfast, lunch, and snacks. Closed in July. 116 Rue Mouffetard (at Rue de l'Arbalète). Métro: Place-Monge. 43.31.42.50

69 St.-Médard This rustic village church, built in 1773, is an architectural conglomeration of flamboyant Gothic and Renaissance styles and has a story for every predilection. French literature majors may remember this as the church in which **Jean Valjean** accidentally encounters **Javert** in **Victor Hugo's** *Les Misérables.* Trade unionists point out that St.-Médard was turned into the *Temple of Labor* during the Revolution. Art historians will recall the notorious painting of **Sainte Geneviève,** which for centuries was erroneously ascribed to **Watteau.** And finally, the occultists in the crowd will appreciate a most famous corpse buried here, that of Saint Médard's deacon, a young Jansenist named **François Paris,** who died in 1727. Within two years, crowds of more than 800 hysterical convulsionists flocked to his grave where they groaned and trembled in hopes of miraculous cures. (The frenzied gatherings were finally outlawed by **Louis XV** in 1732, but Paris' tomb remains beneath the unmarked stones of what is now the Chapel of the Virgin.) The majority of the church's construction was financed by fines imposed on Protestants; the money ran out while the vaulted ceiling was being installed, so it was completed in wood. At least that's how the story goes. ♦ 141 Rue Mouffetard. Métro: Censier-Daubenton

70 A la Bonne Source (At the Good Spring) The bas-relief of two boys drawing water dates from the time of **Henri IV** (1589-1610) and is the oldest house sign on the street. ♦ 122 Rue Mouffetard (between Rues de l'Arbalète and Edouard Quenu). Métro: Censier-Daubenton

70 Facchetti & Co. Charcuterie Fine Although it's a first-rate gourmet Italian delicatessen, the main reason for stopping here is not to buy pasta and Parmesan but to admire the bucolic outdoor mural of peasants at work below a pair of stags and wild boars. ♦ Tu-Th 8:15AM-1PM, 4-7:30PM; F-Sa 8:15AM-3:30PM; Su 8:15AM-1:30PM. 134 Rue Mouffetard (between Rues de l'Arbalète and Edouard Quenu). Métro: Censier-Daubenton. 43.31.40.00

71 Le Petit Marguery ★★$$ This lively 1900s-style neighborhood bistro presents such inventive dishes as leeks with truffles and venison with celery root. ♦ Lunch and dinner. Closed Sunday, Monday, and in August. 9 Blvd de Port-Royal (between Avenue des Gobelins and Rue Pascal). Reservations recommended. Métro: Gobelins. 43.31.58.59

Napoléon, or, more correctly, Bonaparte, as he was then known, first came to national attention at the siege of Toulon, where his bravery and innovative use of artillery caught the attention of Robespierre's younger brother. Born in Corsica, Napoléon had a sensational career—the most stunning of the 19th century. His rise from relative obscurity to emperor of Europe was made possible by the Revolution; indeed, he often said he was its heir. By a coup d'état in 1799, he made himself the Republic's First Consul and, soon afterwards, First Consul for life. In 1804 he crowned himself emperor.

72 Gobelins Tapestry Factories The factory, the avenue, and the neighborhood all take their name from the brothers **Jean** and **Philibert Gobelin,** who in the 15th century established their famous dye works along the stinking **Bièvre River.** Although the name *Gobelins* has become synonymous with tapestry, the two brothers never wove a thread. Their claim to fame in the tapestry world was making a special scarlet dye. In 1662 **Jean-Baptiste Colbert, Louis XIV's** famous minister, persuaded the king to take over the Gobelins property. There, under the management of court painter **Charles Le Brun,** Colbert assembled a craft colony of about 250 Flemish weavers. His goal was twofold: to compete with Flanders' tapestry industry and to cover the vast expanse of walls in the Sun King's sumptuous palace at Versailles. (Within Gobelins' first courtyard stands a marble 1907 statue of Le Brun by **Cardier,** followed in the next courtyard by an 1894 statue of his boss, Colbert, by **Aube.**) In time, Gobelins became so celebrated that **Marie Antoinette** and **Louis XVI** (in 1790) and the **Pope** (in 1895) paid personal visits to the humble workshops.

Today scores of weavers at the Gobelins factory manufacture tapestries with the ancient techniques, working on century-old wooden looms. Using wools from a palette of 14,920 colors, weavers may spend two to four years completing woven panels, the designs of which are based on modern paintings by artists such as **Matisse, Picasso,** and **Miró.** Three days a week, the state-owned Gobelins mills offer 75-minute guided tours of the tapestry factory and the allied **Savonnerie** (carpet) and **Beauvais** (horizontal loom weaving) workshops, a treat for anyone interested in weaving and crafts. You can visit the studios where weavers, trained from the age of 16, work quietly, occasionally glancing up at mirrors before them to view the reverse side of the tapestry. If you can't get to the factory, you can see Gobelins tapestries hanging at Versailles as well as other places reserved for the privileged: the Paris Opéra, the National Library, the Elysée Palace, and the Luxembourg Palace. ◆ Tours: Tu-Th 2-3PM. To arrange group tours, call Caisse Nationale des Monuments Historiques at 44.61.20.00. 42 Ave des Gobelins (at Rue Croulebarbe). Métro: Gobelins. 43.37.12.60

73 Mobilier National (National Storehouse) What is as supersecret as the French CIA, answers directly to the president, and is littered with Napoléon-era love seats and andirons? Answer: the Mobilier National, the nation's attic. This singular institution was created in 1667 by **Colbert** as a royal storehouse when he was transforming the Gobelins factory. It is the state's interior decorator, responsible for furnishing government ministries and embassies with everything from inkwells to curtains. The

institution, which at one time also kept the crown jewels, is quartered within the Gobelins complex in an unremarkable redbrick structure designed by **Auguste Perret.** In 1964 **André Malraux,** then Minister of Culture, offered studio space in the Mobilier National to contemporary French furniture designers who would be willing to create and sell their prototypes to French manufacturers. Thus, the Mobilier National takes credit for the boldly modern furniture used in former president **Georges Pompidou's** office at the **Elysée Palace.** You can pass by the Mobilier National on the Gobelins tour, but the warehouse is off-limits to the public. ◆ Rue Berbier-du-Mets (at Rue Emile Deslandres). Métro: Gobelins

74 La Tuile à Loup Run by the affable **Marie-France** and **Michel Joblin,** this crowded shop specializes in French regional arts and crafts. You will find earthenware dishes, hand-carved wooden bowls, toys by well-known French artist **Roland Roure,** and a vast selection of books on French folklore, rural architecture, and ecology. ◆ Tu-Sa 10:30AM-1PM, 3-7:30PM; Su 10AM-1PM (call ahead to confirm Sunday hours). 35 Rue Daubenton (between Rues Candolle and Monge). Métro: Censier-Daubenton. 47.07.28.90

75 Place Monge This square is named for the mathematician **Gaspard Monge** (1746-1818), who in 1794 founded the prestigious Ecole Polytechnique. Near the bustling small farmers' market is the old barracks of the **Garde Républicaine,** whose famous Horse Guards parade up the **Champs-Elysées** on Bastille Day, 14 July. ◆ Market: W, F, Su 7AM-1PM. Métro: Place-Monge

76 Arènes de Lutèce (Roman Arena) After the Roman Baths, this enormous first-century amphitheater is the city's most important Roman ruin. The 325- by 425-foot oval once seated 15,000 spectators, and it was accidentally discovered (and partially destroyed) in 1869. With its surrounding gardens and benches, the arena provides an island of tranquility for young parents pushing strollers and old men playing *boules;* in summer, campy medieval jousts take place in the arena. It's a nice spot for a picnic lunch of sourdough rye bread and charcuterie from the Place-Monge Market. ◆ Enter at Rues de Navarre and des Arènes. Métros: Cardinal-Lemoine, Jussieu, Place-Monge

77 Hôtel Jardin des Plantes $$ Guests of this quiet hotel can enjoy breakfast surrounded by flowers on the rooftop terrace. Many of the rooms have views of the magnificent botanical garden nearby. ♦ 5 Rue Linné (between Rues Lacépède and des Arènes). Métros: Jussieu, Place-Monge. 47.07.06.20

78 La Mosquée de Paris This Moorish ensemble of soaring minarets, pink marble fountains, and crescent moons is the oldest mosque in France. It was constructed in 1926 by Arab artisans and three French architects. In gratitude for North African support during World War I, France gave the French Arab community the funds to build the mosque. Arabs from the poor Belleville and Barbès quarters gather at this enclave of Islam to read the Koran at the **Muslim Institut.** During Ramadan, hundreds of North Africans kneel facing Mecca and pray to Allah on a sea of Persian carpets spread beneath the mosque's delicately carved dome. Nearby, behind a dark curtain, the women intone their prayers. A guided tour (unfortunately brief) of the building, central courtyard, and Moorish garden offers a worthwhile introduction to Islam. You may leave feeling as though you've passed the afternoon in Riyadh or Istanbul. ♦ M-Th, Sa-Su 9AM-noon, 2-6PM. Place du Puits-de-l'Ermite (at Rue Quatrefages). Métro: Place-Monge. 45.35.97.33/34/35

78 Café de la Mosquée ★$ Flaky Moroccan pastries, sweet mint tea, and Turkish coffee are served during the summer on a white patio shaded by leafy fig trees. In winter warm up with tea in a quiet lounge adjoining the *hammam* (Turkish steam bath). No alcohol is served. ♦ Lunch, dinner, and snacks. Closed in August. Baths: (for women) M, W 11AM-8PM, Th 11AM-9PM, Sa 10AM-9PM; (for men) F 11AM-8PM, Su 10AM-8PM. 2 Rue Daubenton (at Rue Geoffroy-St.-Hilaire). Métro: Censier-Daubenton. 43.31.18.14

79 Jardin des Plantes It was begun in 1626 by **Louis XIII** as a royal medicinal herb garden planted on an old rubbish heap. Today the 74-acre botanical garden hosts a floral orgy of peonies, irises, roses, geraniums, and dahlias from April through October. The garden, bounded by streets named after great French naturalists and botanists (**Jussieu, Geoffroy St.-Hilaire, Daubenton, Buffon,** and

Lacépède), contains a pedestal inscribed to the French scientist **Lamarck,** the founder of the doctrine of evolution (tough luck, **Charles Darwin**) and another honoring **Chevreul,** the director of the Gobelins dye factory who lived to 103 and whose color-spectrum research informed the Impressionist painters.

Within the park is France's oldest public zoo, a menagerie with a rather pathetic history. Established shortly after the Revolution to display survivors from the Royal Menagerie at Versailles (one hartebeest, one zebra, one rhinoceros, and a sheepdog), it was originally called the **People's Democratic Zoo.** In 1795 the first elephants arrived, in 1805 the bear pit opened, and in 1827 an Egyptian prince gave the Jardin des Plantes its first giraffe. The zoo grew in size and popularity until the Siege of Paris in 1870 and1871, when the poor beasts were eaten. For several weeks, it is said, the privileged of Paris dined on elephant steaks the size of manhole covers. The zoo has never recovered from the slaughter, and conditions remain on the shabby side (animals are still jailed in Second-Empire pavilions and rumors of stray cats being fed to snakes and reptiles proliferate). However, children still seem to love visiting the zoo.

Legend holds that the park's famous *Cedar of Lebanon,* now 40 feet in circumference, traveled in 1735 as a seedling in the hat of naturalist **Bernard de Jussieu,** who had carefully preserved it during confinement as a prisoner of war. But in truth, it was given to him after his release.

The park's **Museum of Natural History** has four departments, Paleontology, Paleobotany, Mineralogy, and Entomology, and it possesses one of the world's richest mineral collections and some of the oldest fossilized insects on earth. The Zoology exhibit, closed since 1965, is scheduled to reopen in the spring of 1994. ♦ Garden: daily 8AM-8PM. Zoo: daily 9AM-6PM. Greenhouses: M, W-Su 1-5PM. Museum: daily 10AM-5PM. Enter at Rue Buffon, Rue Cuvier, or Place Valhubert. Métros: Gare d'Austerlitz, Jussieu, Place-Monge. 40.79.30.00

80 Musée de Sculpture en Plein Air This outdoor sculpture museum, built in 1980, was once **Henri IV's** bathing beach. The king would pour water here from a royal hat over the young Dauphin as the preamble to a swimming lesson. Today this spot on the banks of the Seine holds permanent and temporary exhibitions. But don't come after dark; a less desirable brand of exhibitionist prowls then. ♦ Quai St.-Bernard. Métros: Gare d'Austerlitz, Jussieu

80 L'Institut du Monde Arabe Opened in December 1987, this sociocultural institution was established to promote relations between France and the Arab world. It contains a library, an exhibition space, and a top-floor restaurant that serves Lebanese specialties. The architect, **Jean Nouvel,** who received the Agha Kahn prize for his design, has given Islamic references a stunning space-age interpretation. Notice Nouvel's treatment of the south facade: the wall is made up of thousands of cameralike shutters that open and close automatically, according to the sun's brightness, to regulate the amount of light let inside the building. ♦ Institute: Tu-Su 1-6PM. 23 Quai St.-Bernard (at Blvd St.-Germain). Métros: Jussieu, Cardinal-Lemoine. 40.51.38.38 (general information)

Within L'Institut du Monde Arabe:

Fakhr el Dine ★★$$ The river view from this rooftop Lebanese restaurant is better than that of **La Tour d'Argent**—at half the price. You may want to make a meal of the hot and cold hors d'oeuvres, which include *hummus, baba ghanoush,* falafel, grilled chicken wings marinated in garlic and lemon, lamb brochettes, and Lebanese bread stuffed with cheese, tomato, and mint. Linger at a table on the terrace on balmy summer evenings. ♦ Lunch and dinner. Closed Monday. 1 Rue des Fossés-St.-Bernard (at Blvd St.-Germain). 43.25.88.51, 46.33.00.55

Bests

Baron Eric de Rothschild
Co-owner/Manager, Château Lafitte Rothschild Bordeaux Wines

Strolling in the **Albert Kahn Gardens** in Boulogne.

Having tea and chocolate cake in one of the little bistros in the **Parc des Buttes-Chaumont.**

Sunday lunch in the **Parc Montsouris.**

Seafood at **Le Duc** on the Boulevard Raspail with Rieussec (dry white wine) for dinner.

Feasting on pot-au-feu for lunch on Saturday at **Balzar.**

Perusing the wine list at **Benoît** on Rue St.-Martin.

Rudolph Chelminski
American Author

The view at night of the islands and the Left Bank, from the point where the Pont des Arts jumps over the Seine from the Institut de France to the Right Bank. Anyone who sees this and doesn't instantly agree that Paris is the most beautiful city in the world is a churl or a New Yorker, which is usually the same thing, anyway.

A four-corner, right-of-way blockage at an intersection where everyone has *priorité* over everyone else and refuses to budge. In one beautiful flash, you entirely understand French civilization.

A walk through the **Marais** ending at the **Place des Vosges** and wondering why in hell you didn't have the brains to buy an apartment there 25 years ago.

A Christmas dinner of oysters, *dinde aux marrons,* and champagne in **La Coupole** (the brasserie side, of course).

The third girl from the left in the **Crazy Horse Saloon's** chorus line. For sheer beauty it's a toss-up between her and the **Ste.-Chapelle,** but the chorus girl's more kinetic.

The **Pont Alexandre III** at twilight, when the Belle Epoque lanterns have been turned on but there is enough sky left to give a Magritte effect.

Watching the murderous old men playing a game of *boules* in **Luxembourg Gardens.**

All the open-air markets, especially the **Buci** and the **Mouffetard.**

Père-Lachaise, the cemetery that makes death seem like fun.

Dinner at **Taillevent, Vivarois,** or **Lucas-Carton,** if some rich publisher is buying. If not, any of the following will do just fine: **L'Aquitaine, Chez les Anges, Chez Georges, Le Cochon d'Or, Aux Charpentiers, L'Entrecôte, Léon, La Providence, Le Récamier,** or **Le Val d'Or.** And that's just a start.

Françoise Gilot
Artist

Walking along **Le Canal St.-Martin** (built by Gustave Eiffel, who built the Eiffel Tower) with its small bridges and waterlocks.

The charming **Place des Vosges** for its early 17th-century architecture, the **Victor Hugo Museum** (which is a curiosity rather than a full-fledged museum), and all the small shops and restaurants around the square. The **Coconnas** has always been popular, although recently it hasn't quite lived up to its reputation.

Some of architect **François Ledoux's gates** to the city of Paris built in the 17th century, particularly the one at the **Jaurès** métro station, or those at **Denfert-Rochereau** or **Monceau.**

One of the enclosed galleries at the **Passage des Panoramas** and the nearby **Musée Grevin,** which is the Parisian equivalent of Madame Tussaud's. The **Passage Choiseul** is also interesting.

The old section of the **Père-Lachaise** cemetery. It's romantic in the springtime, with trees growing everywhere and statues tilting in one direction or another.

Gustave Moreau Museum, located in the artist's home and studio on Rue de la Rochefoucauld.

Rue Réaumur, where you can see the many Art Nouveau, Art Deco, and purely outrageous buildings along the street. Newspapers are published here, and, at the turn of the century, this was the headquarters for the textile magnates.

Restaurants/Clubs: Red **Hotels:** Blue
Shops/ Outdoors: Green **Sights/Culture:** Black

In the 1950s, Jean-Paul Sartre and Simone de Beauvoir held Existential court at **Café de Flore**—a great place to savor a real bacon-and-eggs breakfast

Ⓜ Solférino

Make advance reservations to tour the extraordinary **Glass House** (see page 60)

Ⓜ Rue du Bac

Ⓜ St.-Sulpice

Ⓜ Sèvres-Babylon

A small bronze replica of the Statue of Liberty graces the gardens here

The site of a beekeeping school run by an Esperanto-speaking Dominican friar

St.-Germain

The tree-lined **Boulevard St.-Germain** originates near the tip of Ile St.-Louis, then traverses the heart of literary Paris, and finally arrives back at the Seine at the **Pont de la Concorde** in that noble faubourg fashionable during the reign of **Louis XV**. This is the home of the **Académie Française**, the world's oldest café (**Le Procope**), prestigious publishing houses, bookbinders, and that conclave of intellectual watering holes where **Fitzgerald**, **Hemingway**, and other American scriveners wrote or drank away rejection-slip depression. And in the 1950s, this is where **Sartre** gave birth to existentialism.

L'Hôtel—the hotel where Oscar Wilde expired is the refined favorite of Robert de Niro, Julie Christie, and countless honeymooners

Pablo Picasso painted *Guernica* here on Rue des Grands-Augustins in 1937

M St.-Michel

Place St.-Michel—a popular rendezvous for students, bikers, and drug-pushers

M Odéon

St.-Séverin Church—Paris' richest example of flamboyant Gothic architecture

Pub St.-Germain-des-Prés—24 varieties of beer on draft and 450 international kinds in bottles

Place de Furstemberg—a hidden courtyard that attracts French filmmakers, flamenco guitar players, and harpists who come for the extraordinary acoustics. Also the site of Eugène Delacroix's old atelier (studio), now a museum displaying his paintings, sketches, and letters

Théâtre de l'Odéon—formerly the home of playwright Molière's Comédie Française

Don't miss the church caretaker's rooftop garden on the southeast corner of **St.-Sulpice**

M Luxembourg (RER)

Bandstand for summer afternoon concerts

Sylvia Beach, a famous Hemingway and James Joyce colleague, hid from the Nazis for two years in a top-floor kitchen on 93 Boulevard St.-Michel

Guided tours of Marie de Médici's **Luxembourg Palace** are offered the first Sunday of each month

Toy sailboat regattas take place in the octagonal basin

Pony rides and a marionette theater for children are offered on weekends

M St.-Germain-des-Prés

M = Métro

The St.-Germain quarter is also the home of the inviting **Luxembourg Gardens,** the **Ecole des Beaux-Arts,** and a plethora of art galleries. In this neighborhood, the painter **Corot** walked the quays; **Manet** lived on **Rue Bonaparte;** and **Delacroix** resided in the **Place de Furstemberg. Ingres, Baudelaire,** and **Wagner** stayed on **Quai Voltaire,** and **Picasso** painted *Guernica* on **Rue des Grands-Augustins.**

The St.-Germain itinerary covers half of the boulevard—the most interesting portion is in the vicinity of the church of **St.-Germain-des-Prés,** where the remains of the city's oldest abbey stand. The promenade takes you down alleys where bookshops, poster stores, antique dealers, and picture restorers do business side by side with chic dress shops and cafés frequented by students.

This is a stroll you can make in blue jeans and a sweater. Start at the **Musée d'Orsay,** a former Belle Epoque train station that is now devoted to art and culture, spanning the era from 1848 to World War I. En route to the Boulevard St.-Germain, take Rue du Bac and stop at **Deyrolle,** an amusing taxidermy shop. On the boulevard, you'll encounter **Madeleine Gély's** handmade-umbrella shop, an essential for those frequent April downpours. You might consider having an early lunch and watching the world go by at one of those literary shrines: **Lipp, Flore,** or **Deux Magots.** When you can't eat another bite of Lipp's *choucroute* (sauerkraut), visit the shaded Place de Furstemberg to look for the old studio of **Delacroix,** browse for antiques along **Rue Jacob,** or tour the African art galleries along **Rue de Seine.**

The narrow **Cour du Commerce St.-André** is where the guillotine was invented and where the firebrand **Marat** had his printing press. You'll pass Le Procope, where **Voltaire** and **Robespierre** were among the regulars, and the **Buci Market,** where Picasso bought his sausages. At **Rue de Tournon,** nature lovers will want to detour through the Luxembourg Gardens, one of the **Queen Marie de Médici** legacies to the city.

At the day's end, consider dining at a classic, old-world bistro such as **Allard.** Or you could catch an early Cary Grant film at the **Action Christine,** then dine in the splendor of **Jacques Cagna** around the corner on Rue des Grands-Augustins. After dinner, wander toward the river via **La Palette,** where you can have a beer at the bar, or venture into the hole-in-the-wall **Caveau de la Boulée** to sit in on a midnight game of chess.

1 Hôtel Solférino $$ This hotel has Oriental rugs, pastel walls, floral wallpaper, small rooms, and a veranda where you can enjoy breakfast. ♦ 91 Rue de Lille (between Rue de Solférino and Blvd St.-Germain). Métro: Solférino-Musée d'Orsay. 47.05.85.54

Mrs. Allonby: They say, Lady Hunstanton, that when good Americans die they go to Paris.

Lady Hunstanton: Indeed? And when bad Americans die, where do they go?

Lord Illingworth: Oh, they go to America.

Oscar Wilde, *A Woman of No Importance*

2 Palais de la Légion d'Honneur Built by **Pierre Rousseau** for German **Prince Frédéric III de Salm-Kyrbourg** in 1786, this palace (pictured above) is architecturally the most significant **Louis XVI** building in Paris. In 1804 **Napoléon** acquired it for the *Légion d'Honneur.* (The city of San Francisco built a copy of the palace and turned it into an art

Restaurants/Clubs: Red **Hotels:** Blue
Shops/ 🌳Outdoors: Green **Sights/Culture:** Black

museum.) The *légion* was a society started by Napoléon to honor men, and later women, who greatly served France. Members may wear a woven bud of red wool stitched to their left lapel. ♦ Admission. Légion museum: Tu-Su 2-5PM. 2 Rue de Bellechasse (at Quai Anatole-France). Métro: Solférino-Musée d'Orsay

3 Musée d'Orsay In December 1986 a long train of effort chugged into the Gare d'Orsay, and when the steam cleared, there stood a magnificent museum, a Paris showcase for 19th-century art and culture. The Musée d'Orsay houses the art that chronologically links the Louvre collections with those at the Pompidou Center, bridging the end of Romanticism and the origins of Modern Art. The museum transports us back to a time of grace and wit with the works of such geniuses as **Henry James, Edouard Manet, Sarah Bernhardt,** and **James McNeill Whistler.**

The Musée d'Orsay collection (see diagram) includes all the Impressionist paintings formerly in the **Jeu de Paume;** the post-Impressionist and Nabi works from the **Palais de Tokyo** (among them are 400 paintings by **Odilon Redon**); and selected works that were formerly in the Louvre, including paintings and sculptures by artists such as **Courbet** and **Millet,** who were born after 1820, and various late paintings by **Delacroix, Corot, Ingres,** and the **Barbizon landscape painters.**

The Quai d'Orsay site was once occupied by the **Palais d'Orsay,** a government building that was devastated (as were the Hôtel de Ville and the Tuileries Palace) by the May 1871 fires set by the Commune at the end of France's tragic civil war period. The Orléans Rail Company bought the property and hired **Victor Laloux** (1850-1937), the architect who had rebuilt the Hôtel de Ville, to design a railway station and hotel. Construction lasted from September 1898 to July 1900 and was accomplished by a crew of 380 men working in round-the-clock shifts.

Upper Level

Middle Level

Main Entrance

Information Area

Ground Level

Painting	Bookstore
Sculpture	Rooftop Café
Decorative Arts	Art Nouveau
Architecture	Birth of the Filmmaker
Temporary Exhibitions	Restaurant

At one time, 200 trains a day used the Gare d'Orsay, but the growing electrification and lengthening of trains made Orsay's short platforms obsolete in the late 1930s. Over the years, the station took on other functions. Prisoners of war were garrisoned here after the l iberation; **General de Gaulle** announced his return to power at the Gare d'Orsay hotel on 19 May 1958; **Orson Welles** made a film

Musée d'Orsay

version of the **Franz Kafka** book *The Trial* here in 1962; and in 1970, **Bernardo Bertolucci** used it as a setting for part of his film, *The Conformist.*

As early as 1961, plans to raze the station and build a modern 870-room hotel complex were nearly realized; **Le Corbusier** even competed for the design job. But in 1971 the station was declared a historic landmark. In 1979 **ACT Architecture** (a group of three associated architects: **Pierre Colboc, Renaud Bardon,** and **Jean-Paul Philippo**) was selected to renovate the building for use as a museum. The famed Italian designer **Gae Aulenti** planned the interior.

Ground Level This floor features painting, sculpture, photography, and decorative arts dating from 1848 to 1870. The front of the gallery contains sculptures by **Rude, Préault,** and **Pradier,** and a great animal bronze by **Barye.** At the rear of the gallery stands *The Dance* by **Carpeaux.** Rooms at the end of the courtyard are dedicated to the **Paris Opéra** and its architect, **Charles Garnier.**

To the right of the courtyard are paintings by Romantics such as **Delacroix** and **Ingres,** as well as works by the eclectics and symbolists such as **Puvis de Chavannes** and **Gustave Moreau,** along with the pre-1870 work of **Edward Degas.** To the left of the courtyard are works by Realists, including **Daumier, Corot, Millet,** and the **Barbizon painters.** They are neighbors to the masterpieces of **Edouard Manet,** such as *Olympia* and *Déjeuner sur L'Herbe,* in addition to the pre-1870 work of **Monet, Bazille,** and **Renoir.**

Upper Level The tour jumps to the upper level (to follow the chronological order of the artwork), where the light streaming through the museum's glass roof shows off the post-1870 flowering of Impressionism. Here **Manet, Degas, Monet,** and **Renoir** are joined by **Sisley, Pissarro, van Gogh,** and **Cézanne.** Nearby, post-Impressionists such as **Seurat, Signac, Cross,** and **Gauguin** are shown with the Pont Aven and Nabi schools, including **Denis, Bonnard, Vallotton,** and **Vuillard.** There's also a special room devoted to graphic arts and photography from 1880-1914, including the works of early photographers **Atget, Emerson, Steichen,** and **Stieglitz,** as well as **Bonnard** and Degas, who are best known for their painting. After you have feasted your eyes on this floor's treasures, go downstairs for **Nadar, Legray, Baldus, Carroll,** and **Cameron.**

Middle Level The terraces above the courtyard display the sculpture of **Rodin, Maillol,** and **Bourdelle.** The rooms along the Seine have figures created during the Third Republic, including works by symbolists **Burne-Jones** and **Delville.** Eight rooms are devoted to the sinuous era of Art Nouveau, with works by the Belgians **Horta** and **van de**

Velde, by **Gallé** and **Majorelle** of the Nancy School, and pieces by **Guimard** and **Thonet,** the dean of bentwood furniture. On the Rue de Lille side, you will find the 20th-century paintings of **Klimt** and **Matisse,** heralding the advent of Modern Art. Also on this level is an exhibition showing the evolution of the film industry.

Impressionists The famous French Impressionist collection is displayed on the ground and upper levels. The term "Impressionism" was coined by a derisive critic after seeing Monet's painting *Impression: Sunrise.* The name stuck, and the movement effected as dramatic a change in the course of art history as the Renaissance had. Instead of choosing heroes, mythic deities, or saints for their subject matter, the Impressionists painted ordinary people in cafés as well as trains chugging into Gare St.-Lazare with vivid color and undisguised brush strokes.

Americans in Paris The Orsay collection also includes paintings by more than 36 American artists, including **John Singer Sargent, William Merritt Chase, Robert Henri,** and **Winslow Homer,** many of whom worked and studied in Paris. And this is where you can visit that emblem of American art, *The Artist's Mother,* by Whistler. A rooftop café, a bookstore, and a 380-seat auditorium round out the museum. ◆ Admission. Tu-W, F-Sa 10AM-6PM; Th 10AM-9:30PM (opens at 9AM, 20 June-20 Sept); Su 9AM-5:30PM. Closed Christmas day and 1 May. 1 Rue de Bellechasse (at Quai Anatole-France). Métro: Solférino-Musée d'Orsay. 40.49.48.14, 45.49.11.11 (recorded information)

Within Musée d'Orsay:

Museum Restaurant ★$$ Housed in the dining room of the old hotel, the restaurant is an ornately gilded period piece that has a ceiling covered with painted deities by **Gabriel Ferrier,** winner of the 1872 *Prix de Rome.* The decor is the real attraction here, not the food. Don't bother asking the waiter for absinthe, but try Pernod on ice. ◆ Lunch and afternoon tea; Thursday dinner. Closed Monday. 45.49.47.03

4 **Bonpoint** This pricey chain store offers a touch of couture for the little darlings in your life. Sister stores are nearby. ◆ M-Sa 10AM-7PM. 67 Rue de l'Université (between Rues de Solférino and de Bellechasse). Métro: Rue du Bac. 45.55.63.70

5 **Rue du Bac** The barracks that housed the swashbuckling heroes of *The Three Musketeers* by **Alexandre Dumas** were located on this street, which was built in 1564 and named after the *bac* (ferry) that used to transport Vaugirard quarry stone across the Seine to the construction site of the Tuileries Palace. ◆ Métro: Rue du Bac

JEAN SAFFRAY

6 **Jean Saffray** Buy an ice cream bust of your favorite French politician, whether it's François Mitterrand, Georges Marchais, Jacques Chirac, or Valèry Giscard d'Estaing. ♦ Tu-Sa 7AM-8PM; Su 7:30AM-7PM. Closed in August. 18 Rue du Bac (at Rue Verneuil). Métro: Rue du Bac. 42.61.27.63

7 **Lefèbvres Fils** Among the former shoppers at this century-old firm selling earthenware china and fanciful trompe l'oeil dishes were **Victor Hugo, Marcel Proust,** and **Georges Feydeau.** ♦ M-Sa 10AM-1PM, 2-7PM. Closed in August. 24 Rue du Bac (between Rues de l'Université and de Verneuil). Métro: Rue du Bac. 42.61.18.40

Christian Constant

7 **Christian Constant** ★$ This tearoom-cum-chocolate-and-pastry shop serves 36 kinds of tea accompanied by five varieties of sugar, acacia honey, and fresh brioches, as well as great lemon meringue tarts, but the pièce de résistance is its pure bittersweet chocolate bars. ♦ Daily 8AM-8PM. Tearoom: breakfast, lunch, and tea. 26 Rue du Bac (between Rues de l'Université and de Verneuil). Métro: Rue du Bac. 47.03.30.00

7 **50 Rue de l'Université** This is the former site of the **Hôtel de l'Intendance,** where **Edna St. Vincent Millay** wrote her Pulitzer prize-winning poem, *The Ballad of the Harp-Weaver,* in 1921. ♦ Between Rues du Bac and de Poitiers. Métro: Rue du Bac

8 **Tan Dinh** ★★★$$$ The most elegant—and expensive—Vietnamese restaurant in Paris is conveniently located around the corner from the Musée d'Orsay. Delicate smoked-goose ravioli, light noodles with piquant shrimp, and lobster *beignets* of *coquilles St.-Jacques* with ginkgo are prepared by the affable **Vifian** brothers, who alternate nights in the kitchen. Exotic sorbets and remarkable Bordeaux are memorable diversions from the entrées. ♦ Lunch and dinner. Closed Sunday and in August. 60 Rue de Verneuil (between Rues du Bac and Poitiers). Dinner reservations recommended. Métro: Rue du Bac. 45.44.04.84

8 **Maxoff Restaurant** ★$$ The menu's highlights include *tarama,* a Baltic salad, beef stroganoff, Russian caviar, *caviar d'aubergines,* Ukrainian borscht, strudels, and blintzes. ♦ Lunch and dinner; dinner only on Saturday. Closed Sunday and in August. 44 Rue de Verneuil (between Rues du Bac and de Poitiers). Reservations recommended. Métro: Rue du Bac. 42.60.60.43

8 **Ravi** ★★$$$ Spicy and pricey, this aptly named Indian restaurant (*Ravi* means *sun* in Hindi) outshines its competitors with Madras curries, kabobs, and outstanding Tandoori prawns. ♦ Lunch and dinner. Closed Sunday. 50 Rue de Verneuil (between Rues du Bac and de Poitiers). Reservations recommended. Métro: Rue du Bac. 42.61.17.28

9 **Le Rideau de Paris** After 40 years in business, this crowded little linen shop has cornered the neighborhood market in true one hundred-percent French cotton dishtowels and lace bistro curtains. ♦ M-F 10AM-6:30PM; Sa 2:30-6:30PM. 32 Rue du Bac (between Blvd St.-Germain and Rue de l'Université). Métro: Rue du Bac. 42.61.18.56

9 **Nina Borowski-Archéologie** A world-renowned dealer in rare Greek and Near Eastern antiquities, Borowski also works in New York by appointment. She numbers among her clients the great museums of Europe and America. Don't miss her collection of ancient Greek and Roman rings and other jewelry. ♦ M 2-7PM; Tu-Sa 10:30AM-12:30PM, 2-7PM. Closed in August. 40 Rue du Bac (between Blvd St.-Germain and Rue de l'Université). Métro: Rue du Bac. 45.48.61.60

10 **Galerie Adrien Maeght** The owner of this bookstore/gallery comes from a famous family of art dealers and sells drawings and prints by modern artists from **Matisse** to **Cucchi,** as well as **Calder** posters, **Miró** T-shirts, and deluxe art books. ♦ Tu-Sa 10AM-1PM, 2-7PM. 42 and 46 Rue du Bac (between Blvd St.-Germain and Rue de l'Université). Métro: Rue du Bac. 45.48.45.15

10 **Deyrolle** A 150-year old taxidermy shop with everything from mounted polar bears, tigers, and bewildered baby elephants to cobras and many other citizens of Noah's Ark, all staring out of glass eyes. Deyrolle also acquires rare butterflies, tastefully stuffed cocker spaniels, and just about every crystal, geode, and mineral on earth. Kids could be left here for hours. The question is, when you retrieve them, will they have glass eyes, too? ♦ M-F 9AM-12:30PM, 2-6PM; Sa 9AM-6PM. 46 Rue du Bac (between Blvd St.-Germain and Rue de l'Université). Métro: Rue du Bac. 42.22.30.07

10 **Lenôtre** The owner, **Gaston Lenôtre,** wrote the book on pastry, and this is only one of his five outlets in Paris. You can almost gain weight just by looking in the shop window, so why not slip inside and sample the *palet d'or* or go for broke with the delectable Concorde chocolate meringue cake? ♦ M-Sa 9AM-8PM; Su 9AM-1PM. Closed in August. 44 Rue du Bac (between Blvd St.-Germain and Rue de l'Université). Métro: Rue du Bac. 42.22.39.39

11 Trente Quatro ★★★$$ Charming **Francesca Ciardi** serves delectable Italian fare in her cozy dining room. Ricotta and spinach ravioli, risotto with apples and watercress, and veal in white wine or lemon vodka sauce are all worthy entrées, and if you have any room left, share the rich zabaglione and blueberries with someone. ♦ Lunch and dinner; dinner only on Sunday. Closed Saturdays in August. 34 Rue de Bourgogne (between Rues de Grenelle and Las-Cases). Reservations recommended. Métros: Varenne, Assemblée Nationale. 45.55.80.75

12 L'Oeillade ★★$$ An ever-changing, moderately priced three-course menu is offered by chef **Jean-Louis Huclin,** who makes all the sausages, terrines, and pasta himself. He also serves perfectly stewed pot-au-feu salad, cassoulet in a gleaming copper saucepan, succulent roast chicken, and mousse au chocolat. Wine options are limited but affordable. ♦ Lunch and dinner; dinner only on Saturday. Closed Sunday. 10 Rue St.-Simon (between Rue de Grenelle and Passage de la Visitation). Métro: Rue du Bac. 42.22.01.60

12 Hôtel Duc de St.-Simon $$$ A Swedish couple runs this cozy antique-furnished 34-room hotel on a hidden street just off the Boulevard St.-Germain. Popular among transatlantic diplomats and intellectuals (**Edward Albee,** author of *Who's Afraid of Virginia Woolf?,* stays here). Reservations for newcomers may be difficult, but keep trying. Garden lovers should ask for room No. 25, which has a flower-bedecked terrace. ♦ 14 Rue St.-Simon (between Rue de Grenelle and Passage de la Visitation). Métro: Rue du Bac. 45.48.35.66

13 The General Store Homesick Americans can comfort their taste buds with Paul Newman's spaghetti sauce, Hellman's mayonnaise, taco shells, Cheerios, maple syrup, peanut butter, and pecans, thanks to the General Store. Stuffed turkeys and homemade pumpkin pies are sold during Thanksgiving week, and French gourmands researching recipes for meat loaf or succotash will find cookbooks such as *La Cuisine Américaine.* ♦ M-Sa 10AM-7:30PM. 82 Rue de Grenelle (between Rues du Bac and St.-Simon). Métro: Rue du Bac. 45.48.63.16

Tourists often hum "April in Paris" with great hopes of clear weather, but Parisians know sunshine and spring don't hit town until May, when three long weekend holidays (Labor Day, Ascension, and Pentecost) give a taste of the summer vacations ahead. May is also the month for polo matches at the Club de Paris (otherwise closed to the public) and the glamorous French Tennis Open at Roland-Garros (but tickets are as rare as counterfeits are rife: center court seats are sold out by January to corporate clients).

14 Superlatif Not as elegant as its former incarnation, **Papier +,** this stationery shop sells colored paper, designer pens, and assorted doodads. ♦ M 1-7PM; Tu-Sa 10AM-7PM. 86 Rue du Bac (between Rues de Grenelle and de Varenne). Métro: Rue du Bac. 45.48.84.25

14 Olivier de Sercey This tiny printing and engraving shop makes those dignified business cards dealt out by the ambassadors and government ministers whose offices are nearby. Wedding and party invitations are made here as well. ♦ M-F 9AM-7PM. Closed in August and on holidays. 96 Rue du Bac (between Rues de Grenelle and de Varenne). Métro: Rue du Bac. 45.48.21.47, 45.49.20.80

14 La Boîte à Musique This antique shop specializes in 19th-century music boxes from France, England, and Switzerland. ♦ M 2-7PM; Tu-Sa 11AM-7PM. Closed in August. 96 Rue du Bac (between Rues de Grenelle and de Varenne). Métro: Rue du Bac. 42.22.01.30

LA COUR DE VARENNE

15 La Cour de Varenne The back door of this snobbish antiques store opens onto a lovely courtyard where the servants' quarters of **Madame de Staël** still stand (see illustration above). There are two floors of carved wooden columns, clocks, 17th- and 18th-century furniture, Japanese lacquer, mother-of-pearl-framed mirrors, and early 19th-century paintings of hot-air balloons. ♦ Tu-F 10AM-1PM, 2-7PM; Sa 10AM-1PM, 2-6PM. Closed in August. 42 Rue de Varenne (between Rues de Bellechasse and du Bac). Métros: Rue du Bac, Sèvres-Babylone. 45.44.65.50

16 Musée Rodin The **Hôtel de Biron,** which houses the **Rodin Museum,** is a Regency masterpiece of columns and pediments originally built in 1730 by **Jean Aubert** and **Jacques-Anges Gabriel** for a wealthy wigmaker named **Abraham Peyrenc.** In 1753 it was bought by the **Maréchal-Duc de Biron,** who indulged quite a passion for gardening in the years before he went to the guillotine during the Reign of Terror; he spent 200,000 livres each year on tulips alone. During an unfortunate tenure as a convent school, the hotel's gold-and-white wood paneling was ripped out by the mother superior: she deemed it too baroque and materialistic.

In 1908, after the Hôtel de Biron was subdivided into a cluster of artists' studios, **Auguste Rodin** (1840-1917) moved in and stayed until his death. His neighbors in the hôtel included German poet **Rainer Maria Rilke,** French artist **Jean Cocteau,** American dancer **Isadora Duncan,** and French painter **Henri Matisse.**

After you have entered the front door and seen the ground-floor exposition, bear left and gradually spiral upstairs. The works are displayed so you may follow Rodin's career chronologically, beginning with his academic paintings and his sketches in both classic and modern modes. Notice Rodin depicts only right hands, except that of Satan crushing humanity in *The Hand of the Devil.*

The room containing Rodin's *Sculptor with his Muse* also displays several works by **Camille Claudel,** the talented sculptor who became Rodin's muse, model, and lover at the age of 17. Her portrait of Rodin, executed in 1888 at the peak of their affair, when he was nearly 50, reveals a rather cold man with small eyes.

Upstairs is a series of studies of **Balzac** created in the early 1890s. In one of them, a bronze, the writer stands stark naked and is 90 percent paunch. In the final version, which stands at the corner of Rue Vavin and Boulevard Montparnasse, Rodin draped Balzac in a concealing cloak.

The Hôtel de Biron's garden, the third largest of any of the hôtels in Paris (after those of the **Elysée Palace** and the **Hôtel de Matignon**) provides the setting for Rodin's best-known works. On 30 January 1937, **Helen Keller** visited here and was permitted to touch the sculptures with her hands. Of *The Thinker,* she said: "In every limb I felt the throes of emerging mind." Until recently, across the garden stood the *Six Burghers of Calais,* who surrendered their lives to the English to save their city. Helen Keller said this heroic group was "sadder to touch than a grave." Sadder still, in 1988 a Japanese museum bought the figures for $2.5 million. ♦ Admission. Tu-Su 10AM-5:45PM Apr-Sept; Tu-Su 10AM-5PM Oct-Mar. 77 Rue de Varenne (between Blvd des Invalides and Rue Barbet de Jouy). Métro: Varenne. 47.05.01.34

16 L'Arpège ★★★$$$$ Daring but respectful of tradition, young chef **Alain Passard** concocts unusual dishes such as *crème de truffe aux oeufs et Parmesan,* sweet and sour Brittany lobster with rosemary, white tuna with herbs and spicy butter, and *canard Louise Passard.* Desserts include a heavenly *soufflé de citron* as well as wild strawberries and raspberries in a light hibiscus sauce.

L'Arpège's skillful servers may perform the final touches at your table. The wine list is one of the best in Paris. ♦ Lunch and dinner; dinner only on Sunday. Closed Saturday. 84 Rue de Varenne (between Blvd des Invalides and Rue de Bourgogne). Reservations required. Métro: Varenne. 47.05.09.06, 45.51.47.33

17 110 Rue du Bac After the sale of *The Artist's Mother* to the French government in 1893, **James McNeill Whistler** moved into a ground-floor apartment here and consorted with his artist-intelligentsia friends such as **Henry James, Edgar Degas, Edouard Manet,** and **Henri Toulouse-Lautrec.** ♦ Between Rues de Babylone and de Varenne. Métro: Rue du Bac

18 La Pagode Those **François Truffaut** and **Jean Renoir** classics you've always sighed over may demand a new orientation in this authentic Chinese pagoda, the most unusual cinema in Paris. ♦ 57 bis Rue de Babylone (between Rues Monsieur and Vaneau). Métro: St.-François-Xavier. 47.05.12.15

19 Au Bon Marché The oldest department store in Paris is especially famous for its *épicerie* (food market), which is the largest of its kind in the city (2,750 square meters) and sells everything from fresh oysters to foie gras. ♦ M-Sa 9:30AM-6:30PM. Epicerie: 8:30AM-9PM. 22 Rue de Sèvres (between Rues du Bac and Velpeau). Métro: Sèvres-Babylone. 44.39.80.00. Epicerie: 44.39.81.00

20 La Vie Naturelle This beauty salon-cum-health food store run by the talented coiffeur and ex-Le Mans race-car driver **Jean-Pierre Régnier** proffers everything from honey and carrot cake to a smart haircut. ♦ M 1-7PM; Tu 10AM-7PM; W-Th 9:30AM-7PM; F 10AM-7:30PM; Sa 9AM-noon. 101 Rue du Bac (between Rues de Varenne and de Commaille). Métro: Rue du Bac. 45.48.90.58

Parlez-Vous Anglais?

If English is your first—or only—language, and you need a book fix in Paris, here are the English-language bookstores of choice:

Albion 13 Rue Charles-V 42.72.50.71

Attica 23 Rue Jean-de-Beauvais 46.34.62.03

Brentano's 37 Avenue de l'Opéra 42.61.52.50

Galignani 224 Rue de Rivoli 42.60.76.07

Shakespeare and Company
37 Rue de la Bûcherie 43.26.96.50

Village Voice 6 Rue Princesse 46.33.36.47

W.H. Smith and Son 248 Rue de Rivoli .. 44.77.88.99

Restaurants/Clubs: Red   Hotels: Blue
Shops/ ♠Outdoors: Green   **Sights/Culture:** Black

21 Diners en Ville Tablecloths, candlesticks, china, earthenware, flatware—here's everything for the well-dressed table. ◆ M 2-7PM; Tu-Sa 11AM-7PM. 27 Rue de Varenne (at Rue du Bac). Métro: Rue du Bac. 42.22.78.33

22 Kenzo Everyone's favorite Japanese designer splashes gorgeous colors over these amusing, informal clothes and accessories. ◆ M 11AM-7PM; Tu-Sa 10AM-7PM. 17 Blvd Raspail (at Rue de Grenelle). Métro: Rue du Bac. 45.49.33.75

23 Fontaine des Quatre-Saisons The Four Seasons Fountain was designed in 1730 by **Bouchardon** to supply water to aristocrats in the wealthy Faubourg St.-Germain. This sculpture's magnificence is, as **Voltaire** once complained, squandered on a narrow street. ◆ 57-59 Rue de Grenelle (between Rue du Bac and Blvd Raspail). Métro: Rue du Bac

23 Roland Barthélemy Fromager The Elysée Palace buys its cheese at Barthélemy, which offers more than 50 kinds of fresh goat cheese, the finest Vacherin (from October to February), and its special *boulamour,* a ball of enriched cow's cheese covered with kirsch-soaked raisins. ◆ Tu-F 8:30AM-1PM, 4-7:30PM; Sa 8:30AM-1:30PM, 3:30-7:15PM. 51 Rue de Grenelle (between Rue du Bac and Blvd Raspail). Métro: Rue du Bac. 45.48.56.75

24 Issey Miyake Artist **Shiro Kuramata's** white-plaster drapes make a stunning backdrop for Miyake's sculptural clothes. A fashion purist, this Tokyo-based designer creates all his own fabrics and dresses his followers for maximum comfort and ease of motion. Nearby are two other Miyake boutiques: **Hommes** (the men's store at 33 Blvd Raspail) and **Plantation** (the moderately priced unisex line at No. 17 Blvd Raspail). ◆ M-Sa 10AM-12:30PM, 1:30-7PM. Closed three weeks in August. 201 Blvd St.-Germain (at Rue de Luynes). Métro: Rue du Bac. 45.48.10.44, 45.44.60.48

25 Hotel Lutetia $$$ Fashion designer **Sonia Rykiel** spruced up the interior of this turn-of-the-century luxury hotel with elegant gray and violet fabrics as well as Art Deco frescoes. ◆ 45 Blvd Raspail (at Rue de Sèvres). Métro: Sèvres-Babylone. 45.44.38.10

26 Atelier Guillaume Martel Have a special 17th-century portrait or modern print you need framed? Martel, a graduate of the prestigious **Ecole du Louvre,** specializes in *dorure froide* for both antique and contemporary prints. ◆ Tu-Sa 9-11AM, 3-7PM. Closed in August. 2 Rue du Regard (at Rue du Cherche-Midi). Métro: Sèvres-Babylone. 45.49.02.07

27 Café Parisien ★★★$ This modest café has garnered a large reputation. Its weekend brunches, pot-au-feu, hearty *plats du jour,* and *tarte tatin* draw a lively, often literary, throng. ◆ Lunch and dinner; Saturday and Sunday brunch. 15 Rue d'Assas (between Rues de Rennes and de Vaugirard). Reservations recommended. No credit cards. Métro: Rennes. 45.44.41.44

28 Le Petit Bacchus ★★$$ The Left Bank wine bar owned by **Steven Spurrier** offers a respectable selection of Bordeaux, Côtes-du-Rhône, and Loire Valley wines. Delicious quiches, vegetable tarts, Auvergne charcuterie, country cheeses, and wines by the glass are further temptations. ◆ Lunch, snacks, and dinner. Closed Sunday and Monday. 13 Rue du Cherche-Midi (between Rue d'Assas and Carrefour de la Croix-Rouge). Métro: Sèvres-Babylone. 45.44.01.07

28 Jule des Prés Ravishing dried-flower sculptures are designed by the much-imitated shop that opened nearly a decade ago in the Marais. Each piece is signed with a red-wax seal. ◆ M-Sa 11AM-7PM. 19 Rue du Cherche-Midi (between Rue d'Assas and Carrefour de la Croix-Rouge). Métros: St.-Sulpice, Sèvres-Babylone. 45.48.26.84

29 Soleil de Provence This friendly shop imports virgin olive oil, *tapenade,* almond soap, and herbs from Provence. Quite simply, it has much of the best that the sunbathed southern French province has to offer. ◆ Tu-Sa 10AM-7PM. Closed in August. 6 Rue du Cherche-Midi (between Rue d'Assas and Carrefour de la Croix-Rouge). Métro: Sèvres-Babylone. 45.48.15.02

29 Poilâne The most famous baker in France, if not the world, **Lionel Poilâne** continues a family tradition started by his Norman father, **Pierre,** in 1933. The round sourdough country loaf baked in wood-fired ovens is served in some 400 Parisian restaurants and flown daily to expensive gourmet shops in New York and Tokyo. **Catherine Deneuve** and **Pierre Cardin** order specially decorated loaves for their parties, and **King Hussein** has it jetted to his palace.

If he's not too busy and you ask politely, Lionel may even take you down into the bakery's 12th-century cellars, where a bare-chested baker in shorts and a cap, like a Daumier cartoon, feeds lumps of dough to a wood-burning brick oven. ◆ M-Sa 7:15AM-8:15PM (delivery 24 hours). 8 Rue du

Cherche-Midi (between Rue d'Assas and Carrefour de la Croix-Rouge). Métro: Sèvres-Babylone. 45.48.42.59

30 Le Récamier ★★★$$$ Situated in a serene cul-de-sac in the well-trodden St.-Germain shopping district, this elegant restaurant caters to the Paris publishing crowd and has one of the city's most peaceful outdoor terraces. Owner and certified wine expert **Martin Cantegrit** features dishes from his native Burgundy: fricassee of snails and wild mushrooms, beef Bourguignon *sans pareil,* chateaubriand Récamier, as well as salmon tartare, an excellent summer starter. Cantegrit's wine list, which he calls "my little Bible," merits the appellation. ♦ Lunch and dinner. Closed Sunday. 4 Rue Récamier (at Rue de Sèvres). Métro: Sèvres-Babylone. 42.22.51.75

31 Au Sauvignon ★$ This trendy old wine bar is predictably papered with maps of French wine regions. Still, in summer, it's not such a bad thing to order a plate of country-cured ham, some Cantal cheese, and a Sancerre rosé while sitting at one of the sidewalk tables watching the world stroll by. ♦ Breakfast, lunch, dinner, and snacks. Closed Sunday and in August. 80 Rue des Sts.-Pères (at Rue Grenelle). No credit cards. Métro: Sèvres-Babylone. 45.48.49.02

32 Maude Frizon More than 1,500 styles of handcrafted footwear are carried here. Next door at **Maude Frizon Club,** the shoes are almost as pretty, but they're machine-made and one-third the price. ♦ M-Sa 10:30AM-7PM. 83 Rue des Sts.-Pères (at Rue de Grenelle). Métro: Sèvres-Babylone. 45.49.20.59

32 Cassegrain There's nothing quite like a proper thank-you note or an engraved-in-gold place card. This stationer has been setting the standard since 1919. ♦ 81 Rue des Sts.-Pères (at Rue de Grenelle). Métro: Sèvres-Babylone. 42.22.04.76

33 31 Rue du Dragon The **Académie Julian,** which was once here, admitted hundreds of aspiring American painters who were hoping to study on the GI bill after World War II but were unable to meet the stricter entrance requirements of the **Ecole des Beaux-Arts.** ♦ Between Rues du Four and Bernard-Palissy. Métro: St.-Germain-des-Prés

33 Chez Claude Sainlouis ★$ For more than 25 years, the unfailingly popular restaurant of ex-stuntman **Claude Piau** has played it safe, serving an unchanging menu: steak, lamb chops, salad, and chocolate mousse. ♦ Lunch and dinner. Closed Sunday, Saturday dinner in August, one week at Easter, and one week at Christmas. 27 Rue du Dragon (between Rues du Four and Bernard-Palissy). Reservations recommended. No credit cards. Métro: St.-Germain-des-Prés. 45.48.29.68

33 Yakijapo Mitsuko ★★$$ One of the best sushi bars in Paris also serves sashimi and *yakitori* (broiled skewered meats and vegetables) at reasonable prices. ♦ Lunch and dinner. 8 Rue du Sabot (between Rues du Dragon and de Rennes). Métro: St.-Germain-des-Prés. 42.22.17.74

33 Via Palissy ★$$ Climb to the tiny, crooked dining room of this Italian restaurant to sample risotto Milanese, gnocchi with Gorgonzola, and homemade *tiramisù.* ♦ Lunch and dinner. Closed Sunday and three weeks in August. 11 Rue Bernard-Palissy (between Rues de Rennes and du Dragon). Reservations recommended. Métro: St.-Germain-des-Prés. 45.44.02.52

34 Brasserie Lipp ★★$$ This famous Alsatian brasserie counts among its clients **Yves Saint Laurent** and **François Mitterrand.** A literary landmark, where waiters still dress in black waistcoats and long white aprons, Lipp is always replete with editors (from *Grasset, Gallimard,* and *Hachette*) and politicians. **De Gaulle** and **Pompidou** used to lunch at these tables, and **Ben Barka,** a Moroccan militant, was arrested here.

The ceilings are covered with buxom nudes; the walls are festooned with Art Nouveau ceramics and conveniently hung with mirrors so large you never need to crane your neck to watch the celebrities pass by. Lipp used to be run by the formidable **Roger Cazes** (whose father bought the establishment in 1920 from an Alsatian named **Lippman**), who didn't seem to care for Americans of less cultural stature than **William Styron.** The best ploy for getting seated was to arrive on a rainy day in February just before 2AM—or shortly after a morning bomb scare. Anyone who was anyone sat on the main floor; upstairs was more or less Siberia. After Cazes' death, the new management restored the second floor so diners there need no longer feel banished.

It is, of course, always possible to enjoy a Bavarian dark beer or cup of hot chocolate on the terrace; just don't tell anyone that's where you sat. The food is solid, though often disappointing. Stick with oysters, smoked salmon, and potato salad: they're hard to ruin. ♦ Breakfast, lunch, snacks, dinner, and late-night. 151 Blvd St.-Germain (between Rues de Rennes and du Dragon). Reservations required. Métro: St.-Germain-des-Prés. 45.48.53.91

34 Le Drugstore ★$ Here you can enjoy such French delicacies as le hamburger, le ice cream, and le Coca-Cola. Downstairs you can buy le newspaper, *The International Herald Tribune,* which arrives at 1AM the morning of publication. ♦ Store: daily 10AM-2AM. Restaurant: daily 9AM-2AM. 149 Blvd St.-Germain (between Rues de Rennes and du Dragon). Métro: St.-Germain-des-Prés. 42.22.92.50

35 Korean Barbecue ★$ The cook-it-yourself fare includes marinated beef and vegetables that you grill over a gas stove at your table. ♦ Lunch and dinner. 1 Rue du Dragon (between Blvd St.-Germain and Rue Bernard Palissy). No credit cards. Métro: St.-Germain-des-Prés. 42.22.26.63

36 Baxter Old prints, etchings, and lithographs abound in this charming shop that specializes in European architectural and botanical illustrations from the 17th to 19th centuries. The friendly staff has both a knowledge of and affection for the wares. Framing services are available. ♦ M 1-7PM; Tu-Sa 10AM-7PM. 15 Rue du Dragon (at Rue Bernard Palissy). Métro: St.-Germain-des-Prés. 45.49.01.34

37 Yohji Yamamoto Shop for an outfit that's actually both fashionable and comfortable. This Japanese designer creates baggy high-style clothes for men as well as women. ♦ M-Sa 10:30AM-7PM. 69 Rue des Sts.-Pères (between Blvd St.-Germain and Rue de Grenelle). Métros: St.-Germain-des-Prés, St.-Sulpice. 45.48.22.56

37 Sts.-Pères $$$ The tastefully renovated hotel was designed in 1658 by **Alphonse Daniel Gittard**, who founded the Academy of Architecture under **Louis XIV** and whose portrait hangs behind the reception desk. If dozing off while staring up at a 17th-century ceiling painting of the *Crowning of Jupiter* is your idea of luxury, ask for Room No. 100. ♦ 65 Rue des Sts.-Pères (between Rue de Grenelle and Blvd St.-Germain). Métro: Sèvres-Babylone. 45.44.50.00

37 Sabbia Rosa Sexy teddies and other alluring lingerie can be purchased for or by the femme fatale. ♦ M-Sa 10AM-7PM. Closed last half of August. 71-73 Rue des Sts.-Pères (between Rue de Grenelle and Blvd St.-Germain). Métro: St.-Sulpice. 45.48.88.37

38 The Twickenham ★★$$ A favorite haunt of contemporary French philosopher and best-selling author **Bernard Henry Levy,** this English-style pub/restaurant is dimly lit, with plush red-leather booths and an elegant varnished bar. ♦ Lunch and dinner. Closed Sunday and in August. 70 Rue des Sts.-Pères (between Rue de Grenelle and Blvd St.-Germain). Métro: Sèvres-Babylone. 42.22.96.85

39 La Maison de Verre (Glass House) Seeing the extraordinary glass house of **Pierre Charreau** and **Bernard Bijovet** is a must for any student of 20th-century design. You can get a glimpse of the exterior from the courtyard, but for a look at the inside of the early 1930s building—a tour de force in glass-block-and-steel construction—you must make a reservation in advance. ♦ Send requests to: A.P. Vellay-Dalsace, 31 Rue St.-Guillaume (between Blvd St.-Germain and Rue de Grenelle), 75007 Paris. Métro: Sèvres-Babylone

40 Madeleine Gély Since 1834 the finest umbrella shop in Paris has been selling and repairing handmade *parapluies.* You needn't have a limp to buy one of Madeleine Gély's 400 unusual canes, which include duck- and bulldog-headed canes, watch canes, whiskey-flask canes, and even a cane to measure the withers of a horse. ♦ Tu-Sa 9:30AM-7PM. Closed in August. 218 Blvd St.-Germain (between Rues St.-Guillaume and St.-Thomas d'Aquin). Métro: Rue du Bac. 42.22.63.35

41 Hôtel Montalembert $$$$ The newest and best of the Left Bank's luxury hotels is popular with people from the worlds of publishing, fashion, and fine art. When the building was renovated a few years ago, designer **Christian Liaigre** selected the tasteful furnishings of the lobby and 56 rooms; there's a wondrous attention to detail, from handcrafted leather furniture to cast-bronze door handles. The modern rooms with customized furniture will suit guests who prefer contemporary style, while the Louis Philippe rooms with finely restored period furniture will please traditionalists. Everyone staying here should plan a few long, bubbly soaks in the luxurious bathrooms, done in gray marble and chrome. ♦ 3 Rue de Montalembert (between Rues du Bac and de l'Université). Métro: Rue du Bac. 45.48.68.11

Within the Hôtel Montalembert:

Restaurant Montalembert ★★★$$$ The congenial atmosphere and the creations of chef **Arnaud Vincent** have made this intimate café a popular meeting place for Parisians. You can't go wrong with the warm artichoke salad, veal with mushrooms and baked potatoes, grilled lamb chops, scampi ravioli with herbs, or grilled salmon with tomato butter. ♦ Breakfast, lunch, and dinner; Sunday brunch. Reservations recommended. 45.48.68.11

42 Le Cabinet de Curiosité Lined with panels from a late 18th-century pharmacy, this amusing shop displays scientific instruments, ancient technical books, monkey skeletons from Madagascar, brass hourglasses, ladies' shoes from the Louis XVI epoch, and an exquisite collection of Gothic keys and locks. Owner **Jean-Claude Guerin** is an expert in fine wrought iron. ♦ M-Sa 11AM-7PM. Closed in August. 23 Rue de Beaune (between Rues de Ville and de Verneuil). Métro: Rue du Bac. 42.61.09.57

43 Bistrot de Paris ★★$$ Michel Oliver, whose father owns the Grand Véfour, created this chic bistro, which has an innovative one-two punch: ravishing 1880s decor with Belle Epoque mosaics and a classic menu of crab soup, braised pig's feet, stewed beef in wine sauce, and reliable Bordeaux. ♦ Lunch and dinner; dinner only on Saturday. Closed Sunday. 33 Rue de Lille (between Rues de Beaune and du Bac). Reservations recommended. Métro: Rue du Bac. 42.61.16.83

44 Quai Voltaire This quay honors Voltaire, whose triumphant return in 1778 from 30 years of exile was greeted by a torchlight parade that wound from the **Comédie Française** (where his tragedy *Irène* had just opened) across the river to **No. 27**, where he died months later on 30 May 1778. The quay's history involves many artists: **Jean-Dominique Ingres** died on 14 January 1867 at **No. 11; Delacroix** and **Corot**, at different times, rented the top-floor studio at **No. 13**; in the hotel at **No. 19, Baudelaire** penned *Les Fleurs du Mal* in 1857; and **Wagner** composed *Die Meistersinger* here between 1861 and 1862. Today, it is a bazaar of first-rate antiques shops and galleries. Side by side are well-known dealers such as **H. Berès Bailly** (No. 25), **Jean Max Tassel** (No. 15), and **Michel Segoura** (No. 11). ♦ Métro: St.-Sulpice

44 Sennelier The Left Bank's finest painters patronize this celebrated art-supply store. Even if you couldn't draw an apple to save your life, step inside and rub shoulders with the Beaux-Arts students shopping for linseed oil, blocks of brilliantly colored pastel chalks, and wooden palettes. ♦ M 9AM-noon, 2-6:15PM; Tu-Sa 9AM-6:15PM. 3 Quai Voltaire (between Rues de Beaune and des Sts.-Pères). Métro: Rue du Bac. 42.60.72.15

44 Quai Voltaire $$ Charles-Pierre Baudelaire, Oscar Wilde, Richard Wagner, and Jean Sibelius each came to this hotel looking for a room with a view. Do the same: ask for a front room (if you don't mind the traffic noise) and wake up to a vista of the Seine and the Tuileries. ♦ 19 Quai Voltaire (between Rues de Beaune and des Sts.-Pères). Métro: Solférino. 42.61.50.91

45 7 Rue de Beaune **Henry James,** whose classic novel *The Ambassadors* featured American expatriates in Paris, came to visit **James Lowell** here in 1872 and as an added bonus found **Ralph Waldo Emerson** and his daughter, **Ellen,** in the sitting room. ♦ Between Rue de Ville and Quai Voltaire. Métro: Rue du Bac

45 9 Rue de Beaune While living here at the Hotel Elysée in July 1920, **Ezra Pound**

convinced **James Joyce** to move from Trieste and bring his family to Paris, where they lived nearby in a small hotel at **9 Rue de l'Université.** ♦ At Rue de Ville. Métro: Rue du Bac

46 Université $$$ This smugly stylish hotel in a 17th-century town house is embellished with tapestries, antiques, and a small courtyard. ♦ 22 Rue de l'Université (between Rues de Beaune and des Sts.-Pères). Métro: Rue du Bac. 42.61.09.39

46 2-4 Rue de l'Université In 1776 **Benjamin Franklin** lived here at the former **Hôtel d'Entragues** while he was drumming up support for the American Revolution. ♦ At Rue des Sts.-Pères. Métro: Rue du Bac

47 Lenox $$$ The then 22-year-old **T.S. Eliot** spent a romantic summer here in 1910 on the old man's money, just before he took a job in a London bank and wrote "The Love Song of J. Alfred Prufrock." Restored with chic simplicity and a slightly new wave bar, the Lenox is a favorite of visiting fashion models. The women come and go talking of Valentino. ♦ Bar: daily 5PM-2AM. 9 Rue de l'Université (between Rues de Beaune and des Sts.-Pères). Métro: Rue du Bac. 42.96.10.95

48 Debauve and Gallais This wood-paneled chocolate shop with a semicircular counter began as a pharmacy nearly 200 years ago when medicated chocolate was a nostrum for flatulence, anemia, and other ills. Today, in addition to delicious nonmedicinal chocolate, Debauve and Gallais sells such delights as *croquamandes* (almonds roasted with caramelized sugar), hot chocolate mix, and real chocolate gift boxes. The old metal tea canisters date from 1804. ♦ M-Sa 10AM-7PM. Closed last week of July, and August. 30 Rue des Sts.-Pères (between Rues Perronet and de l'Université). Métros: Rue du Bac, St.-Germain-des-Prés. 45.48.54.67

49 Coffee Parisien ★★$$ An American brunch is served all day. Franco-New Yorker **Jonathan Goldstein** (who manages **Le Coffee Shop** across the street) serves pancakes with maple syrup, hash browns, bagels and cream cheese, eggs Benedict, bacon cheeseburgers, and more. Goldstein's personal collection of Americana, which includes a 1950s Lucky Strike ad and the *New York Times* front page from 22 November 1963—the day President John F. Kennedy was assassinated in Dallas—decorates the walls. ♦ Lunch, brunch, and dinner. 5 Rue Perronet (between Rues des Sts.-Pères and St.-Guillaume). Reservations recommended. Métro: St.-Germain-des-Prés. 40.49.08.08

Restaurants/Clubs: Red **Hotels:** Blue
Shops/ Outdoors: Green **Sights/Culture:** Black

49 Than ★★$ Don't let the crowds in the aisle or the swordfish teeth on the wall scare you away. This tiny Asian canteen is a popular bargain in the pricey St.-Germain quarter. For 24 years the affable Mr. Than has been serving delicious and affordable Cantonese and Vietnamese specialties to neighborhood editors, publishers, and medical students. He brags about the lacquered duck and caramelized spare ribs. ♦ Lunch and dinner; dinner only on Monday. Closed Sunday. 42 Rue des Sts.-Pères (between Blvd St.-Germain and Rue Perronet). Métro: St.-Germain-des Prés. 45.48.36.97

50 Jean-Michel Beurdeley and Cie Proprietor of one of the boulevard's most inviting Asian art galleries, Beurdeley displays 18th-century Japanese paintings and eighth-century Chinese porcelain figures, but his most treasured item is an enormous second-century BC bronze drum from Southwest Asia. ♦ M-Sa 10AM-noon, 2:30-7PM. Closed in August. 200 Blvd St.-Germain (between Rues St.-Guillaume and des Sts.-Pères). Métro: Rue du Bac. 45.48.97.86

50 Galerie André-François Petit This fanciful surrealist gallery has brass door handles, whimsically designed by an artist named **Jette,** that look like a typesetter's nightmare. ♦ Tu-Sa 10:30AM-noon, 2:30-6:30PM. Closed 14 July-15 Sept. 196 Blvd St.-Germain (between Rues St.-Guillaume and des Sts.-Pères). Métro: Rue du Bac. 45.44.64.83

50 Relais St.-Germain ★★$$ Dine on respectable cuisine at prices even struggling writers can afford. Profitérole addicts swear by this place. ♦ Lunch and dinner. 190 Blvd St.-Germain (between Rues St.-Guillaume and des Sts.-Pères). Reservations recommended. Métro: Rue du Bac. 42.22.21.35, 45.48.11.73

51 Rue des Sts.-Pères Known in the 13th century as the **Chemins aux Vaches** (Cow Path), this street became **Rue de St.-Pierre** in the 16th century because of a nearby chapel dedicated to Saint Peter. By 1652, people had worn the name down to Rue des Sts.-Pères. ♦ Métros: Rue du Bac, St.-Germain-des-Prés

52 St.-Vladimir le Grand Come on a Sunday morning and watch the rosy grandmothers wearing babushkas enter this Ukrainian church. ♦ 49-51 Rue des Sts.-Pères (at Blvd St.-Germain). Métros: Rue du Bac, St.-Germain-des-Prés

53 Rue Jacob This street named after the Old Testament patriarch is chock-full of book and antique shops selling everything from autographs and old manuscripts to theater props and scientific instruments. ♦ Métro: St.-Germain-des-Prés

53 Alain Brieux This eclectic curio shop specializes in prints, Arabic astrolabes, and rare medical books that date back to the 14th century. Everything in the store is for sale except the alligator hanging from the ceiling. This item was a traditional feature in old apothecaries and alchemists' labs. ♦ M-F 10AM-1PM, 2-6:30PM. Closed in August. 48 Rue Jacob (between Rues des Sts.-Pères and Bonaparte). Métro: St.-Germain-des-Prés. 42.60.21.98

53 Angleterre $$$ Formerly the English Embassy, **Benjamin Franklin** refused to enter the building to sign the U.S. Declaration of Independence because he considered it British soil. Angleterre is now a picturesque hotel with a garden patio (**Hemingway** once lived in a small second-floor room). Ask for the large front room, No. 7. The bar and piano lounge are open 24 hours for hotel clients only. ♦ 44 Rue Jacob (between Rues des Sts.-Pères and Bonaparte). Reservations required. Métro: St.-Germain-des-Prés. 42.60.34.72

53 Il Casanova ★★$ A smiling waiter serves visiting graduate students delicious tomato and mozzarella salad, minestrone soup, lasagna, and tortellini with mushrooms at this small, inexpensive Italian restaurant. ♦ Lunch and dinner; dinner only on Tuesday. Closed Monday. 42 Rue Jacob (between Rues des Sts.-Pères and Bonaparte). Dinner reservations recommended. Métro: St.-Germain-des-Prés. 42.60.36.83

54 Démons et Merveilles You'll find folk costumes from Romania, Hungary, Poland, Afghanistan, Tibet, and India, and all the garb you need to run away with the Gypsies here. **Faty,** the Tunisian owner, ran away from his law practice to start this shop. ♦ M-Sa 10AM-8PM. 45 Rue Jacob (between Rues des Sts.-Pères and St.-Benoît). Métro: St.-Germain-des-Prés. 42.96.26.11

55 Le Petit St.-Benoît ★★$ Offering indigent Left Bank intellectuals the same menu for 125 years now (including a respectable roast veal with mashed potatoes), this popular coach-house bistro has prices that are difficult to beat. And, as a bonus, the WC features a celebrated blue-and-white checked washbowl. ♦ Lunch and dinner. Closed Saturday and Sunday. 4 Rue St.-Benoît (between Rue Jacob and Blvd St.-Germain). No credit cards. Métro: St.-Germain-des-Prés. 42.60.27.92

56 Le Muniche ★$$ Delicious fish soup, grilled sardines, fresh briny oysters, four kinds of sauerkraut, and an honest plate of liver and onions are some of the fare at this crowded Alsatian bistro. In summer, reserve a table on the sidewalk. ♦ Lunch, dinner, and late-night. 22 Rue Guillaume Apollinaire (between Rues St.-Benoît and Bonaparte). Métros: Mabillon, Odéon. 44.34.01.06

57 Shu Uemura If you like art supply and stationery stores, you'll love this Japanese cosmetics shop, which has some of the fascination of both. Compacts, lipstick, nail polish, creams, and brushes in every hue and shape imaginable are on display. This is but one of an international 6,000-shop chain created 20 years ago by makeup artist Shu Uemura, who embellished the faces of Japan's most famous movie stars. ♦ M 11AM-7PM; Tu-Sa 10AM-7PM. 176 Blvd St.-Germain (between Rues des Sts.-Pères and St.-Benoît). Métro: St.-Germain-des-Prés. 45.48.02.55

57 Café de Flore ★★$$ Jean-Paul Sartre wrote of hanging out in this great café during World War II: "**Simone de Beauvoir** and I more or less set up house in the Flore. We worked from 9AM till noon, when we went out to lunch. At 2PM we came back and talked with our friends till 4PM, when we got down to work again till 8PM. And after dinner, people came to see us by appointment. It may seem strange, all this, but the Flore was like home to us: even when the air-raid alarm went, we would merely feign leaving and then climb up to the first floor and go on working." You don't have to be Sartre, **Camus,** or any other brainy Flore regular to divine that the drink to order here in winter is hot grog (rum, tea, and lemon slices). And ask for extra slices because they never bring enough. If you're an early bird, the Flore is an excellent place to scrutinize *Le Monde* and have a *real* breakfast of *oeufs sur le plat* (fried eggs), bacon, and croissants. ♦ Breakfast, lunch, dinner, and late-night. 172 Blvd St.-Germain (at Rue St.-Benoît). No credit cards. Métro: St.-Germain-des-Prés. 45.48.55.26

If you've noticed Parisians toting baguettes with the last two inches munched off, you have witnessed the tradition of eating *le croutôn,* the crusty end, before the baguette makes it home. Serious baguette fans know the baking schedule of their neighborhood boulangerie, and time their visit for when the bread is fresh from the oven.

The ornate Luxembourg Gardens employs 80 gardeners, which translates into more than one gardener per acre. Each year, this army plants or transplants 350,000 flowers, and in winter places into safekeeping 150 palm and orange trees, some 200 years old, to shelter them from the cold.

57 Le Montana Piano-Bar ★★$ Champagne at dawn, *pourquoi pas?* The surly, therefore authentic, bartender serves a seductive *Montana Fantaisie* made of pears, grenadine, orange juice, and champagne, enhanced by live jazz in the evenings. ♦ Lunch, dinner, late-night, and early-morning. 28 Rue St.-Benoît (at Blvd St.-Germain). Métro: St.-Germain-des-Prés. 45.48.93.08

57 Le Bilboquet ★$$ On the former site of **Club St.-Germain,** an old existentialist haunt, this upbeat dinner-jazz club serves grilled rack of lamb and sides of beef. ♦ Dinner and late-night. Jazz: 11PM-2:45AM. 13 Rue St.-Benoît (between Rue Jacob and Blvd St.-Germain). Métro: St.-Germain-des-Prés. 45.48.81.84

57 Aux Deux Magots ★★★$$ If you've read *The Sun Also Rises,* you never need to be alone at this café. This is where Jake Barnes meets up with Lady Brett, and it is peopled with fictitious memories. **Hemingway** and his cronies met here to drink away the sting of rejection slips, a pastime he later reminisced about in *A Moveable Feast.*

The name of the café has nothing to do with fly larvae, but comes from the two statues of paunchy Chinese commercial agents—*magots*—that hang high on one of the pillars. They sit on money boxes. So does the new manager of Aux Deux Magots, who paid some $1.4 million in 1985 to purchase this literary mecca. Boasting that the Deux Magots is "The Rendezvous of the Intellectual Elite," the menu offers 25 kinds of whiskey and little pots of strong espresso. From May through August, the sidewalk entertainment on the terrace opposite the St.-Germain-des-Prés bell tower is always amusing and occasionally brilliant. ♦ Breakfast, lunch, dinner, and late-night. 6 Place St.-Germain-des-Prés (at Blvd St.-Germain). Métro: St.-Germain-des-Prés. 45.48.55.25

Restaurants/Clubs: Red   **Hotels:** Blue
Shops/ ☂Outdoors: Green   **Sights/Culture:** Black

58 La Hune Wedged between Café de Flore and Aux Deux Magots is one of the liveliest bookstores in Paris. La Hune provides literary sustenance to the Parisian men and women of letters (and those trying to resemble them) who frequent shrines to caffeine-driven cogitation. ♦ M 2PM-midnight; Tu-F 10AM-11:45PM; Sa 10AM-7:30PM. 170 Blvd St.-Germain (at Rue St.-Benoît). Métro: St.-Germain-des-Prés. 45.48.35.85

58 Arthus-Bertrand This 150-year-old establishment casts reproductions of some of the Louvre's treasures in sterling or in 18-karat gold. It also supplies 80 percent of the military medals and decorations for African nations. (Business is usually brisk owing to the high turnover in excellencies.) For $6,000 to $20,000, Arthus-Bertrand custom-designs the ceremonial swords worn by the "immortals" accepted into the Académie Française. The firm has a seriousness and a price list that will curb any idle browser. ♦ Tu-F 10AM-6:15PM; Sa 10AM-12:30PM, 2-6:15PM. 6 Place St.-Germain-des-Prés (west side, between Rue Guillaume Apollinaire and Blvd St.-Germain). Métro: St.-Germain-des-Prés. 42.22.19.20

59 Embâcle This sculpture (whose name means "blockage" in French) is not a ruptured water main but a practical joke of a fountain by **Charles Daudelin.** It was created in 1985. ♦ Blvd St.-Germain (at Rue de Rennes). Métro: St.-Germain-des-Prés

60 Annick Goutal This ivory- and gold-toned boutique offers original perfumes, precious oils, lotions, and soaps. Goutal's beautifully packaged products celebrate nature with such women's and men's fragrances as Eau d'Hadrien, Eau du Ciel, Gardénia Passion, and Rose Absolute. The knowledgeable salespeople will cheerfully assist you in choosing the right scent. ♦ M-Sa 10AM-7PM. 12 Place St.-Sulpice (between Rues Bonaparte and des Canettes). Métros: St.-Sulpice, Mabillon, St.-Germain-des-Prés. 46.33.03.15

61 Hôtel de l'Abbaye $$$ Stone arches, antique furniture, and fresh-cut flowers enhance this peaceful 18th-century convent-turned-hotel. Ground-floor rooms Nos. 2 and 3 open onto the trellised garden. ♦ 10 Rue Cassette (at Rue de Mézières). Reservations required. Métro: St.-Sulpice. 45.44.38.11

62 58 Rue Madame The oldest brother of Gertrude Stein, **Michael Stein,** and his artist wife, **Sarah,** moved here in 1903 and began buying the canvases of their close friend **Henri Matisse.** Within two decades, the Steins had assembled in this apartment one of the finest collections of Matisses, **Renoirs, Gauguins,** and **Picassos** in the world. ♦ Between Rues de Fleurus and d'Assas. Métro: St.-Placide

63 Perreyve $$ A quiet, newly renovated hotel, Perreyve is just a minute's stroll from the Luxembourg Gardens. ♦ 63 Rue Madame (at Rue de Fleurus). Métro: St.-Placide. 45.48.35.01

64 Hôtel de l'Avenir $$ This small hotel near the Luxembourg is tremendously popular with students. ♦ 65 Rue Madame (at Rue de Fleurus). Métro: St.-Placide. 45.48.84.54

65 La Table de Fès ★★$$ Excellent North African couscous, chicken and lemon *tajine* (stew), and peppery *merguez* (lamb sausage) keep this Moroccan restaurant crowded and hopping. The spicy change of pace from all those French buttery cream sauces is welcome. This spot is best late at night. ♦ Dinner. Closed Sunday and 15-31 August. 5 Rue Ste.-Beuve (between Blvd Raspail and Rue Notre-Dame-des-Champs). Reservations recommended (call after 5PM). Métro: Vavin. 45.48.07.22

65 Hôtel Ste.-Beuve $$ This handsome hotel, ideally situated equidistant from La Coupole and the Luxembourg Gardens, was decorated by master designer **Christian Badin.** Any advice (on restaurants, gallery openings, concerts) received from **Alain** at the front desk is golden. ♦ 9 Rue Ste.-Beuve (between Blvd Raspail and Rue Notre-Dame-des-Champs). Métro: Vavin. 45.48.20.07

66 26 Rue Vavin This luxury terraced apartment building was designed in 1925 by French architect **Henri Sauvage.** The splendid blue-and-white tile complex, complete with ground-floor shops and indoor parking, was an early attempt at a self-contained building: what Le Corbusier would call *unité d'habitation.* ♦ Between Blvd Raspail and Rue Notre-Dame-des-Champs. Métro: Vavin

66 Marie-Papier Attracting customers from Los Angeles to Tokyo, this famous French stationery store promotes an elegant line of colored paper in single sheets or large albums. ♦ M-Sa 10:30AM-7PM. Closed first two weeks in August. 26 Rue Vavin (between Blvd Raspail and Rue Notre-Dame-des-Champs). Métro: Vavin. 43.26.46.44

66 Rouge et Noir Games galore! This handsome shop sells finely crafted miniature billiard tables, roulette wheels, hand-carved dominoes, Chinese checkers, Monopoly, and, yes, even Trivial Pursuit. ♦ Tu-Sa 10:30AM-1PM, 2-7PM. 26 Rue Vavin (between Blvd Raspail and Rue Notre-Dame-des-Champs). Métro: Vavin. 43.26.05.77

67 La Coupole ★★$$ Along with the Brasserie Lipp and Le Balzar, La Coupole is the most popular café with a history. **Jean-Paul Sartre** dined here, as did **Eugène Ionesco,** who liked his coffee *liégeois.* **Alberto Sordi** lost himself in the curry while **Roman Polanski** played coy behind his menu. **Josephine Baker** frequented La Coupole accompanied by her lion cub. Novelists **Hemingway, Fitzgerald,** and **Joyce** also consorted here. When American breakfasts were the specialty at La Coupole, **Henry Miller** would come for his morning porridge. **Man Ray, Matisse,** and the famous **Kiki** of Montparnasse were part of the local fauna, too.

La Coupole was conceived in 1926 by **René Lafond.** While working at the Dôme Café, he negotiated a 20-year lease on the wood and coal depot across the street. He transformed the building with red-velvet booths, jazz-age chandeliers, and a dozen columns painted by Montparnasse's artistic community. The story goes that the painter **Auffray,** whose studio was in Montparnasse, first suggested that real artists paint the Coupole's 12 columns. Lafond paid for the supplies and gave each artist a few good meals as an honorarium. **Léger's** contribution is to the left of the bar; the black rat dancing on the head of a flutist is by **Vassilief.** Other columns were painted by **Gris, Ribiera, Soutine, Chagall, Delaunay, Brancusi,** and **Foujita.** Matching the artist with his pillar has been a favorite diversion over dessert at La Coupole ever since.

Purchased for more than $10 million and restored by brasserie czar **Jean-Paul Boucher,** the cavernous dining room is classified as a historic monument, and therefore its columns have been preserved. La Coupole today is a watering hole for politicos, neighborhood merchants, aspiring actors, wandering poets, Scandinavian models, editors, and, most recently, the suburban hordes that invade the Montparnasse movie theaters on Saturday nights. La Coupole, so it is said, has the densest population of beautiful women in Paris here on weeknights; it is most chic, however, to make an appearance Sunday night. But on any night the atmosphere will be smokily festive. Expect a good time, but don't expect haute cuisine. The fare is simple and serviceable. In the basement is an enormous ballroom where dancers literally kick off their shoes. ♦ Breakfast, lunch, dinner, and late-night. Ballroom: F-Sa 9:30PM-4AM (tea dancing: Su 3-7PM). 102 Blvd du Montparnasse (at Rue Delambre). No reservations taken after 8:30PM. Métro: Vavin. 43.20.14.20

68 Dominique ★★$$ This restaurant/deli is as Russian as balalaikas. Grab a stool at the counter and snack on smoked salmon, pressed caviar, hot borscht, and blintzes with sour cream. Takeout is available ♦ Lunch and dinner. Closed mid-July to mid-August and one week in February. 19 Rue Bréa (between Rue Vavin and Blvd du Montparnasse). Reservations recommended. Métro: Vavin. 43.27.08.80

69 Académie de la Grande-Chaumière Any closet Cézannes, budding Bonnards, or rising Renoirs in your traveling party? At this modest art academy you can draw or paint your own masterpiece from live models and carry it home for less than the cost of those imitation Toulouse-Lautrec posters sold on Rue de Rivoli. ♦ Painting and drawing: M-Sa 9AM-noon. Sketching: M-Sa 3-6PM; closed in August. 14 Rue de la Grande-Chaumière (between Blvd du Montparnasse and Rue Notre-Dame-des-Champs). Métro: Vavin. 43.26.13.72

The French Are Famous for More Than Just Fries

Where would the world be without the croissant, the omelet, and mayonnaise, not to mention these other culinary gifts from the French:

Bouquet Garni—First used in French recipes in the mid-17th century, the combination of thyme, bay leaf, and parsley is a staple for sauces and soup stocks.

Chicken Fricassee—The French method of frying chicken in fat, then adding a little liquid to create a sauce, has been around since the 15th century.

Food Processor—Created in 1964 by **Pierre Verdun,** this machine and its descendants revolutionized food preparation.

Peach Melba—**August Escoffier** created this luscious dessert in 1899 for singer **Nellie Melba:** a ripe peach with vanilla ice cream and fresh raspberry sauce.

Pressure Cooker—Invented in 1679, it was first called a "steam digester" by its creator, **Denis Papin.**

Soufflé—This most French of recipes made its first appearance in a 1730 cookbook.

70 La Caméléon ★★$$ A bohemian bastion for famished painters in the 1960s, La Caméléon has changed (regrettably retaining its black wallpaper, however) into a thriving neighborhood bistro serving classic veal stew, hot sausage, smoked haddock, and a wide selection of salads. Those with a sweet tooth swoon for the white chocolate mousse and iced tea (with fresh mint) soufflé, a recipe the owners borrowed from their children, who operate **Gerard et Nicole,** a first-rate Montparnasse restaurant. Splurge on a delicious old Bourgueil wine with your meal. ♦ Lunch and dinner. Closed Sunday, Monday, and in August. 6 Rue de Chevreuse (between Blvd du Montparnasse and Rue Notre-Dame-des-Champs). Dinner reservations recommended. No credit cards. Métro: Vavin. 43.20.63.43

71 La Closerie des Lilas ★★$$ This legendary restaurant is where lilacs once bloomed, where **Hemingway** and **Henry James** hung out, where the defenders of Dreyfus plotted, and where **Gide, Verlaine, Chateaubriand, Ingres,** and **Trotsky** expounded. (Trotsky, **Lenin,** and the Russian crowd actually preferred La Rotonde, which opened down the street around 1911, 103 years after La Closerie des Lilas. Serious drinkers convened at Le Dôme Café, and the American crowd hung out at La Coupole—both are located down the block.) Today La Closerie des Lilas is frequented by young French film stars and other constellations of the pretty and chic. It's expensive and a little pretentious, but not bad for an after-dinner drink or a weekend lunch in the mottled light of its outdoor terrace, especially during

August when the rest of Paris shuts down. Try the steak tartare, *pigeon de Bresse rôti, rumsteck Hemingway flambé au Bourbon,* or the best-selling *turbotin grillé*. The piano kindles a certain warmth as well. ♦ Lunch, dinner, and late-night. 171 Blvd du Montparnasse (at Ave de L'Observatoire). Reservations required. Métro: Port Royal (RER). 43.26.70.50, 43.54.21.68

72 93 Boulevard St.-Michel During World War II, the Nazis searched for two years for **Sylvia Beach,** founder of the famous Paris **Shakespeare and Company** bookstore (see page 68), who hid here in a top-floor kitchen. ♦ Between Rues Royer-Collard and Abbé-de-l'Epée). Métro: Luxembourg (RER)

72 Le Petit Journal Jazz of every stripe, from Dixieland to fusion and back again to bebop, can be heard in **Claude Bolling's** favorite club. Other performers here include **Sacha Distel, Bill Coleman, Sugar Blue, Doctor Feelgood,** and the **Metropolitan Jazz Band.** ♦ Daily 10PM-2AM. Closed in August. 71 Blvd St.-Michel (at Rues Royer-Collard and Gay Lussac). Métro: Luxembourg (RER). 43.26.28.59

73 Dalloyau ★★$$ To sip a civilized cup of Chinese tea and indulge in a scoop of homemade ice cream or a delicate pastry while gazing over the Luxembourg Gardens from Dalloyau's terrace is to taste the luxury and leisure of an earlier, more gracious era. ♦ Breakfast, lunch, and afternoon tea. 2 Place Edmond-Rostand (between Rue de Médicis and Blvd St.-Michel). Métro: Luxembourg (RER). 43.29.31.10

73 Rue Monsieur-le-Prince *Monsieur-le-Prince* is what every French king's brother was traditionally called. During the last century, this street was a veritable American alley, as evidenced by the events that took place at the following addresses. **No. 14:** in March 1959 **Martin Luther King, Jr.,** visited black novelist **Richard Wright** in his third-floor apartment. **No. 22:** in 1892 **James McNeill Whistler** had a studio on the courtyard, where he completed a portrait of **Count Robert de Montesquieu** (years later, the count sold the painting for an exorbitant sum, thereby greatly offending Whistler. The portrait now hangs in the Frick Museum in New York). **No. 49:** the poet **Henry Wadsworth Longfellow** lived here in June 1826. He made his contribution of $36 a week to the Parisian economy, which gained him not only a room in the *pension de famille* of **Madame Potet,** but also French lessons with her daughters and free laundry service. **No. 55: Oliver Wendell Holmes** lived here (now the site of the **Lycée St.-Louis**) from 1833 to 1835 while he studied to be a doctor. To be on the safe side, the following year he obtained a second medical degree from Harvard. ♦ Métro: Odéon

74 Slice ★★$ If you crave mozzarella and an aroma of Manhattan, Slice serves the best New York pizza in town. You will also find highly respectable chocolate chip cookies and brownies and a moist banana-chocolate cake. ♦ Lunch, dinner, and snacks. Delivery: noon-2:30PM, 6:30-11PM anywhere in Paris. 62 Rue Monsieur-le-Prince (between Rue de Vaugirard and Blvd St.-Michel). No credit cards. Métros: Luxembourg (RER), Odéon. 43.54.18.18

75 Luxembourg Gardens As a part of his draconian remodeling of Paris, **Baron Haussmann** had a plan to change this precious green expanse but was thwarted when 12,000 Parisians signed a petition to save the park. In the heart of the Left Bank, the 60-acre playground is graced with fountains, sculptures, ponds, flower beds, tennis courts, pony rides, a marionette theater, and outdoor band concerts. The open-air café is dappled with a light filtering through the leaves of the surrounding trees that recalls the most pleasant moods of Impressionism. The park is under heavy surveillance by officious *gardiens* enforcing regulations stating that "the park is out of bounds to the drunk, beggars, and the indecently dressed; the playing of cards is restricted to the northwest corner of the gardens; the kicking of balls and sitting on the grass is prohibited entirely; and the park must be vacated precisely 30 minutes before sunset." These uniformed guards trill their whistles to chase lingerers from the gardens.

As for those ever-amusing Americans in Paris: in 1900 **Isadora Duncan** was wont to dance here at 5AM, when the gardens opened, and **Hemingway's** destitute painter protagonist in *Islands in the Stream* captured and strangled pigeons for lunch. Do not miss the Luxembourg's many hidden delights: the small bronze replica of the Statue of Liberty; a series of statues of French queens and famous 19th-century women standing among the crocuses, daffodils, and azaleas; a beekeeping school run by Esperanto-speaking Dominican friar

René-Jean Marmou, curator of the apiary, who gives practical classes from April to September through the Centrale d'Apiculture (41 Rue Pernety, 45.42.29.08); and the *pétanque* bowlers and chess players sequestered in their respective corners of the gardens. On weekends, smartly dressed Latin Quarter grade-schoolers romp here and compete in the park's tricycle races and toy sailboat regatta held in the octagonal basin at the center of the park. ♦ Métros: Luxembourg (RER), Notre-Dame-des-Champs, St.-Sulpice

76 Médici Fountain At the end of a long, somewhat slimy pool filled with goldfish is one of the few Italianate stonework remnants of **Marie de Médici's** day. White marble nude lovers, *Acis* and *Galatea*, are eyed from above by the bronze Cyclops *Polyphemus,* who waits to do the Greek mythic version of kicking sand in the face of the 98-pound weakling before making off with the girl. Notice the trompe l'oeil effect of having the water appear to flow uphill into the grotto. On the back side of the fountain is a delightful bas-relief of *Leda and the Swan* by **Valois.** ♦ 15 Rue de Vaugirard. Métro: Luxembourg (RER)

77 Luxembourg Palace In 1610, the assassin **Ravaillac** could hardly have imagined that his murder of **Henri IV** would result in the creation of this splendid palace and gardens. (Indeed, he didn't live long enough after committing his dastardly deed to imagine much of anything.) The widow of Henri IV, **Queen Mother Marie de Médici,** tired of the Louvre, decided to build a palace that would recall her native Italy. She bought this vast property at the southern edge of the city from **Duke François de Luxembourg** and dispatched an architect to Florence to study her family residence, the Pitti Palace, before making plans for the new palace. Obediently, **Salomon de Brosse** designed Luxembourg Palace for her. Work began in 1615, but, ironically, by the time the residence reached completion in 1631, Marie had been banished by her own son, **Louis XIII,** for turning against **Cardinal Richelieu.** She died penniless in Cologne 11 years later. During the Revolution, the palace served a short stint as a prison; it was here that "Citizen Paine," the American **Thomas Paine,** languished as an enemy Englishman for more than 10 months during the 1793 Reign of Terror and narrowly escaped execution.

Subsequently, Luxembourg Palace was re-modeled to house the newly created French Senate, which met for the first time in 1804 and still resides here. Few of the trappings of Marie de Médici's time remain; the 19th-century architect **Chalgrin** (who also designed the Arc de Triomphe) made sure of that in his democratic remodeling. The 24 images of the queen's life story created by **Rubens** were moved to the Louvre and the Uffizi Gallery in Florence. Chalgrin festooned the library with the paintings of **Delacroix** in homage to Virgil,

Homer, and Dante. On the one day each month that the palace is open, visitors queue around the block, looking disturbingly like a bread line. ♦ Closed to the public except the first Sunday of each month at 10:30AM (call 44.61.21.68 to make a reservation for the guided tour). 15 Rue de Vaugirard. Métro: Luxembourg (RER)

78 Théâtre de l'Odéon City architects **Marie-Josephe Peyre** and **Charles de Wailly** designed this rather clumsy building (pictured above) in 1782, intending it to look like an antique temple. With 1,913 seats, it was the largest theater in Paris. **Beaumarchais'** *Marriage of Figaro* premiered here on 27 April 1784 in an atmosphere of success and scandal; the author was jailed. After World War II, **Jean-Louis Barrault** and **Madeleine Renaud** revived interest in the theater with their productions of works by **Beckett, Ionesco, Albee,** and **Claudel,** which became the talk of the town and, for a short period, made the theater the most popular in Paris. ♦ Ticket office: daily 11AM-6:30PM. 1 Place Paul-Claudel. Métro: Luxembourg (RER). 44.41.36.36

79 Le Moniteur The best shop in Paris for books on architecture and landscape design also has a large selection of international design magazines and an array of unusual guidebooks and postcards. ♦ M-Sa 10AM-7PM. 7 Place de l'Odéon (at Rue Corneille). Métro: Odéon. 43.25.48.58

80 Polidor ★★$ For more than a century, Polidor's home-cooking has lured writers such as **Hemingway, Joyce, Valéry,** and **Verlaine** out of their garrets for the earthy consolations of pumpkin soup, chicken in cream sauce, bacon and lentils, and rabbit in mustard sauce. Since its founding in 1845, little has changed; Polidor still has the classic bistro decor, lace curtains, and tiny wooden drawers where the regulars store their linen napkins. One customer has dined here every evening for 40 years. Even the prices have stayed within a garret-dweller's means. ♦ Lunch and dinner. 41 Rue Monsieur-le-Prince (between Rues Racine and de Vaugirard). No credit cards. Métros: Luxembourg (RER), Odéon. 43.26.95.34

81 Chez Maître Paul ★★$$ Like a country cottage hidden deep in the Franche-Comté region of eastern France, this restaurant comes with white tablecloths and a warm welcome from the **Gaugain** family. The kitchen is famous for its variety of wine sauces and a winning way with chicken and veal. ♦ Lunch and dinner. Closed Monday, Sunday, Christmas, New Year's Day, and in August. 12 Rue Monsieur-le-Prince (at Rue Casimir-Delavigne). Reservations recommended. Métros: Luxembourg (RER), Odéon. 43.54.74.59

81 Grand Hôtel des Balcons $$ This comfortable, reasonably priced hotel is down the street from the Théâtre de l'Odéon. ♦ 3 Rue Casimir-Delavigne (between Place de l'Odéon and Rue Monsieur-le-Prince). Métros: Luxembourg (RER), Odéon. 46.34.78.50

82 La Mediterranée ★$$ This old haunt of **Marlene Dietrich** and **Jean Cocteau** serves seafood specialties such as marinated mussels, bouillabaisse, and *barre grillé*. ♦ Lunch and dinner. 2 Place de l'Odéon (between Rues de l'Odéon and Crébillon). Métro: Odéon. 43.26.46.75

83 12 Rue de l'Odéon From 1921 to 1940 this was the famous bookstore **Shakespeare and Company,** run by **Sylvia Beach,** daughter of a Presbyterian minister from Princeton, New Jersey. Her shop was a Parisian hearth and home for American and British writers such as **Ezra Pound, Archibald MacLeish, Thornton Wilder,** and **F. Scott Fitzgerald,** to whom she served as guardian angel. She was constantly lending books and money to **Ernest Hemingway,** who came to Paris in 1921 and, after the publication of *The Sun Also Rises,* became the city's most famous expatriate writer.

Beach was devoted to literature in general and to one writer in particular: **James Joyce.** If it hadn't been for this amazing woman, the most important literary event of the day might never have happened: the publication, in full, of *Ulysses.* Beach accomplished that feat by becoming Joyce's secretary, editor, agent, and banker. She nearly went blind typing his illegible manuscript, and the publishing costs practically bankrupted Shakespeare and Company. ♦ Between Place de l'Odéon and Blvd St.-Germain. Métro: Odéon

84 19 Rue de Tournon In May 1790 the American Revolutionary naval officer **John Paul Jones,** having served a year in the Russian navy, moved to Paris, where he was welcomed as a national hero for his epic 1779 capture of the *Serapis,* a British warship. Jones died destitute in this second-floor flat on 18 July 1792. The fact that he received a full-scale state funeral paid for by the French government was no consolation and no small irony. ♦ Between Rues St.-Sulpice and de Vaugirard. Métro: Luxembourg (RER)

85 Grand Hôtel des Principautés Unies $$ In a top-floor flat, **William Faulkner** set to work on his first novel, *The Mosquitoes,* in the summer of 1925. Perhaps you will be equally inspired here. ♦ 42-44 Rue de Vaugirard (at Rue Servandoni). Métro: St.-Sulpice. 46.34.11.80

Artists' Ateliers

If you'd like to see where many museum master-pieces began, the following artists' studios are open to the public:

Emile-Antoine Bourdelle This conglomeration of workshops, galleries, and gardens pays homage to the work of the sculptor who spent 15 years with **Rodin** as pupil, assistant, collaborator, and friend. The museum, which is run by his daughter, **Madame Rhodia Dufet-Bourdelle,** contains 21 studies of **Beethoven,** with whom he was fascinated, as well as casts of his sculptures and busts of **Ingres, Rodin,** and **Rembrandt.** ♦ Admission. Tu-Su 10AM-5:40PM. 18 Rue Antoine-Bourdelle. Métros: Falguière, Montparnasse-Bienvenue. 45.48.67.27

Constantin Brancusi The sculptor willed his Montparnasse atelier and its contents of more than 110 works to France on the condition that they be maintained in his home of 30 years. His wishes were met, in spirit. The former four-room Montparnasse atelier has been reconstructed in the Beaubourg and has been dubbed the **Pompidou Center's** potting shed. ♦ Admission. M, W-F noon-10PM; Sa-Su 10AM-10PM. Georges Pompidou Center. Métros: Hôtel-de-Ville, Rambuteau. 42.77.11.12, 42.77.12.33

Eugène Delacroix In 1857, Delacroix took these rooms for their proximity to St.-Sulpice and for their privacy. He had given up the profligate ways of youth for painting. "I go to work as other men run to their mistresses," he said. ♦ Admission. M, W-Su 9:45AM-12:30PM, 2-5:15PM. 6 Place de Furstemberg. Métro: St.-Germain-des-Prés. 43.54.04.87

Gustave Moreau No starving artist, Moreau moved into this elegant town house with his parents in 1854 and stayed here until he died in 1898. The four-story mansion contains more than 1,100 paintings, drawings, and illustrations. ♦ Admission. W-Su 10AM-1PM, 2-5PM. 14 Rue de la Rochefoucauld. Métro: Trinité. 48.74.38.50

86 Au Bon St.-Pourçain ★★$$ This is one of the few remaining authentic Lyonnais bistros in Paris. Chef **Daniel Pesle** fuels his regulars from the neighborhood with aioli, cassoulet, and his quick wit. ♦ Lunch and dinner. Closed Saturday and Sunday. 10 bis Rue Servandoni (between Rues de Vaugirard and Palatine). Métro: Mabillon. 43.54.93.63

87 Rue Férou Stroll down the street of the following artistic addresses. **No. 2:** painter/photographer **Man Ray** occupied an atelier with a high ceiling here in 1951; **No. 6: Hemingway** lived in this sphinx-protected *hôtel particulier* in 1926 while writing *A Farewell to Arms,* having left his wife, **Hadley,** for French *Vogue* staffer **Pauline Pfeiffer;** and **No. 13:** painter **Henri Fantin-Latour** had an apartment here in 1858, where he was sketched by his friend **James McNeill Whistler** (whose drawing was later purchased by the Louvre). ♦ Métro: St.-Sulpice

88 Place St.-Sulpice One of the most serene squares in Paris has a café, pink-flowering chestnut trees, and the marvelous stone *Fountain of the Cardinal Points* by **Visconti** (pictured above), featuring four famous French clergymen oriented north, south, east, and west, with four regal lions snarling at their feet. Once flanked by shops peddling ivory crucifixes, rosary beads, and clerical garments, the square today is graced by two **Yves Saint Laurent** boutiques and hosts antique and book fairs in summer, and, for many, the finest of the Bastille Day balls. ♦ Métro: St.-Sulpice

Although classy restaurants do not take kindly to babies or young children (and Parisians know better than to bring them), a warm welcome is always extended to man's best friend, *le chien.*

For the French, *la politesse* is a way of life, so it is best to respect their custom and address them formally: for example, say *"Bonjour Monsieur," "Pardon Madame,"* and *"S'il vous plaît Madame,"* rather than simply *"Bonjour," "Pardon,"* or *"S'il vous plaît."*

88 Church of St.-Sulpice Interrupted by insurrection, insolvency, and even bolts of lightning, the construction of this church (see illustration above) required the services of architects, including the notable **Louis Le Vau,** over a span of 134 years. Its dramatic classical style was the inspiration of **Giovanni Servandoni,** a Florentine known for his theater and stage-set designs. The disparity of the two towers, an odd couple indeed, was the result of shifting architectural sands and patronly indecision. Named after **Saint Sulpicius,** the sixth-century archbishop of Bourges, and dubbed the Temple of Victory during the Revolution, the church hosted a lavish banquet for 1,200 after **Napoléon** returned from his victories in Egypt. Inside the front door are two holy water stoups made from enormous shells given to **François I** by the Venetian Republic. The first chapel on the right was frescoed by an aging **Eugène Delacroix.** In a chapel at the rear of the church is the extraordinary *Virgin and Child* by **Jean-Baptiste Pigalle.** The organ, designed in 1776 by **Chalgrin,** with 6,588 pipes, numbers among the largest in the world.

In the floor, running along the north-south transept, is a bronze meridian line, a testament to France's 19th-century passion for science. Three times a year, on the equinoxes and the winter solstice, sunlight strikes the line so precisely that light runs along the metal strip, glances off an obelisk and globe at its top, and finally illuminates a cross. The inscription on the obelisk translates, more or less, as "Two Scientists with God's Help." Outside on the sunny southeast corner of the church you can glimpse the caretaker's rooftop garden; during particularly hot summers, he sells his bumper crop of strawberries and tomatoes to tourists. ♦ Daily 8AM-7PM. Place St.-Sulpice. Métro: St.-Sulpice. 46.33.21.78

89 Djuri ★★$$ In his intimate basement club, venerable guitarist and singer **Djuri Cortez** performs Russian, Yiddish, Romanian, and Gypsy folk music into the wee hours. Nice things happen here: for example, the ravishing Yugoslav at the next table may entice you to dance. Djuri's upstairs restaurant serves Hungarian goulash, chopped liver, stuffed peppers, and Transylvanian cabbage. ◆ Dinner. Closed Monday and in August. Club: Tu-Su 10:30PM-1:45AM. 6 Rue des Canettes (between Rue du Four and Place St.-Sulpice). Métro: Mabillon. 43.26.60.15

89 Chez Georges ★★$ On an alley called Duckling Street, surrounded by a wealth of Italian restaurants, the footloose walker stumbles onto this classic old French bar wallpapered with mug shots of the singers who perform in the cabaret downstairs. It's a nice place for a glass of Côtes-du-Rhône or Beaujolais before dining on cannelloni and pizza down the street. ◆ Lunch and late-night. Closed Sunday, Monday, and in August. 11 Rue des Canettes (between Rues du Four and Guirsade). No credit cards. Métro: Mabillon. 43.26.79.15

89 The Village Voice In the intelligent tradition of those famous Left Bank bookstore/salons run by women such as Sylvia Beach and Adrienne Monnier, the English bookshop of **Odile Hellier** is a busy crossroads for anglophone writers, artists, and literati in Paris. Hellier has something for everyone: a fine selection of classical, contemporary, and small-press fiction, exceptional author readings, and the latest issues of *The New York Review of Books, The New Yorker,* and (naturally) *The Village Voice.* ◆ M 2-8PM; Tu-Sa 11AM-8PM. 6 Rue Princesse (between Rues du Four and Guirsade). Métro: Mabillon. 46.33.36.47

89 Bistro Henri ★★$ The first-rate neighborhood bistro is known for its delicious *magret de canard,* green bean vinaigrette, *foie de veau,* baked goat-cheese salad, au gratin potatoes, and homemade tarts. ◆ Lunch and dinner; dinner only on Monday. Closed Sunday. 16 Rue Princesse (between Rues du Four and Guirsade). Reservations required. No credit cards. Métro: Mabillon. 46.33.51.12

89 Birdland The jazzy bar serves chili con carne and plays classic **John Coltrane** and **Charlie Parker.** ◆ M-F 7PM-dawn; Sa 10PM-dawn. 20 Rue Princesse (between Rues du Four and Guirsade). Métro: Mabillon. 43.26.97.59

90 Castel's ★$$$ The most private of the city's private clubs, Castel's caters to dandies, back-biting gossips, the most clean-cut "BCBGs" (the French term for yuppies), and former cabinet ministers with socialite dream girls on their arms. Technically, no one crosses **Jean Castel's** threshold unaccompanied by a card-carrying member (some 2,500 privileged people), but if you're dressed acceptably (coat and tie) and speak some French to **Corinne** at the box office window . . . *peut-être.* The decor is tacky, the food unremarkable, and the dance floor crowded—so what's all the fuss about? ◆ Dinner and late-night. Closed Sunday. Disco: M-Sa 11:30PM-dawn. 15 Rue Princesse (between Rues du Four and Guirsade). Métro: Mabillon. 43.26.90.22

90 Aux Charpentiers ★★$$ Formerly the lunch hall of an 18th-century carpenters guild, this reasonably priced bistro serves chef **Pierre Bardeche's** simple but well-prepared bacon and lentils, beef stew, sautéed veal, and other daily specials. ◆ Lunch and dinner. Closed Sunday. 10 Rue Mabillon (between Rues du Four and Guirsade). Reservations recommended. Métro: Mabillon. 43.26.30.05

90 Guy ★★$$ Brazilian music, spicy shrimp with pepper, and the delicious (but unpronounceable) *empajadas de camarao* and *feijoada churrascos* lure expatriates from Rio. A live Brazilian band plays during Saturday lunches. ◆ Dinner; Saturday lunch. Closed Sunday and in August. 6 Rue Mabillon (between Rues du Four and Guirsade). Reservations required. No credit cards. Métro: Mabillon. 43.54.87.61

91 Marché St.-Germain The old covered market is being renovated to house a new commercial center. The cobblers, fishmongers, and dairymaids can still be found in the next-door building on the Rue Lobineau. Next to the market are an underground basketball court and a 25-meter public swimming pool, the Piscine St.-Germain. ◆ Market: Tu-Sa 9AM-1PM, 4-7:30PM; Su 9AM-11PM. Pool: hours vary greatly; call 43.29.08.15. Rue Mabillon (at Rue Lobineau). Métro: Mabillon

92 Le Petit Vatel ★★$ One of Paris' smallest and cheapest restaurants is filled with famished students and artists seated around three tables. The tiny room used to be dominated by a large lavender stove until it was judged to be a fire hazard and authorities forced the owner, Mary, to remove it. Now a photograph on the wall is all that's left of the famous stove, but fortunately the food hasn't suffered. Tasty daily specials include Brazilian red beans, ratatouille, moussaka, roast pork, poached fish, and chocolate cake. ◆ Lunch and dinner. Closed Sunday and one week at Christmas. 5 Rue Lobineau. Métro: Mabillon. 43.54.28.49

The Piscine Deligny, a floating swimming pool on the Seine at Quai Anatole-France and a Paris landmark since 1785, sank into the river in 1993. No one was hurt when the 165-by-50-foot pool, constructed on 12 attached barges, broke away from its supports and touched bottom. The carcass now sits on the riverbed 12 feet underwater.

93 **Marie Mercié** The custom-made hats in Marie's summer and winter collections range from classic chapeaux to the amusing befeathered, beribboned fantasies which are earning her an international reputation. ♦ Tu-Sa 11AM-7PM. 23 Rue St.-Sulpice (between Rues de Tournon and Garancière). Métros: Odéon, Mabillon. 43.26.48.83

94 **Hôtel de Fleurie** $$ This renovated 18th-century town house in the heart of St.-Germain-des-Prés offers quiet, airy rooms, including some in the attic with high ceilings and wood beams. Downstairs is a handsome stone-vaulted breakfast room, where the **Marolleau** family serves an excellent Continental breakfast—slices of *quatre-quarts* (French pound cake), crisp baguettes, cheese, and freshly squeezed orange juice. ♦ 32-34 Rue Grégoire de Tours (between Blvd St.-Germain and Rue des Quatres-Vents). Métro: Odéon. 43.29.59.81

94 **Casa Bini** ★★$$ Recommended by the concierges at the Montalembert and George V hotels, this casual, friendly Tuscan restaurant run by **Anna Bini** and her family has prepared meals for **Catherine Deneuve** and **Marcello Mastroianni.** Florentine appetizers include *crostini* with mascarpone and salmon, and swordfish carpaccio with herbs. There are new meat, fish, and pasta specials every day, but the Pasta Casa Bini, a filling fettuccine and salmon dish, is always available. The shop next door sells many of the Tuscan products used in the restaurant, including pastas and sauces. Ask about Madame Bini's tours to Italy. ♦ Lunch and dinner; dinner only on Saturday. Closed Sunday, three weeks in August, and one week at Christmas. 36 Rue

Grégoire de Tours (between Blvd St.-Germain and Rue des Quatres-Vents). Reservations recommended. Métro: Odéon. 46.34.05.60

95 **Au Savoyard** ★★$$ For 35 years this colorful restaurant has been serving authentic French Alpine cuisine in the midst of Paris. The wooden chairs, wild-game trophies, paintings of mountain scenes, and peacock feathers provide an appropriately rustic setting for raclette (melted raclette cheese, potatoes, and ham), Savoyard fondue, and smoked Savoie sausages. Au Savoyard is a regional gem. ♦ Lunch and dinner. Closed last two weeks in July and all of August. 16 Rue des Quatres-Vents (between Carrefour de l'Odéon and Rue Grégoire de Tours). Reservations recommended. Métro: Odéon. 43.26.20.30

96 **Carrefour de l'Odéon** A crossroads of sorts is ruled over by a great pigeon-christened bronze of **Danton.** This Revolutionary leader's statements such as "We need audacity, more audacity, audacity forever . . . " cost him his head when he was sent to the guillotine by **Robespierre** in 1794. ♦ Métro: Odéon

Jazz Joints

In the 1940s and 1950s, when the Latin Quarter's underground dives resonated to the sounds of saxophones, Paris was the undisputed jazz capital of the world. In the next three decades, cities in the United States and Japan laid claim to that fame, but now Paris is staging a comeback. Here are some of the city's hottest spots for jazz:

Le Bilboquet 13 Rue St.-Benoît 45.48.81.84

Au Duc des Lombards
42 Rue des Lombards 42.33.22.88

L'Eustache 37 Rue Berger 40.26.23.20

Jazz Club Lionel Hampton Hôtel Meridien, 71 Boulevard Gouvion-St.-Cyr 40.68.34.34

Latitudes 7-11 Rue St.-Benoît 42.61.53.53

Le Montana 28 Rue St.-Benoît 45.48.93.08

Montgolfier Hôtel Sofitel,
8 Rue Louis Armand 40.60.30.30

New Morning 7-9 Rue des
Petites-Ecuries 45.23.51.41

Le Petit Journal/Montparnasse 13 Rue du Commandant Rene Mouchotte 43.21.56.70

Le Petit Opportun 15 Rue des Lavandieres Ste.-Opportune 42.36.01.36

Slow Club 130 Rue de Rivoli 42.33.84.30

Le Sunset 60 Rue des Lombards 40.26.46.60

La Villa 29 Rue Jacob 43.26.60.00

Restaurants/Clubs: Red	**Hotels:** Blue
Shops/ 🌳Outdoors: Green	**Sights/Culture:** Black

96 Christian Tortu After eight years, Tortu is still one of the hottest florists in town, creating opulent and original designs with flowers and vegetables. Garden furniture is also sold. ◆ M-Sa 9AM-8PM. 6 Carrefour de l'Odéon. Métro: Odéon. 43.26.02.56

97 Rue de l'Ecole de Médecine During the Revolution, **Jean-Paul Marat** founded the biting journal *L'Ami du Peuple* and was forced to hide in the Paris sewers. The radical democrat was elected to the National Convention three years later with the support of **Danton** and **Robespierre** but soon learned that you can't please all of *le peuple* all of the time. On 13 July 1793 Marat was stabbed while taking a bath in his house along this street. His killer was Girondist **Charlotte Corday,** who had hidden a knife in her bodice. For the surprisingly ungory details of the assassination see **David's** painting in the Louvre's Salle des Etats. ◆ Métro: Odéon

98 Le Procope ★★$$ Founded in 1686 by Sicilian **Francesco Procopio dei Coltelli,** and assured success by the 1689 opening of the **Comédie Française** in a tennis court-turned-theater across the street, the Procope advertises itself as the world's oldest café (the second star in its rating is for its history). Customers have included Olympian talents **La Fontaine, Rousseau,** and **Voltaire;** 18th-century revolutionaries including **Benjamin Franklin, Thomas Jefferson, Robespierre, Danton, Bonaparte,** and **Marat;** ageless literati like **Victor Hugo, Honoré de Balzac, Paul Verlaine, George Sand,** and **Mallarmé;** and in the 1950s, when the tavern/café became a restaurant, **Simone de Beauvoir** and **Jean-Paul Sartre.** These days, the best part of dining at Le Procope is adding your name to the distinguished guest list. Its 18th-century decor, red walls, and crystal chandeliers never seem to compensate for the slow service and disappointing cuisine. Safest bets are the classics: pot-au-feu and grilled lamb. ◆ Breakfast, lunch, and dinner. Closed in July. Jazz: M-Sa 11PM-2AM. 13 Rue de l'Ancienne-Comédie (between Blvd St.-Germain and Rue St.-André-des-Arts). Métro: Odéon. 43.26.99.20

99 Vagenende ★★$$ With a full effulgence of 1885 Belle Epoque and Tiffany glass decor, this poor man's Maxim's has starred in films such as *Travels with My Aunt* and *Murder on the Orient Express.* Homemade foie gras, fresh shellfish, and pot-au-feu are several good dishes to try. ◆ Lunch and dinner. 142 Blvd St.-Germain (between Rues de Seine and Grégoire de Tours). Métro: St.-Germain-des-Prés. 43.26.68.18

100 La Boutique Layrac Traiteur The windows at this expensive late-night delicatessen/caterer are capable of bringing any passing gourmand to a dead stop. Duck *à l'orange,* curried chicken, ornamented whole poached salmon, and impeccable pastries join a fine selection of wines, liqueurs, breads, and regional French specialties. ◆ Daily 9:30AM-3AM. 29 Rue de Buci (between Rue de Seine and Blvd St.-Germain). Métros: Mabillon, Odéon, St.-Germain-des-Prés. 43.25.17.72

101 Rue des Ciseaux Named after a scissors craftsman who once resided here, this short street is home to three Japanese restaurants and an Italian pizzeria. ◆ Métro: St.-Germain-des-Prés

102 St.-Germain-des-Prés For more than 15 centuries a church has stood on this corner, which in Roman times was *prés* (open pasture). The first church, built in AD 452 by Merovingian **King Childebert,** was repeatedly destroyed by invading Normans and finally rebuilt to last in 1163. The Romanesque western gate tower is faintly reminiscent of the great abbeys on the outskirts of Paris. During the Middle Ages, the St.-Germain-des-Prés, named after Saint Germanus (AD 496-576), bishop of Paris, became a focal point for Easter fairs, with hundreds of stalls, performing theater troupes, and dancing bears. (None of this has changed today save the dancing bears, which have been replaced by street musicians of the imitation-Dylan school.)

Inside the church of St. Germain is an altar dedicated to the victims of the September 1793 massacre, a shameful chapter of French history, when Paris was ruled by a bloodthirsty mob called the *sans culottes* (because they wore linen trousers instead of aristocratic knee breeches). In 1793, after a mock trial on the weekend of 2-3 September, almost 200 prisoners sequestered in the church were led into the courtyard (at the corner of what is now **Rue Bonaparte** and **Blvd St.-Germain**), where they were stabbed and hacked to death by hired killers. Ministers of **Louis XVI,** his father confessor, and the Swiss Guards were slaughtered. The carnage was followed by an auction of the victims' personal effects. The skull of **René Descartes,** the 17th-century mathematician and philosopher, along with the body of **John Casimir,** a 17th-century king of Poland who was abbot of St.-Germain, are buried inside the church.

Today, however, the edifice is best known for its evening concerts of classical music. It provides a cool place to meditate on muggy summer days. ♦ Daily 8AM-8PM. Guided tours Tu, Th 1-5PM. Place St.-Germain-des-Prés. Métro: St.-Germain-des-Prés. 43.25.41.71

102 Picasso Sculpture In the small park to the left of the main portal of St.-Germain-des-Prés is a bronze bust of a woman by **Pablo Picasso,** given to the city in 1958 in memory of his friend, the poet **Guillaume Apollinaire** (1880-1918), who lived and died at 202-204 Boulevard St.-Germain. (A short street nearby also honors Apollinaire.) Of Polish origin (his last name was **Kostrowitzki**), Apollinaire wrote the famous *Alcools* in 1913 and was an early leader of the Paris avant-garde. Eventually renowned for his poetry, Apollinaire was best known in his time as the man who stole the *Mona Lisa.* The scandal began when Apollinaire's former personal secretary lifted two inconsequential Phoenician statues from the Louvre and sold them to Picasso. Coincidentally, the *Mona Lisa* disappeared shortly afterwards. Apollinaire, trying to protect his secretary and Picasso from suspicion and incarceration, turned in the statues and was jailed for four days. The *Mona Lisa* eventually resumed her place in the Louvre, and Apollinaire was exonerated. He never, however, recovered his self-esteem. ♦ Métro: St.-Germain-des-Prés

103 St.-Germain-des-Prés $$ In the heart of bustling St.-Germain, this small hotel is convenient but hardly tranquil. Breakfast is served in the garden room. ♦ 36 Rue Bonaparte (between Rue Jacob and Blvd St.-Germain). Métro: St.-Germain-des-Prés. 43.26.00.19

103 Librairie Le Divan The bookstore of the Gallimard publishing house has works by all its latest authors, plus other literature and a large collection of *bandes dessinés* (comic books), such as *Tin Tin Chez le Psychanalyste.* Also notable are the black-and-white author photos tacked to the walls. ♦ M-Sa 10AM-7:30PM. 37 Rue Bonaparte (at Rue de l'Abbaye). Métro: St.-Germain-des-Prés. 43.26.84.73

103 Réunion des Musées Nationaux It's Tuesday. You forgot to buy a poster or catalog at the Louvre to take home, and now the museum is closed. Don't fret. This bookstore stocks all the catalogs and posters published by the national museums in France since 1966. ♦ M-F 9AM-12:30PM, 2-5PM. Closed three weeks in August. 10 Rue de l'Abbaye (between Rues Bonaparte and de Furstemberg). Métro: St.-Germain-des-Prés. 43.29.21.45

104 24 Rue Bonaparte In the spring of 1928, **Henry Miller** stayed here with his wife **June.** ♦ Between Rue Jacob and Quai Malaquais, across from Rue Visconti. Métro: St.-Germain-des-Prés

105 Ecole des Beaux-Arts The city's **School of Fine Arts** was established by **Louis XIV** and trained many of the architects and artists who have designed and decorated Paris over the centuries. It's worth a quick detour to view the lovely Renaissance archway, fountain, and sculpture, and the changing exhibitions of student work. Two well-known architects, **Richard Morris Hunt** and **Bernard Ralph Maybeck,** were among the first Americans to be educated here, and each employed his own version of the Beaux-Arts style in the U.S. during the late 19th century. ♦ 14 Rue Bonaparte (between Quai Malaquais and Rue Jacob). Métros: Rue du Bac, St.-Germain-des-Prés. 42.61.81.11

106 8 Rue Bonaparte The young Corsican conqueror once lived here, but this street wasn't named for him until 1852, when his nephew, **Napoléon III,** became emperor. ♦ Between Quai Malaquais and Rue des Beaux-Arts. Métro: St.-Germain-des-Prés

107 Restaurant des Beaux-Arts ★★$ Established in 1850, this bargain canteen is usually filled with art students. Go early to miss the lines but not the coq au vin, beef Bourguignonne, *confit de canard,* and rabbit in mustard sauce. ♦ Lunch and dinner. 11 Rue Bonaparte (between Quai Malaquais and Rue des Beaux-Arts). No credit cards. Métro: St.-Germain-des-Prés. 43.26.92.64

107 Robert Duperrier Here you'll find a lively combination of Indonesian, North American, and African art, from Gambian amulets to Ibo statues. ♦ M-Sa 10AM-12:30PM, 3-7PM. Closed in August. 14 Rue des Beaux-Arts (between Rues Bonaparte and de Seine). Métro: St.-Germain-des-Prés. 43.54.38.64

107 Franco Maria Ricci Editore This is the Paris headquarters of the celebrated Milan publisher whose eclectic and elegant series of fine arts books and literature ranges in subject from decorative ceramics and iconography to deluxe Italian re-editions of **Saki, Kafka, Borges,** and **Poe.** ♦ Tu-Sa 10AM-1PM, 2:30-7PM. 12 Rue des Beaux-Arts (between Rues Bonaparte and de Seine). Métro: St.-Germain-des-Prés. 46.33.96.31

107 L'Hôtel $$$$ This pretentiously generic name is befitting for a hostelry with true snob appeal—the snug and refined favorite lodgings of **Robert de Niro, Glenn Close, Julie Christie**, and countless honeymooners. Formerly the **Hôtel d'Alsace**, this is where **Oscar Wilde** stayed in 1899 after his release from Reading Gaol (the prison). He expired here the following year, sighing, "I am dying beyond my means." *Dorian Gray* fans can actually occupy the room where Wilde lived out his last days. Or, if you prefer, book the Art Deco bedroom of dance-hall belle **Mistinguett**. The hotel's seven-story light well is a triumph of Directoire architecture. All in all, it's a unique hotel with a seductive ambience. ♦ 13 Rue des Beaux-Arts (between Rues Bonaparte and de Seine). Reservations required. Métro: St.-Germain-des-Prés. 43.25.27.22

Within L'Hôtel:

Le Belier ★★$$$ This romantic restaurant maintains a reputation for excellent, convivial service. The specialties include veal tournedos with mozzarella, sole and salmon in saffron, and meringue with mangoes and chocolate. ♦ Lunch and dinner. Reservations recommended. 43.25.27.22

Bar de l'Hôtel Young art and antique dealers bring their fancy American friends here to experience the Parisian scene and enjoy the piano bar. ♦ Daily 6AM-2AM. 43.25.27.22

107 Galerie Claude Bernard One of the city's best, this internationally known gallery shows such modern heavyweights as **Balthus, Giacometti, David Hockney, Louise Nevelson**, and **Jim Dine**. ♦ Tu-Sa 9:30AM-12:30PM, 2:30-6:30PM. Closed in August. 7-9 Rue des Beaux-Arts (between Rues Bonaparte and de Seine). Métro: St.-Germain-des-Prés. 43.26.97.07

107 5 Rue des Beaux-Arts Edouard Manet was born here in 1835. A wall plaque commemorates that truly blessed event. ♦ Between Rues Bonaparte and de Seine. Métro: St.-Germain-des-Prés

108 Roger-Viollet With more than eight million black-and-white and color photographs, these archives document the history of mankind from antiquity to the present. Stored here are glossies of the Temple of Ramses at Abou Simbel, the interior of a 14th-century baker's shop, **Louis Armstrong**, and the demolition of the Berlin Wall. Curious tourists shouldn't amble in, but journalists, students, and other researchers are welcome. ♦ M-F 9AM-1PM, 2-6PM. 6 Rue de Seine (between Rues des Beaux-Arts and Mazarine). Métros: Odéon, St.-Germain-des-Prés. 43.54.81.10, 43.54.32.90

109 24 Rue Visconti This was once the home of **Racine**. According to a historian's account, the brilliant 17th-century dramatist died here on 21 April 1699 of a combination of dysentery, erysipelas, rheumatism, a liver ailment, and, possibly, "the chagrin of no longer being in favor with the king." ♦ Between Rues Bonaparte and de Seine. Métro: St.-Germain-des-Prés

109 17 Rue Visconti Young **Balzac** set up his print shop at this cultural address. A few years later, in 1836, **Delacroix** moved in. It was here that he painted his portraits of **George Sand** and her lover **Frédéric Chopin**. ♦ Between Rues Bonaparte and de Seine. Métro: St.-Germain-des-Prés

110 Atelier Depretz In a courtyard off Rue Jacob, **Jean-Claude Depretz**, a master-painting restorer, repairs damaged canvases with rabbit-skin glue while his assistant camouflages the scars. ♦ M 10:30AM-12:30PM, 2-7PM; Tu-F 9AM-12:30PM, 2-7PM; Sa 9AM-12:30PM. Closed in August. 30 Rue Jacob (between Rues Bonaparte and de Seine). Métro: St.-Germain-des-Prés. 43.26.60.14

110 Claude Boullé Some of the cut and polished stones at this gallery are the mineral counterparts of **J.M.W. Turner's** seascapes on canvas. ♦ M-Sa 10:30AM-12:30PM, 2-7PM. 28 Rue Jacob (between Rues Bonaparte and de Seine). Métro: St.-Germain-des-Prés. 46.33.01.38

110 La Maison Rustique Green thumbs will enjoy browsing in this agricultural and horticultural bookstore. ♦ M-Sa 10AM-7PM. 26 Rue Jacob (between Rues Bonaparte and de Seine). Métro: St.-Germain-des-Prés. 43.25.67.00

110 14 Rue Jacob German opera composer **Richard Wagner** lived here from 1841-42. ♦ Between Rues Bonaparte and de Seine. Métro: St.-Germain-des-Prés

111 La Villa $$$ If you want to stay on the Left Bank but rustic decor doesn't charm you, this newly refurbished hotel has a slick contemporary look. After 10:30PM (except on Sunday) you'll find an international assortment of beautiful people downstairs in the Club la Villa, listening to live jazz and munching on caviar and foie gras. American filmmaker **Spike Lee** stays here. ♦ 29 Rue Jacob (between Rues Bonaparte and de Furstemberg). Métro: St.-Germain-des-Prés. 43.26.60.00

111 27 Rue Jacob The prestigious French publishing house, **Editions du Seuil,** has its offices in the building where **Ingres,** the master of French classical painting, lived more than 150 years ago. ♦ Between Rues Bonaparte and de Furstemberg. Métro: St.-Germain-des-Prés

Restaurants/Clubs: Red   Hotels: Blue
Shops/ 🌳Outdoors: Green   **Sights/Culture: Black**

111 Les Marronniers $$ Named after the two chestnut trees in its garden, this charming hotel, classified as a national monument, is set back on a peaceful courtyard that was once part of the monastery of the church of St.-Germain-des-Prés. It is justly popular. ♦ 21 Rue Jacob (between Rues Bonaparte and de Furstemberg). Reservations required. Métro: St.-Germain-des-Prés. 43.25.30.60

111 Yveline Tucked away in the **Furstemberg Square** (pictured above) is a charming antique shop. ♦ M-F 11AM-6:30PM; Sa 1-6:30PM. Closed in August. 4 Rue de Furstemberg (between Rues Jacob and de l'Abbaye). Métro: St.-Germain-des-Prés. 43.26.56.91

111 Delacroix Museum The old atelier of **Eugène Delacroix,** where he lived, worked, and in 1863, died, is now a museum displaying his paintings, sketches, and letters. A quick tour will give you some idea of why **Baudelaire** described Delacroix as a "volcanic crater artistically concealed beneath bouquets of flowers." ♦ Admission. M, W-Su 9:45AM-12:30PM, 2-5:15PM. 6 Rue de Furstemberg (between Rues Jacob and de l'Abbaye). Métro: St.-Germain-des-Prés. 43.54.04.87

111 7 Rue Jacob In 1656, at the age of 17, **Racine** lived here with his uncle. ♦ Between Rues Bonaparte and de Furstemberg. Métro: St.-Germain-des-Prés

111 Librairie Maritime et d'Outre-Mer This bookstore specializes in maritime books. ♦ M-Sa 10AM-7PM. 17 Rue Jacob (between Rues Bonaparte and de Furstemberg). Métro: St.-Germain-des-Prés. 46.33.47.48

111 Studio V.O./ V.F. Want to star in the next Polanski thriller set in Paris? Need to gesticulate more effectively at surly waiters and postal clerks? Adult acting classes in French or English are taught here by highly professional American and French drama instructors. ♦ Tu-F 9AM-5PM. Closed July and August. 11 Rue Jacob (between Rues Bonaparte and de Furstemberg). Métro: St.-Germain-des-Prés. 40.46.01.92

112 Manuel Canovas A wallpaper and fabric designer whose sumptuous work is often featured in *Vogue* and *Architectural Digest,* Manuel Canovas sells to professional and amateur decorators alike. ♦ M-Sa 9:30AM-6:30PM. 7 Rue de Furstemberg (between Rues Cardinale and de l'Abbaye). Métros: Mabillon, St.-Germain-des-Prés. 43.25.75.98

112 La Boutique Manuel Canovas Shoes, handbags, place mats, linens, and scarves fashioned from the cheery fabrics of Manuel Canovas, the next-door neighbor, are featured here. ♦ M-Sa 10AM-7PM. 5 Rue de Furstemberg (between Rues Cardinale and de l'Abbaye). Métros: Mabillon, St.-Germain-des-Prés. 43.26.89.31

112 2 Rue Cardinale The Black Sun Press operated at this address under the aegis of **Harry** and **Caresse Crosby,** a couple of wild surrealists of the 1920s. They were the first to publish the **D.H. Lawrence** book *Sun.* Harry, who was a nephew of **J.P. Morgan,** died in a double suicide with his mistress at the **Hôtel des Artistes** in New York. ♦ Off Rue Furstemberg. Métro: Mabillon

112 Place de Furstemberg Named after **Egon de Furstemberg,** a 17th-century abbot of St.-Germain-des-Prés, this hidden treasure attracts French filmmakers, flamenco guitar players, and harpists who like to play in the courtyard with its extraordinary acoustics. At the center of the square is a white-globed lamppost and four paulownia trees that **Henry Miller** described in *Tropic of Cancer* as having "the poetry of T.S. Eliot." In spring the trees burst into fragrant lavender bloom; Paris never smells as sweet anywhere else. ♦ Métro: St.-Germain-des-Prés

113 Hôtel de Seine $$ Once a family run pensione, this recently renovated hotel has lost its bohemian charm. Beat poet **Lawrence Ferlinghetti,** owner of City Lights Bookstore in San Francisco, used to stay here. ♦ 52 Rue de Seine (between Rues de Buci and Jacob). Métro: Odéon. 46.34.22.80

113 Mimi La Sardine A rainbow variety of velours has been stitched into everything from headbands to skirts. ♦ M 2-7:30PM; Tu-Sa 10AM-7:30PM. 54 Rue de Seine (between Rues de Buci and Jacob). Métro: Odéon. 46.34.11.66

113 Cosi ★★$ This gourmet Italian sandwich and salad counter serves everything from salmon carpaccio to roasted red peppers—all on bread baked in wood-fired pizza ovens. Tuscan wines, opera by Verdi, and daily editions of *La Repùbblica* lend to Cosi's Latin charm. Take your order elsewhere or, if you

prefer, eat here in the upstairs seating area.
♦ Lunch and dinner. 54 Rue de Seine (between Rues de Buci and Jacob). Métros: Odéon, St.-Germain-des-Prés. 46.33.35.36

114 L'Echaudé ★$$ Yet another romantic lace-curtain restaurant run by the brother and sister team of **Philippe** and **Martine Layrac,** this one is off the Rue de Buci. Chef **Bruno Sense** makes a *filet de rascasse de pomme de terre,* sweet-and-sour duck, and *cassoulet d'escargots* that will provide more than sufficient memories to fill your next postcard home. ♦ Lunch and dinner. 21 Rue de l'Echaudé (at Rue de l'Abbaye). Reservations required. Métro: Mabillon. 43.54.79.02

114 Le Chai de l'Abbaye ★★$ This is one of the few good wine bars in Paris not crawling with yuppies. ♦ Breakfast, lunch, dinner, and late-night. 26 Rue de Buci (at Rue du Bourbon le Château). Métros: Mabillon, Odéon. 43.26.68.26

114 2 Rue du Bourbon le Château Buzz yourself in and have a look at the circular-well courtyard in this 1824 structure. (L'Hôtel on Rue des Beaux-Arts is another example of this architectural device.) Try to imagine how items such as grand pianos are hoisted up to the fifth floor through the windows. ♦ Between Rues de Buci and de l'Echaudé. Métro: Mabillon

115 Rhumerie Martiniquaise ★$ Upper-crust rum imbibers, along with the rabble out for a good time, keep this place packed. However, the stiff punches made with 130 kinds of the sugarcane elixir make it worth fighting for a table. In addition to the usual daiquiris and planter's punch, try the *Père Serge,* which is named after a priest at St.-Germain-des-Prés and is made with rum, lemon, and sugarcane syrup. ♦ Lunch, snacks, and late-night. 166 Blvd St.-Germain (between Rues de Buci and de l'Echaudé). No credit cards. Métro: St.-Germain-des-Prés. 43.54.28.94

116 Buci Market One of the prettiest street markets is named after **Monsieur Buci,** president of the French Parliament during the Renaissance. The intersection of Rue de Buci and Rue de Seine is thronged with operatic hawkers hustling endives, homemade fettuccine, freshly ground Colombian coffee, wild strawberries, fresh cherries, hot baguettes, and pink tulips. From here, Rue de Seine shoots off toward the river, becoming a thoroughfare of art galleries. Bear that in mind when passing by in the early evening: a crowded gallery is most likely hosting a *vernissage* (literally a "varnishing"), or exhibition opening. Manifest your best French accent, join the party, and talk art while sipping a glass of champagne. ♦ Tu-Sa 9AM-1PM, 4-7PM; Su 9AM-1PM. Métro: Odéon

116 Le Fournil de Pierre In the vanguard of the new artisanal bakeries, Le Fournil de Pierre takes pride in its whole-grain breads. Its *pain de six céréales* possesses more fiber than a Presto log and might even inspire you to buy a toaster for your hotel room. ♦ M 11AM-8PM; Tu-Sa 8AM-8PM; Su 8:30AM-1PM. 64 Rue de Seine (between Rue de Buci and Blvd St.-Germain). Métro: Odéon. 46.34.17.59

116 La Louisiane $$ If you want to stay right in the heart of Paris, there's no better choice than this hotel. Located around the corner from the Rue de Buci street market, the Louisiane has hosted some very famous French literati, including **Jacques Prévert** and **Jean-Paul Sartre.** The noise level is likely to be high at all times, so light sleepers should go elsewhere. ♦ 60 Rue de Seine (between Rue de Buci and Blvd St.-Germain). Métros: Mabillon, Odéon. 43.29.59.30, 43.29.79.30

117 Galerie Documents Opened in 1954 by **Michel Romand** and now run by his daughter **Mireille,** this is the city's most distinguished antique poster shop, specializing in *affiches* from 1875 to 1930, particularly the works of **Toulouse-Lautrec, Grasset, Mucha,** and **Steinlen.** ♦ Tu-Sa 10:30AM-12:30PM, 2:30-7PM. 53 Rue de Seine (between Rues de Buci and Jacques-Callot). Métro: Odéon. 43.54.50.68

117 Librairie Fischbacher Along with a stunning collection of fine arts editions, this shop has books on history and primitive arts, and autobiographies in French, English, and German. ♦ M-F 9AM-7PM; Sa 10AM-7PM. 33 Rue de Seine. (between Rues de Buci and Jacques-Callot). Métro: Odéon. 43.26.84.87

118 La Palette ★★$ This bohemian café is right out of a Jean Rhys novel. In fact, **James Ivory** filmed part of that down-and-out tale *Quartet* (with **Alan Bates, Maggie Smith,** and **Isabelle Adjani**) here in 1981. The artists' palettes that hang on the wall are more interesting than the paintings themselves, but don't miss the humorous 1920s tiled murals in the back room. House specialties include Gruyère omelet, chef's salad, country ham served on Poilâne country bread, and a delicious *tarte tatin.* Bearded waiter **Jean-François** is grouchy but kindhearted and plays the part of a little Bonaparte. You must order quickly and without indecision or he'll ignore you until you've learned your lesson. The WC is an "authentic porcelain kangaroo trap," as one Aussie regular calls the crouch-style toilet. ♦ Breakfast, lunch, snacks, and late-night. Closed in August. 43 Rue de Seine (at Rue Jacques-Callot). No credit cards. Métro: Odéon. 43.26.68.15

118 Galerie Arts des Amériques If pre-Columbian art from Central and South America is your passion, this gallery has treasures in store for you. ♦ M 2-5PM; Tu-Sa 10:30AM-12:30PM, 2-5PM. Closed in August. 42 Rue de Seine (between Rues Visconti and Jacob). Métros: Mabillon, St.-Germain-des-Prés. 46.33.18.31

119 Marie & Fils ★★★$$ Marie Steinberg owned her first Left Bank restaurant, Chez Marie, for ten years. As the name of her new culinary venture implies, she now has a partner, her son Guillaume Barclay. The team has created a refreshing menu with a range of prices, which in turn has drawn a range of customers. Local artists, editors, and gallery owners lunch here, and at dinnertime the belle clientèle arrive, including such neighborhood residents as Catherine Deneuve. Selections change every two months except for two first-class standbys: roast beef with mashed potatoes, and foie de veau à la sauce aigre-douce (veal liver in a sweet-and-sour sauce), Guillaume's preference. The atmosphere is warm and spirited. ♦ Lunch and dinner; dinner only on Monday. Closed Sunday. 34 Rue Mazarine (between Rues Jacques-Callot and de Seine). Reservations recommended. Métros: Odéon, St.-Germain-des-Prés. 43.26.69.49

119 12 Rue Mazarine Here the young Molière made his acting debut and later, with an inherited nest egg, opened a theater in an abandoned tennis court; this was the genesis of the Comédie Française. In 1673, after he died on stage, the company was orphaned and evicted. But the troupe started anew in another old tennis court at 14 Rue de l'Ancienne Comédie after more than a decade of inactivity. ♦ At Rue de Seine. Métro: Odéon

120 Institut de France Situated across the Pont des Arts from the Louvre, this 17th-century masterpiece (pictured below), designed by Louis Le Vau at the same time he was working on the Louvre, houses the prestigious Académie Française. The academy began in 1635 as a salon of intellectuals who gathered informally to discuss French rhetoric and usage. Shortly thereafter, Cardinal Richelieu charged them with the protection and proliferation of the French language, hoping that Parisian French would eventually obliterate the less-refined regional dialects. Academy membership is limited to 40 "immortals." At their induction ceremonies, the members wear silver-embroidered green robes and cocked admirals' bonnets and carry jeweled swords. The immortals don their robes for secret meetings, which are held every Thursday afternoon. Among their responsibilities are safeguarding the mother tongue and preparing new editions of the academy's dictionary, which first appeared in 1694.

Election to the academy is reserved for great writers, and even the list of runners-up comprises a pantheon of French literature: Descartes, Diderot, de Maupassant, Balzac, Flaubert, Verlaine, Stendhal, and Proust among them. Molière, the playwright/director/actor, was invited to join the academy on the condition that he give up acting. He refused the honor. No actor has ever been admitted to date. Emile Zola campaigned unsuccessfully for election 13 times; Nobel prize winners André Gide and Albert Camus never even tried. In 1981, history was made when Marguerite Yourcenar was inducted into the sacred ranks of the academy and

Institut de France

became the first female immortal (her cloak was personally designed by **Yves Saint Laurent**). The left wing of the institute (toward the mint building) is the site of the notorious **Tour Nesle,** from where, according to **Dumas, Queen Margot** (the first wife of **Henri IV**) would catapult that night's lover into the Seine. Among the exemplary statuary in the institute rotunda is a nude **Voltaire.**
♦ Métro: Odéon

121 Pont des Arts Providing a pedestrian crossing between the **Institut de France** and the **Louvre,** this wooden-planked structure with its latticed arches was the first iron bridge in Paris. Designed by an engineer named **Dillon** in 1804, this footbridge was originally landscaped with potted orange trees, rosebushes, and hothouses full of tropical plants. Hordes of easel-toting artists from the nearby **Ecole des Beaux-Arts** come here to sketch and paint that familiar compact view spanning the **Ile de la Cité,** the rose-gray facade of **Place Dauphine,** the dignified form of the **Pont-Neuf,** and the spires of **Notre-Dame** and **Ste.-Chapelle** in the distance.
♦ Métro: Odéon

122 Galerie Granoff Larock One of the city's most reputable modern art galleries sells works of the masters. ♦ M 2-7PM; Tu-Sa 10AM-7PM. 13 Quai de Conti (at Impasse Conti). Métros: Pont-Neuf, St.-Germain-des-Prés. 43.54.41.92

122 Impasse de Conti On this street in 1792, a young Corsican named **Napoléon Bonaparte** rented an attic room in the **Hôtel de Guénégaud,** built by **François Mansart** in 1659. Twelve years later, he conquered Europe and crowned himself emperor of France. ♦ At Quai de Conti. Métro: Odéon

123 Hôtel des Monnaies The austere classical-style French mint (pictured above) is where the nation's centime and franc coins are designed and struck. In 1775, shortly after the original mint by **Jules Hardouin-Mansart** was demolished, the present edifice was built by **Jacques-Denis Antoine.** The **Musée des Monnaies** traces the history of French coins back to **Charlemagne's** day and houses a collection of medals, currency, and commemorative coins. Hundreds of gold and silver medals are also for sale in the nearby museum shop (M-F 9AM-5:30PM; Sa 9AM-1PM, 2-5:30PM. 2 Rue Guénégaud. 40.46.56.66). ♦ Museum tours: Tu-Su 1-6PM.

Free tours of production area: Tu, Th 2PM, 3PM. Group tours: 40.46.55.35, 40.46.55.27. 11 Quai de Conti (at Rue Guénégaud). Métro: Odéon. 40.46.58.92

124 Le Balto ★$ Local architecture students pass their afternoons playing table soccer at this animated bar, which is best for Gruyère on Poilâne bread or a nightcap standing up. Every Wednesday at 9:30PM the **Fanfare des Beaux-Arts,** a rowdy horn ensemble, performs. ♦ Breakfast, lunch, and snacks. 15 Rue Mazarine (at Rue Guénégaud). Métro: Odéon. 43.26.02.29

124 Michel Cachoux Dig through the fossils, lapis, amethysts, and star-shaped calcites—there's something for everyone's hard-rock fantasy here. ♦ Tu-Sa 11AM-12:30PM, 2:30-7:30PM, or by appointment. Closed in August. 16 Rue Guénégaud (between Rue Mazarine and Quai de Conti). Métro: Odéon. 43.54.52.15, 43.25.46.20

124 Galerie Couvrat Desvergnes The last time you saw such an elegant Art Deco setting was probably in an Ernst Lubitsch film. If you can afford it, this is the place to start your own collection of French Art Deco furniture and accessories designed by period luminaries such as **Rhulmann, Charreau,** and **Cheuret.** Imagine a bronze *torchère* by **Brandt** with light filtering through an alabaster shade in your living room. ♦ Tu-Sa 11AM-1PM, 2-7PM. Closed in August. 12 Rue Guénégaud (between Rue Mazarine and Quai de Conti). Métro: Odéon. 43.29.72.70

125 La Cafetière ★★$$ Co-owner **Jean Romestant** greets you with a voice meant for a Truffaut movie. The specialties of his warmly lit restaurant are the *canard sauvage* (wild duck) and hot apple crêpes. *Cafetière* means coffeepot, hence the collection that's scattered about. ♦ Lunch and dinner. 21 Rue Mazarine (between Rue Guénégaud and Passage Dauphine). Reservations required. Métro: Odéon. 46.33.76.90

125 Galerie Isy Brachot From the vast repertoire of jokes deriding Belgians, you might conclude that the French lack respect for the people of that country. This quite respectable gallery reflects the Belgian view of surrealism (representing the artists **Magritte** and **Delvaux**) and is worthy of a lingering look. ♦ Tu-Sa 11AM-1PM, 2-6:30PM. Closed 10 July-10 September. 35 Rue Guénégaud (at Rue Mazarine). Métro: Odéon. 43.29.41.71

126 Rue de Nevers This 13th-century alley ends near a remnant of the **King Philippe Auguste** city wall (circa 1200) and passes beneath an arch chiseled with an excerpt of the 17th-century poem *Le Paris Ridicule,* by **Claude Le Petit,** which forecasted the collapse of **Henri IV's** noble Pont-Neuf. The paper edition of this caustic verse was publicly burned in the **Place de Grève,** along with its author.
♦ Métro: Odéon

127 Le Monde en Marche Step into a magical world of wooden toys, puppets, and puzzles that are gaily colored and made by hand. ♦ Tu-Sa 10:30AM-7:30PM. Closed in August. 34 Rue Dauphine (between Passage Dauphine and Carrefour Buci). Métro: Odéon. 43.26.66.53

127 Hôtel le Régent $$ This recently renovated 25-room hotel is nicely located midway between the Seine and Rue de Buci, which proffers the prettiest outdoor market in Paris. ♦ 61 Rue Dauphine (between Rues Mazet and St.-André-des-Arts). Métro: Mabillon. 46.34.59.80

128 Pub St.-Germain-des-Prés ★★$$ Along with 24 brands of draft beer and 450 international varieties of bottled brew, this 600-seat pub offers such basic grub as mussels and beef cooked with—guess what?—beer. By the end of the evening, you may feel that you have been similarly stewed yourself. Open 24 hours a day, it's a favorite of American students abroad. ♦ Breakfast, lunch, dinner, and late-night. 17 Rue de l'Ancienne-Comédie (between Blvd St.-Germain and Rue St.-André-des-Arts). Métro: Odéon. 43.29.38.70

128 Rue St.-André-des-Arts Running from Rue Mazarine to Place St.-Michel, this eclectic little street seems more like a pedestrian mall and is always host to a few guitar duos passably imitating Simon and Garfunkel. ♦ Métro: Odéon

128 St.-André-des-Arts $$ A friendly staff runs this comfortable, modest pensione. ♦ 66 Rue St.-André-des-Arts (between Rues Mazet and des Grands-Augustins). Métro: Odéon. 43.26.96.16

128 Le Mazet Street musicians, lowlifes, and professional pinball players frequent this down-and-out bar. You know the scene: beer-foamed mustaches, numerous dogs underfoot, and a pall of cigarette smoke in the air. If you choose to slum here, watch your billfold. ♦ Daily 10AM-2AM. 61 Rue St.-André-des-Arts (between Rues Mazet and des Grands-Augustins). No credit cards. Métro: Odéon. 43.54.68.81

128 Cour du Commerce St.-André Built in 1776, the city's first covered shopping mall was a hive of activity during the Revolution and inspired 17 other *passages* that sprang up on the Right Bank in the 19th century. Through the windows at **No. 4,** you can glimpse the remains of one of the towers in the city wall. At **No. 8** in 1789, **Marat** printed revolutionary exhortations in his inflammatory journal *L'Ami du Peuple.* Nearby, a German carpenter named **Schmidt** patiently perfected the hideous guillotine (named after **Dr. Guillotin,** who recommended this philanthropic apparatus for decapitation). Schmidt practiced on sheep, and the street ran red with the blood of the unfortunate beasts. It was also here that the artist **Balthus** had a studio and painted his famous picture *Le Passage du Commerce St.-André* in 1954 (don't look for the shop he painted with the golden key; it has long since been abandoned). ♦ 59-61 Rue St.-André-des-Arts (at Passage du Commerce St.-André). Métro: Odéon.

Within the Cour du Commerce St.-André:

Monsieur Baudrillart If you decide to have your Paris journal re-covered in leather, the bookbinding shop of Monsieur Baudrillart is the place to go. ♦ M-F 9AM-noon, 2-7PM. 46.33.19.88

A La Cour de Rohan ★★$ This British tearoom is decorated in garden-fresh whites and greens and offers lobster bisque, broiled goat cheese on toast, savory tarts, toothsome cakes, scones, crumbles, exotic teas, and a 17th-century heirloom recipe for spicy marmalade. No smoking allowed. ♦ Lunch and afternoon tea; Saturday dinner. Closed Monday and 15-30 August. No credit cards. 43.25.79.67

128 La Datcha des Arts ★$$ The proprietor of this Central European restaurant keeps a guitar on the wall for those who prefer their own singing to the piped-in mazurkas. Start with borscht and a lemon vodka, a dollop of beluga caviar, then move on to the *Assiette Datcha* (Danish salmon, sprats, *tarama,* eggplant caviar, and three kinds of Baltic herring with fresh blintzes). He also sells 15 kinds of vodka, Matroszka dolls, and blintzes to go. ♦ Lunch and dinner. 56 Rue St.-André-des-Arts (between Rues Dauphine and des Grands-Augustins). Métro: Odéon. 46.33.29.25

129 Jacques Cagna ★★★$$$$ In his elegant old inn, Jacques Cagna features traditional French cuisine with a nouvelle flourish. The prices are heavy, but the sauces are light and the vegetables are treated with the gentleness they deserve. Specialties include asparagus, lobster, and wild mushrooms in puff pastry; poached turbot in hollandaise sauce with puréed peas; Scottish beef filet with Périgord truffles; duck with red Burgundy and orange; veal sweetbreads with almonds and herbs; and a layered meringue and raspberry cake. The wine cellar stocks 60,000 bottles in 550 varieties. ♦ Lunch and dinner. Closed Saturday (except two Saturday nights per month from September to November), Sunday, holidays, 23 December to 2 January, and in August. 14 Rue des Grands-Augustins (at Rue Christine). Reservations required. Métro: Odéon. 43.26.49.39

Restaurants/Clubs: Red | **Hotels:** Blue
Shops/ Outdoors: Green | **Sights/Culture:** Black

129 Relais Christine $$$$$ A 16th-century monastery was converted into this plush, well-run, fashionable hotel in 1980. It offers modern and antique rooms as well as single or split-level apartments, some of which have luxurious marble bathrooms and access to a secluded courtyard. The basement breakfast room alone is worth the visit to this splendid hotel. ◆ 3 Rue Christine (between Rues Dauphine and des Grands-Augustins). Reservations required. Métro: Odéon. 43.26.71.80

129 5 Rue Christine After being ignominiously kicked out of their apartment on Rue de Fleurus, **Gertrude Stein** and **Alice B. Toklas** moved here in 1938. During the war, they fled to the countryside; in their absence, 5 Rue Christine was visited by the Gestapo, who attached a note to one of Stein's **Picasso** paintings reading "Jewish trash, good for burning." Stein died on 19 July 1946, and Toklas lived on here for another 18 years. The two women are buried side by side in the **Père-Lachaise** cemetery. ◆ Between Rues Dauphine and des Grands-Augustins. Métro: Odéon

129 La Rôtisserie d'en Face ★★★$$ Across the street from **Jacques Cagna's** famous namesake restaurant is his unpretentious new bistro, where good, simple meals can be enjoyed in an agreeable setting. The menu features meats cooked on the rotisserie—chicken served with mashed potatoes, rabbit with rosemary, and Scottish lamb with thyme. Cagna's mother has contributed family recipes, including *joues de cochon aux carottes at pommes fondantes,* which translates inelegantly as pig cheeks with carrots and mashed potatoes. For dessert, the specialty is *Vacherin glacé au caramel et noix,* a cheese ice cream with caramel and walnuts; meanwhile, the bistro's chocolate mousse and crème brûlée rival the best. ◆ Lunch and dinner; dinner only on Saturday and Sunday. 2 Rue Christine (between Rues Dauphine and des Grands-Augustins). Reservations recommended. Métro: Odéon. 43.26.40.98

129 Action Christine Two adjacent revival houses keep aficionados of **Hitchcock** and **Lubitsch,** as well as fans of **Bogie** and **Bacall** classics, happy. ◆ Daily 2-10:30PM. 4 Rue Christine and 10 Rue des Grands-Augustins. Métro: Odéon. 43.29.11.30

130 7 Rue des Grands-Augustins From 1936 to 1955, **Pablo Picasso** lived in this imposing house, where he painted *Guernica* in 1937. His friends **Gerald** and **Sara Murphy,** the quintessential American expatriates in the 1920s, had an apartment in the pink building around the block on the Quai des Grands-Augustins. It was Picasso who got them work painting sets for **Diaghilev** and the **Ballet Russe.** They were also the models **Fitzgerald** used for Dick and Nicole Diver in *Tender Is the Night.* ◆ Between Quai des Grands-Augustins and Rue de Savoie. Métro: Odéon

130 Quai des Grands-Augustins In 1313, one of the first *quais* (embankments) in Paris was constructed next to the monastery of **St.-Augustin.** Hundreds of years later, **Thomas Jefferson** idled away many an afternoon here, browsing along this stretch of riverside, which is still known for its book- and print-sellers. ◆ Métro: St.-Michel

130 Lapérouse ★★$$$ Chef **Gabriel Biscay** is attracting multitudes of gourmands to this Old World quayside restaurant with culinary sonnets such as lobster lasagna, lobster soup with julienne of vegetables, and warm apple tarts. ◆ Lunch and dinner; lunch only on Sunday. Closed Monday. 51 Quai des Grands-Augustins (at Rue des Grands-Augustins). Reservations required. Métro: St.-Michel. 43.26.68.04

131 46 Rue St.-André-des-Arts Sixty years ago, in a building housing two bookshops, **e.e. cummings** rented a single room. ◆ Between Rues des Grands-Augustins and Seguier. Métros: Odéon, St.-Michel

132 28 Rue St.-André-des-Arts In *Satori in Paris,* **Jack Kerouac** described pleasant evenings spent here at what was then a bar called **La Gentilhommière** (circa 1962) and is now a pizzeria. ◆ At Rue Gît-le-Coeur. Métros: Odéon, St.-Michel

133 Allard ★★$$ One of the old-time, honest bistros, Allard has two zinc bars, sawdust-strewn floors, and a rotating selection of *plats du jour* as perennial as the clientele. The **Allard** family, who played host here to the **Aga Khan, Brigitte Bardot,** and **Georges Pompidou,** have sold the restaurant, but it retains much of the old feeling. ◆ Lunch and dinner. Closed Saturday, Sunday, holidays, and in August. 41 Rue St.-André-des-Arts (at Rue de l'Eperon). Reservations required. Métros: Odéon, St.-Michel. 43.26.48.23

134 Maroussia ★$ Formerly **La Tchaika,** this Russian tea salon has a drawing-room atmosphere in which Chekhov, Tolstoy, or any princeling for that matter, would have been comfortable. Slavic hors d'oeuvres such as borscht, *tarama,* caviar, blintzes, and smoked salmon are served, along with cheesecake. It's perfect for an afternoon tea or a quick meal. ◆ Lunch and dinner; dinner only on Saturday. Closed Sunday. 9 Rue de l'Eperon (between Rues Suger and Serpente). Métros: Odéon, St.-Michel. 43.54.87.50

135 La Lozère ★★$$ This crowded canteen with bare wooden tables is a trip straight to the Lozère region in France's heartland. Try one of the robust regional specialties such as *confit de porc,* mutton tripe vinaigrette, and *aligot d'Aubrac* (a heavenly concoction of mashed potatoes, garlic, and Cantal cheese, served only on Thursday), or snack on slices of country ham, herb sausage, and *Bleu d'Auvergne.* ♦ Lunch and dinner. Closed Sunday, Monday, August, and last week of December. 4 Rue Hautefeuille (between Place St.-Michel and Rue des Poitevins). Reservations recommended. Métro: St.-Michel. 43.54.26.64

136 Rue Gît-le-Coeur The name means "Where the heart lies," a French phrase that's a good deal more romantic than the street's preceding moniker: **Gilles-le-Cook.** Nos. 1-9 were originally one mansion, built in the 16th century by **François I** for his love at the time, the **Duchess d'Etampes.** ♦ Métro: St.-Michel

136 Hôtel de Vieux Paris $$$ In the 1950s this was a pay-as-you-go crash pad for the American Beat generation. **John Dos Passos, e.e. cummings,** and **William S. Burroughs** all hung out here at various times and discussed what existentialist effronteries might be perpetrated next. In 1991 it was renovated into a comfortable three-star hotel and has lost its beatnik charm. ♦ 9 Rue Gît-le-Coeur (between Quai des Grands-Augustins and Rue St.-André-des-Arts). Métro: St.-Michel. 43.54.41.66

136 Caveau de la Bolée ★$$ A wooden door leads into a 13th-century dungeonlike cavern filled with late-night chess and checkers players. Dinner is served upstairs starting at 9PM. Downstairs a cabaret act plays nightly (except Sunday) starting at 10:30PM. ♦ Dinner and late-night. 25 Rue de l'Hirondelle (between Rue Gît-le-Coeur and Place St.-Michel). Métro: St.-Michel. 43.54.62.20

136 L'Ecluse ★★$ This wine bar overlooking the Seine offers a spectrum of 70 reds (18 of which can be ordered by the glass). Bordeaux is the specialty, a wine that goes wonderfully with the plates of smoked goose, carpaccio, and Chavignol crottin cheese served here. ♦ Lunch, dinner, snacks and late-night. 15 Quai des Grands-Augustins (between Place St.-Michel and Rue Gît-le-Coeur). Reservations recommended. Métro: St.-Michel. 46.33.58.74

137 Boulevard St.-Michel This was one of the great boulevards of **Baron Haussmann,** scythed through the Left Bank from the edge of the Seine in a broad, tree-lined swath. The street was named in 1867 in memory of the ancient chapel of **St.-Michel** that stood here once upon a time. ♦ Métro: St.-Michel

137 Place St.-Michel A relatively nonviolent crowd of students, bikers, and drug-pushers gathers here on hot Saturday nights. The passable restaurants around the square cater to pizza- and souvlaki-eaters. ♦ Métro: St.-Michel

137 St.-Michel Fountain In 1860 **Gabriel Davioud** designed this 75-foot-high and 15-foot-wide spouting monster (pictured above). The bronze of Saint Michael fighting the dragon is by **Duret.** ♦ Métro: St.-Michel

137 St.-Michel Métro This is one of the Art Nouveau métro entrances designed by **Hector Guimard** in 1900. ♦ At Rues Danton and St.-André-des-Arts

Le St. Séverin

137 Le St.-Séverin The best people-watching perch in Place St.-Michel has ice cream from the famous Berthillon. The hot chocolate isn't bad either. ♦ Daily 7AM-2AM. 3 Place St.-Michel (at Rue de la Huchette). Métro: St.-Michel. 43.54.19.36

138 Rue de la Harpe Named after **Reginald the Harper,** this medieval street, along with **Rue de la Huchette,** is one of the city's oldest. A youthful air emanates from the cheap restaurants jammed with students along this bustling street. ♦ Métro: St.-Michel

138 Rue de la Huchette In medieval times this ancient thoroughfare was called Street of Roasters, because it had a plethora of barbecue pits. Couscous and shish kebab joints continue the carnivorous tradition by roasting whole lambs and pigs in their front windows. You can always find cheap, sometimes risky, street food here. ♦ Métro: St.-Michel

138 28 Rue de la Huchette Outside the **Hôtel Mt.-Blanc** is a plaque commemorating a World War II Resistance fighter in the Rainbow unit that reads "Here fell Jean-Albert Bouillard, dead in the course of duty, killed by the Gestapo 17 May 1944 at 20 hours." ♦ Between Place St.-Michel and Rue Xavier-Privas. Métro: St.-Michel

138 Théâtre de la Huchette Ever since **Eugène Ionesco** finished them in the mid-1950s, two of his plays, *The Bald Soprano* and *The Lesson,* have been running nonstop at this 85-seat theater. ◆ 23 Rue de la Huchette (between Place St.-Michel and Rue Xavier-Privas). Métro: St.-Michel. 43.26.38.99

138 Caveau de la Huchette This is another crowded, dingy jazz cellar on a street that once rang with bebop. ◆ Cover. M-Th, Su 9:30PM-2:30AM; F 9:30PM-3AM; Sa 9:30PM-4AM. 5 Rue de la Huchette (between Place St.-Michel and Rue Xavier-Privas). Student discount available. Métro: St.-Michel. 43.26.65.05

138 10 Rue de la Huchette For several months here in 1795, a young brigadier general languished in a sparsely decorated back room. Unemployed, unloved, and (he thought) dying of hunger, he saw no hope for the future. Soon thereafter, he dispersed a mob by firing grapeshot into its midst, and from then on **Napoléon Bonaparte** was never ignored. ◆ Between Place St.-Michel and Rue Xavier-Privas. Métro: St.-Michel

139 Rue du Chat-qui-Pêche The Street of the Fishing Cat, most likely named after a medieval fishmonger, is one of the narrowest and, arguably, grungiest alleys in Paris. ◆ Métro: St.-Michel

140 Rue de la Parcheminerie This narrow street was crammed with scribes, copyists, and parchment peddlers in the Middle Ages. ◆ Métro: St.-Michel

140 St.-Séverin This lesser-known edifice (illustrated below), which was constructed around 1220 on the burial site of a sixth-century hermit named **Séverin,** is the official church of the **University of Paris.** Recognized as the city's richest example of flamboyant Gothic architecture, it was expanded between 1414 and 1520 with a bullet-shaped nave, a gaggle of gargoyles, and a five-aisled symphony of ribbed vaulting and stained glass. In 1673, the distinguished **Jules Hardouin-Mansart** tried his hand at enhancing the church, adding a small communion hall.

Don't miss the double ambulatory's slender medieval columns that shoot into vaulted arches, creating an effect that **Joris-Karl Huysmans** compared to being in a palm grove. The modern windows are by **Jean Bazaine,** the French abstract painter who created the mosaics for the UNESCO building and the Cluny-Sorbonne métro station. **Saint-Saëns** and **Fauré** performed on the 18th-century rococo organ in front of the west window; today the organ is frequently used for recitals. ◆ M-F 11AM-1PM, 3:30-7:30PM; Sa 11AM-11PM; Su 9AM-8PM. Rue des Prêtres-St.-Séverin. Métro: St.-Michel

St.-Séverin

Bests

Jim Dine
American Artist

Every time I visit Paris, I immediately go to the **Bon Marché** department store and make a complete tour of it because it's the kind of dopey store you used to be able to find in Cincinnati in the 1940s. There's a salesclerk in the luggage department who must think I'm some kind of pervert because she sees me looking at luggage all the time. She sells blue metal trunks and those aluminum suitcases that were once used by soldiers. I buy espadrilles, art supplies, and great stationery there. I go to their bicycle and sports department, and to the hardware department, which is where I found a very good etching tool (a rotary sanding disk on Velcro that enables you to erase without creating circular marks).

I also always visit the **Rodin Museum** because it's on the way from my hotel to Crommelynck's (my printer). I like to admire the roses in the garden.

I used to go to the **Bois de Boulogne** everyday to ride my bike, but my back is so bad now that I don't. It's great because you can see the prostitutes flashing in the woods.

I shop along the **Avenue de la Grand-Armée,** which is the continuation of the **Champs-Elysées,** because that's where some very good bike shops are located.

St.-Sulpice's Delacroix murals are always worth a visit!

I always go to the **Café de Flore** for breakfast and order toast. My wife, Nancy, and I like their soft-boiled eggs. We also dine at **Brasserie Balzar,** and we have tea at **Christian Constant,** where they've got the finest cocoa I've ever tasted.

I go to the **Louvre** to look at antiquities and tour the Pavillon de Flore, which houses Spanish paintings and French bronzes by Barais.

The **Picasso Museum** is tastefully designed and is a great homage to the artist. I love the **Giacometti** furniture and the lighting fixtures—although everything about the museum is beautiful.

Christopher Evans and Victor Wong
Designers, Evans and Wong

Your basic needs are perfectly fulfilled in Paris:

Air: the blossoming trees during the month of June.

Water: the waterfall in the artificial grotto at the **Parc des Buttes-Chaumont.**

Food: shopping for fresh produce on **Rue du Faubourg-St.-Denis.**

Shelter: protection from the elements provided by the canopy of any neighborhood café.

Clothing: all you need to make your own at the **Marché St.-Pierre.**

Love: anywhere, anytime, anyway—after all, it's Paris.

Sandra and Jay Lampros
Sculptor and Architect

Place des Vosges—especially in the spring when the trees sprout their tiny green leaves and children gather to play.

Au Petit Fer à Cheval—our local café and rendezvous point.

Michelangelo's *Slaves* in the southwest wing of the **Louvre.**

After-dinner walks around the Ile St.-Louis when the sun lies low against **Notre-Dame.** Any physical effort is easily rewarded with a double scoop of Berthillon ice cream.

Vieux Saigon—a Vietnamese restaurant where the service allows time to catch a movie at the Bastille.

The gardens of the **Palais Royal,** after a long Parisian stroll.

Fresh foie gras with a glass of Loupiac at **Au Cru de Bourgogne** in Les Halles.

The walls lined with every variety of tea imaginable at **Mariages Frères.**

An *andouillette frites* at **Ma Bourgogne** on the **Place des Vosges.**

The garden of the **Hôtel Sully.**

Mina Gondler
Painter/Sculptor

When roses are blooming I always go to the **Bagatelle** in the **Bois de Boulogne**—it's a haven of beauty and perfumes.

The Musée Dapper, 50 Avenue Victor-Hugo, is a private foundation that presents exquisite exhibitions of African art.

Once a week I tour the galleries of St.-Germain-des-Prés and visit the famous bookstore **La Hune,** next to **Aux Deux Magots.** Then I meet friends at **La Palette,** the painters' café on the Rue de Seine.

Walking along the Seine and observing the Paris sky is always a meditation for me.

From time to time it's important to go to the **Musée Marmottan.** One can really appreciate **Monet's** paintings in that calm atmosphere.

In warm weather, I dine with friends in the garden of **L'Espace Restaurant,** opposite the American Embassy, or in the garden of **La Closerie des Lilas** in Montparnasse.

A concert at **Ste.-Chapelle** is a double pleasure for the spirit. You can enjoy the chapel's stained-glass windows and the excellent music at the same time.

"The French do not go to priests, doctors, or psychiatrists to talk over their problems. They sit over a cup of coffee or a glass of wine and talk to each other."

Eric Sevareid, *"Town Meeting of the World,"* CBS-TV (1 March 1966)

Restaurants/Clubs: Red   **Hotels:** Blue
Shops/ Outdoors: Green   **Sights/Culture:** Black

Legrand—a renowned wine store with a ceiling made of thousands of wine corks

Louis XIV—a Lyonnais bistro where four-pound, help-yourself blocks of butter are passed from table to table

Chez Georges—classic handwritten menus, and waitresses in black dresses

Au Père Tranquille and **Le Bon Pêcheur**—great cafés for people-watching

Rue St.-Denis—Paris' red-light district

Joe Allen—hamburgers and apple pie for homesick Americans

Pharamond—the tripe restaurant, if you can stomach it

Forum des Halles—the "belly of Paris" has been turned into a modern mall

Le Cochon à l'Oreille—turn-of-the-century working-class bar and café that opens at 7AM

Ⓜ **Les Halles**

Horoscope Tower—where Ruggieri, Catherine de Médici's astrologer, gazed at the stars

Au Cochon d'Or—the classic bistro that puts the "French" in french fries

La Tour de Montlhery—24-hour bistro frequented by lawyers, local butchers, and English novelists

Les Trottoirs de Buenos Aires—take a tango lesson or just watch the pros do it

On 14 May 1610, Ravaillac assassinated King Henri IV on Ironmongers Row

Order a Blue Lagoon in **Café Costes**, Philippe Starck's architectural triumph

Aux Délices de Chine—the Chinese restaurant where you must order your lacquered duck 48 hours in advance

Ⓜ **Hôtel-de-Ville**

Marais & Les Halles

This district traverses 16 centuries of Parisian history. Begin exploring at the city's oldest square, **Place des Vosges,** a section of the Marais that was once a snarl of medieval streets inhabited by rich viscounts and poor Jews. Then move on to the **Georges Pompidou Center,** the department store of modern culture that is flanked by the trendy, high-voltage glitter of **Les Halles,** once the site of the great marketplace that **Emile Zola** called "the belly of Paris." A good ending point is **Place des Victoires,** where the Marais flavor of the Middle Ages and Renaissance gives way to the baroque configurations of central Paris.

Ⓜ *Arts-et-Métiers*

Ⓜ *Rambuteau*

Archives Nationales—*Joan of Arc's letters, Napoléon's will, and more, all on 175 miles of shelves*

Musée Picasso—*world's largest collection of the artist's work: 203 paintings, 30 sketchbooks, and 1,500 drawings. Not to be missed*

La Maison des Bonbons—*try a caramel au beurre salé in this neighborhood candy shop*

Place de la Bastille—*on 14 July 1789, 633 people stormed and demolished the fortress, sparking the French Revolution*

A l'Impasse—*the best-kept secret in the Marais*

Gambrinus—*sells 400 brands of beer and 200 kinds of whiskey*

Hôtel des Ambassadeurs de Hollande—*you're greeted by howling Medusa heads carved in the magnificent doors*

Rue Pavée—*one of the first paved streets in Paris*

Rue des Rosiers—*the spine of the Jewish Quarter*

Ma Bourgogne—*try the Auvergnat sausage for Sunday breakfast*

Notice the trompe l'oeil bricks on the facade

Hôtel de Sully—*the place to rent a château in France*

PLACE DE LA

Colonne de Juillet

Ⓜ BASTILLE

Kick off your day with a breakfast of eggs and auvergnat sausages at **Ma Bourgogne,** then browse in the boutiques of Place des Vosges, or visit the **Musée Carnavalet** (the Historical Museum of the City of Paris) to peruse its collection of Revolution memorabilia and 18th-century shop signs, both of which are a big hit with children. Have lunch at one of the many tea salons (**Le Loir dans la Théière,** for example) or pick up a quick falafel or pastrami sandwich somewhere on **Rue des Rosiers,** the main artery of the old Jewish quarter, which is lined with storefront synagogues and kosher bakeries (remember that much of the street closes on Saturday, the Jewish Sabbath). Your dessert will be the **Picasso Museum** in the **Hôtel-Salé** on Rue de Thorigny. (If visiting the Marais during summer, inquire about the **Festival du Marais,** a series of opera, chamber music, and drama performances in the district's exquisite 17th-century mansions.)

Upon reaching the Pompidou Center, you'll find abundant late-night restaurants, cafés, and clubs around Les Halles. **Au Cochon d'Or, Le Maraîcher,** and **L'Escargot Montorgueil** are three classic French restaurants for dinner. Great dancing is afoot at the funky **Les Bains Douches** or the more Latin **Le Tango.** Complete your Les Halles rite of passage by sipping a Blue Lagoon at midnight on the terrace at **Café Costes** or indulging in a steak at 3AM at **La Tour de Montlhery.**

Marais

Since Roman times, this district in eastern Paris has been known as the *Marais* (marsh). It was once a vast, oozy swamp on the northern branch of the Seine. In the 12th century the marsh was drained, making it habitable for humans but inhospitable to all the creatures who wanted it wet. Like New York's fashionable SoHo district, the Marais is now a mélange of ruin and restoration, past and present. The historically rich neighborhood possesses at least one Roman road (along Rues François-Miron and St.-Antoine), what may be the city's oldest house (a 14th-century, half-timbered house at 3 Rue Volta), the site of the (long-since destroyed) Bastille prison, and numerous twisting, huddled medieval streets.

Among those streets are three (Rues des Rosiers, des Ecouffes, and Ferdinand-Duval) that are the backbone of the celebrated Jewish quarter, formed in the 13th century when **King Philippe Auguste** "invited" the Jewish merchants living in front of Notre-Dame to move outside of his new city wall.

Seven French kings resided in the Marais, starting with **Charles V** (1337-1380). **Henri II** (1519-1559) was the last; he died during a freak jousting accident when the shattered lance of **Montgomery,** the captain of his Scots Guards, pierced the visor of his helmet. Henri's wife, **Catherine de Médici,** tried to ease her grief by having their royal **Maison des Tournelles** in the Marais demolished.

A half-century after the accident, **Henri IV** chose to construct the **Place Royale** on the leveled crown land in the Marais. Its name was changed in 1800 to **Place des Vosges** to honor the Vosges in eastern France, which was the first provincial department to pay its taxes after the Revolution. "It's the blow of Montgomery's lance," **Victor Hugo** later wrote, "that created the Place des Vosges."

The Marais and Place Royale (Vosges) figured prominently in Henri IV's building boom in the 17th century, which also included **Pont-Neuf, Place Dauphine,** and **Ile St.-Louis.** In the Marais, the king employed the leading architects of the day: **Louis Le Vau, François Mansart,** and **Jules Hardouin-Mansart.**

During this era, **Molière, Racine, Voltaire,** and **Madame de Sévigné** were exchanging witty party conversation in the great salons of the Marais that Molière parodied in his play *Précieuses Ridicules.* Within a century the former swamp had become the heart of intellectual Paris. In 1630 **Cardinal Richelieu,** a Marais resident, founded the **Académie Française** here, and years later a seven-year-old Mozart played his first Paris concert in Marais. This area became an island of urban civility and sophistication, far removed from the wild boars and party boors of Versailles.

After the Revolution the elegant town houses were abandoned or carved into small factories and rooming houses. Squatters took over, and the Marais fell into a shocking state of ruin. Over the centuries, 29 of the grand *hôtels particuliers* were destroyed; nearly one hundred remained, dilapidated and on the verge of collapse. In 1964 **André Malraux,** Minister of Culture under **Charles de Gaulle,** came to the rescue and designated the Marais the first historic preservation district in Paris. Within its boundaries are 1,500 architecturally important structures, making the Marais the largest historic district in France.

Many of the old buildings have been given new life, as you'll see when you visit the **Archives Nationales, Musée Carnavalet** (the city's historical museum), the famous Place des Vosges, and the **Picasso Museum.** The Marais quarter, a juxtaposition of splendor and squalor, is on a fashionable rebound.

Place de la Bastille On 14 July 1789, 633 people stormed the **Bastille** (the French counterpart to the Tower of London), captured its ammunition depot, released its prisoners (only seven, and none political), lynched its governor, and demolished the fortress, thus sparking the French Revolution. Every year the 14th of July is celebrated in Paris with parades and dancing in the streets.

The eight-towered Bastille was built in 1370 by Provost **Hugues Aubriot** as a fortified palace for **Charles V,** and was later transformed by **Cardinal Richelieu** into a holding tank where political prisoners were detained without trial. During its baleful history, the Bastille held **Voltaire,** who was imprisoned for penning his biting verse, as well as the **Marquis de Sade** and the notorious, enigmatic "Man in the Iron Mask." The paving stones, laid where Rue du Faubourg-St.-Antoine intersects the square, mark the site of the original towers. The figure perched on top of the 170-foot **July Column** (pictured above) is not an allegory of Liberty as many suppose, but a winged Mercury.
♦ Métro: Bastille

1 Opéra Bastille Not long ago, the French government appointed **Carlos Ott,** a Canadian-Uruguayan architect, to design what was to be the largest opera house in the world on the Place de la Bastille (illustrated above). The facility, billed as the "people's opera house," entertains an estimated 960,000 ticket-holders a year and includes an amphitheater and a stage for smaller performances. Its opening was planned in

conjunction with the July 1989 bicentennial of the storming of the Bastille and the French Revolution, but dissension among administrators, including the axing (figuratively at least) of the director, delayed the opening of the amphitheater until 1991. The opera house finally opened in 1992. ♦ 120 Rue de Lyon (at Rue de Charenton). Métro: Bastille. 44.73.13.99, 44.73.13.00

2 Pavillon de l'Arsenal This building's heavy stone facade hides a glass and steel structure constructed in 1879 for **Laurent-Louis Borniche,** an art lover and patron, as a place to display his almost 2,000 canvases. Borniche didn't live to see his museum open, his daughter sold the building, and over the years it was used for various purposes, including workshops for the Samaritaine department store and archival storage for the City of Paris. Renovated in 1988 by **Bernard Reichen** and **Philippe Robert,** it now houses a fascinating museum that looks at the urban development of Paris. In addition, it has a center for documentation on current architectural projects, and a photographic library.

By presenting drawings and models of local urban design and architectural projects, the museum aims to enhance the public's understanding of the city's continual evolution. On permanent display is a model of Paris connected to a computer; at a visitor's request, the videodisc shows one of 30,000 images (of canals, monuments, green spaces, sectors under development, etc.) while a laser ray spots the corresponding locus on the model. There is also an exhibit on the successive phases of the city's construction, from the wall of **Philippe Auguste** to Haussmann's Paris and beyond to present-day developments. The changing exhibitions concentrate on contemporary urbanization. ♦ Exhibitions: Tu-Sa 10:30AM-6:30PM; Su 11AM-7PM. Library: Tu-F 2-6PM. 21 Blvd Morland (at Rue de Schomberg). Métro: Sully-Morland. 42.76.33.97

3 Statue of Beaumarchais The 18th-century comedies of **Caron de Beaumarchais** (1732-1799), *The Barber of Seville* (1775) and *The Marriage of Figaro* (1784), were transformed by **Rossini** and **Mozart** respectively into operas whose factotum hero was regarded as dangerously, even revolutionarily, independent. The radical sympathies of Beaumarchais were played out in real life, too: his office was secretly running guns to American revolutionaries. In keeping with the dramatist's satiric tradition, residents of the Bastille neighborhood are constantly dressing up his statue in outrageous costumes. ♦ At Rues St.-Antoine and des Tournelles. Métro: Bastille

4 Le Maraîcher ★★$$ It's authentic in every detail, from the wooden beams and old photos of the Marché St.-Antoine to the patron himself. **Valentin Corral** studied cooking with Alain Senderens, decoration and presentation at Ledoyen, and fine wines in Bordeaux. Hence the exotic flowers, the well-chosen wine list, and, above all, the seasonally inspired menu with gems such as *pot-au-feu de canette au coriandre, magret de canard* with honey and spices, and scallop ravioli with zucchini and thyme. Just as impressive are the prices, with an incredibly inexpensive lunchtime menu. ◆ Lunch and dinner; dinner only on Monday. Closed Sunday. 5 Rue Beautreillis (between Rues St.-Antoine and Charles-V). Reservations recommended. Métro: Sully-Morland. 42.71.42.49

5   Hôtel St.-Louis Marais $$ A rustic 15-room hotel is all that remains of the 18th-century Hôtel des Celestins that belonged to the **Celestins Convent.** Around the corner on Rue Beautreillis is the original entrance to the convent, a stone portal with a weathered wooden door. Beware: the five-story hotel's landmark status prevents the owners from installing an elevator. ◆ 1 Rue Charles-V (at Rue du Petit-Musc). Métros: St.-Paul, Sully-Morland. 48.87.87.04

6   Albion Pick up a few paperback classics in English to read at cafés and on train rides. French people who are trying to learn English buy their books here. ◆ M-F 9:30AM-7PM; Sa 10AM-6PM. Closed last three weeks in August. 13 Rue Charles-V (between Rues St.-Paul and Beautreillis). Métros: St.-Paul, Sully-Morland. 42.72.50.71

7   Thanksgiving ★★$ Americans who long for familiar tastes can content themselves with barbecued chicken or chocolate chip cookies at this American-food boutique and restaurant. The shop carries packages of Cracker Jacks, Oreos, and Pop-Tarts, as well as Alpo for your dog (at foie-gras prices). When Thanksgiving approaches, fresh turkey (cooked if you call ahead), pumpkins, and cranberries are on hand. ◆ Lunch, brunch, and late-afternoon snacks. Closed Monday. Shop: M-Sa 11AM-8PM; Su 11AM-6PM. 20 Rue St.-Paul (at Rue Charles-V). Métros: St.-Paul, Sully-Morland, Pont-Marie. 42.77.68.29

Some of the original stones of the Bastille prison can be found in the small Henri-Galli square in the 4th arrondissement.

l' **E NOTECA**

7   L'Enoteca ★★★$$ The Italian food served here, beneath colorful glass lamps and wood beams, often varies in specifics but never in quality. Neighborhood residents come for veal scaloppini with endives and thyme or baked trout filet with mushrooms, tomato sauce, and basil. The wine bar is a pleasant place to pass the afternoon or late evening, with more than 300 Italian wines as well as Italian cheeses for nibbling. ◆ Lunch and dinner. Wine bar noon-2AM. 25 Rue Charles-V (at Rue St.-Paul). Reservations recommended. Métros: St.-Paul, Sully-Morland, Pont-Marie. 42.78.91.44

Village St.-Paul This jumble of antique shops crammed into a courtyard often becomes a lively outdoor market. It's one of the few places in Paris to shop on Sunday. ◆ M, Th-Su 11AM-7PM. Between Rues St.-Paul, des-Jardins-St.-Paul, and de l'Ave Maria. Métros: St.-Paul, Sully-Morland, Pont-Marie

9   Hôtel de Sully The most richly decorated private mansion in Paris dates from the time of **Louis XIII** and was designed in 1630 by architect **Androuet du Cerceau** for the notorious gambler **Petit Thouars,** who is said to have lost his entire fortune in one night. Ten years later, the mansion was bought by the **Duc de Sully,** a minister to **Henri IV.** Inside at the information office of the Caisse Nationale des Monuments Historiques et des Sites (Bureau of Historic Monuments and Sites), you may rent any of 40 châteaus or historic mansions throughout France for private receptions, weddings, or conventions. ◆ M-F 9AM-noon, 2-6PM; Sa 10:30AM-noon, 2-6PM. 62 Rue St.-Antoine (between Rues de Turenne and de Birague). Métro: St.-Paul. 44.61.20.00

10   Hôtel de la Place des Vosges $$ Just down the street from the King's Pavilion entrance to the famous square sits this cozy, rather than regal, hotel. ◆ 12 Rue de Birague (between Rue St.-Antoine and Place des Vosges). Métro: St.-Paul. 42.72.60.46

11   A l'Impasse ★★$$ One of the best-kept secrets in the Marais can be found tucked away in a narrow alley. This old neighborhood bistro serves delightful meals in a pleasantly renovated dining room. Baked goat cheese salads, terrines of rabbit and chanterelle mushrooms, filet of duck in blueberry sauce, and rich chocolate profitéroles are offered here at bargain prices. The service is warm and attentive. ◆ Lunch and dinner; dinner only on Saturday. Closed Sunday and two weeks in August. 4 Impasse Guéménée (off Rue St.-Antoine). Reservations recommended. Métros: Bastille, St.-Paul. 42.72.08.45

Restaurants/Clubs: Red   **Hotels:** Blue
Shops/ 🌳Outdoors: Green   **Sights/Culture:** Black

12 Bofinger ★$$ Among the oldest and most overrated brasseries, Bofinger dates from 1864; house legend holds it was the first in the city to pour draft beer. Specialties are nostalgia, *fruits de mer*, Alsatian *choucroute*, wine from the Côtes-du-Rhône, and more nostalgia. It's popular with Americans, whom the restaurant segregates from its French regulars as a matter of course. ♦ Lunch and dinner. 5-7 Rue de la Bastille (between Blvd Beaumarchais and Rue des Tournelles). Reservations recommended. Métro: Bastille. 42.72.87.82

13 Coconnas ★$$ Boasting a Louis XIII dining room and sidewalk terrace overlooking the mansions and garden of the Place des Vosges, this casual restaurant (run by **Claude Terrail** of La Tour d'Argent) has built its reputation on serving Good King Henri's *poule-au-pot* (commemorating Henri IV's famous political promise of a chicken in every pot) and *marquise au chocolat*. American tourists and expatriates predominate. ♦ Lunch and dinner. Closed Monday, Tuesday, and 15 Dec to 15 Jan. 2bis Place des Vosges (at Rue de Birague). Reservations recommended. Métros: Bastille, St.-Paul. 42.78.58.16

13 Musée Victor Hugo
This museum was the French writer's home from 1833 until 1848, when **Napoléon III** came to power and Hugo's voluntary exile in the Channel Islands began. The museum's eclectic assortment of Hugo mementos includes the cap he wore during the 1871 Siege of Paris, his bust sculpted by **Rodin,** and a model of an elephant sculpture that he proposed for Place de la Bastille. Haunting postage stamp-size pen-and-ink doodles of Rhine castles and ships at sea along with macabre sketches of witches, demons, and the hanging of John Brown show a nightmarish side to the author of *The Hunchback of Notre-Dame* (1831) and *Les Misérables* (1862).

The drawings are counterbalanced by the hodgepodge of Oriental furnishings Hugo designed for the Guernsey home of **Juliette Drouet,** his mistress for more than half a century. Don't leave the museum without viewing the Place des Vosges from one of Hugo's upstairs windows and glancing at the **Nadar** photo of an old but ageless Hugo on his deathbed, 22 May 1885. ♦ Admission. Tu-Su 10AM-5:40PM. 6 Place des Vosges. Métros: Bastille, St.-Paul. 42.72.10.16

14 Place des Vosges The oldest and perhaps most beautiful square in Paris, this symmetrical ensemble of 36 matching pavilions with red and gold brick and stone facades, steep slate roofs, and dormer windows was designed in 1612 by **Clément Metezeau.** For the first time in Paris an arcade was used to link houses, and balconies were employed for more than decorative purposes.

Commissioned by **Henri IV,** the square's original function was to house a silk factory and its workers. The goal was to provide **Marie de Médici,** his estranged queen, with lingerie cheaper than what could be imported from Genoa. Despite Henri's good intentions, his silk workers' housing project was gentrified before the last brick was laid. Into the apartments with 16-foot-high ceilings, red marble fireplaces, and parquet floors moved **Richelieu, Corneille, Molière,** and a covey of courtiers, cavaliers, ministers, and marquises.

It remained a high-class neighborhood until the summer of 1686, when **Louis XIV** moved to Versailles and the French aristocracy followed. In the early 18th century the Marais continued to decline and eventually became the city's industrial East End. Heavy machinery was bolted to the elegant floors of the great spaces, and magnificent salons were subdivided into minuscule apartments. The neighborhood was not pulled out of its nosedive until the early 1960s, when Minister of Culture **André Malraux** had the Place des Vosges and the Marais declared a historic district. Nowadays in the Place des Vosges you will find, weather permitting, grandmothers knitting, toddlers digging in the dirt, or perhaps a group of North African immigrants enjoying an impromptu soccer game beside an equestrian statue of a smirking **Louis XIII.** ♦ Métros: Bastille, St.-Paul

15 Issey Miyake Something of an art gallery for clothes, the newest boutique in the Place des Vosges shows the latest looks from the Japanese master. Many of these pieces are made in limited editons, while the boutique at 201 Boulevard St.-Germain sells Miyake's regular lines. ♦ M-Sa 10AM-7PM. Closed two weeks in August. 3 Place des Vosges. Métros: St.-Paul, Bastille. 48.87.01.86

15 Hôtel de Coulanges The **Marquise de Sévigné,** whose correspondence with her daughter in Provence became one of the most famous series of letters in French literature, was born here on 6 February 1626. It's a private residence. ♦ 1 Place des Vosges. Métros: St.-Paul, Bastille

15 3 Place des Vosges The newer buildings constructed on the square are masterpieces of trompe l'oeil. The facades are made of plaster on wood framing, and you have to get pretty close to notice that the bricks are painted on. ♦ Métros: St.-Paul, Bastille

16 La Chope des Vosges ★$$ Architects working on restorations in the historic district hang out in this simple café/restaurant. Not found on any gourmet's restaurant roster, it serves a sumptuous foie gras with a warm welcome. ♦ Breakfast, lunch, and dinner. Closed Monday and Sunday dinner from October through April. 22 Place des Vosges. Reservations recommended. Métros: Bastille, St.-Paul. 42.72.64.04

16 Mythes et Légendes This museumlike shop sells antiques and archaeological artifacts, bronze Buddhas, Flemish tapestries, and magnificent Mayan and Aztec pieces. ♦ M-Sa 10AM-12:30PM, 2-7PM. Closed two weeks in August. 18 Place des Vosges. Métros: Bastille, St.-Paul. 42.72.63.26

16 18 and 23 Place des Vosges These are two of the best portals on the square. Also, don't miss the door knockers at **No. 4** and **No. 17.** ♦ Métros: Bastille, St.-Paul

17 Pavillon de la Reine $$$ One of the most elegant hotels in the Marais, this 17th-century mansion, discreetly distanced by its own garden courtyard, is quietly opulent, with antique tapestries, Persian carpets, grand fireplaces, marble floors, and soft leather couches. The Pavillon de la Reine is operated in conjunction with the chic **Relais Christine** across the Seine. ♦ 28 Place des Vosges. Métros: Bastille, St. Paul. 42.77.96.40

17 Jardin de Flore Founded by renowned French architect **Fernand Pouillon,** this remarkable small publishing house reissues deluxe limited editions of antique manuscripts, illustrations, and maps. Pouillon employs Renaissance bookmaking techniques and prints on handmade paper. The books are bound in tooled, gold-leaf leather, and illustrations are colored by hand. Among the wares on display are the masterful *Apocalypse* engravings (1498) of **Albrecht Dürer,** the illustrated *Venise* (1610) by **Giacomo Franco,** and the famous three-foot-diameter globes that Venetian cartographer **Vincenzo Maria Coronelli** created for **Louis XIV** in 1693. In 1984 another French head of state, **President François Mitterrand,** ordered a pair of these globes (at $12,000 apiece) for his Elysée Palace office—personalized with his portrait floating in the South Atlantic. The Art Nouveau doorway of ersatz marble is by sculptor and jeweler **Jean Filhos.** ♦ Tu-Su 2-6PM. 24 Place des Vosges. Métros: Bastille, St.-Paul. 42.77.61.90

17 André Bissonnet Some years ago, a butcher named André Bissonnet laid down his meat cleaver, redecorated his *boucherie,* and began buying antique musical instruments and restoring them in his cold-storage room. On any given day he might be working on a 1747 viola da gamba, a 17th-century harp, a porcelain trumpet, ancient hurdy-gurdies, or a black serpent, a bizarre 18th-century horn used to accompany chanting priests. Bissonnet claims to be an accomplished player of the Breton bombardon and upon request will proudly bleat out a few bars. ♦ M-Sa 2-7PM or by appointment. Closed in August. 6 Rue du Pas-de-la-Mule. Métros: Bastille, St.-Paul. 48.87.20.15

18 21 Place des Vosges Cardinal Richelieu (1585-1642), the French prime minister under **Louis XIII** and the founder of the **Académie Française,** lived here. ♦ Métros: Bastille, St.-Paul

18 La Guirlande de Julie ★$$$ At his newest restaurant on the square, **Claude Terrail,** owner of the celebrated Tour d'Argent, presents a small seasonally inspired menu. Start with something light, such as the *terrine de poisson,* followed by the excellent pot-au-feu or *viennoise de saumon* and a bottle of wine from the Cave de la Tour d'Argent. Conclude with the popular nougat glacé in caramel sauce. In summer reserve a table outside beneath the brick arcade. ♦ Lunch and dinner. Closed Tuesday and in January. 25 Place des Vosges. Reservations recommended. Métros: Bastille, St.-Paul. 48.87.94.07

19 Ma Bourgogne ★★$$ Owned by **Aimé Cougoureux,** this arcade-sheltered café is where the locals go for Sunday breakfast. Specialties include sausages from Auvergne, foie gras *des Landes, andouillette,* veal tripe, and spicy steak tartare. Sample one of the sublime Burgundies from the 15,000-bottle wine cellar. ♦ Breakfast, lunch, dinner, and late-night. Closed in February and one week in March. 19 Place des Vosges (at Rue des Francs-Bourgeois). No credit cards. Métros: Bastille, St.-Paul. 42.78.44.64

19 L'Ambrosie ★★★$$$$ One of the few Michelin three-star restaurants in Paris is L'Ambrosie. The small menu of owner and chef **Bernard Pacaud,** who trained under Claude Peyrot at Le Vivarois, fulfills the promise of the restaurant's name. The ambrosia changes every two or three months; some past favorites that haven't been forgotten are artichokes with foie gras, red pepper mousse, skate with sliced cabbage, veal sweetbreads with shallots and fresh pasta, and the puff-pastry desserts. ♦ Lunch and dinner. Closed Monday and Sunday, two weeks in February, and three weeks in August. 9 Place des Vosges. Reservations required. Métros: St.-Paul, Bastille. 42.78.51.45

20 Bar de Jarente ★★$ Whether you come for coffee and a croissant in the morning or an aperitif before hitting one of the neighboring restaurants, do as the locals do and let the energetic and feisty **Madame Renée** take care of you. You will see why her hospitality is known throughout the *quartier*. ♦ Breakfast, lunch, and snacks. Closed Sunday and in August. 5 Rue de Jarente (at Rue Caron). Métro: St.-Paul. No phone

20 Auberge de Jarente ★$$ This simple restaurant serves such Basque specialties as *piperade* and paella at modest prices. ♦ Lunch and dinner. Closed Monday, Sunday, and in August. 7 Rue de Jarente (between Rues de Sévigné and Caron). Reservations recommended. Métro: St.-Paul. 42.77.49.35

21 Jean-Pierre De Castro Antique silver and silver-plated articles such as champagne buckets, candelabras, and sugar tongs are the specialties of this busy boutique. Forks and spoons are displayed by the basketful and sold by the kilogram. ♦ M 2-7PM; Tu-Sa 10:30AM-7PM; Su 11AM-7PM. 17 Rue des Francs-Bourgeois (between Rues de Sévigné and de Turenne). Métro: St.-Paul. 42.72.04.00

22 Rue des Francs-Bourgeois Originally called *Rue des Poulies* (Street of Spools) after a local community of weavers, this thoroughfare became known as the *Street of the Free Citizens* in the 14th century, when the local parish built an almshouse (on the site of 34-36 Rue des Francs-Bourgeois) for citizens so poor they were *francs* (free) of any obligation to the state tax jackals. ♦ Métro: St.-Paul

22 Carnavalette Old newspapers, political cartoons, fin-de-siècle theater programs, 19th-century satirical newspapers, and fashion catalogs from the 1930s are for sale here. ♦ Daily 10:30AM-6:30PM. 2 Rue des Francs-Bourgeois (at Rue de Turenne). Métro: St.-Paul. 42.72.91.92

22 Les Bourgeoises ★★$$ Dining here on the baked St. Marcellin cheese on toast, fresh raviolis stuffed with herbed cheese, lamb stew with coriander and ginger, or Indian specialties such as chicken tandoori is like dining in the living room of owner **Martine Robin's** grandmother, and for good reason: the oil paintings, chairs, and tables all come from her grandparents' antique shop. The homemade raspberry liqueur aging in a jar by the front window is, unfortunately, purely decorative. ♦ Lunch and dinner. Closed Monday and Sunday. 12 Rue des Francs-Bourgeois (between Rues de Sévigné and de Turenne). Reservations recommended. Métro: St.-Paul. 42.72.48.30

23 La Maison des Bonbons Crammed with glass jars of chocolate pralines, hazelnut rabbits, and colorful candy letters of the alphabet, **Anne** and **Josef Laurence's** shop is a child's dream come true. Take home some sugared doves, ladybugs, and teddy bears to decorate your child's next birthday cake, and before leaving with your goodies, fortify yourself with a chewy *caramel au beurre salé.* ♦ M-F 11AM-7PM; Sa-Su 2:30-7PM. 46 Rue de Sévigné (between Rues des Francs-Bourgeois and du Parc-Royal). Métros: St.-Paul, Chemin-Vert. 48.87.88.62

23 Romeo Gigli In this sunny showroom, the Italian fashion designer's jewel-like pieces seem to float. Gigli, trained as an architect, is known for fanciful outfits in luminous colors and richly textured fabrics. ♦ Tu-Sa 11AM-7PM. 46 Rue de Sévigné (between Rues des Francs-Bourgeois and du Parc-Royal). Métros: St.-Paul, Chemin-Vert. 48.04.57.05

One look at the kamikaze traffic around the Arc de Triomphe or Place de la Concorde and you'll understand why France leads the Mediterranean in traffic fatalities. According to Pierre Karli, noted Parisian brain specialist and author of the book *L'Homme Aggressif,* French drivers use their automobiles to express their high opinion of themselves and their low estimation of others. In 1988, 1,600 pedestrians were killed and 30,000 were injured; half of those accidents occurred on or within a few meters of a pedestrian crossing.

Many of the streets in Paris have gutters running down the middle, a holdover from the Middle Ages, when water was channeled through to wash them.

Parisians who arrive late to work are hard-pressed to blame the Métro. At rush hour, the subway arrives once every 80 seconds. All cars undergo a weekly maintenance to insure against mechanical breakdowns.

Window-shopping is a favorite pastime everywhere; in France it's known as *léche-vitrine*—which translates literally as "lick the window."

Ground Floor

24 **Carnavalet Hôtel et Musée** The laughing carnival mask sculpted in stone above the gate (facing the Rue des Francs-Bourgeois) of this splendid mansion is a misleading visual pun: this 16th-century building does not conceal a midway of clowns or a family of dancing bears. A truer clue to the building's contents is found in the ship (the symbol of Paris) on the gate (illustrated above). In 1880, the Hôtel Carnavalet was put into service as the Historical Museum of the City of Paris, and today it vividly displays four centuries (1500-1900) of Parisian life. The Hôtel Carnavalet's original 1540 design is attributed to **Pierre Lescot,** who was then architect of the Louvre. The *hôtel* (mansion) was spruced up in 1655 by **François Mansart,** the architect memorialized by the term *mansard* roof. The building's name evolved from an early owner's name, the widow of the Breton **Sire de Kernevency,** whose surname Parisians constantly mispronounced and permanently corrupted to its present form.

The museum has something for everyone, even the most fidgety youngster. On the ground floor (see diagram above) is an entire roomful of old metal shop signs and 18th-century billboards, dating from an age of mass illiteracy. The baker advertised himself with a golden sheaf of wheat, the butcher with a suckling pig, and the locksmith with an ornate iron key. There is also a lively show-and-tell description of the French Revolution; the royal family's itemized laundry bill; the young dauphin's penmanship book; the rope ladder used by a political prisoner to escape from the Bastille; a model of the guillotine; a pair of drums banged by the Revolutionaries; a *Who's Who* of the Revolution in portraits (from crazed **Marat** to stern **Robespierre**); and, finally, perhaps foreshadowing the end of the Reign of Terror, the penknife **Napoléon Bonaparte** used during the Egyptian campaign.

On the second floor (see diagram at right) are exhibitions of fashionable furnishings from the reigns of the last Bourbon kings (**Louis XIV, Louis XV,** and **Louis XVI**), salon murals by **Jean-Honoré Fragonard** and **François Boucher,** and the apartments of **Madame de Sévigné** (1626-96). This "Grande Dame of the Marais" (who was born, baptized, and married in the district) lived at the Hôtel Carnavalet for the last 19 years of her life. Here she entertained the greatest thinkers of the day and,

in her famous *Lettres,* inscribed her witty, incisive observations on the court of Louis XIV. Her association with the royals was not forgotten by well-read Revolutionary hotheads, who a century later exhumed her remains, beheaded the corpse, and triumphantly paraded through Paris with her skull. On your way out, catch Louis XIV, looking rather silly decked out as a Roman general with a wig (the **Antoine Coysevox** courtyard statue was brought here from the Hôtel de Ville), and pass through the current exhibition rooms on the ground floor.
♦ Admission. Tu-Su 10AM-5:40PM. 23 Rue de Sévigné (between Rues des Francs-Bourgeois and du Parc-Royal). Métros: Chemin-Vert, St.-Paul. 42.72.21.13

Second Floor

Maison SUBA

25 Maison Suba A stone's throw from the Place des Vosges you will find a shop full of delicious red pepper conserves and oak-smoked Hungarian sausages. Don't pass up the Tokaji wine, so loved by **King George V**, the father of **Queen Elizabeth II**, that he ordered it in industrial quantities. ♦ Tu-Sa 9AM-1PM, 3-7PM. Closed in August. 11 Rue de Sévigné (between Rues des Francs-Bourgeois and St.-Antoine). Métro: St.-Paul. 48.87.46.06

26 Synagogue The sinuous facade of the only synagogue (1913) designed by **Hector Guimard,** the Art Nouveau architect best known for his sculptural métro entrances, suggests an open book, perhaps the Torah. ♦ Services on Saturday. 10 Rue Pavée (between Rues du Roi de Sicile and des Rosiers). Métro: St.-Paul

26 Rue des Rosiers *Rosiers* means rosebushes and refers to the roses that bloomed nearby within the old medieval city wall, but the fragrances wafting along this narrow, crooked street today are anything but floral. Scents of hot pastrami, steaming borscht, chopped chicken livers, and fresh matzos emanate from the kosher butcher shops, delicatessens, and bakeries that line this street, the *Platzel* of the Jewish quarter since the Middle Ages. The adjoining **Rue des Ecouffes** takes its name from the Lombardian pawnbrokers who were derided as *écouffes,* French for kite, a rapacious bird. A terribly haunting souvenir of the district's history was a plaque that until recently hung outside an elementary school on the street. It read: "165 Jewish children from this school, deported to Germany during World War II, were exterminated in Nazi camps. Never forget." Down this street the Nazis and Vichy French marched and dragged away 75,000 Jews to concentration camps. In **Jo Goldenberg,** the most famous delicatessen on the street, there occurred a more recent tragedy: on 9 August 1982, masked gunmen killed six customers. The PLO took credit, and the gunmen were never caught. ♦ Métro: St.-Paul

26 Le Loir dans la Théière ★★$ With its flea-market furniture, sprung-out sofas, wooden tables, and raffish air, this comfortable tea salon could be in Seattle or Berkeley. The name, "Dormouse in the Teapot," recalls *Alice's Adventures in Wonderland,* as does the mural of other characters from the **Lewis Carroll** fantasy. Yet the light tasty salads and fine homemade cakes and tarts are very real. ♦ Lunch, afternoon tea, and snacks. 3 Rue des Rosiers (between Rues Pavée and Ferdinand-Duval). No credit cards. Métro: St.-Paul. 42.72.90.61

26 Jo Goldenberg ★★$$ The sweet aroma of spiced meat, the clatter of dishes, and, particularly on Sunday afternoon, the babble of strong, animated voices fill this Jewish delicatessen/restaurant. Try the *foie haché* (chopped liver), *poisson farci* (gefilte fish), Cracovian sausages, and strudel, washed down with a cold Pilsen. ♦ Breakfast, lunch, and dinner. Closed Yom Kippur. 7 Rue des Rosiers (at Rue Ferdinand Duval). Reservations recommended. Métro: St.-Paul. 48.87.20.16, 48.87.70.39

27 Rue Pavée The construction of one of the city's first paved (*pavée*) streets was a pioneer achievement in the 14th century, when the city's sinking muddy roads also served as open sewers and pigsties. ♦ Métro: St.-Paul

27 Bibliothèque Historique de la Ville de Paris Designed in 1611 by **Baptiste du Cerceau,** the **Hôtel Lamoignon** (pictured above) has, since 1969, housed the Historical Library of Paris and is a mecca for French historians. The mansion was originally the property of **Diane de France,** the bastard daughter of **Henri II.** As the story goes, young Henri, while traveling in Italy, was in hot pursuit of the **Duchess of Angoulême.** When she refused to leave her house, he burned it down and had her kidnapped and taken to France. Out of their tumultuous union, Diane was born. At age seven, she was legally adopted by the king and given all the rights of nobility, among them this mansion, where she lived until her death at age 82.

This was the city's first private mansion and is adorned with a colossal order of Italianate pilasters. The low triangular pediment is embellished with a stag with antlers, a tribute, naturally, to **Diana,** goddess of the hunt. On a rainy day, the library is one of the best places in Paris to read about Paris. Once in the courtyard, bear right, up the steps to the reading-room door. If you manage to convince

---

Restaurants/Clubs: Red   Hotels: Blue

Shops/ ☂ Outdoors: Green   **Sights/Culture:** Black

the guard you are a visiting scholar, he will give you a reader's card. Take a seat at one of the long wooden tables and gaze up at the gilded beams, one of which is ornamented with a painting of Diana and the hunt. ◆ M-Sa 9:30AM-6PM. Closed holidays and last two weeks of August. 24 Rue Pavée (between Rues des Rosiers and Mahler). Métro: St.-Paul. 42.74.44.44

28 La Tartine ★★★$ This is the oldest wine bar in Paris, owned for 70 years by the family of **Monsieur Bouscarel**, who selects the stock of more than 60 wines himself. He buys directly from Burgundy, Bordeaux, Rhône, and Loire Valley producers, keeping the prices down and the quality up. The café is always filled with a vibrant mix of ages and personalities, happily sipping wine and munching on *tartines*, simple sandwiches on *pain poilâne* filled with pâté, cheese, ham, or sausage. ◆ Breakfast, lunch, and snacks; lunch and snacks only on Wednesday. Closed Tuesday. 24 Rue de Rivoli (between Rues des Ecouffes and Ferdinand-Duval). Métros: Hôtel-de-Ville, St.-Paul. 42.72.76.85

29 Le Roi du Falaffel-Rosiers Alimentation North African grocers offer *hummus,* Israeli dishes, and falafel sandwiches to go. ◆ M-F, Su 10AM-8:30PM; M-F, Su 10AM-10PM in winter. 34 Rue des Rosiers (between Rues Pavée and Vieille-du-Temple). Métro: St.-Paul. 48.87.63.60

30 Finkelsztajn Since 1851 a Jewish bakery has operated at this address, and today **Sacha Finkelsztajn** carries on the tradition, producing the richest cheesecake this side of Manhattan's Second Avenue. The affable baker offers newcomers a free taste of her Polish herring, chicken liver, and eggplant purée. ◆ W-Su 9:30AM-1:30PM, 3-7:30PM. Closed 1 July to mid-August, and one week in winter. 27 Rue des Rosiers (between Rues Vieille-du-Temple and des Ecouffes). Métro: St.-Paul. 42.72.78.91

30 Au Petit Fer à Cheval ★★★$ Named after its 1903 marble-topped horseshoe *(fer à cheval)* bar, this neighborhood café offers lunchtime *plats du jour* in its back room, where one of the booths is an old wooden métro seat. ◆ Breakfast, lunch, and snacks; lunch and snacks only on Saturday and Sunday. 30 Rue Vieille-du-Temple (between Rues du Trésor and des Rosiers). Métros: Hôtel-de-Ville, St.-Paul. 42.72.47.47

31 Le Loft A faint fragrance of fresh polish permeates this three-story warehouse of English antique imports. French Anglophiles

shop here for old pine towel rails and three-door wardrobes. ◆ M-Sa 10AM-7PM. 17bis Rue Pavée (between Rues des Rosiers and Mahler). Métro: St.-Paul. 48.87.46.50

32 Smart/Société des Métiers d'Art Hand-painted tiles and ceramics by a score of French craftspeople scattered from Alsace to Provence are sold here. You can reconstruct the Place des Vosges in terracotta tile miniatures of the 17th-century town houses or assemble a fantasy Gallic village with little tiles of a French bakery, café, butcher shop, pharmacy, school, and church. Other items on Smart's bestseller list are Marseillaise tarot cards in tile, and brass European faucets. A victim of its own success, it is now open only by appointment. ◆ Closed in August. 22 Rue des Francs-Bourgeois (between Rues Elzévir and Payenne). Métro: St.-Paul. 42.77.41.24

32 Marais Plus Formerly a bookstore and tea salon, this jumble is now a *boutique en movement,* with an ever-changing stock of postcards, globes, dolls, stuffed animals, Christmas decorations, and handmade ceramic tea services. Alas, the books have disappeared, but the tearoom still serves delicious tarts, salads, and desserts, plus brunch on Sunday and plum pudding at Christmas. ◆ Daily 10AM-7PM. 20 Rue des Francs-Bourgeois (at Rue Payenne). Métro: St.-Paul. 48.87.01.40

33 Luthier François Perrin buys, sells, makes, and restores violins, violas, bows, guitars, harps, and old instruments in these quarters of the **Hôtel de Savourny**. ◆ M-F 9:30AM-noon, 2:30-6:30PM; Sa 9:30AM-12:30PM, 2:30-7PM. 4 Rue Elzévir (between Rues des Francs-Bourgeois and du Parc-Royal). Métro: St.-Paul. 42.77.68.42

33 Musée Cognacq-Jay This marvelously complete collection of 18th-century art was acquired by the husband-and-wife team of **Louise Jay** and **Ernest Cognacq,** who created the Samaritaine department stores and boasted of never having set foot in the Louvre. The collection was moved to the five-story, 16th-century **Hôtel Donon,** and the works of **Boucher, Tiepolo, Watteau, Fragonard, Greuze, La Tour, Rembrandt, Gainsborough,** and **Reynolds** are as well-displayed here as they were in their old home on Boulevard des Capucines. There's also a remarkable set of perfume cases and snuffboxes as well as **Meissen** porcelain statuettes. ◆ Admission. Tu-Su 10AM-5:40PM. 8 Rue Elzévir (between Rues des Francs-Bourgeois and Barbette). Métro: St.-Paul. 40.27.07.21

33 Maison Mansart The ground floor of the house **François Mansart** built for himself (and inhabited until his death in 1666) now houses **Alain Thiollier's** stark, high-ceilinged gallery, which exhibits contemporary works by an international group of artists. Thiollier's mother lives upstairs in Mansart's old flat, and on the second floor is a strange positivist chapel (with an altar inscribed to "Humanism") built by a Brazilian follower of French positivist **Auguste Comte.** The chapel is not open to the public, but inquire about the occasional string-quartet concerts. ♦ Gallery: Tu-Sa 3-7PM. 5 Rue Payenne (between Rues des Francs-Bourgeois and du Parc-Royal). Métro: St.-Paul. 45.74.45.90. Gallery: 48.87.41.03

34 Musée Bricard et Musée de la Serrure/ Bricard Showrooms Roman door knockers, medieval chastity belts, and the key of the now-destroyed **Cimetière des Innocents** may be seen in the changing exhibits of this small, quirky museum, established by the time-honored locksmithing company Bricard and housed in the **Hôtel Libéral Bruant.** (Architect Bruant built this mansion as his personal residence, and it is considered his most important work after the **Hôtel des Invalides** and the **Salpêtrière** chapel.) The museum has been relegated to the building's vaulted cellar while the Bricard showrooms upstairs are happy to sell you handmade replicas of some of the museum pieces, such as the lock to **Marie Antoinette's** Versailles apartments. Here you can also examine the rich detailing and historical styles of other Bricard products. ♦ Museum: M-F 2-5PM. Showroom: M-F 8:30AM-12:30PM, 1:30-5:30PM. 1 Rue de la Perle (at Rue Elzévir). Métros: Chemin-Vert, St.-Paul. Museum: 42.77.79.62. Showroom: 42.77.71.68

35 Musée Picasso The museum was opened by French **President François Mitterrand** on 23 September 1985. It had taken two other French presidents, five ministers of culture, and 11 years to establish. In the first month alone, it received 80,000 visitors.

"Give me a museum and I'll fill it up," said **Pablo Picasso,** perhaps the 20th century's most important and prolific painter. His wish was granted posthumously in the form of the **Hôtel Salé.** The man who epitomized outlaw modernism yet preferred ancient houses would have been happy with this 17th-century building. Today the mansion enshrines the artist's collection of his own works, the largest in the world: 203 paintings, 158 sculptures, 16 collages, 29 relief paintings, 88 ceramics, 30 sketchbooks, more than 1,500 drawings, and numerous prints, including the *Vollard Suite,* his neoclassical etchings created in the 1920s. The museum also houses Picasso's personal art collection, including works by **Matisse, Renoir, Cézanne, Braque, Balthus,** and Le Douanier **Rousseau.**

In December 1912 at the age of 31, Picasso began to hoard his own work. He wrote his dealer, **Daniel Henry Kahnweiler,** that he would keep five paintings a year, as well as his self-portraits, family portraits, and most of his sculpture. For 70 years Picasso also made a habit of holding on to the works he painted during the week of his birthday, 25 October.

When Picasso died on 8 April 1973 with no will, France's tax collectors were quick to pounce on his estate. In lieu of $65 million in inheritance taxes, Picasso's heirs donated one-quarter of his collection to the state. **Dominique Bozo** (former chief curator of the Museum of Modern Art at the Pompidou Center) and a team of Picasso experts carved up the artist's pie for France. Ironically, as late as 1945, France owned only three Picassos in public collections, a handful far outnumbered by the many in the possession of the Museum of Modern Art in New York.

The Hôtel Salé has but a few of Picasso's masterpieces: *Still Life with Caned Chair, Two Women Running on Beach,* and the neoclassical *Pipes of Pan* among them. However, his collection is exhibited chronologically, and the work affords an extraordinary odyssey through the artist's growth and psyche. Furthermore, revealing Picasso memorabilia are sprinkled throughout the museum: photos of Picasso at bullfights, posing on the beach with a fig leaf, hoisting a bull's skull at the beach of Golfe-Juan, playing with his children, and consorting with friends such as **Jean Cocteau** and **Max Jacob.**

Throughout the museum are portraits of the women in Picasso's life: **Olga Kokhlova,** the Russian dancer; **Marie-Thérèse Walter,** the 17-year-old earth mother; **Dora Maar,** the intellectual; **Françoise Gilot,** the painter; and his widow, **Jacqueline.** Picasso wrote, "1935-1939 was the worst time of my life." But it was the best time for his art. During those years, he broke with Olga, fathered a child with Marie-Thérèse, and then turned to

Dora Maar. The pictures he produced in that period are particularly violent, such as *Cat Seizing a Bird* and the grotesque feminine figure of *Woman in a Red Chair.* Personal anguish mixed with outrage at Franco's butchery in Picasso's native Spain is expressed in his surreal print *The Dream and Lie of Franco,* which presages the theme and force of his masterwork, *Guernica.*

You could spend the entire day wandering through the museum, but if it's 11:30AM and you've got a 1PM lunch date, it is best to concentrate on the second-floor collection, then sample the sculpture in the basement on your way out. Here are a few highlights: **Room 1** brings you face-to-face with one of his Blue Period masterpieces, the wintry 1901 *Self-Portrait at Age 20,* which shows him looking gaunt in a mangy beard and an overcoat to ward off the drafts that doubtlessly plagued his bohemian existence. The influences of **Toulouse-Lautrec** and **van Gogh** are particularly evident in the Expressionist deathbed portrait of the poet **Casagemas**. **Rooms 2** and **3** contain sketches and drawings inspired by **Cézanne's** geometrical style and by the primitive sculpture from Africa and New Caledonia that so fascinated Picasso and ultimately led to the creation of *Les Demoiselles d'Avignon.* **Room 4,** especially *Still Life with Caned Chair,* portrays his years of cubist inquiry (1909-1917) with **Georges Braque.** The next several rooms feature his paper collages and three-dimensional paintings made of cigar-box wood, newspapers, and metal shards. Musical instruments, such as guitars and mandolins, recur throughout Picasso's work, but as he once told a friend: "Music has never interested me." It was the womanly shape of the guitar rather than its sound that sparked his imagination. **Room 5** contains the best of the 60 works in Picasso's collection: masterpieces by **Matisse, Braque, Rousseau,** and **Cézanne.** Of the latter, Picasso told the photographer **Brassaï** in 1943: "Do I know Cézanne! He's my one and only master."

The museum crescendos in **Room 6** with *La Lecture de la Lettre* and *The Pipes of Pan* from his classical period. The minuscule side room (**6B**) is devoted entirely to Picasso's theater and costume designs, created in collaboration with **Cocteau, Massine, Stravinsky,** and **Diaghilev.** Near the end of his life, Picasso's art became childlike and cartoonish. The last painting in the collection, dated 14 April 1972, is called *Young Painter,* a sketchy thing of a smiling dauber. In his final years the artist confessed, "It has taken all my life to learn how to paint like a child again." Picasso's playfulness is perhaps most evident in his sculpture, which is fashioned from an amusing assortment of odds and ends. En route to the exit, descend into the museum's basement to find his sculpture collection, with originals of his celebrated monkey, goat, and skipping girl.

Hôtel Salé was built from 1655 to 1659 by architect **Jean Bouillier** for **Pierre Aubert de Fontenay,** a man who got rich collecting taxes on salt (hence *Salé*) for the king. With the fall of **Nicolas Fouquet** (1615-1680), **Louis XIV's** greedy finance minister, Aubert lost his job, his house, and finally, in 1668, his life.

Later the Hôtel Salé was leased to the embassy of the Venetian Republic and the naval minister of **Louis XVI.** After the Revolution, in 1793, it became a boys school (**Balzac** studied here), a science laboratory, and, from 1887 to 1964, an exhibition hall for a bronze foundry. After Picasso's death, Minister of Culture **Michel Guy** secured a 99-year lease on the building from the City of Paris, and the government spent some 65 million francs on its restoration.

Roland Simounet, winner of the 1977 Grand Prix for Architecture, was selected to design the museum. Simounet's plan preserved the architectural integrity of the building while doubling its interior space from 3,000 to 6,000 square meters. A design detail lost on most visitors: the museum's extraordinary benches, tables, and light fixtures were fashioned by the late **Diego Giacometti,** brother of artist **Alberto.** ♦ Admission. M, Th-Su 9AM-5PM (ticket window closes at 4:30PM); W 9AM-10PM (ticket window closes at 9:15PM). 5 Rue de Thorigny (between Rues de la Perle and des Coutures-St.-Gervais). Métros: St.-Paul, St.-Sébastien-Froissart. 42.71.25.21

Within the Musée Picasso:

Museum Restaurant ★$ A small, attractive tea salon serving salads, quiche, soups, grilled salmon, and fruit tarts. ♦ Breakfast, lunch, and afternoon tea. Closed Tuesday. 42.71.25.21

36 Galerie Philippe Uzzan The only gallery in Paris devoted to architecture, Uzzan shows the work of international designers who have become as famous for their concepts as for their constructions. Videos, photos, drawings, sketches, models, and installations are all used to explain the process architects go through. The projects of **Thom Mayne, Diller and Scofidio, Daniel Liebeskind, Michele Saee, Peter Eisenman, Steven Holl,** and partners **Odile Decq** and **Benoît Cornette** are exhibited here. ♦ Tu-F 3-7PM; Sa noon-7PM. 11 Rue de Thorigny (between Rues des Coutures-St.-Gervais and Debelleyme). Métro: St.-Sébastien-Froissart. 44.59.83.00

36 Galerie Yvon Lambert Works by **Lewitt, Twombly, Oppenheim, Schnabel,** and **Christo** are showcased here. ♦ Tu-F 10AM-1PM, 2:30-7PM; Sa 10AM-7PM. Closed in August. 108 Rue Vieille-du-Temple (between Rues Debelleyme and des Coutures-St.-Gervais). Métro: St.-Sébastien-Froissart. 42.71.09.33

37 A l'Image du Grenier sur l'Eau Brothers **Yves** and **Sylvain Di Maria** have spent the last decade assembling this remarkable collection of more than one million vintage postcards of locales from Avignon to Zaire and a universe of images in between, each one for sale. They also carry French publicity photos from the 1950s and the same turn-of-the-century aristocratic illustrations that decorate the walls of Maxim's. ♦ M-F 10AM-7PM; Sa 2-7PM. 45 Rue des Francs-Bourgeois (between Rues Hospitalières-St.-Gervais and Malher). Métro: St.-Paul. 42.71.02.31

37 Janine Kaganski Exquisite 18th-century hand-painted wedding chests and armoires from France, Austria, and the Rhine Valley are presented in this shop. ♦ M-Sa 11AM-6:30PM; Su by appointment. 41 Rue des Francs-Bourgeois (between Rues Hospitalières-St.-Gervais and Malher). Métro: St.-Paul. 48.87.94.73

38 Boutique Filofax Here you'll find everything to gratify your Filofax fetish. The famous pocket-size, three-ring English notebooks come in myriad styles, from black leather to rubber, and with notepaper of every hue. Also in stock are sheaves of maps, calendars, and metric conversion charts to store in your portable file cabinet as well as a beautiful collection of handmade sterling silver pens. ♦ M-Sa 11AM-7PM. Closed in August. 32 Rue des Francs-Bourgeois (between Rues Vieille-du-Temple and Elzévir). Métro: St.-Paul. 42.78.67.87

39 Jules des Prés The most extraordinary dried flower arrangements in Europe are created here. The hyper-affluent clientele, which includes designers **Christian Lacroix**, **Karl Lagerfeld**, and **Christian Dior**, doesn't flinch at spending $1,200 on a basket of cinnamon sticks, bay leaves, and juniper berries. After all, it's an investment and won't wilt or need watering. ♦ M-Sa 11AM-7PM. Closed in August. 46 Rue du Roi-de-Sicile (between Rues des Ecouffes and Vieille-du-Temple). Métro: St.-Paul. 48.04.79.49

40 Mariage Frères ★★★$$ Everything that involves tea is treated as an art at this tea boutique and *salon de thé*. The handsome shop sells hundreds of teas stored in smart black canisters lining the walls, along with teapots, sugars, spices, tea cakes, and jams. In the dining room, tea is served with a selection of scones, muffins, and pastries, as well as a superb brunch and lunch. ♦ Tea salon: Brunch, lunch, and afternoon tea. Shop: 10:30AM-7:30PM. Closed Mondays in August. 30-32 Rue du Bourg-Tibourg (between Rues Ste.-Croix-de-la-Bretonnerie and du Roi-de-Sicile). Métros: St.-Paul, Hôtel-de-Ville. 42.72.28.11. Also at: 13 Rue des Grands-Augustin. 40.51.82.50

41 Hôtel des Ambassadeurs de Hollande When this baroque mansion (built in 1660) was named, there were no Dutch

ambassadors to France, and none has ever lived here. Subsequently rebuilt by **Pierre Cottard**, the *hôtel's* most famous resident was **Caron de Beaumarchais,** author of *The Marriage of Figaro* and *The Barber of Seville.* The great wooden doors are embellished by what looks like howling Medusas or perhaps a pair of baritones warming up. ♦ 47 Rue Vieille-du-Temple (between Rues Ste.-Croix-de-la-Bretonnerie and des Blancs-Manteaux). Métro: St.-Paul

42 Le Dômarais ★$$$ Covered by a glass rotunda, sumptuously adorned with scarlet walls and bronze statues, this trading house-turned-restaurant oozes romance. Tucked away on a quiet courtyard, it provides the perfect setting for an intimate dinner. ♦ Lunch and dinner; dinner only on Sunday. Closed Monday, Saturday, and in August. 53bis Rue des Francs-Bourgeois (between Rues Vielle-du-Temple and des Archives). Reservations recommended. Métro: Rambuteau. 42.74.54.17

42 Crédit Municipal de Paris Paris' first municipal pawnshop is still a place for hocking ("putting it on the nail," as the French say). Auctions, especially for jewelry, are frequent and well-attended; check the notices posted outside. ♦ 55 Rue des Francs-Bourgeois (between Rues des Archives and Vieille-du-Temple). Métro: Rambuteau. 42.71.25.43

Gourmet Take-Away

Whether you're purchasing hors d'oeuvres for the holidays or preparing a romantic picnic for two, here's where you can buy some of France's finest food:

Beauvilliers Celebrate the holidays with delicacies from this superb spot in Montmartre. 52 Rue Lamarck, 42.54.54.42.

Fauchon This renowned supermarket can fulfill all your gastronomic needs. 24 Place de la Madeleine, 47.42.60.11.

Lenotre Foie gras and *bûches de Noël* (traditional French cakes shaped like Yule logs) are among the holiday specialties at this shop in St.-Germain. 44 Rue d'Auteuill, 45.24.52.52.

Guy Savoy Near the Arc de Triomphe, this famous restaurant makes excellent foie gras. 18 Rue Troyon, 43.80.40.61.

Vigneau-Desmarets An excellent St.-Germain address for turkey and *poulet de Bresse* (guinea hen). 107 Rue de Sèvres, 45.48.04.73.

Vignon Wonderful *boudin blanc* (white sausage) with truffles is among the delicious offerings at this Champs-Elysées restaurant. 14 Rue Marbeuf, 47.20.24.26.

Restaurants/Clubs: Red	Hotels: Blue
Shops/ ♦Outdoors: Green	**Sights/Culture:** Black

Picard Surgelés Who said the French are all food snobs? The brave new world of French frozen food is displayed in this chilly, sterile mart (one of a chain of stores in Paris) that sells microwave ovens and anything you might want to defrost in them. Press your nose against the glass, watch Parisians wheel shopping carts around yellow, blue, and red freezers looking for tonight's TV dinner, and ask yourself what Julia Child would say. ♦ M-W, F-Su 9AM-7:30PM; Th 9AM-8PM. 48 Rue des Francs-Bourgeois (between Rues Vieille-du-Temple and des Archives). Métros: Rambuteau, Hôtel-de-Ville. 42.72.17.83

43 Archives Nationales/Musée de l'Histoire de France The letters of **Joan of Arc** and **Voltaire,** the wills of **Louis XIV** and **Napoléon I,** a papyrus signed by Merovingian **King Dagobert** (622-638), the Edict of Nantes, the Declaration of the Rights of Man, and six billion other documents are stored on 175 miles of shelves in this admirable 18th-century mansion, the former **Hôtel Soubise.** Even if you have no interest in scrapbook French history, the museum's fortified turrets, colonnaded courtyard (72 Corinthian columns in all), and the riot of rococo in the **Oval Salon** make a visit worthwhile. Designed by **Alexis Delamaier** for **François de Rohan,** the prince of Soubise, the ornate interior (1739) was engineered by **Germain Boffrand,** a pupil of François Mansart. Boffrand hired the best artists of the day, among them **François Boucher** and **Charles Natoire,** to decorate the *hôtel.* The archives, housed in the Hôtel Soubise since 1808, took over the adjacent **Hôtel de Rohan** in 1927. ♦ Admission. M-F 9AM-5PM. 60 Rue des Francs-Bourgeois (at Rue des Archives). Métros: Hôtel-de-Ville, Rambuteau. 40.27.60.00

44 Hôtel de Rohan In 1705 the son of **François de Rohan,** prince-bishop of Strasbourg, commissioned **Alexis Delamaier** to build a mansion opposite the **Hôtel Soubise,** where his parents lived. In the courtyard to the right, above the entrance to the former stables, is one of the masterpieces of 18th-century French sculpture: **Robert Le Lorrain's** superb relief-sculpture *The Watering of the Horses of the Sun.* The building sometimes houses temporary exhibitions. ♦ 87 Rue Vieille-du-Temple (between Rues des Francs-Bourgeois and des Quatre-Fils). Métro: Rambuteau

45 Rue des Archives For generations, the lower section of this street bore the name *Rue où Dieu fut boulli* (The street where God was boiled) after the legend of the moneylender who stabbed a communion wafer with his knife, then threw it into a steaming pot, where to his astonishment it began to bleed. ♦ Métro: Hôtel-de-Ville

45 Musée de la Chasse et de la Nature (Museum of the Hunt) Housed in a portion of the **Hôtel de Guénégaud** (1654) and designed by **François Mansart,** this museum presents three floors full of hunting paraphernalia and related items, including crossbows, muskets, game trophies, whole stuffed animals, and paintings of hunting dogs and animals by the likes of **Rubens** and **Brueghel.** Among the most lavish paeans to the slaughter are the paintings of **Desportes,** the court artist employed by **Louis XIV** to portray the royal hunts at Versailles. This museum is a favorite of children.
♦ Admission. M, W-Su 10AM-12:30PM, 1:30-5:30PM. 60 Rue des Archives (at Rue des Quatre-Fils). Métros: Hôtel-de-Ville, Rambuteau. 42.72.86.43

Les Halles

The area known as *Les Halles* (the marketplace) takes its name from the great wholesale food market that began here in 1100. The market operated until the mid-1970s, when it was moved to Rungis near Orly Airport, leaving behind *le trou* (the hole, which later was filled by an underground shopping mall known as the **Forum des Halles** and a perimeter consisting of the **St.-Eustache Church** and several old all-night restaurants serving onion soup and pig's feet.

As recently as a few decades ago, it was occupied by a run-down garment district and slum that stretched between the St.-Merri Church and the old food market. The opening of the Forum des Halles and the **Georges Pompidou Center** in the late 1970s brought new commercial life into the area (as well as architectural controversy). Retired food vendors now share their turf with hordes of tourists, mall-bound French youths, and upscale professionals who come to take in the local color.

The inclined plaza west of the Georges Pompidou Center is now home to an impromptu circus of folksingers, hypnotists, kerosene garglers, sword-swallowers, Hare Krishnas, rowdies, acrobats, jugglers, and (may you be forewarned) purse snatchers and panhandlers who prey on gawking tourists.

46 Gambrinus A beer drinker's paradise, Gambrinus offers 400 kinds of brew-to-go from 34 countries and 200 sorts of whiskey, enough to please the sophisticated sipper or the gargantuan guzzler. ♦ M 3-8PM; Tu, Th-F 11AM-1:30PM, 3-8PM; W 11AM-1:30PM, 3-10PM; Sa 9AM-1:30PM, 3-8PM. 13-15 Rue des Blancs-Manteaux (at Rue Aubriot). Métro: Rambuteau. 42.76.03.52

47 Rue de la Verrerie This narrow street, which takes its name from the 11th-century glassblowers guild, is where **Jacquemin Gringoneur** once lived. He invented playing cards to amuse **King Charles VI** ("The Beloved"), who ruled from 1380 to 1422. ♦ Métro: Hôtel-de-Ville

48 Lescene-Dura Since 1875 this sprawling wine-lover's warehouse has been offering all manner of enological paraphernalia, from corkscrews to champagne buckets. ♦ Tu-Sa

9:30AM-1PM, 2-7PM. Closed two weeks in August. 63 Rue de la Verrerie (between Rues du Renard and du Temple). Métro: Hôtel-de-Ville. 42.72.08.74

49 Vieux Marais $$ Redecorated with Chinese carpets and floral wallpaper, this 30-room hotel always gives guests a warm welcome. ♦ 8 Rue du Plâtre (between Rues du Temple and des Archives). Métro: Rambuteau. 42.78.47.22

50 The Studio ★★$$ In the adjoining dance studio courtyard, this Tex-Mex canteen throws the hottest Fourth of July party in Paris. ♦ Dinner; lunch Saturday and Sunday. 41 Rue du Temple (between Rues St.-Merri and Simon-le-Franc). Métro: Rambuteau. 42.74.10.38

51 Café de la Cité ★★$ No wider than a bowling alley, this café/luncheonette has become one of the most popular pit stops in the area. Decorated with wooden pinwheel fans and prints of old Breton sailing vessels (the owner comes from Brittany), this is where you can get tasty *plats du jour,* and the management boasts that you can order, eat, and head out the door in less than 30 minutes. ♦ Breakfast, lunch, and dinner. Closed Sunday. 22 Rue Rambuteau (between Rues Beaubourg and du Temple). Reservations required for dinner. Métro: Rambuteau. 42.78.56.36

52 Musée de la Musique Mécanique This private collection features more than one hundred music machines, from mechanized trumpets to the curious pianola for which **Debussy** and **Stravinsky** composed some works. ♦ Admission. Sa-Su, holidays 2-7PM. Impasse Berthaud (off Rue Beaubourg). Métro: Rambuteau. 42.71.99.54

52 Galerie Daniel Templon Modeled after New York's SoHo galleries, Daniel Templon helped launch conceptual art, language art, and a good deal of the "Support Surface" movement in France. ♦ Tu-F 10AM-1PM, 2:30-7PM; Sa 10AM-7PM. Closed in August. 30 Rue Beaubourg (between Rues Rambuteau and Michel-le-Comte). Métro: Rambuteau. 42.72.14.10

53 Le Tango To dance here cheek-to-cheek among Brylcreem dandies and perfumed widows is to enter a time warp that leads back to 1906, when the tango first hit Paris. Calypsos, salsas, beguines—any beat but disco—are danced to all night long. This club is authentic and cheap. ♦ W-Sa 11PM-5AM. 13 Rue au Maire (at Rue Volta). Métro: Arts-et-Métiers. 42.72.17.78

54 404 ★★★$$ The small open kitchen puts bowls of exotic spices, plates of delicate pastries, and simple cooking techniques on display, all of which infuse this North African restaurant with an artistic ambience and heavenly aromas. Tasting one of the *tagines,* succulent stews of delicately blended meats with fruit, vegetables, and spices served in ceramic pots, is pure bliss. Choose a bottle of Moroccan wine to go with your meal, lean back on the plump pillows, observe the hip-looking Parisians at the tables around you, and try to guess the source of the restaurant's name (unless you're a car buff, you'll fail; the Peugeot 404 was a very popular car in both France and North America in the 1960s). ♦ Dinner. Closed Sunday and last two weeks of August. 69 Rue des Gravilliers (between Rues Beaubourg and St.-Martin). Métro: Arts-et-Métiers. 42.74.57.81

55 Rue du Vert-Bois The remains of the walls of **St.-Martin-des-Champs** date from 1270. An inflammatory letter from **Victor Hugo** is said to have saved the wall from demolition. ♦ Métro: Temple

56 St.-Nicolas-des-Champs Construction on this church began in the 12th century, and it has acquired distinguished features throughout the ages: a flamboyant Gothic facade, a Renaissance doorway, and many 17th-, 18th-, and 19th-century paintings. ♦ M-Sa 9AM-7PM; Su 9:30AM-noon. 254 Rue St.-Martin (at Rue Réaumur). Métro: Arts-et-Métiers. 42.72.92.54

57 Musée National des Techniques This extraordinary collection of 80,000 machines traces the evolution of science from the 16th century onward. Housed in an Orwellian juxtaposition of religion and technology, part of the museum is in the remains of the **St.-Martin-des-Champs** priory, one of the finest naves to survive the Middle Ages. The museum is undergoing a complete renovation and is scheduled to reopen in 1995. The project has been slowed because workers came across important archaeological artifacts in the museum's chapel, many of them dating from before the 10th century. The Laboratory Antoine-Laurent, showing the origins of modern chemistry from the end of the 18th century, will continue to stay open during the period of renovation. ♦ Admission. Tu-Su 10AM-5:30PM. Closed holidays; free on Sunday. 292 Rue St.-Martin (at Rue Réaumur). Métros: Réaumur-Sebastopol, Strasbourg-St.-Denis. 40.27.23.71, 40.27.22.20, 40.27.23.31

58 Porte St.-Martin In 1674 **Pierre Bullet** constructed this arch after plans made by **François Blondel** for Porte St.-Denis. These two triumphal arches, astride the most important routes leading to the north, were erected by the Sun King to announce the grandeur of the French capital to visitors at the very time he had moved to Versailles and was tearing down the 13th-century city wall. ♦ Métro: Strasbourg-St.-Denis

59 La Chope des Artistes ★★$ This simple café and cocktail bar is a place to relax. Artists, actors, and neighborhood residents sip Long Island Ice Teas and toss back B52s while disheveled songwriter **Jacques Delaporte** plays the piano. Equilibrate the drinks with light meals such as *salade de chèvre chaud, tagliatelles au saumon,* and country ham sandwiches. ♦ Breakfast, lunch, dinner, and late-night. Closed Sunday. 48 Rue du Faubourg-St.-Martin (between Passage du Marché and Blvd St.-Martin). Métro: Strasbourg-St.-Denis, Château-d'Eau. 42.02.86.76

60 Porte St.-Denis At the intersection of Rue St.-Denis and Boulevard Bonne-Nouvelle stands this consciously Roman-style triumphal arch (illustrated above) celebrating **Louis XIV's** victorious battles in Flanders and the Rhineland. **François Blondel** modeled the gigantic arch after the Arch of Titus in Rome; **Charles Le Brun's** allegorical sculptured adornments were inspired by the reliefs on Trajan's Column. ♦ Métro: Strasbourg-St.-Denis

61 Café Café/Art Blue Café ★★$$ Skip the overpriced, overrated pre-show dinner at the nearby Folies Bergère and head for this relaxed, candlelit spot run by the agreeable **Charles-Eric Plante** and his dog **Lou Lou.** This café-cum-art gallery-cum-restaurant offers a refuge in the heart of the bustling wholesale clothing district, a lively neighborhood that is quickly being rediscovered by the arty crowd. The diverse café sports monthly *cercles de poésies* (poetry readings) and *vernissages* (gallery openings) that include dinner with the artist and live piano music. Homestyle dishes that would please a French grandmother include *cassolette d'escargots forestière* (wild mushroom and escargot casserole) and *poulet de Marengo* (the meal Napoléon ate after his victory at Marengo). Among the dessert highlights are *aumonière au Grand Marnier* (a crêpe envelope containing Grand Marnier-soaked cake) and homemade fruit

tarts. ♦ Breakfast, lunch, dinner, and late-night. Closed Sunday. Call for information on poetry readings and gallery openings. 27 Rue d'Enghien (between Rues d'Hauteville and du Faubourg-St.-Denis). Métros: Bonne-Nouvelle, Château-d'Eau. 44.79.02.02

61 Folies Bergère This music hall institution has showcased high-kicking, semi-nude women since 1868. Times have changed, but this cabaret hasn't noticed. Newly renovated, the Folies Bergère has revamped its variety show to give more of a Latin twist to the choreography. But, not to worry—the women may be wearing fewer sequins, but underneath the pompoms and feathers, they're still *au naturel.* All is not salacious, however. The first act includes impersonators who pay tribute to legendary French entertainers **Edith Piaf, Maurice Chevalier, Josephine Baker,** and **Mistinguett.** ♦ Pre-show/dinner at 7:30; Show at 9:30. Closed Monday. 32 Rue Richer (between Rues Saulnier and Trévise). Reservations are required. Métros: Cadet, Rue Montmartre. 44.79.98.98

62 Ambassade d'Auvergne ★★$$ Run by Italian **Joseph Petrucci** and his auvergnat wife, this rustic restaurant is adorned with flickering oil lamps, a roaring fire, and cured hams dangling from heavy wood beams. Hearty *Massif Central* cuisine is served here, from *loulus* (pot-au-feu) and *loujus* (roast suckling pig) to lentil cassoulet and blood sausage with chestnuts. ♦ Dinner. 22 Rue du Grenier-St.-Lazare (between Rues St.-Martin and Beaubourg). Reservations recommended. Métro: Rambuteau. 42.72.31.22

63 Defender of Time Inspired by the Rathaus clock in Munich, the one-ton **Jacques Monestier** kinetic sculpture (1975) in oxidized brass sends a sword-brandishing warrior to do battle with a bird, a crab, and a dragon (representing the three elements: air, water, and earth). As every hour strikes, one of the beasts attacks, and at noon, 6PM, and 10PM, the Defender of Time is forced to take on all the creatures at once, always emerging victorious. A bit kitschy (as is this whole mini-shopping mall, the **Quartier de l'Horloge**), but young children love it. ♦ Rue Brantôme (at Rue Bernard de Clairvaux). Métro: Rambuteau

The length of the average French business lunch is 124 minutes, compared to the average American business lunch of 67 minutes.

Restaurants/Clubs: Red   **Hotels:** Blue

Shops/ 🌳Outdoors: Green   **Sights/Culture:** Black

64 Espace Vit'Halles
This popular health club, started in 1983 by French Olympic wrestler **Christophe Andanson** and his wife, **Claudy,** has become one of the hottest underground (in a literal sense) singles spots in the district. Among the more than one thousand members are Pompidou Center staffers flocking to aerobics classes and young Bourse financiers pumping iron as a respite from lusting after gold. The clean and affordable facilities include a sauna, a Jacuzzi, tanning rooms, bodybuilding equipment, and a juice bar. Memberships are available for one day, one week, and longer. ♦ M-F 8AM-10PM; Sa 11AM-7PM; Su 11AM-3PM. 48 Rue Rambuteau (at Rue Brantôme). Métro: Rambuteau. 42.77.21.71

ESPACE VIT'HALLES

65 Centre Georges Pompidou/Centre National d'Art et Culture Critics took to calling the five-story jumble of glass and steel the "gasworks" and wondered "who forgot to take the scaffolding down?" Still, this surrealistic Tinkertoy of modern culture is the biggest attraction in Paris, outdrawing both the Louvre and the Eiffel Tower. One million people visited in 1977 during the first seven weeks it was open; more than half the visitors are under age 25. Created at the behest of then **President Georges Pompidou** (1911-1974) and designed by Italian **Renzo Piano** and Englishman **Richard Rogers** (whose proposal was selected from among a field of 681), the revolutionary (some say revolting) structure houses a modern art museum, the city's largest public library (with more than half a million books), one of the world's most advanced computer music centers, a language library, a children's theater and dance workshop, and a fifth-floor restaurant with a four-star view. Pompidou, who was a patron of modern art as well as a politician, is immortalized by **Victor Vasarely** in a hexagonal portrait that hangs on the ground floor.

The high-tech design concept of the center celebrates the building's functional parts (heating ducts, ventilator shafts, stairways, and elevators) by brightly color-coding them: red means vertical circulation, green means water, blue is for air, yellow for electricity, and white for structure. An escalator in a Plexiglas tube snakes up the front of the Pompidou. Even if you aren't moved by the **Salvador Dalí** portrait of **Lenin** dancing on piano keys, which is exhibited on the fourth floor, you should still ride up and, once there, scan one of the city's best-loved vistas, the view over the Right Bank rooftops. Unfortunately, innovation and popularity carry a price: the Pompidou is showing wear and tear in tarnished steel, peeling paint, and shredded carpets. Architects blame not just the crowds but the design. "To put the bones and intestines outside the skin," said one, "is to invite health problems." ♦ M, W-F noon-10PM; Sa-Su 10AM-10PM. Métros: Châtelet-Les Halles, Hôtel-de-Ville, Rambuteau. 44.78.12.33

Within the Centre Georges Pompidou:

Musée d'Art Moderne The third and fourth floors of the Pompidou Center display one of the world's largest collections of modern and contemporary art. Beginning with **Rousseau's** *Snake Charmer* and ending with the museum's up-to-the-minute acquisitions, the collection includes works by the greatest artists of the 20th century: **Picasso, Bonnard, Matisse, Kandinsky, Mondrian, Chagall, Pollock, Magritte, Calder, Moore,** and **Bacon.** Exhibitions are splendidly mounted. ♦ Admission; free on Sunday 10AM-2PM

Cinémathèque Française This famous film archive and cinema, located on the fifth floor, presents three international classics daily. The cinémathèque's other auditorium is at the National Cinema Museum in the **Palais de Chaillot** (Place du Trocadéro, 44.05.39.10), where there is also an exhibition of movie memorabilia, such as dresses worn by **Greta Garbo,** the tunic **Rudolph Valentino** wore in *The Sheik,* and one of the robots from the 1926 **Fritz Lang** film *Metropolis.*

Centre Georges Pompidou/Centre National d'Art et Culture

66 IRCAM (Contemporary Institute of Musical and Accoustic Research) One of the world's most advanced computer music centers is located at the bottom of what looks like another métro entrance on the Place Igor-Stravinsky. Toiling away in IRCAM's underground reaches, **Pierre Boulez's** studio of composers and electronic engineers is creating the music of the future. You can take in one of the frequent lectures or even a concert by **L'Ensemble Intercontemporain.** ♦ Admission by application only. 1 Place Igor-Stravinsky. Métros: Châtelet-Les Halles, Hôtel-de-Ville. 42.77.12.33

66 Rites of Spring Fountain A fantastic and frivolous ballet of animals, serpents, and musical notes floats in this lively fountain created by **Niki de Saint-Phalle** and **Jean Tinguely,** making this a great spot for an urban picnic. ♦ Place Igor-Stravinsky. Métros: Châtelet-Les Halles, Hôtel-de-Ville

66 Café Beaubourg ★★$$ This more intellectual cousin of Café Costes offers a vantage point on the local wildlife roaming around the Pompidou Center. You'll find palatable sandwiches, daily copies of *Le Monde* and *Libération,* and a stray cat to lend a personal style to this **Christian de Porzamparc** creation. ♦ Breakfast, lunch, snacks, dinner, and late-night. 100 Rue St.-Martin (at Rue St.-Merri). Métros: Châtelet-Les Halles, Hôtel-de-Ville. 48.87.63.96

67 Les Brichères de Saint-Merry What a treat to find an old-time bakery in this modish neighborhood, complete with a rosy-cheeked baker proudly displaying his fresh brioches, croissants, and tarts on the white marble counters. ♦ M, W-Sa 8:30AM-8PM; Su 9:30AM-7:30PM. 81 Rue St.-Martin (between Rues des Lombards and de la Reynie). Métros: Hôtel-de-Ville, Châtelet-Les Halles. 42.72.04.96

The Bastille's Bustling Bistros and Bars

The area around the Bastille, rejuvenated by the relatively new opera house and scores of art galleries, is called the SoHo of Paris. Formerly a working-class haven for painters and other bohemians, the neighborhood has undergone a mind-boggling transformation. The once seedy Rue de Lappe, just off the Place de la Bastille, is now dubbed "the trendiest street in Paris." Quite a change from 1944, when Somerset Maugham wrote in *The Razor's Edge* that even as you enter Rue de Lappe, "you get the impression of sordid lust." Back in the 1930s, the street was filled with *bougnats,* auvergnat dispensaries of wine and coal. Nowadays, however, the streets are replete with oh-so-trendy bars and cafés, including these favorites:

Le Bar à Nenette ★★$ At the turn of the century this friendly café was a traditional auvergnat *bougnat.* The original wood stove, still in working order, has become the café's centerpiece and is surrounded with artists and antique dealers dining on hearty salads and light meals. Oddly delicious, the café's auvergnat cheese platter is served provençal style, drenched in olive oil and fresh herbs. ♦ Lunch, dinner, and late-night; dinner and late-night only on Saturday. Closed Sunday. 26bis Rue de Lappe. Métro: Bastille. 48.07.08.18

Café Iguana This corner bar has a woody interior and the muddiest draft Guinness this side of Dublin. ♦ Daily 9AM-2AM. 15 Rue de la Roquette. Métro: Bastille. 40.21.39.99

L'Entre-Pots The decor of this dark cavernous bar suggests Paris in the 1940s. Hip French students sip expensive American cocktails and lip-sync to booming Otis Redding and Madonna tunes. ♦ Daily 7PM-2AM. 14 Rue de Charonne. Métro: Bastille. 48.06.57.04

La Palette 1900 ★★$ Like its artsy namesake on the Rue de Seine, this corner café is an architectural jewel. It opened in 1907 as a bistro/billiard hall and retains the original Eiffel-era girders, carved wood panels, and peeling gold-leaf lettering. Have a *pastis* on the terrace and luxuriate in the faded fin de siècle elegance. ♦ Breakfast, lunch, dinner, and late-night. 116 Avenue Ledru Rollin. Métro: Bastille. 47.00.34.39

Chez Paul ★★$$ Though the customers look trendy, Chez Paul is unpretentious and old-fashioned, serving authentic bistro fare, such as lamb with rosemary and rabbit stuffed with goat cheese and mint. ♦ Lunch and dinner. Closed Sunday. 13 Rue de Charonne (at Rue de Lappe). Métro: Ledru-Rollin. 47.00.34.57

China Club ★★$$ This Shanghai-chic club mixes cocktails for the new gentry of the east side. Its exotic interior includes a cozy drawing room with soft leather sofas, a 46-foot-long bar, and a Chinese restaurant. Bourgeois from the conservative west side like to venture here for a night out. ♦ Dinner and late-night. 50 Rue de Charenton (between Ave Ledru-Rollin and Place de la Bastille). Reservations recommended. Métros: Ledru-Rollin, Bastille, Gare-de-Lyon. 43.43.82.02

Café de l'Industrie ★★★$ Miniature palm trees, subdued lighting, and warm colors create a calm atmosphere where anyone can sip a Brazilian cocktail or a glass of banana juice. Chili con carne, carpaccio, and roast beef with potatoes provide sustenance. The owner doesn't advertise and even closes down on Saturdays so as to preserve this tranquil spot. ♦ Lunch, dinner, and late-night. Closed Saturday. 16 Rue St.-Sabin (between Blvd Richard-Lenoir and Rue de la Roquette). Métros: Bréguet-Sabin, Bastille. 47.00.13.53

Casbah Three bouncers at the door decide who will get into this nightclub, where everything from jeans to tuxedos is acceptable as long as you have "the look." Those who pass muster can soak in an atmosphere created by rich colors, dim lighting, and incense, but don't even think of arriving before midnight. ♦ 9PM-dawn. 18-20 Rue de la Forge-Royale (between Rues du Faubourg-St.-Antoine and Chanzy). Métros: Ledru-Rollin, Faidherbe-Chaligny. 43.71.71.89

67 Hôtel St.-Merri $$ A quirky 13-room hostelry is attached to the medieval **St.-Merri Church**. Specializing in irreligious caprice, this hotel uses communion rails as banisters and has a room with a flying buttress and another with a confessional-as-clothespress. ♦ 78 Rue de la Verrerie (at Rue St.-Martin). Métros: Châtelet-Les Halles, Hôtel-de-Ville. 42.78.14.15

68 Benoît ★★$$$ You need not take the train to Lyon to savor blood sausage with apples and roast potatoes, duckling with turnips, or mussel soup. This attractive 1912 bistro is frequented by families in the evening. ♦ Lunch and dinner. Closed Saturday, Sunday, and in August. 20 Rue St.-Martin (at Rue Pernelle). Reservations required. No credit cards. Métro: Châtelet-Les Halles. 42.72.25.76

69 Aux Délices de Chine ★$ Lacquered duck, stuffed pigeon with swallow's nest, and Chinese hot pot are **Victor** and **Suzanne Chau's** specialties. The decor is nothing fancy, unlike some of the dishes that are so elaborate they must be ordered 48 hours in advance. If your stomach can't plan that far ahead, there are also items on the menu that do not demand lengthy preparations. ♦ Lunch and dinner. Closed Sunday. 26 Rue des Lombards (between Blvd de Sebastopol and Rue Quincampoix). Reservations recommended. Métro: Châtelet-Les Halles. 42.78.38.62

69 Rue Quincampoix The Scottish financier **John Law** founded a bank on this street in 1719 after he became France's controller general, prompting a brief rash of speculation in this part of the city. In more recent times, the street has been a magnet for *les femmes de la nuit*, women photographed so remarkably by **Brassaï** in the early 1930s. ♦ Métros: Rambuteau, Châtelet-Les Halles

70 Pacific Palisades ★★$$ A Les Halles version of Californian nouvelle cuisine is served by French waiters who act like they just stepped off the beach at Malibu. In summer, the terrace is splendid. Any season of the year, the piano bar downstairs is smoky and the crowd trendy. ♦ Lunch, dinner, and late-night. 51 Rue Quincampoix (between Rues Aubry-le-Boucher and de Venise). Reservations recommended. Métro: Rambuteau. 42.74.01.17

70 46 Rue Quincampoix This complex contains a cinema, a theater, and the Cultural Center of Yugoslavia. Don't miss the startling entryway sculpture of an army of nudes bursting through the seams in the wall. ♦ Between Rues Aubry-le-Boucher and de Venise. Métro: Rambuteau

70 Galerie Jean Fournier The ideal art dealer, Jean Fournier is always amenable to showing and discussing his selections. American artists represented here include **Sam Francis, Shirley Jaffe,** and **Joan Mitchell**. The gallery includes a bookstore specializing in painting as well as ancient and contemporary art. ♦ M-Sa 10AM-1PM, 2-7PM. Closed in August. 44 Rue Quincampoix (between Rues Aubry-le-Boucher and de Venise). Métro: Rambuteau. 42.77.32.31

70 Galerie Zabriskie This is Paris' outpost of New York's first-rate Fifth Avenue photo gallery. ♦ Tu-Sa 11AM-7PM. Closed in August. 37 Rue Quincampoix (between Rues Aubry-le-Boucher and de Venise). Métro: Rambuteau. 42.72.35.47

70 Galerie Alain Blondel Risen from the ashes of the defunct Luxembourg Gallery, Blondel features early 20th-century works, large canvases from the 1930s, trompe l'oeil, and realism. ♦ Tu-F 11AM-7PM; Sa 2-7PM. 4 Rue Aubry-le-Boucher (at Rue Quincampoix). Métro: Rambuteau. 42.78.66.67

71 Passage Molière For now, this ramshackle 19th-century alley with its tiny one-room flats and cheap tailor shops offers a glimpse, in contrast to the glitter and glamour of Les Halles, of what the Beaubourg quarter was like before it got malled. ♦ Off Rue Quincampoix (between Rues Rambuteau and aux Ours) Métro: Rambuteau

72 Clair Obscur This whimsical bookstore/gallery specializes in marionettes, Venetian masks, and books on theater and cinema. Ask the owner to crank up the mechanical performing circus, complete with lion tamer, acrobats, and hypnotist. ♦ M-Su 11AM-7:30PM. 161 Rue St.-Martin (between Passage Molière and Rue aux Ours). Métro: Rambuteau. 48.87.78.58

73 Les Bains-Douches ★$$$ Architectural whiz kid **Philippe Starck** transformed these old public Turkish baths with their 1900 facade into one of the trendiest discos and restaurants in Les Halles. What would former baths patron **Marcel Proust** have to say? ♦ Dinner and late-night. Disco: daily 11PM-dawn. 7 Rue du Bourg-l'Abbé (between Blvd de Sebastopol and Rue St.-Martin). Métro: Etienne-Marcel. 48.87.01.80

74 Duthilleul et Minart For more than a century, this store has sold uniforms and work clothes, from waiters' aprons to chefs' toques, plus an array of uniquely French occupational garb. This is a great spot for gifts, too, such as the popular French watchmakers' smocks. ♦ M-Sa 9AM-7PM. 14 Rue Turbigo (at Rue Etienne-Marcel). Métros: Etienne-Marcel, Les Halles. 42.33.44.36

75 St.-Leu-St.-Gilles A 14th-century church of interest less for its unimposing exterior than for its unusual interior. On a street epitomizing voyeurism, the glass doors of the church appropriately provide their own peep show of medieval architecture. ♦ M 5-10PM; Tu-F 1-10PM; Sa 1:30-10PM; Su 10AM-12:30PM. 92 Rue St.-Denis (between Rues du Cygne and de la Grande-Truanderie). Métro: Les Halles

76 Rue de la Cossonnerie On this 13th-century street, **Giovanni Boccaccio** (1313-1375), considered one of the founders of the Italian Renaissance, was born. He was the author of *Filocolo* and the *Decameron*. ♦ Métro: Les Halles

77 Au Père Tranquille ★$ French teenagers wearing penny loafers and fake American varsity-letter jackets crowd this late-night corner café. On a warm evening, order a Kir on the terrace while you sit and watch the Les Halles parade pass by. **e.e. cummings** set Act III of his play *Him* here. ♦ Breakfast, lunch, dinner, and late-night. 16 Rue Pierre-Lescot (at Rue Rambuteau). Métro: Les Halles. 45.08.00.34

77 Le Bon Pêcheur ★$ When the adolescents at Au Père Tranquille grow up, they graduate to this smoky café across the street. Le Bon Pêcheur is decorated with orange neon lights, mirrored columns, a zinc bar, and maps of Brazil on the wall. It offers salsa on the stereo, *caipirinha* (the fiery Brazilian drink), and quiche Lorraine for the hungry. ♦ Breakfast, lunch, dinner, and late-night. 14 Rue Pierre-Lescot (at Rue Rambuteau). Métro: Les Halles. 42.36.91.88

78 Rue St.-Denis Once the route by which France's kings entered Paris to be crowned and exited to be buried in the basilica at St.-Denis, this street now unfurls a lurid panoply of Parisian sleaze: peep shows, prostitutes, and fast-food joints such as the **Love Burger.** ♦ Métro: Les Halles

78 Aux Deux Saules ★★$ The Two Willows, a remnant of old Les Halles in a wasteland of gaudy neon-splashed sex shops, offers simple fare such as onion soup, sausages, *pommes frites*, and cheap wine served on outdoor wooden tables. Inside are gorgeous ceramic murals. ♦ Lunch and dinner. Closed Tuesday. 91 Rue St.-Denis (at Rue Rambuteau). Métro: Les Halles. 42.36.46.57

78 Chez Vong aux Halles ★★$$$ Refined Cantonese and Szechuan dishes may be found in the company of excellent French wines at this attractive Chinese bistro. Dim sum, beef in oyster sauce, and lacquered pigeon are good choices. ♦ Lunch and dinner. Closed Sunday. 10 Rue de la Grande-Truanderie (between Rues Pierre-Lescot and St.-Denis). Reservations recommended. Métro: Les Halles. 40.39.99.89

79 Joe Allen ★$$ One of the most popular restaurants in Les Halles, this is a replica of its Los Angeles and Manhattan namesakes, right down to the old photographs on the dark brick walls. The menu, also a replica, offers spareribs, chili con carne, black bean soup, and apple pie. It's terribly American, or at least the beautiful Parisians think so. ♦ Lunch, dinner, and late-night. 30 Rue Pierre-Lescot (between Rues du Cygne and Etienne-Marcel). Métro: Les Halles. 42.36.70.13

80 Chez Pierrot ★★★$$ Walk through the doors of this bistro and you'll find yourself back in the old Les Halles market days. It's been decorated in period and everything is done to excess. A cornucopia of hors d'oeuvres is followed by grilled kidneys and marinated mackerel. Customers prefer cheese to desserts, insists Pierrot's owner, so they can order another hearty Bordeaux. ♦ Lunch and dinner. Closed Saturday and Sunday. 18 Rue Etienne-Marcel (between Rues Française and de Turbigo). Métro: Etienne-Marcel. 45.08.05.48

81 Pharamond ★★$$ Try the *tripes à la mode de Caen*, cooked in apple cider in classic Normandy fashion and served in old-fashioned charcoal-fired brass braziers. Nobody simmers it better. ♦ Lunch and dinner; dinner only on Monday. Closed Sunday. 24 Rue de la Grande-Truanderie (between Rues Mondétour and Pierre-Lescot). Reservations required. Métro: Les Halles. 42.33.06.72, 42.36.51.29

Furniture Fantastique

Unlike in America, haute-couture furniture houses in Paris are open to the public, and showcase stores devoted to the work of avant-garde designers are becoming as popular for furniture as for fashion. Hot spots for top-of-the-line French furnishings include the following:

Ecart Opened by Andrée Putman in 1978, this shop offers reeditions of furniture by such 20th-century designers as Robert Mallet-Stevens and Eileen Gray, as well as new designs. ♦ M-Sa 9AM-6PM. 111 Rue St.-Antoine. Métro: St.-Paul. 42.78.88.35

Edifice Philippe Starck got his start in this showroom, and his iconoclastic design spirit lives on in the work of such young designers as Marie-Christine Dorner and Shiro Kuramata. ♦ M-Sa 10AM-7PM. 27bis Boulevard Raspail. Métro: Sèvres-Babylon. 45.48.53.60

Mobilier International A pioneer of importing and marketing 20th-century design since 1950, this company features the work of French designer Jean-Michel Wilmotte as well as other European designers and such 20th-century design doyens as Charles Eames. ♦ M-F 9:30AM-12:30PM, 2-4:30PM. 166 Rue du Faubourg-St.-Honoré. Métro: St.-Philippe-du-Roule. 43.59.08.40

Neotu This is the place for whimsical furniture-as-sculpture, where any material is fair game, from bags of stones to molded plastic. ♦ M-Sa 11AM-1PM, 2-7PM. 25 Rue du Renard. Métros: Hôtel-de-Ville, Rambuteau. 42.78.91.83

81 Batifol ★$$ While the pre-World War II decor remains, the Royal Mondétour and the beloved Bonnenfant family, alas, are no longer. They have been replaced by more professional (and more mercenary) *patrons* who turn out acceptable, affordable bistro fare (hot chèvre salad, pot-au-feu, coq au vin, and *tarte tartin* with Calvados), but rush diners in the interest of squeezing in a second and sometimes even a third seating each night. ♦ Lunch, dinner, and late-night. 14 Rue Mondétour (between Rues de la Grande-Truanderie and Rambuteau). Reservations recommended. Métro: Les Halles. 40.28.02.98, 40.28.04.22

82 Forum des Halles Architect **Victor Baltard's** 12 marvelous 19th-century iron-and-glass food halls were torn down in the 1970s after the 800-year-old wholesale market was moved near Orly Airport in 1969. In its place, architects **Claude Vasconi** and **Georges Pencreach** designed a four-level underground shopping mall along the lines of an inverted hollow pyramid. This crater of consumerism is a labyrinth of walkways, cinemas, snack bars, cafés, 12 restaurants, more than 200 boutiques (the most chic of which are located on the top levels), and a branch of **FNAC,** a popular hangout where French teenagers congregate to buy concert tickets and peruse the latest *bande-dessinées* (hardcover comic books). According to a survey conducted by the McDonald's here, 80,000 pedestrians walk past its doors every day.

Recently, a Japanese insurance company dished out more than $80 million for a 32.7 percent stake in the Forum, which will earn it one-third of the annual rent paid by the Forum's shops and movie theaters ($463 million in 1988 alone). Beneath the Forum is the **Châtelet-Les Halles** métro station, the world's largest underground train station, providing direct access to the métro, the RER (to Charles de Gaulle Airport), and to various underground parking lots. ♦ Rues Rambuteau, Pierre-Lescot, Berger, and Les Halles Garden. Métro: Châtelet-Les Halles

82 Kiosque-Théâtre A kiosk in the Châtelet-Les Halles métro station sells half-price tickets to theater, dance, music hall, concert, café theater, and, occasionally, opera events, on the day of performance. ♦ Daily 1-8PM. Métro: Châtelet-Les Halles

83 Café Costes ★★$ What Café de Flore was to St.-Germain-des-Prés in the 1950s, this was to Les Halles in the 1980s. Intelligent, elegant, and chic, Café Costes set the standards for a whole new generation of Paris cafés. Owner **Jean-Louis Costes** hired architectural designer **Philippe Starck,** whose work is definitely worth viewing (including the space-age bathrooms) before sitting down to sip your Blue Lagoon. ♦ Breakfast, lunch, dinner, and late-night. Square des Innocents (at Rues Berger and St.-Denis). No credit cards. Métro: Châtelet-Les Halles. 45.08.54.39

83 Innocents Fountain During the 16th century, Les Halles fishmongers and butchers alike drew their water from this fountain (pictured above), which was commissioned by **Henri II** and designed by **Pierre Lescot** in 1547. An important architectural relic of early Renaissance Paris, it stands on the site of what was once the overcrowded, foul-smelling **Church of the Innocents** cemetery. In 1786 the church was razed and the skeletons of its many inhabitants were transported to a quarry, which was then most appropriately renamed the **Catacombs.** Later, during World War II, the Catacombs was the macabre setting for the headquarters of the French Resistance. Today, the area surrounding the Innocents Fountain is the haunt of tattooed lowlifes and indigent backpackers poring over out-of-print copies of *Europe on $20 a Day.* ♦ Square des Innocents. Métro: Châtelet-Les Halles

84 Les Trottoirs de Buenos Aires The most authentic tango music in town is played here, as evidenced by the largely South American clientele. Crowds are guaranteed after 11PM, so call and reserve a table. Reasonably priced tango classes (private as well as group instruction) with Uruguayan and Spanish dance teachers are offered each evening before the club opens. (If you're looking for a night of tango and salsa dancing, however, try **Le Tango.**) ♦ Shows: Tu-Sa 9:30PM. Classes: Tu, Th by appointment; W 5:30-6:30PM; F 5:30-7:30PM; Sa 1:30-4:30PM. Closed in August. 37 Rue des Lombards (between Rues Ste.-Opportune and St.-Denis). Reservations recommended. Métro: Châtelet-Les Halles. 40.26.28.58

Restaurants/Clubs: Red   Hotels: Blue
Shops/ Outdoors: Green   **Sights/Culture:** Black

105

84 Au Diable des Lombards ★$ A trendy bistro serving cheeseburgers, rabbit terrine, and homemade ice cream, Au Diable is run by **Alain Eclache.** ◆ Lunch, dinner, and late-night. Closed Christmas Eve. 64 Rue des Lombards (between Rues Ste.-Opportune and St.-Denis). Métro: Châtelet-Les Halles. 42.33.81.84

84 Ducs d'Anjou $$ This 30-room hotel sits just off the charming Place Ste.-Opportune. But rooms on the courtyard are somber. ◆ 1 Rue Ste.-Opportune (between Rues des Halles and de la Ferronnerie). Métro: Châtelet-Les Halles. 42.36.92.24

84 Rue de la Ferronnerie Here **Henri IV** was murdered in his carriage on 14 May 1610 as he passed along Ironmongers Row. His assassin, **Ravaillac,** was subsequently quartered by four horses in the Place de Grève, today called Place de l'Hôtel-de-Ville. ◆ Métro: Châtelet-Les Halles

84 Papeterie Moderne If you've got enough patience to sort through this store's marvelous hodgepodge of old Parisian signs (for streets, butcher shops, bakeries, and the like), you can take home a fine souvenir. A copy of anything in the store may be ordered; allow 10 days for pickup. ◆ M-Th, Sa 7:30AM-noon, 1-8PM; F 10:30AM-noon, 1-8PM. Closed two weeks in summer. 12 Rue de la Ferronnerie (between Rues St.-Denis and des Halles). Métro: Châtelet-Les Halles. 42.36.21.72

85 La Tour de Montlhery ★★$$ The owner, **Jacques,** with his white apron and 1890s mustache, serves his loyal clientele of wine merchants, advertising executives, and visiting English novelists stick-to-the-ribs specialties such as stuffed cabbage, mutton with beans, and steak with shallots. Old friends find this a nice place to meet over a bottle of Brouilly. It's open around-the-clock on weekdays. ◆ Breakfast, lunch, and dinner. Closed Sunday and mid-July through mid-Aug. 5 Rue des Prouvaires (between Rues St.-Honoré and Berger). Métro: Les Halles. 42.36.21.82

86 Les Halles Garden The razing of Les Halles market left 106 acres of open space, which has now been transformed into a tree-lined garden and children's playground in the shadow of St.-Eustache Church. Beneath this urban wilderness is **Paul Chemetov's** subterranean sports and culture complex that includes a gymnasium, radio station, billiard hall, art gallery, record-lending library, performing-arts conservatory, and a learning center offering instruction on everything from cooking to magic tricks and bridge. ◆ Olympic swimming pool: Admission. 10 Place de la Rotonde. M 11:30AM-8PM; Tu, Th-F 11:30AM-10PM; W 10AM-7PM; Sa-Su 9AM-5PM. Métro: Les Halles

87 Rue Montorgueil Paris chefs have continued to shop on this lively market street despite the demolition of the old Les Halles markets. It begins at the Rue Rambuteau. ◆ Market: Tu-Su 6AM-1PM. Métro: Les Halles

87 L'Escargot Montorgueil ★★★$$$ One of the most authentic displays of 1830s decor in Paris, the restaurant has a black-and-gilt facade, enormous cut-glass mirrors, tulip chandeliers, and red banquettes. The old cooking allegory gracing the wall came from the dining room of actress **Sarah Bernhardt.** The champagne comes in carafes; the escargots come in mint, curry, Roquefort, or *à la bourguignonne;* and the customers are of the Maxim's, Lasserre, Grand Véfour, and La Tour d'Argent variety. Small wonder. The restaurant is run by **Mademoiselle Saladin-Terrail,** the sister of **Claude Terrail,** who owns La Tour d'Argent. ◆ Lunch and dinner. Closed Monday. 38 Rue Montorgueil (at Rue Mauconseil). Reservations recommended. Métro: Les Halles. 42.36.83.51

88 St.-Eustache Church This massive amalgam of Gothic flying buttresses, rose windows, and flamboyant vaulting with a Renaissance facade was built in 1640 to rival the likes of Notre-Dame. While its dimensions are enormous (346 feet long with a 112-foot-high nave), the church (floor plan below) is better known for its musical legacy than architectural grandeur. The **Berlioz** *Te Deum* and **Liszt** *Grand Mass* were first performed here; composer **Jean-Philippe Rameau** is buried in the church. The Christmas offering of its impressive 8,000-pipe organ and talented church choir at midnight Mass

St.-Eustache Church

outshines even Notre-Dame's. Notable treasures of plastic arts in the church are the **Rubens** *Pilgrims at Emmaus,* the **Pigalle** statue of the Virgin, and a colorful sculpted scene honoring the vegetable vendors forced out of Les Halles in 1969.

The church is dedicated to **Saint Eustache,** a second-century Roman general who converted to Christianity when, like Saint Hubert, he saw a vision of the cross poised between the antlers of a stag. (A sculpted stag's head and cross are beneath the gable in the church's Renaissance transept facade.) Saint Eustache, as the story goes, was gruesomely martyred; he was roasted alive inside an immense bronze bull with his wife and children. This was once the parish church for the merchants of Les Halles and the nobility from the nearby Louvre and Palais Royal. It hosted the infant baptisms of **Cardinal Richelieu, Jean-Baptiste Poquelin (Molière),** and **Madame de Pompadour,** as well as the funerals of fabulist **Jean de La Fontaine, Colbert** (prime minister of **Louis XIV**), Molière, and Revolutionary orator **Mirabeau.** During the Revolution the church was vandalized and renamed the "Temple of Agriculture," doubtless in honor of its proximity to Les Halles market. ◆ M-Sa 8:30AM-7PM; Su 8:30AM-12:30PM, 3-7PM. A 45-minute tour is available Sunday at 3PM. 2 Rue du Jour. Métro: Les Halles

89 Le Cochon à l'Oreille ★★$ Beautiful ceramic murals adorn this authentic turn-of-the-century working-class bar/café. Butchers, foie gras wholesalers, local merchants, and paunchy men of indefinite occupation wearing blue coveralls hang out here. They come for their coffee and Calvados before dawn or to share a *pastis* at the crowded zinc bar in the afternoon. ◆ Breakfast, lunch, and late-afternoon snacks. Closed Sunday. 15 Rue Montmartre (between Rues Etienne-Marcel and St.-Eustache). No credit cards. Métro: Les Halles. 42.36.07.56

90 Marithé and François Girbaud These two young designers, who have revolutionized casual wear in France, are responsible for 10 clothing lines for men, women, and children. Everything is here in this three-story high-tech loft. ◆ M 11AM-7PM; Tu-Sa 10AM-7PM. 38 Rue Etienne-Marcel (between Rues Montmartre and de la Jussienne). Métros: Etienne-Marcel, Les Halles. 42.33.54.69

91 agnès b. These cheerful striped cotton T-shirts, chic silk blouses, pajamas, and skirts are comfortable and colorful. In her three outlets along Rue du Jour, one each for children, men, and women, agnès b. outfits the 1990s generation. Her trademark cotton cardigans with mother-of-pearl snaps in countless colors are *de rigueur* Parisian attire. ◆ M noon-7:30PM; Tu-Sa 10:30AM-7:30PM. 3 Rue du Jour (between Rues Rambuteau and Montmartre). Métro: Les Halles. 42.33.04.13

91 Au Pied de Cochon ★$$ This nostalgic all-night restaurant specializes in *fruits de mer* (chilled shellfish), pig's feet (hence the restaurant's name), and an overrated onion soup *gratinée.* Local night owls gather here at 4AM, but otherwise it's a tourist mecca. Oysters of a dozen varieties are washed down with champagne at the bar for a Parisian version of Sunday brunch. Though open 24 hours, service is as poky as the snails are delicious. ◆ Breakfast, lunch, dinner, and late-night. 6 Rue Coquillière (between Rues Jean-Jacques-Rousseau and du Jour). Métro: Les Halles. 42.36.11.75

91 Au Cochon d'Or ★★$$ A holdover from old Les Halles days, this small, friendly, lace-curtained bistro serves classic *la moelle au pochet* and grilled beef accompanied by the best french fries in Paris. ◆ Lunch and dinner; dinner only on Saturday. Closed Sunday. 31 Rue du Jour (between Rues Rambuteau and Montmartre). Reservations recommended. Métro: Les Halles. 42.36.38.31

107

91 L'Epi d'Or ★★$$ This humble 1950s Les Halles standby serves honest *pomme de ris de veau en cocotte,* salt pork and lentils, and unsophisticated Rhones and Bordeaux.
♦ Lunch and dinner; dinner and late-night on Saturday. Closed Sunday and in August. 25 Rue Jean-Jacques-Rousseau (between Rues Coquillère and Etienne-Marcel). Reservations recommended. Métro: Les Halles. 42.36.38.12

92 La Chambre de Commerce One of the few buildings to escape the Les Halles demolition, the Commercial Exchange (built in 1887) is a graceful birthday cake of iron and glass. Not to be confused with the **Bourse des Valeurs** (the Roman temple to the north that houses the Paris Stock Exchange), here brokers in wheat, sugar, and other commodities do their trading. Beside the Chambre de Commerce is a 101-foot classical column, topped with what appears to be a giant iron birdcage. This curiosity, called the **Horoscope Tower,** was once attached to the **Hôtel de la Reine** of **Catherine de Médici** and accommodated her stargazing astrologer, **Ruggieri,** during the late 16th century. ♦ Between Rues Coquillère and Berger. Reception/information: M-F 8AM-7:30PM. 42.89.70.00. Metro: Les Halles

93 Le Pavillon Baltard ★$ This Alsatian brasserie serves *choucroute* (sauerkraut) with your choice of fish, pork, calf's head, or stuffed pig's tail. Nouvelle cuisine this ain't. Plan a long stroll after dinner. ♦ Lunch, dinner, and late-night. 9 Rue Coquillère. Reservations recommended. Métro: Les Halles. 42.36.22.00

94 Dehillerin Half warehouse, half hardware store, this family-run kitchen emporium has been supplying the great chefs of Europe with cooking vessels and utensils since 1820. Dehillerin even furnishes the French Army with cast-iron frying pans, boxwood knives, spatulas, and the wire skimmers known as "spiders." And mail-order is available to civilians anywhere in the world. Dehillerin also happens to be the city's leading specialist in re-tinning copper pots. The salespeople speak broken English. ♦ M-Sa 8AM-12:30PM, 2-6PM. 18-20 Rue Coquillère and 51 Rue Jean-Jacques-Rousseau. Métros: Les Halles, Louvre. 42.36.53.13

95 La Cloche des Halles ★★$ This wine bar, named after the *cloche* (bronze bell) that for decades signaled the opening and closing of Les Halles market, offers not only superb Sancerres, Morgons, and Côtes-de-Brouillys, but scrumptious plates of baked country ham, assorted regional cheeses, chicken-liver pâté, and homemade fruit tarts. It's crowded with local merchants, journalists, and the folks in dark suits from the Bourse and Banque de France up the street. ♦ Breakfast, lunch, snacks, and dinner. Closed Sunday and two weeks in August. 28 Rue Coquillère (at Rue Coq-Héron). No credit cards. Métros: Les Halles, Louvre. 42.36.93.89

95 Gérard Besson ★★$$$ One of the neighborhood's finest lunch menus begins with owner/chef Besson's thick fish soup, which may be followed by roast Bresse chicken with mushrooms. For dessert, try the *biscuit glacé à la framboise.* The detailed wine list is strong on Bordeaux. ♦ Lunch and dinner. Closed Saturday and Sunday. 5 Rue Coq-Héron (between Rues du Louvre and Coquillière). Reservations recommended. Métros: Louvre, Palais-Royal. 42.33.14.74

96 La Fermette du Sud-Ouest ★★$$ Jacky Mayer reigns supreme over this countrified restaurant. La Fermette is famous for homemade *boudin* (blood sausage) with onions in sautéed potatoes, cassoulet, magnificent entrecotes, and hearty Cahors wines. ♦ Lunch and dinner. Closed Sunday and in August. 31 Rue Coquillière (between Rues Croix-des-Petits-Champs and du Bouloi). Reservations recommended. Métro: Louvre. 42.36.73.55

97 La Coutellerie Suisse You can't miss this consummate cutlery shop with its giant red Swiss Army knife splayed in the window. ♦ M-F 9AM-noon, 2-6PM. Closed in August. 44 Rue Coquillière (between Rues Hérold and Croix-des-Petits-Champs). Métro: Louvre. 42.33.20.92

98 Banque de France The mansion, which became home to the Bank of France in 1812 by order of **Napoléon,** was originally built for the **Comte de Toulouse,** the son of **Louis XIV** and **Mademoiselle de Montespan.** Among its lavish treasures is a first-class work of art, *Fête à Saint Cloud,* which many art historians say is the best of **Fragonard's** landscape paintings. That huge (7-by-10-foot) canvas hangs in the private office of the governor of the bank. Therefore, unless you have specific business with the governor, you will have to content yourself with the smaller Fragonards down the street at the Louvre. ♦ 39 Rue Croix-des-Petits-Champs (at Rue des-Petits-Champs). Métro: Louvre

Before 1640, Parisian town houses had no indoor plumbing. Chamber pots were emptied into the street or courtyard from upper-story windows (hence the expression *gardez l'eau*), and men relieved themselves wherever they pleased (which is why royalty always had a nosegay within reach to cover the stench). The raw sewage made its way back into the Seine, thus explaining Parisians' preference for wine over river water. Today, tap water, referred to in restaurants as *Château de Chirac* (after Mayor Jacques Chirac), is filtered from the Seine and is certainly drinkable.

Restaurants/Clubs: Red   **Hotels:** Blue
Shops/ 🌳 Outdoors: Green   **Sights/Culture:** Black

Place des Victoires Shopping Map

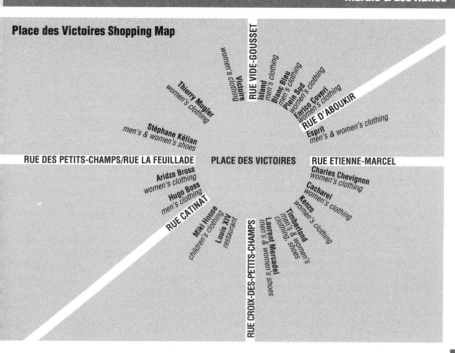

RUE VIDE-GOUSSET

Victoire
women's clothing

Island
women's clothing

Blanc Bleu
women's clothing

Plein Sud
women's clothing

Enrico Coveri
women's clothing

RUE D'ABOUKIR

Thierry Mugler
women's clothing

Esprit
men's & women's clothing

Stéphane Kélian
men's & women's shoes

RUE DES PETITS-CHAMPS/RUE LA FEUILLADE   PLACE DES VICTOIRES   RUE ETIENNE-MARCEL

Aridza Bross
women's clothing

Charles Chevignon
women's clothing

Hugo Boss
men's clothing

Cacharel
women's clothing

RUE CATINAT

Kenzo
women's clothing

Miki House
children's clothing

Timberland
men's & women's
clothing/shoes

Louis XIV
restaurant

Laurent Mercadel
men's & women's shoes

RUE CROIX-DES-PETITS-CHAMPS

Place des Victoires

99 Place des Victoires Like the Place Vendôme, this circle of noble mansions (shown above) was designed by **Jules Hardouin-Mansart** to celebrate a triumph of **Louis XIV,** this time the Treaty of Nimegen that marked his victory over Spain, Holland, Piedmont, and Germany. Originally at its center was a gilded bronze statue (1686) portraying the king being crowned by a goddess of victory, with four bound warriors at his feet representing the conquered nations. Destroyed during the Revolution, the statue was replaced in 1822 with the **Astyanax Bosio** equestrian version of Louis XIV that proudly rears here today. During the 19th century, the Place des Victoires fell into ruin and its buildings were converted into tradesmen's shops, but a recent restoration has turned it into the Right Bank's hub of high fashion.
♦ Métro: Bourse

100 Louis XIV ★★$$ This old bistro in the prettiest building in the Place des Victoires serves generous portions of traditional Burgundy and Lyon dishes such as dandelion greens with bacon, rabbit in mustard sauce, and beef *Bourguignon.* The house Beaujolais comes in pitchers, the pickles in large vats, and a mammoth help-yourself block of butter is passed from table to table. The lunch crowd consists of reporters, bankers, brokers, and fashionable types fueling up to shop at Kenzo and the other smart boutiques nearby. In good weather, reserve a sidewalk table and enjoy the view of Louis XIV, majestic on horseback. ◆ Lunch and dinner. Closed Saturday, Sunday, and in August. 1bis Place des Victoires (at Rue Croix-des-Petits-Champs). Reservations required. Métros: Bourse, Pyramides. 40.26.20.81

100 Kenzo This appealing, natural-wood boutique has some of the most fanciful fashions and friendliest sales help in town. For the young at heart: menswear is downstairs, ladieswear upstairs. ◆ M 11AM-7PM; Tu-Sa 10AM-7PM. 3 Place des Victoires (between Rues Etienne-Marcel and Croix-des-Petits-Champs). Métros: Bourse, Pyramides. 40.39.72.00

100 Cacharel Though company founder **Jean Bosquet** moved into politics long ago, the design flame remains bright with sensible sportswear and cotton paisley print fabrics in collaboration with Liberty of London. Menswear is in the basement. (womenswear is sold nearby at 49 Ave Etienne-Marcel.) ◆ M 11AM-7PM; Tu-Sa 10AM-7PM. 5 Place des Victoires (between Rues Etienne-Marcel and Croix-des-Petits-Champs). Métros: Bourse, Pyramides. 42.33.29.88

101 Hugo Boss With a handsome mahogany interior created by **Philippe Starck,** this Hugo Boss boutique looks more like a private men's club than a clothing store. The unique environment reflects the originality of the German designer's fashions for men. ◆ M-Sa 10AM-7PM. 2 Place des Victoires (at Rue Catinat). Métros: Bourse, Pyramides. 40.28.91.64

102 Lina's ★★$ This airy sandwich bar with its ocher walls, blond-wood trim, and acres of windows is the perfect vantage point for spying on the chic fashion show that promenades in the vicinity of the Place des Victoires. Behind the counter, statuesque men in white shirts and smart neckties offer delicious shrimp-avocado, pastrami, and smoked-salmon sandwiches on crusty country bread (*pain pavé*). ◆ Lunch and late-afternoon snacks. Closed Sunday and Saturdays in August. 50 Rue Etienne-Marcel (at Rue d'Argout). Métro: Bourse. 42.21.16.14

103 Chez Georges ★★$$$ Handwritten menus, beveled mirrors, waitresses in black dresses, and an honest platter of beefsteak and fries are the hallmarks of this classic Parisian bistro. ◆ Lunch and dinner. Closed Sunday and in August. 1 Rue du Mail (at Rue Notre-Dame-des-Victoires). Reservations recommended. Métro: Sentier. 42.60.07.11

104 Victoire Come here to find out what's new in the current fashion scene. Victoire takes pride in being the very first specialty store to discover new Paris talent. ◆ M-Sa 9:30AM-7PM. 10-12 Place des Victoires (at Rue Vide-Gousset). Métros: Bourse, Pyramides. 42.61.09.02

104 Au Panetier Hundreds of crispy sourdough baguettes are baked daily in the wood-fired oven of **Bernard Lebon.** ◆ M-F 8AM-7PM. 10 Place des Petits-Pères (between Rues de la Banque and Notre-Dame-des-Victoires). Métros: Bourse, Pyramides. 42.60.90.23

104 Notre-Dame-des-Victoires Using the plans of **Pierre Le Muet,** in 1740 architect **Sylvain Cartaud** completed this rather undistinguished church, whose name commemorates the **Louis XIII** trouncing of the Protestants in 1628 at La Rochelle. Inside the church are a 1702 bust of the composer **Jean-Baptiste Lully,** who lived down the street at **45 Rue des Petits-Champs,** and an estimated 30,000 tablets blanketing the walls. ◆ M-F 7:30AM-7PM; Sa 8:30AM-12:15PM, 2:30-7:15PM; Su 8:30AM-12:15PM, 4-7:15PM. Place des Petits-Pères (at Rue Notre-Dame-des-Victoires). Métro: Bourse

105 Legrand It's a joy to behold this renowned wineshop's bright red Belle Epoque facade, glass candy jars on the sidewalk out front, and ceiling covered with corks. For three generations, the Legrand family has run this *épicerie* stocked with an intelligent selection of wine, chocolate, tea, coffee, and jam. **Francine Legrand,** the daughter of the late **Lucien,** has a passion for younger, undiscovered (and less expensive) wines from France's smaller vineyards in Burgundy and Bordeaux. Ask her to recommend one: she loves to chat. ◆ Tu-F 8:30AM-7:30PM; Sa 8:30AM-1PM, 3-7PM. 1 Rue de la Banque (at Place des Petits-Pères). Métro: Bourse. 42.60.07.12

The 283-member Senate, France's equivalent of the House of Lords, can be overruled at any time by the National Assembly. If the president of the Republic dies in office, however, the constitution authorizes the president of the Senate to take over the president's responsibilities pending a presidential election, which must be held within 35 days. Ever since World War II, in referendum after referendum, the French have unsuccessfully tried to abolish this elitist provision.

The famous Turgot Map of Paris was completed in 1739 after four years of labor by a team of artists led by Louis Bretez. Commissioned by Michel Etienne Turgot, who was in effect the mayor of Paris at the time, the extraordinary document is architecturally accurate right down to the window bays in the Louvre and the bushes in the Tuileries. The streets, however, are widened to keep them from disappearing behind the buildings. The maps featured at the beginning of each tour outlined in this book were inspired by the Turgot Map.

Restaurants/Clubs: Red   **Hotels:** Blue
Shops/🌳Outdoors: Green   **Sights/Culture:** Black

France's Revolutionary Time Line: 1787 to 1804

Pre-Revolutionary Period (January 1787-May 1789)

February 1787: Louis XVI's realm is in dire financial straits; the First Assembly of Notables refuses to be taxed to raise money.

May 1788: Law courts *(parlements)* refuse to tax privileged orders.

June-July 1788: Revolt of the nobility.

August 1788: Louis XVI calls a meeting of the Estates-General.

January 1789: Sieyès pamphlet, "What is the Third Estate?" is published.

From the Estates-General to the Fall of the Bastille (May 1789-July 1789)

17 June 1789: The Third Estate declares itself the National Assembly.

20 June 1789: The Tennis Court Oath (the National Assembly swears not to disband until a constitution is adopted).

23 June 1789: Louis XVI refuses to recognize the National Assembly; he holds a session of the Estates-General.

27 June 1789: The king orders the first two estates to join the National Assembly.

11 July 1789: Dismissal of Jacques Necker.

14 July 1789: Fall of the Bastille.

The Constituent Assembly (July 1789-September 1791)

17 July 1789: Capitulation of Louis XVI to Paris. The beginning of the Constituent Assembly, the new legislative body that emerged from the National Assembly.

July-August 1789: Massive peasant rebellion called the Great Fear.

4-11 August 1789: Constituent Assembly abolishes feudalism.

26 August 1789: Declaration of the Rights of Man and of the Citizen is adopted by the Constituent Assembly.

5-6 October 1789: Women march to Versailles and bring the king and his family back to Paris.

9 October 1789: Constituent Assembly also relocates to Paris.

2 November 1789: All church property is confiscated.

13 February 1790: All religious orders are abolished.

19 June 1790: Every hereditary title is abolished.

12 July 1790: The church is made subservient to the State.

17 July 1791: Petitioners in the Champ-de-Mars demanding Louis XVI's abdication are attacked; about 50 are killed.

20-25 July 1791: Louis XVI is captured at the border town of Varennes while trying to flee France. He is returned to Paris.

3 September 1791: The new constitution is proclaimed.

14 September 1791: Louis XVI accepts the constitution and is restored to power.

The Legislative Assembly (October 1791-September 1792)

1 October 1791: The new Legislative Assembly meets under the new constitution. Former members of the Constituent Assembly are prohibited from sitting in the new assembly.

20 April 1792: After long debates, war is declared against the king of Bohemia-Hungary.

20 June 1792: Crowds invade Tuileries Palace to intimidate the king into accepting Revolutionary legislation. He refuses.

28 July 1792: A manifesto by the Duke of Brunswick, commanding general of the Austro-Prussian Army, is distributed in Paris. It threatens those refusing to obey Louis XVI.

10 August 1792: Attack on Tuileries, de facto end of the monarchy.

13 August 1792: The royal family is imprisoned in the Temple Tower by the Commune.

19 August 1792: Lafayette defects and is imprisoned in Austria. Prussian troops and French émigrés invade France.

2-7 September 1792: Prison massacres take place in Paris.

20 September 1792: The Prussian advance is halted at the Battle of Valmy.

The Convention Assembly (September 1792-October 1795)

From the Republic to the Terror (September 1792-June 1793)

21 September 1792: The First Republic is proclaimed. The Convention Assembly replaces the Legislative Assembly.

21 January 1793: After months of debate, a trial and a condemnation. Louis XVI is executed.

1 February 1793: The Convention Assembly declares war on Great Britain.

24 February 1793: Military conscription is decreed.

March 1793: Royalist-Catholic rebellion (or counterrevolution) breaks out on the Vendée.

5 April 1793: General Dumouriez deserts to the Austrians.

6 April 1793: The Committee of Public Safety is decreed.

The Terror
(June 1793-July 1794)

31 May-2 June 1793: Twenty-nine Girondin deputies are purged from the Convention Assembly.

24 June 1793: The "Jacobin" constitution is completed (adopted on 4 August but never applied).

27 July 1793: Robespierre is elected to the Committee of Public Safety.

27 August 1793: Touloun, the French naval headquarters for the Mediterranean, falls to the British.

4-5 September 1793: The Hébertist uprising in Paris forces emergency measures on the Convention Assembly. The constitution is suspended.

17 September 1793: Law of Suspects is decreed.

4 December 1793: Law of Frimaire centralizes all activities of the Revolutionary Government.

26 February-3 March 1794: The Laws of Ventôse authorize the seizure and redistribution of the property belonging to the suspects.

March 1794: Execution of the Hébertists.

April 1794: Execution of the Dantonists.

4 June 1794: Robespierre elected president of the Convention.

10 June 1794: Law of 22 Prairial is decreed, inaugurating the final phase of the Terror.

26 June 1794: Battle of Fleurus liberates Belgium from the Austrians and ends the foreign military threat to the Revolution.

27 July 1794: Fall of Robespierre. He is executed the next day.

After Robespierre's Fall
(July 1794-October 1795)

18 September 1794: Church and State are separated.

12 November 1794: Paris' Jacobin Club is closed.

22 August 1795: A new constitution is approved; it provides for a Directory government.

5 October 1795: Napoléon puts down a royalist revolt in Paris.

26 October 1795: Napoléon is named commander in chief of all armies in France.

From the Directory to the Empire
(October 1795-December 1804)

27 October 1795: Directory government succeeds the Convention.

2 March 1796: Napoléon named commander in chief of the French Army in Italy.

1 July 1798: Napoléon launches his Egyptian campaign.

1 August 1798: Nelson defeats the French fleet at Aboukir Bay.

16 October 1799: Napoléon arrives in Paris.

9-10 November 1799: Napoléon's coup d'état. He becomes First Consul of the Consulate government.

15 December 1799: Constitution of the Consulate is issued.

2 December 1804: Napoléon is crowned emperor in the Notre-Dame Cathedral. End of the First French Republic.

David P. Jordan
Reprinted with permission from *France Magazine*

Evelyne de Normandie
Author/Songwriter

To live in **Montmartre** and to breathe the best air in the city.

To meet my friends in its characteristic cafés: **Le Progrès, Le St.-Jean, Le Sancerre,** and **La Cantina,** the liveliest Mexican restaurant in the quarter.

In summer, to dine alongside the hill at **Le Soleil de la Butte** or at **Les Canons de Montmartre**—my favorite terraces.

To descend to **Place Pigalle,** cross the boulevard, and breathe *l'air du temps* at the fashionable bar **Le Moloko.**

To descend farther into Paris and, if I'm in the mood, attend either a ballet at the **Paris Opéra** or a rock concert at **Olympia Music Hall.**

To walk a little farther on to the **Rex,** and dance all night at their special metallic jungle evenings.

To rest in the gardens of the **Musée Rodin,** taking in its beautiful sculptures.

To walk along the quay of the **Port de L'Arsenal** and watch the little pleasure boats in the tranquil canal.

Marc Mimram
Engineer/Architect

The **Seine** is always the best way to discover the interior of the city: Travel by car from the Pont au Change to the Pont de Bercy, or by *bateau mouche* from the **Eiffel Tower.** Night or day, stop in front of the **Tuileries** or **Musée d'Orsay**—the **Passerelle Solferino** connects the two.

Have a drink at the **Closerie des Lilas** or the **Select** on Boulevard Montparnasse.

In the evening, buy a book at **La Hune** near **Café de Flore** on the Boulevard St.-Germain.

Find the best cigars at **A la Civette** on Rue St.-Honoré and then go to Pigalle and listen to some good music at **La Cigale** on Boulevard Rochechouart.

Before you turn in for the night, enjoy a drink at **Lili la Tigresse's** bar on Rue Blanche or at **Les Bains-Douches.**

You can spend the night at the **Hotel du Quai Voltaire** or the **Hotel des Grands Hommes** at the Pantheon.

The next day take your *petit déjeuner* at **Café Costes** before seeing the latest exhibition at the **Georges Pompidou Center** in Beaubourg.

Guy Castelain Perry
Architect/Developer

The business day in the **Place Vendôme/Opéra/Madeleine** area.

Shopping at **Ermenegildo Zegna.**

A Mexican beer at **La Perla** in the Marais.

Chinese, Thai, and Vietnamese food at **Nouillaville** in the Belleville quarter. Don't miss the Thai-style sticky rice or the fish wrapped in banana leaves.

Inexpensive Chinese food at **Dalat** in Belleville; try the *soupe Vietnamienne* and *vermicelle au boeuf.*

Italian wine and pasta at **L'Enoteca** in the Marais.

Save a few francs for later: have lunch at **La Tour d'Argent,** rather than dinner.

A walk along the quays of **Ile St.-Louis** on a damp evening.

Sleeping on the rooftops of the Marais.

An evening in the west (by car):

Dinner at **Les Salons de l'Arc.**

To aid digestion, a convertible or limo ride up and down the "Grand Axe" from **Place de la Concorde** to **La Défense** before the lights go out.

Return to **Les Salons** (downstairs) or go to **Le Niels.**

An evening in the east (on foot):

Linger on Rue St.-Antoine from **Eglise St.-Paul** to **Place de la Bastille** in the early evening.

Dinner at **Bofinger,** the oldest brasserie in Paris.

Drinks upstairs at the **China Club.**

The **Casbah** after 1AM (the neighborhood looks the part).

How to get away from it all . . .

Within the city:

The **Parc André Citroën** in the 15th arrondissement. This impressive modern landscape is on par with the traditional ones for which the French arc most famous.

In the suburbs:

The view from the château at **St.-Germain-en-Laye.** (Take the A line on the RER.)

In the countryside (go on a weekday to avoid traffic and crowds):

Relaxing on the lawn at the far end of **Vaux-le-Vicomte's** gardens.

The timeless poetry of the gardens of **Courances.**

Thirty-six holes of golf at **Le Prieuré,** an 800-year-old clubhouse set in the Vexin countryside, preserved as it should be.

Jean Nouvel
Architect

Notre-Dame—The history, the stained-glass windows.

Ste.-Chapelle—A marvel of light.

Driving on the streets along the quays, under the bridges of Paris.

Tête Défense—What a sight!

Le Louvre—The underground portion, above all.

L'Hôtel Industriel—A new office building of transparent glass by **Dominique Perrault.**

La Cité de la Musique in **La Villette**—The music conservatory that is a small town of music by Christian De Porzamparc.

L'Institut du Monde Arabe (The Institute of the Arab World)—The geometry and the light of Islam.

La Fondation Cartier (Cartier Foundation)—The trees and the sky on the facade of the building at this park and sculpture garden outside of Paris.

Beaubourg—A monument from the 1970s.

The "Borel" building in Belleville—A low-income apartment complex in a popular district.

The finest restaurants and bistros—**Café Pigalle, Café Costes, Café Beaubourg, Chez Julien,** and **Le Restaurant 15 Montaigne.**

Alain P. Zivie
Egyptologist/Archaelogist/Research Director, National Scientific Research Center

To be in different neighborhoods during the week, when they are full of activity. The weekend will not give you an accurate impression of Paris, except for early Sunday morning when the town is empty.

The Seine and the light from the *bateaux mouche* reflecting on the houses along the banks of the river, thinking about the books of Patrick Modiano, the great poet of Paris. During these times the town resembles a theater set.

The authentic cafés with their authentic 1950s decor.

Delacroix's studio and garden on the Rue Furstenberg. The African, Chinese, and Arabic neighborhoods, including the **Boulevard Barbès** and **Port d'Ivry.** The **Palais Royale** on an ordinary day. The bar at the **Plaza Athenée,** the **Raphael** bar, and **La Cité Bergère.**

The winter nights when the city is blanketed with snow. The **Passy station** and its gardens that meet the Seine. The American in Paris in the 1950s. The square courtyard of the **Louvre** seen from the Egyptian rooms on the first floor. The artisans and shopkeepers. The retirees who play cards in the **Cafe de la Republique.** Paris, city of memories and nostalgia, as well as possibility.

Louvre & Champs-Elysées

This superlative stroll includes the largest museum in the Western world (the **Louvre**), the world's most famous boulevard (the **Champs-Elysées**), the most ancient monument in Paris (the 3,300-year-old Egyptian **Obelisk of Luxor**), the best 360-degree view of Paris (from **La Samaritaine's** rooftop café), the grandest hotels (the **Meurice, Crillon,** and **George V**), the city's oldest métro station (**Franklin-D.-Roosevelt**), the most elegant tea salon (**Angélina**), the best English paperback bookshop (**W.H. Smith and Son**), one of the world's most magnificent squares (**Place de la Concorde**), the largest concert hall in Paris (**Théâtre du Châtelet**), the "hautest" of haute couture (the boutiques along **Avenue Montaigne**), the sexiest cabaret in Paris (**Crazy Horse Saloon**), the city's best restaurant (**Taillevent**), and the world's biggest triumphal arch (**L'Arc de Triomphe**). That's a lot to absorb in one day, so get an early start, put on your most comfortable shoes, and *bon courage*—that's French for "keep a stiff upper lip."

Monday may be the best day to visit this area, for it's the only day the **Hôtel de Ville** (City Hall) is open and the lines at the Louvre Museum slack off (on Sunday, when admission to the Louvre is free, it's a mob scene). Monday is also discount night at the cinemas on the Champs-Elysées. Begin your tour with the Hôtel de Ville, then pass along the Seine by the pet and plant shops on **Quai de la Mégisserie** and stop for morning coffee and a spectacular panorama atop La Samaritaine department store. Next comes the Louvre Museum. Ask someone to hold your place in the museum's ticket line so you can run across the street to peek at the Louis XIV royal pew in the artists' church of **St.-Germain-l'Auxerrois.** Then prepare yourself for a two- to three-hour whirlwind tour of the history of Western art that includes those three remarkable Mediterranean ladies *Venus de Milo, Winged Victory of Samothrace,* and *Mona Lisa.* After the Louvre take a break at the nearby **Tuileries Gardens,** then either splurge for lunch at Gaston Lenôtre's **Elysée Lenôtre** or join the fashion models with fierce sweet cravings who order the Mont Blanc dessert at Angélina. En route to Place de la Concorde, you might stop at W.H. Smith and Son for the latest *New Yorker* or an English novel to read on the plane home.

From the base of the Obelisk of Luxor, it is a mile to the Arc de Triomphe. If you need motivation to keep walking, consider the delights that lie ahead: the Vermeer and Rembrandt paintings at the **Petit Palais,** and chef Deligne's hot oysters with truffles at Taillevent. The eastern half of the Champs-Elysées is bordered by gardens (designed by **André Le Nôtre**, a gardener for Louis XIV, who also landscaped Versailles) that have not changed since novelist **Marcel Proust** played there as a child. On the right, you pass behind three fine properties: the **British Embassy,** the **Japanese Embassy,** and the **Palais de l'Elysée.** At **Rond Point,** a roundabout in the east end of the Champs-Elysées, shoppers should veer left to Avenue Montaigne, the high-fashion row, while art buffs and stamp collectors will want to go directly to the galleries on **Avenue Matignon** and to the stamp stalls on **Avenue Gabriel.**

The last stretch of the Champs-Elysées, which leads up to Napoléon's triumphal arch, is meant to be strolled in the evening when the city lights are glittering, upholding Paris' reputation as the "City of Light." High rollers will want a cocktail on the terrace at **Fouquet's,** and dinner at Taillevent, **Chiberta,** or, perhaps, upstairs at **Lasserre,** where the ceiling rolls back for stargazing between courses. Those who are on a tighter budget might catch a first-run movie at the **Gaumont,** or a Beckett play at the **Théâtre Renaud Barrault,** and then enjoy a late-night raclette (melted cheese on bread) at **La Boutique à Sandwiches.** When the day's strolling is over, you may feel like you've ridden in the Tour de France the world's greatest bicycle race, which finishes each July on the Champs-Elysées where you too will complete your one-day Tour de Paris.

Hôtel de Ville

1 Place de l'Hôtel-de-Ville The present seat
of the Paris city government, this square is
where **Etienne Marcel**, one of the first mayors
of Paris, established his city council in 1357.
Marcel incited a mob to rise against the
monarchy and storm the royal palace on **Ile de
la Cité.** The next year he was killed—not by
the king but by his fellow Parisians. Centered
in the granite on the square is the image of a
boat, the city symbol, adopted from the 13th-
century coat of arms of the Boatmen's Guild.
♦ Métro: Hôtel-de-Ville

2 Hôtel de Ville The City Hall (pictured above)
is another example of late 19th-century
architectural eclecticism. Part Renaissance
palace, part Belle Epoque fantasy, its exterior
is lavished with 146 statues, among them
bronze effigies of the sentries who patrolled
the perimeter of the city wall during the Middle
Ages. Visitors on guided tours of the **State
Rooms** are shown the splendid staircase by
Philibert Delorme, murals by **Puvis de
Chavannes,** and a lesser-known **Rodin**
sculpture, *La République.* ♦ Tours: M
10:30AM, starting from the information desk
at 29 Rue de Rivoli, but call ahead the previous
Friday to confirm hours. Métro: Hôtel-de-Ville.
42.76.40.40

A L'OLIVIER

2 A l'Olivier Founded in 1860, this shop still
sells every oil imaginable—hazelnut oil for
vinaigrettes, almond-honey oil shampoo, and
apricot-nut oil for massages. Tarragon
mustard and dried figs are also sold. The

classic bottles alone are worth taking home,
and the giant pottery casks for olive oil are not
to be missed. ♦ Tu-Sa 9:30AM-1PM, 2-7PM.
23 Rue de Rivoli (between Rues des Ecouffes
and Ferdinand Duval). Métro: Hôtel de Ville.
48.04.86.59

3 Bazar de l'Hôtel-de-Ville Need a floor
sander or new drapes for your hotel room?
A spare tire for your rental car? BHV is every
Parisian's hardware store, its five floors
replete with the wherewithal to do it yourself.
This is a paradise for Monsieur Fix-It. ♦ M-Tu,
Th-Sa 9:30AM-7PM; W 9:30AM-10PM. 52-64
Rue de Rivoli (at Rue du Temple). Métro:
Hôtel-de-Ville. 42.74.90.00

4 Avenue Victoria One of the shortest
avenues in Paris doesn't commemorate any
military victory, but rather the royal visit of the
dowager **Queen of England** to Paris. ♦ Métro:
Hôtel-de-Ville

5 Tour St.-Jacques This 1522 architectural
anomaly was the Gothic belfry of **St.-Jacques,**
a church that was destroyed in 1802; the
tower was spared to become a factory for
manufacturing lead musket balls. Cast your
eyes up and you will see meteorological
equipment lurking among the gargoyles. The
tower now doubles as a weather station,
appropriately enough, for at the tower's base
is a statue of **Blaise Pascal** (1623-62), one of
France's first weather forecasters. In 1648, at
the top of this very tower, he used a barometer
to calculate the weight of air. ♦ Métro:
Châtelet-Les Halles

6 Place du Châtelet Named after a fortress
and prison that once stood on this site,
Châtelet is the principal crossroads of Paris, a
hub of east-west and north-south traffic. The
Châtelet Fountain in the center of the square,
flanked by French sphinxes, was designed in
1808 to celebrate the triumphant Egyptian
campaign of **Napoléon.** Below ground five
métro lines intersect, making Châtelet-Les
Halles the world's largest underground
station. ♦ Métro: Châtelet-Les Halles

Charles-de-Gaulle-Etoile Ⓜ

Taillevent—one of Paris' best restaurants

Ⓜ **George-V**

GRANDE ARMÉE

100

104

103

101

99

102 **95**

97

96

94

93

91

90

89 **88**

87

65

64

Ⓜ **Kléber**

98

92

85

86

84

83

82

66

67

68

81

79

80

78

73

76 **77**

71

72

74

70

69

59

58

56

57

75

Avenue Foch—the widest street in Paris, where Aristotle Onassis, the composer Charles Debussy, the Shah of Iran, and Prince Rainier have had mansions

L'Arc de Triomphe—had Napoléon not changed his mind at the last minute, this grand-daddy of triumphal arches would have been a 160-foot-high elephant

Stuck without a room for the night? Try the **Paris Tourist Office,** where you can make same-day hotel reservations

PLACE DE L'ALMA

QUAI DE LA CONFERENCE

COURS ALBERT 1ER

Bateaux Mouches

Nina Ricci—the most beautiful lingerie in the world

Ⓜ **Franklin-D.-Roosevelt**

The oldest métro station— on 4 October 1898 engineer Fulgence Bienvenue and his crew broke ground here for this métro

FDR learned to drive while honeymooning at **37 Avenue George-V** in 1905

Crazy Horse Saloon—catch Paris' classiest strip show

Purchase a wall-size métro map, Seine navigation charts, or maps of Paris in 1618 at the **Institut Geographique National**

Ⓜ **Alma-Marceau**

During World War II, **7 Rue François Premier** was the head-quarters of the American Red Cross

Pont de l'Alma—Bateaux Mouche tours of the Seine leave from here. See if the river has reached the Zouave soldier's britches

Avenue Montaigne— this street is to haute couture what the Louvre is to art

Ⓜ = **Métro**

Le Berkeley—the classic oysters-and-champagne, steak-and-fries restaurant

American Embassy

W.H. Smith and Son—a bonanza of English paperbacks and magazines

Avenue Matignon—gallery alley for Right Bank art

L'Espace Restaurant—a Pierre Cardin-designed restaurant with neo-1950s Miami Beach decor favored by international TV and film glitterati

Place de la Concorde—on Sunday, 21 January 1793, King Louis XVI was guillotined here; in the following months the Nation's Razor trimmed the heads of Marie Antoinette, Madame du Barry, Charlotte Corday, Danton, and thousands of others

Restaurant Laurent— the parking lot is always crowded with chauffeured limousines bearing diplomatic license plates

On 6 February 1778, Louis XVI and Benjamin Franklin signed a treaty at the Hôtel Crillon that recognized the independence of the 13 American states

(M) Champs-Elysées-Clemenceau

Maxim's—feeling like nobility? Dazzlingly extravagant? Here's an evening of bona fide Gay Paree

Jeu de Paume— first an ancient tennis court, then a famous Impressionist museum, and now a gallery of changing exhibitions

Pont Alexandre III— an architecturally giddy Belle Epoque bridge

Watch a legislative session of the French National Assembly at the Palais-Bourbon

The only remains of the demolished Tuileries Palace stand anonymously behind the Jeu de Paume

Petit Palais—this "Little Palace" houses the city's Fine Arts Museum

Champs-Elysées—the world's most famous boulevard. If you fancy pomp and pageantry, show up here on Bastille Day (14 July), on Armistice Day (11 November), in December (for the Christmas lights), or early in summer for the finish of the Tour de France bicycle race

L'Orangerie— the former citrus nursery now houses 144 masterworks, including Monet's Water Lilies series

Grand Palais—an exuberance of stone, steel, and glass showing Art Nouveau at its excessive zenith

Palais de la Découverte is a sprawling museum with Jacques Cousteau film festivals, holography exhibitions, and 9,000 stars twinkling in its celebrated planetarium

Pont de la Concorde, a five-arched bridge, was constructed with stones taken from the 1789 demolition of the Bastille

Obelisk of Luxor—at 3,300 years old, unquestionably the most ancient monument in Paris

Musée National des Arts de la Mode—Brigitte Bardot's wedding dress, Anne of Austria's 17th-century gloves, a robe designed for Sarah Bernhardt, plus 90 dresses by Elsa Schiaparelli are displayed here

L'Arc du Carrousel—use this arch like a gunsight to line up the grand alley of the Tuileries Fountains, the Obelisk, the Champs-Elysées, and the Arc de Triomphe, more than two miles away. In 1809, this arch was crowned with four bronze horses Napoléon looted from Venice. The originals were returned to the Venetians; these are copies

Tuileries Gardens—designed for Louis XIV by André Le Nôtre, the king's gardener, who also created the gardens at Versailles, Chantilly, and the Château Vaux-le-Vicomte

Cour Napoléon—this courtyard is the site of I.M. Pei's pyramid

Hôtel Meurice—in immense Suite No.108, Nazi Commandant General von Cholitz, after disobeying Hitler's orders to burn Paris, surrendered to the Allies in August 1944

Buried in **St.-Germain-l'Auxerrois** (the artists' church) are architects Le Vau, Gabriel, and Soufflot; the sculptor Coysevox; and painters Coypel, Boucher, and Chardin. Organ concerts are held here every Sunday evening

Angélina—the Rolls-Royce of Parisian tea salons

(M) **Louvre**

The **Louvre Métro Station** is Paris' prettiest—an underground gallery with illuminated copies of the museum's sculptures

(M) **Tuileries**

(M) **Palais-Royal**

Rue de Rivoli—named after the Italian town where Napoléon thrashed the Austrians in 1797

From the **Pont des Arts**, easel-toting artists sketch and daub an unexcelled vista of Paris' islands

Louvre Museum—gallop through the history of Western art (from the Venus de Milo to the Mona Lisa), displayed in the largest palace in Europe

(M) = Métro

6 Théâtre de la Ville de Paris Formerly the **Sarah Bernhardt Theatre,** this mid-19th-century stage is now devoted to contemporary dance, jazz, and classical theater, but still preserves the dressing room of the "Divine Sarah." ♦ Box office: M, Su 11AM-7PM; Tu-Sa 9AM-8PM. 2 Place du Châtelet (at Quai de Gesvres). Métro: Châtelet-Les Halles. 42.74.22.77

7 Pont au Change The **Money-Changers' Bridge** was the ninth-century forerunner of American Express: a spot where travelers and foreigners came to change money. Today this Second-Empire bridge is flanked by identical state-owned theaters, both built by architect **Davioud** in 1862. ♦ Métro: Châtelet-Les Halles

8 Quai de la Mégisserie Once a malodorous *mégisserie* (sheepskin tannery), today this spot is rife with booksellers, pet shops, fish-tackle dealers, and plant stores where mice and goldfish are sold alongside dahlias and fertilizer. The cacophony of the parakeets, turkeys, and guinea fowls, whose cages clutter the pavement, vies pleasantly with that of the

automobile traffic nearby. Even if you don't fancy house pets or have a green thumb, a stroll here will treat you to splendid views of **La Conciergerie,** the towers of **Notre-Dame,** and the spire of **Ste.-Chapelle.** ♦ Métro: Châtelet-Les Halles

9 Théâtre du Châtelet This third-largest auditorium in Paris, after the **Opéra Bastille** and the **Palais des Congrès,** was built in 1862. Seating half as many people as the Opéra Garnier, the theater is primarily a venue for operas, ballets, and symphonies. On 21 May 1910, the **New York Metropolitan Opera Company** made its Paris debut here with *Aida.* **Toscanini** conducted, **Caruso** sang, and the audience, which included most of the French diplomatic corps, the **Vanderbilts,** and **Louis Cartier** (who estimated that more than $3 million worth of jewelry was worn that evening), went wild. ♦ Box office: daily 11AM-7PM. Closed last two weeks in July and all of August. 1 Place du Châtelet (at Quai de la Mégisserie). Métro: Châtelet-Les Halles. 40.28.28.28

10 Le Petit Opportun This popular jazz club headlines such names as **Clark Terry, Slide Hampton,** and **Pepper Adams.** Don't expect the cigarette haze that usually hangs around jazz nightclubs: smoking is not permitted during performances. Buy your tickets at least a half hour in advance. ♦ Shows: 8:30PM and 11PM. Closed Sunday and Monday. 15 Rue des Lavandières-Ste.-Opportune (between Rues de Rivoli and Jean-Lantier). No credit cards. Métro: Châtelet-Les Halles. 42.36.01.36

11 Grand Hôtel de Champagne $$ Small, comfortable rooms characterize this hotel, which is a short walk from the Place du Châtelet, the Louvre, Ste.-Chapelle, Notre-Dame, and the Ile de la Cité. ♦ 17 Rue Jean-Lantier (at Rue des Orfèvres). Métro: Châtelet-Les Halles. 42.36.60.00

12 Slow Club Dixieland jazz is alive and well in Paris. ♦ Daily 10PM-3AM. 130 Rue de Rivoli (between Rues du Pont-Neuf and des Bourdonnais). No credit cards. Métros: Châtelet-Les Halles, Pont-Neuf. 42.33.84.30

13 USA Records This is the best place in Paris—perhaps in Europe—to buy vintage rock oldies and blues from the 1950s and 1960s. ♦ M 3-7PM; Tu-Sa 11AM-1:30PM, 3-7PM. 50 Rue de l'Arbre-Sec (between Rues de Rivoli and St.-Honoré). Métros: Louvre, Pont-Neuf. 42.97.42.35

14 Chez la Vieille ★★$$$ Chef **Adrienne Biasin** prepares a cuisine that seems to come from the kitchen of a French country grandmother: pork liver pâté or sautéed chicken livers, followed by sautéed lamb, veal Marengo, or her special peasant pot-au-feu, and, for dessert, a traditional chocolate mousse or chocolate cake. ♦ Lunch. Closed Saturday, Sunday, and in August. 37 Rue de l'Arbre-Sec (between Rues de Rivoli and Bailleul). Métros: Louvre, Pont-Neuf. 42.60.15.78

15 Rue de l'Arbre-Sec This short street is long and rich in history. **D'Artagnan** of the **Three Musketeers** lived at **No. 4** (formerly the Hôtel des Mousquetaires, now **La Samaritaine** department store); at **No. 52** is the **Hôtel de Trudon,** the former home of Louis XV's wine steward; nearby is the **Hôtel de François Barnon,** named after Louis XIV's barber. The name *arbre-sec* (which literally means dry tree) suggests that a gibbet once stood in the street. ♦ Métro: Pont-Neuf

16 La Samaritaine One of the city's oldest department stores and possibly its most confusing, La Samaritaine takes its name from an old Pont-Neuf water pump decorated with an image of the woman of Samaria offering Jesus a drink of water. Today the store sprawls through four grand old buildings offering everything from pop psychiatry books to kitchen sinks, and at bargain prices. Its best deal, however, is the rooftop panorama. On a pleasant summer day, walk into **Store**

No. 2 (designed by **F. Jourdan**) and ride the elevator to the ninth floor. Sip a *café crème* or *citron pressé,* then mount the stairs and enjoy a 360-degree view of Paris annotated by a ceramic legend that locates points of interest. ♦ Store: M-W, F-Sa 9:30AM-7PM; Th 9:30AM-10PM. The café is open the same hours in the summer months. 19 Rue de la Monnaie (at Quai de la Mégisserie). Métro: Pont-Neuf. 40.41.20.20

𝔓âtisserie 𝔖t·𝔊ermain·l'𝔄uxerrois

17 Pâtisserie St.-Germain-l'Auxerrois This one-hundred-year-old pastry shop and tea salon, elegant with crystal chandeliers, gilded pillars, and marble tables, makes all its sweets and ice creams in a basement factory. Be sure to buy a few treats to munch on while you wait in the Louvre ticket line. Try the chocolate pastries (*la mousseline* and *le cador*) or a flaky *palmier* and *tuile.* ♦ Tu-Su 9AM-7:30PM. Closed two weeks in August and two weeks in September. 2 Rue de l'Admiral-de-Coligny (at Rue de Pretres de St.-Germain-l'Auxerrois). No credit cards. Métros: Louvre, Pont-Neuf. 45.08.19.18

18 Place du Louvre In 52 BC, between the present site of the Louvre and St.-Germain-l'Auxerrois, **Labienus,** a lieutenant of Caesar, bivouacked here with his troops before capturing the settlement of **Lutetia.** ♦ Métros: Louvre, Pont-Neuf

18 St.-Germain-l'Auxerrois On Saint Bartholomew's Day (24 August) in 1572, at the orders of **Catherine de Médici** and **Charles IX,** the pealing bells of St.-Germain-l'Auxerrois (illustrated above) signaled the beginning of a brutal religious massacre. Some 3,000 Huguenots, Protestant wedding guests of **Henri de Navarre** and **Marguerite de Valois,** were slain in their beds. The 38-bell carillon in the neo-Gothic tower is the only truly ancient one in Paris. (All the others were melted down during the Revolution.) The bells still ring out every Wednesday afternoon, a grave reminder of the mass murder.

The gargoyle-laden edifice that was designed in 1220 by **Jean Gaussel** takes its name from **Saint Germain,** the bishop of Auxerre (378-448). This holy man claimed **Saint Patrick** of Ireland, **Saint Illtyd** of Wales, and **Sainte Geneviève** of Paris among his students. When **Louis XIV** and his court moved to Versailles, the artists colony he had established there took over the Louvre, and St.-Germain-l'Auxerrois became its parish church.

Among the luminaries buried here are architects **Louis Le Vau, Jacques-Ange Gabriel,** and **Jacques-Germain Soufflot;** the sculptor **Antoine Coysevox;** and painters **Nöel Coypel, François Boucher,** and **Jean-Baptiste Chardin.** Every Ash Wednesday a service is held to pray for artists throughout the world who will die in the coming year. Royalists flock here annually to a Mass said for **Louis XVI** on the anniversary of his 21 January 1793 execution. Be sure to notice the ornately canopied and sculpted oak bench on the right side of the aisle and imagine Louis XIV and his family contemplating the sermon, enthroned in this red-velvet pew designed in 1682 by painter **Charles Le Brun.** ♦ Daily 8:30AM-8:30PM. Organ recitals: Su 5:30PM. Bells: W 1:30PM (call to check schedule for masses in English). 2 Place du Louvre. Métros: Louvre, Pont-Neuf. 42.60.13.96

19 Louvre Métro Station The platform is a museum in itself, with softly illuminated copies of the sculptures found aboveground in the Louvre. This and the **Varenne Métro Station** (with replicas of **Rodin** sculptures) are two of the prettiest in Paris. ♦ Corner of Rues du Louvre and de Rivoli

19 Rue de Rivoli On this arcaded street, an incongruous mix of luxury hotels and tacky souvenir shops lies demurely behind a graceful but rather monotonous First-Empire colonnade designed by **Charles Percier** and **Pierre Fontaine** in 1811 at the behest of **Napoléon.** The street was named after an Italian town where the emperor thrashed the Austrians in 1797. Strict rules pertaining to the arcades forbade leasing shops to any entrepreneur using ovens or metal tools, thus excluding such artisanal riffraff as bakers and butchers.

Restaurants/Clubs: Red   **Hotels:** Blue
Shops/ ♣ Outdoors: Green   **Sights/Culture:** Black

20 Louvre Museum The Louvre is the single largest building in Paris, the largest palace in Europe, the largest museum in the Western world, and probably the most dominating symbol of art and culture the world has ever known. "I never knew what a palace was until I had a glimpse of the Louvre," said 19th-century American author **Nathaniel Hawthorne.** It has 224 halls, and its enormous **Grande Galerie** is longer than three football fields. It took seven centuries to build, spanning the lives of 17 monarchs and countless architects.

History The origin of the word *louvre,* though obscure, is believed to be a derivation of the Old French word *louverie,* which meant wolf lodge; from a corruption of the word *l'oeuvre,* meaning a work of art; or from an Old Flemish word meaning fortress. In 1190 **King Philippe Auguste** began surrounding Paris with a 30-foot-high city wall that included the fortified Louvre. More than three centuries later, **François I** agreed to live in this fortress at the request of Parisian citizens who had ransomed him from captivity in Italy. In 1527 he tore down most of the old structure, and by 1546 he had constructed the **Cour Carrée** (Square Court).

In 1578 **Catherine de Médici** built a new palace, the **Tuileries,** at the far end of the present Louvre. The two palaces were joined by **Henri IV,** who created a number of apartments in the **Long Gallery** for the use of court painters and their families in 1608. This same Henri was stabbed by an assassin in 1610 and became the only king to die within the Louvre's walls. **Colbert,** a minister of finance to **Louis XIV,** hired the Roman architect **Bernini** to redesign the Louvre. When Bernini suggested knocking the whole place down and starting from scratch, Colbert sent the famous Roman packing. Louis XIV proceeded to reconstruct the Cour Carrée to his own tastes, consulting with the architect **Le Vau,** the painter **Le Brun,** and **Claude Perrault,** a Parisian physician whose brother Charles was the author of *Puss 'n Boots.* After renovating the Louvre, Louis XIV established an art colony there with painters such as **Coustou, Boucher,** and **Coypel.** Louis XIV left Paris for Versailles in 1678, and without royal occupants, the place fell into disrepair. Overrun by freeloaders and squatters, it soon became a slum, and a shantytown of bars and brothels sprang up outside its walls.

Louis XVI was narrowly dissuaded from tearing it down, and shortly before he and **Marie Antoinette** were beheaded in 1793, he magnanimously put some of the royal art collection on display, thus reviving the Louvre's function as a gallery. Following his rise to power, **Napoléon** moved into the Tuileries Palace and built **Rue de Rivoli** for quick access to the Louvre. (Napoléon also built the **Arc du Carrousel,** which he crowned with the famous bronze horses of San Marco that were plundered from Venice during one of his military campaigns. After Waterloo, the horses and other looted works of art were returned to their owners.) During the Second Empire, Napoléon's nephew **Napoléon III** and **Baron Georges-Eugene Haussmann,** the radical urban planner, completed the Louvre (or so they thought) by building the **North Wing** and the **Flore** and **Marsan** pavilions now adjoining the main palace to the Tuileries.

Collection The Louvre's art collection (floor plan at right) began with 12 paintings, including works by **Titian, Raphael,** and **Leonardo da Vinci** that **François I** had looted from Italy (He not only took the *Mona Lisa* but also the man who had painted it). By the time of **Louis XIV** (who reigned from 1643 to 1715), the royal collection numbered more than 2,500 items. Until the Revolution, works in the Louvre were strictly for the pleasure of the kings and their courtiers. In 1793, after nearly burning the Louvre to the ground, the Revolutionaries opened the collection to the masses. Today the Louvre possesses more than 400,000 works of art. Only a fraction of these are on exhibit at any given time. In a morning's hoofing, however, you can see many of the Louvre's greatest hits: the *Venus de Milo,* the *Winged Victory of Samothrace, Mona Lisa,* the Crown Jewels, the David Galleries, *Eagle of Sugerius,* Giudia—Law Code of Hammurabi, the Rubens Gallery, Michelangelo's *Slaves,* the *Seated Scribe,* and other highlights of art history.

The Louvre's collection is divided into seven categories: Greek and Roman Antiquities, Oriental Antiquities, Egyptian Antiquities, Sculptures, Objets d'Art, Paintings, and Drawings. Although Greco-Roman, Egyptian, and Oriental Antiquities warrant at the very least a quick look, the Louvre's richest collection consists of paintings.

Louvre Pyramid Adding to the Louvre Museum building seems to be an irresistible French pastime. Based on the designs of Chinese-American architect **I.M. Pei,** now topping the **Cour Napoléon** (Napoléon Court) is a 70.5-foot-tall glass pyramid, flanked by three smaller pyramids, a series of fountains, reflecting pools, and a bronze replica of the **Bernini** statue of **Louis XI.** The largest pyramid (see illustration next page) serves as the central entrance to the museum and as an enormous skylight above a 70,000-square-foot underground cavern.

The pyramid officially opened in April 1989, and its underground space contains an auditorium, an area for temporary art shows, and an exhibition of the 12th-century fortress that was unearthed prior to the pyramid's controversial construction, as well as ticket offices, conference rooms, laboratories, and museum shops. Tunnels lead from under the pyramid to each side of the U-shaped Louvre.

Traditionalists fear this latest addition has marred the Louvre's grandeur with a sort of Hyatt Regency glitz. **Michel Guy,** cultural minister under former French **President Giscard d'Estaing,** said Pei's pyramids turn the Louvre into a "cultural drugstore that looks like an airport." However, the design has garnered fans, and, lest we forget, the Eiffel Tower was also first greeted with guffaws.

The Louvre Museum's Floor Plans

Louvre Museum

The Richelieu Wing, named after the famed 17th-century French cardinal and statesman, opened in November 1993. Once occupied by France's Finance Ministry, the Richelieu Wing connects to the existing museum, and allows the Louvre to display 25 percent more of its art collection.

Excavations At the same time **President François Mitterrand** approved the Pei pyramid project, he also set aside close to $2 million for an immense archaeological excavation of the Louvre's courtyard. This ambitious project brought 70 archaeologists to supervise the dig in the **Cour Napoléon** and expose the ancient dungeons of the **King Philippe Auguste** fortress. More than 11 million objects were retrieved, ranging from Chinese porcelain imported during the Ming Dynasty to coins from the first century AD and an eighth-century human skeleton.The pyramid allows visitors to descend to the 12th-century dungeons and to view about 10,000 of the objects uncovered in the dig. In mid-1990 **Pei, Cobb, Freed, and Partners** began work on a large underground parking garage and bus station that will connect directly to the large pyramid. Aboveground will be a sculpture garden with trees, grass, and 18 **Maillol** sculptures.

A few words of advice for touring the Louvre: **1.** Don't even think about trying to see the museum's entire collection—or even half of it—in one day. Visit your favorite artworks the first time around, and come back for more another day. **2.** In the summer or other high-season months count on a half-hour wait to buy tickets. **3.** Wear comfortable shoes. Check your coat as you enter, but in winter keep a sweater handy because the museum is drafty. **4.** Guided tours in English leave every 20 minutes from the ground-floor information stand. **5.** When fatigue sets in, take a break in the museum cafeteria. If you lunch outside the Louvre and decide to re-enter, you'll need to

buy a new ticket. **6.** Certain exhibitions (for example, the Crown Jewels) close during the lunch hour (noon-2PM) and when there is a shortage of museum guards. ◆ Museum: M, Th-Su 9AM-6PM; W 9AM-9:45PM. Bookstores and postcard shops: M, W-Su 9:30AM-5PM. Place du Carrousel. Métro: Louvre. 40.20.51.51, 40.20.50.50

Within the Louvre Museum:

Cour Carrée The **Carrée Courtyard** in the Louvre becomes a chic circus during the fall and spring, when more than 50 fashion designers parade their ready-to-wear collections through striped tents set up here. ◆ Check at the information stand for a schedule of events

Le Grand Louvre ★★★$$ An exceptional restaurant by any standard, Le Grand Louvre is run by **André Daguin**, the chef and proprietor of the Hôtel de France, 64 kilometers (40 miles) west of Toulouse in Auch. Gascon specialties include foie gras, goose, *confit de canard* with mushrooms, and prune ice cream. ◆ Lunch and dinner. Closed Tuesday. 40.20.53.41

21 Cour Napoléon Under **King Philippe Auguste,** the **Napoléon Courtyard** was a patch of sparsely populated farmland. Over time, it sprouted a church, a charity school, a meat market, a menagerie for wild animals, the castle kitchens, and a street for prostitutes frequented by soldiers from the castle garrison. **Napoléon III** leveled the houses and paved over the courtyard in the late 19th century. ◆ Métro: Louvre

22 Place du Carrousel The square was named to commemorate a *carrousel* (equestrian gala) held by **King Louis XIV** and his court in June 1662 to honor the birth of the king's first child. More than 15,000 spectators watched the king lead a thundering brigade of horsemen dressed as Romans, sporting golden helmets with red plumes, gold breastplates, and red stockings. ◆ Métro: Louvre

Louvre Pyramid

22 L'Arc du Carrousel This marble arch with pink pillars (see above) was built in 1808 by **Napoléon** to celebrate **Austerlitz** and other military victories. It was then crowned with four splendid bronze horses Napoléon had looted from Venice; originally, the horses had stood in the **Temple of the Sun** at Corinth. In 1815, with the fall of Napoléon, Italy recovered the masterworks and copies were placed on top of the **Carrousel Arch.** The arch can be used like a gun sight to line up the grand alley of the **Tuileries Fountains,** the Egyptian **Obelisk of Luxor** in the Place de la Concorde (a half mile to the west), the **Champs-Elysées,** and the **Arc de Triomphe,** more than two miles away. ♦ Métro: Louvre

23 Musée des Arts Décoratifs Exhibiting furnishings that date from the period of **Louis XVI** through the 19th century, the **Museum of Decorative Arts** is something of a composite mansion, with rooms taken wholesale from different periods. Amid too much wallpaper and too many bowlegged chairs from Versailles, the patient and searching eye will discover singular treasures such as a **Tiepolo** painting, an exquisitely carved floral *boiserie* (woodwork) by **Oudry,** and hunting scenes by **Desportes.**
♦ Admission. W-Sa 12:30-6PM; Su noon-6PM. 107 Rue de Rivoli. Métro: Palais-Royal. 42.60.32.14

23 Musée National des Arts de la Mode Located in the Louvre's **Pavillon de Marsan,** the **Fashion Museum's** sleek and chic collection consists of some 10,000 costumes dating back to the 16th century. Among the highlights of the collection are the 17th-century gloves worn by **Anne of Austria, Brigitte Bardot's** wedding dress (made by **Jacques Esterel** in 1958), a robe designed for **Sarah Bernhardt,** and the gown worn by the **Empress Eugénie** to please **Napoléon III** when he returned from a hard day of empire-building. To enjoy everything the museum has to offer, take the elevator to the fifth floor and walk down; the view of the **Tuileries Gardens** from the top is spectacular. The museum boutique sells, among other things, a beret with an instruction sheet showing four ways to wear the classic French cap. ♦ Admission. M,

W-Sa 12:30-6PM; Su noon-6PM. 109 Rue de Rivoli. Métro: Palais-Royal. 42.60.32.14

24 Jeanne d'Arc This gilded equestrian statue by 19th-century sculptor **Frémiet** honors **Joan of Arc** (1412-31), the French national hero and Roman Catholic saint. Born during the **Hundred Years' War** (1337-1453), this charismatic peasant girl claimed she heard the voices of saints urging her to save France from the English. The saints enabled her to convince the **Dauphin Charles VII** to provide her with troops. Under Joan's generalship, the troops took back Orléans and routed the English forces in the Loire. In 1429, during an unsuccessful attempt to liberate Paris from the occupying English army, Joan stationed a cannon on Butte St.-Roch (leveled some three centuries ago as landfill for the Champ-de-Mars) to attack the St.-Honoré Gate (which is now 163 Rue St.-Honoré). A year later Joan of Arc was captured, and the following year she was convicted of witchcraft and heresy, then burned at the stake in Rouen. She was canonized in 1920, and today France honors her with a national holiday. Several years ago, Parisian medical students went on strike and, as part of their protest, wrapped statues throughout Paris with bandages. Joan of Arc was given special treatment: full-length plaster casts on both her legs. ♦ Place des Pyramides. Métro: Tuileries

25 Tuileries Palace Designed in 1564 by **Philibert Delorme,** this palace stood until 1884. It connected the two corner pavilions of the Louvre (paralleling what is today **Avenue du Général Lemonnier**) and took its name from the *tuile* (tile) factories that had previously stood on the site. **Catherine de Médici,** who built Tuileries, moved out after her astrologer, **Ruggieri,** told her she would die close to St.-Germain. (Tuileries was in the parish of St.-Germain-l'Auxerrois.) Catherine therefore built another palace near what is today the **Bourse du Commerce** (Commercial Stock Exchange), and there she died. As for Ruggieri's prediction: the priest who administered the last rites to Catherine de Médici was named **Julien de St.-Germain.**

Napoléon's second wife gave birth in the Tuileries Palace to a short-lived imperial heir, **l'Aiglon,** who was named the king of Rome. Subsequent royal residents included **Charles X** and **Louis-Philippe,** who ruled from 1831 to 1848 and was popularly known as the Grocers' King for his custom of carving the Sunday roast himself. In 1871, during the **Siege of Paris,** the Communards set Tuileries Palace afire. It burned for three days while the Louvre Museum staff worked frantically to save the collections. The palace was razed between 1882 and 1884. A single bay of the old Tuileries Palace was preserved and stands unmarked in a remote corner of the Tuileries Gardens behind the Jeu de Paume. ♦ Métro: Tuileries

26 Tuileries Gardens The gardens, which are undergoing a $50 million face-lift, were designed in 1649 for **Louis XIV** by **André Le Nôtre,** the king's gardener, who was born in a cottage on the royal grounds. Le Nôtre also designed the gardens at **Versailles, Chantilly,** and the **Château Vaux-le-Vicomte.** The Tuileries' violent past during the Revolution seems scarcely possible when you stroll through the manicured hedges and lawns near the 18 bronze nudes by **Aristide Maillol.** Old ladies feed the pigeons while threadbare African immigrants loft mechanical birds into the air in hope of attracting a sale. Kids race sailboats on the fountain under the watchful eyes of their governesses. You will also find four refreshment stands, a small merry-go-round, a swing set, and subdued pony rides for children.

From the upper terrace of the gardens is a splendid view of the Seine, the new **Musée d'Orsay,** and the **Legion d'Honneur,** which was begun by **Napoléon** to laud French accomplishment. Farther in the distance, you can glimpse the stern **Chambre des Députés,** France's congress. The Tuileries terrace has become known as a gathering spot for gay men. ♦ Métro: Tuileries

27 Hôtel Meurice $$$$ Heads of state, vacationing or exiled, have always favored the Meurice. **Alphonse XIII** of Spain stayed for years in Suite 112, and **Salvador Dalí** made the Royal Suite his Paris home for 30 years. During World War II, the Meurice served as Nazi headquarters. Here, in August 1944, in the immense Suite 108, **Commandant General von Cholitz,** after disobeying Hitler's orders to burn Paris, surrendered to the Allies.

Since 1816, when the hotel opened, its list of famous American visitors has included **Herman Melville, Henry James, Henry Wadsworth Longfellow,** and **Wilbur** and **Orville Wright,** who stayed here in 1907 while trying to sell their airplane to the French. (The Wrights used the familiar argument that their invention was the weapon to end all wars. The French military didn't bite on that, but the public was captivated by the Wrights' biplane, which they had shipped all the way to Paris from Dayton, Ohio.) Tea in the **Salon Pompadour** next to the Meurice's charming bar is a discreet pleasure, especially in the late afternoon after the pianist settles at the keys. Note: Owners of dogs must pay for bunking their pets in the hotel, while children under six cost their parents no extra charge. ♦ 228 Rue de Rivoli (between Rues de Castiglione and d'Alger). Métros: Tuileries, Concorde. 44.58.10.10

27 Galignani The classic French bookstore is sprinkled liberally with selections in English. ♦ M-Sa 10AM-7PM. 224 Rue de Rivoli (between Rues de Castiglione and d'Alger). Métros: Tuileries, Concorde. 42.60.76.07

ANGÉLINA

27 Angélina ★★★$$ The Rolls-Royce of Parisian tea salons, Angélina originally went by the name **Rumpelmayer's.** It was founded in 1903 on the former site of the king's stables. Amid marble pedestal tables, landscapes by **Lorrant-Heilbronn,** red carpet, and gilt decor, Angélina's overworked waitresses deliver justly celebrated pastries, sumptuous hot chocolate, and *Mont Blanc,* a weighty concoction of chestnut cream purée (a favorite of the **Aga Khan**). The whipped cream is fresh and the ice water is served on silver trays. In spring and autumn, strive to get a table near **Rue de Rivoli,** where you can watch the flurry of top models and fashion designers returning from the ready-to-wear collections. ♦ Breakfast, lunch, afternoon tea, and snacks. Closed three weeks in August. 226 Rue de Rivoli (between Rues de Castiglione and d'Alger). Métros: Concorde, Tuileries. 42.60.82.00

28 Inter-Continental $$$$ With more than 500 rooms, the Inter-Continental is one of the largest luxury hotels in the world, but size has swamped neither its considerable charm nor its lovely central courtyard. Designed in 1878 by **Charles Garnier** (who built the **Opéra Garnier** and the **Grand Hôtel**), the hotel has three salons (classified as historical landmarks) where the fanciest receptions in town are hosted, including the haute couture collections of **Yves Saint Laurent, Guy Laroche,** and **Jean Patou.** The Inter-Continental has always drawn a varied clientele: **Victor Hugo** and the **Empress Eugénie** liked it, and so does **Jerry Lewis.** ♦ 3 Rue de Castiglione (between Rues de Rivoli and du Mont-Thabor). Métros: Concorde, Tuileries. 44.77.11.11

Within the Inter-Continental:

La Terrasse Fleurie ★★$$$ This pleasant garden atrium offers a delicious Brittany lobster and risotto with black mushrooms or mousseline of rabbit in mustard, among other entrées. Save room for the delicious desserts. No dogs are allowed. ♦ Lunch and dinner. 44.77.11.11

Café Tuileries ★$$ Simple cuisine is served at reasonable prices. ♦ Breakfast, lunch, and dinner. 44.77.11.11

Bar du Lobby The celebrity-studded bar is paneled in dark wood and softly lighted with Tiffany lamps. ♦ Daily 9AM-midnight. 44.77.11.11

The average French filmgoer spends 57 francs a year on movies, whereas the average Parisian spends 330 francs.

Restaurants/Clubs: Red   Hotels: Blue
Shops/ Outdoors: Green   **Sights/Culture:** Black

29 Passerelle de Solférino Scheduled to be finished in the summer of 1995, the city's newest bridge will provide pedestrian passage between the **Tuileries Gardens** and the **Musée d'Orsay.** Constructed of a special type of steel used in naval architecture, the wood-planked *passerelle* (footbridge), designed by engineer **Marc Mimram,** will reflect the construction possibilities of current technology by being the first to span the Seine with only one arch. The bridge will also allow pedestrians a choice of direct access from either the upper or lower quays. ♦ Between Ponts de la Concorde and Royal. Métro: Musée d'Orsay

30 W.H. Smith and Son A bonanza of English paperbacks and magazines is carried here. ♦ M, W-Sa 9:30AM-7PM; Tu 10AM-7PM. 248 Rue de Rivoli (at Rue Cambon). Métro: Concorde. 42.60.37.97

31 Lescure ★★$$ This unspoiled bistro serves duck with cabbage, rabbit and sorrel, dandelion green salad, and delicious tarts. ♦ Lunch and dinner; lunch only on Saturday. Closed Sunday and 23 December to 1 January. 7 Rue de Mondovi (between Rues de Rivoli and du Mont-Thabor). Reservations recommended. Métro: Concorde. 42.60.18.91

32 Hôtel Talleyrand Designed by **Gabriel,** the architect for **Louis XV,** and **Chalgrin,** who built the Arc de Triomphe, this *hôtel* was originally the residence of diplomat par excellence **Charles-Maurice de Talleyrand-Périgord** and subsequently housed **Czar Alexander I,** several French **Rothschilds,** and, during World War II, the German Navy, which kept prisoners of war in the cellars. Today this historic building houses the U.S. cultural and information services, best known among traveling Americans as the office where you replace lost or stolen passports. ♦ 2 Rue St.-Florentin (between Rues de Rivoli and St.-Honoré). Métro: Concorde. 42.61.80.75

33 Galerie National du Jeu de Paume Built in 1853 by **Napoléon III,** the Jeu de Paume has nothing to do with *jus de pomme* (apple juice). Its name refers to a racket sport (see next page). From 1947 until 1986, the museum contained many French Impressionist masterpieces and was the most visited museum in the world relative to its size. The collection has moved across the river to St.-Germain's **Musée d'Orsay** (see page 53), and the renovated Jeu de Paume now hosts changing exhibitions by contemporary artists. On the terrace to the south of the museum is a monument to **Charles Perrault,** the 17th-century fabulist who convinced **Colbert** to make the Tuileries public. ♦ Tu-F noon-7PM; Sa-Su 10AM-7PM. Closed holidays. Jardin des Tuileries, Place de la Concorde. Métro: Concorde. 47.03.12.44, 47.03.12.50

34 Octagonal Fountain and Statues Between the **Jeu de Paume** and **L'Orangerie**

are 18th-century statues representing the Nile, the Tiber, the Loire and Loiret, the Marne, and, of course, the Seine rivers. On the right is a modest bust of **André Le Nôtre,** the landscape architect. The Tuileries is framed from the west by **Coysevox's** two winged horses, erected in 1719. The first human ascent in a hydrogen balloon, on 1 December 1783, was launched beside the octagonal fountain. The flight was made by physician **J.A.C. Charles** and his mechanic, **Noel Robert.** Thousands packed the park to watch the historic flight; among the spectators were **Benjamin Franklin** and French philosopher **Denis Diderot,** who instantly conjectured that one day human beings might go to the moon. The hot-air balloon rose more than 2,000 feet and carried its passengers safely 25 miles to the north of Paris. Now, every New Year's Day, the celebrity-studded **Paris-Dakar** overland motor race across Europe and North Africa begins here. ♦ Métro: Concorde

35 L'Orangerie This former citrus nursery is the permanent home of the **Walter-Guillaume** collection of paintings, including 144 masterworks by such artists as **Renoir, Monet, Cézanne, Soutine, Picasso, Derain,** and **Matisse.** The artists best represented are Pierre-Auguste Renoir (24 works) and André Derain (28 paintings). The Cézannes are exceptional, particularly *Apples and Biscuits,* whose audacious composition is held together by a drawer latch placed dead center in the picture.

On the lower floor, mounted on curved panels, are Claude Monet's eight giant water lily murals, *Les Nymphéas.* Monet's visual kingdom was centered at his house and gardens in Giverny near Paris (see "Day Trips," page 205). ♦ Admission. M, W-Su 9:45AM-5:15PM. Jardin des Tuileries, Place de la Concorde. Métro: Concorde. 42.97.48.16

36 Place de la Concorde The largest square in Paris, covering 21 acres, was a swamp until royal architect **Jacques-Ange Gabriel** was asked by **Louis XV** to find a setting appropriate for an equestrian statue of the king himself. The statue, which was removed during the Revolution, lasted here less than 20 years. On Sunday, 21 January 1793, the guillotine was set up on the Place de la Concorde's west side, near the spot where the statue of **Brest** sculpted by **Cortot** stands today. That done, **Louis XVI** was beheaded, and the 13-month **Reign of Terror** began. Among its thousands of victims were **Marie Antoinette, Madame du Barry, Charlotte Corday,** and **Danton.** On the evening of 28 July 1794, more than 1,300 townspeople gathered here to watch the execution of **Robespierre.** During the Revolution, no fewer than 1,343 victims were executed on the **Place de la Revolution** (as it was known then), and the square reeked so of gore that herds of oxen balked at crossing it. ♦ Métro: Concorde

36 Obelisk of Luxor This 3,300-year-old, 220-ton Egyptian obelisk is unquestionably the oldest monument in Paris. Originally erected around the 13th century BC, the 76-foot-tall monument was a gift to **Louis Philippe** from **Mohammed Ali Pasha,** who was viceroy of Egypt in 1831. (He also gave **Queen Victoria** a slightly shorter obelisk taken from Heliopolis, **Cleopatra's Needle.**) The Paris obelisk, which replaced the equestrian statue of **Louis XV** that was removed during the Revolution, had been taken from the ruins of the Temple of Luxor. (The Louvre has a marvelous set of four sun-worshiping baboons that also came from the temple.)

The pink-granite obelisk traveled 600 miles by barge down the Nile to Alexandria, was towed across the Mediterranean and Atlantic, carted through Normandy, and finally erected at Place de la Concorde in 1836, ending a political squabble over whose monument should adorn the square dedicated to neither a French king nor Napoléon's army. The designs on the pedestal are meant to illustrate the technological wizardry involved in the obelisk's journey from Egypt to Paris. Visitors to this square should be forewarned: pedestrians crossing the Place de la Concorde on foot may be risking their lives. But go ahead; you only live once (however briefly), and the obelisk is worth a close look. What's more, the island surrounding it provides an unobstructed view of the Champs-Elysées. Cross at the light! ◆ Métro: Concorde

From Monks to McEnroe—Tennis Has Come a Long Way

The French court game *jeu de paume,* a complicated precursor of modern lawn tennis, originated when bored 13th-century French monks swatted a wad of rags around a monastery courtyard with their bare hands (*jeu de paume* literally means "a game of the palm"). By the 17th century, it was played with a racket and had become the French national game: Paris alone had 250 courts. The dashing François I constructed a court in the Louvre as well as a floating tennis court on his 2,000-ton warship *La Grande Françoise.*

The kings and nobles who played it used lopsided rackets to send the balls ricocheting off the wall, floor, and sloping gallery roof, or sailing over a net that sagged like a hammock. Points were awarded for swatting balls through portals and striking bells in windows. It was life-size pinball, high-speed chess, and racquetball in a Gothic cathedral all wrapped into one. A player had 40 surfaces to bounce a ball off of, and the ball often traveled in excess of 120 miles per hour.

At its toughest, the royal tennis game proved to be a killer workout for overzealous sovereigns. Half a dozen kings expired from sheer exhaustion and pneumonia after ferocious jeu de paume matches. Another crowned casualty of the game was the affable but maladroit King Charles VIII, who keeled over shortly after a head-on collision with the lintel of the tennis-court door in his château at Amboise.

Jeu de paume became wildly popular and was repeatedly banned by nobles convinced that tennis-playing merchants and yeomen were neglecting their work and the country's defense. In spite of the prohibition, the craze raged on in hundreds of underground *tripots*—athletic speakeasies notorious for bootlegged tennis equipment, cheap wine, and reckless games of chance. (To this day, when the French gamble away their paychecks, they still curse: "*J'ai paumé.*")

In the France of Louis XIV, the game's popularity suffered as a consequence of increasingly repressive legislation and the king's indifference to the sport (he, after all, was a billiards man). Eventually jeu de paume courts were transformed into playhouses or public meeting places. In fact, a meeting held on 20 June 1789 in the court at Versailles changed the course of French history. Deputies of the Third Estate assembled there and took the historic oath that sparked the French Revolution. More than a century later, in 1907, another group of revolutionaries, the painters called Impressionists, commandeered the city's last two royal jeu de paume courts in the Tuileries Gardens to use them as a gallery for their canvases.

Modern tennis owes a great debt to jeu de paume. The very name tennis comes from the traditional warning *Tenez* (Take heed), which French monks shouted before each *serve*—another term added later to the game by nobles who felt it was beneath them to start a game themselves (they ordered a servant to toss the first ball, and then they would join in).

Known as court tennis in the United States, the game is frequently referred to by English purists as "real tennis" or "Tennis with a capital T" to distinguish it from that slam-bang adulteration played at Flushing Meadows and Wimbledon. Although it originated in France, jeu de paume today is unquestionably Anglo-Saxon. Of the world's 34 courts currently in use, Britain boasts 19, the United States 9, and Australia 4. Only two courts remain in France, one in Bordeaux and one in Paris at the Société Sportive de Jeu de Paume et de Racquets on Rue Lauriston. To catch a glimpse of the ancient game, stop by the club in the late afternoon or evening when French and American businesspeople from the fashionable 16th arrondissement stop on their way home to play a friendly set.

Every evening, a steady stream of people toting plastic containers queues up to collect water from the fountain at tiny Square Lamartine, near Avenue Victor Hugo, in the 16th arrondissement. This isn't the fountain of youth, however, just water, "slightly mineralized, and of good quality," drawn directly from an underground well, one of only three in Paris.

36 Sculpture and Fountains Defining **Gabriel's** original octagonal square are several groups of statuary, allegories of **Bordeaux, Brest, Lille, Marseilles, Nantes, Rouen,** and **Strasbourg.** Believe it or not, the tiny two-room pavilions underneath the statues were once rented out as dwellings. North and south of the obelisk stand two fountains, one representing *Maritime Navigation* and the other *River Navigation*. The latter, ironically, is the farthest from the Seine. The sea nymphs and water gods adorning the fountains were replicated from fountains in St. Peter's Square in Rome. ♦ Métro: Concorde

37 North Facade of Place de la Concorde When royal architect **Jacques-Ange Gabriel** designed the **Place de la Concorde,** he made sure that buildings would face only its north side, and in 1757, work began on the two matching neoclassical north facades separated down the middle by Rue Royale. The facade's design was borrowed from the **Louvre Colonnades,** which Gabriel himself had restored. The **Hôtel de la Marine,** part of the facade east of Rue Royale, was intended to be lodging for foreign ambassadors, but became first a royal-furniture storehouse and then, in 1792, the **Admiralty** (now known as the Ministry of the Navy). The building on the opposite corner is now occupied by the prestigious **French Automobile Club** and the very elegant **Hôtel Crillon.** On 6 February 1778, the Crillon was where **Louis XVI** and American diplomats (including **Benjamin Franklin**) signed the Treaty of Friendship and Trade, which recognized the independence of the 13 American states. ♦ Métro: Concorde

37 Hôtel Crillon $$$$ One of the swankest hotels in Paris, its facade was designed in 1758 by **Jacques-Ange Gabriel** for the **Count of Crillon**. The family managed to hold onto the property right through the Revolution, in spite of having the guillotine set up practically on its doorstep. And today the Crillon is the last of the grand four-star hotels in Paris to remain one-hundred percent French-owned. Should you decide that the kids don't really need to go to college after all, rent one of the three royal suites (Red, White, or Blue) and enjoy some of the best views in Paris of the Place de la Concorde, the Seine, and the Eiffel Tower. The management has recently opened the **Marie Antoinette Apartment** (room rates quoted on request), where the queen is said to have taken her music lessons. Among the famous American couples who have romanced in the Crillon: **Mary Pickford** and

Douglas Fairbanks, who stopped here during their 1920 honeymoon, and newspaper magnate **William Randolph Hearst** and his girlfriend, **Marion Davies.** The hotel's proximity to the American and British embassies assures a clientele of well-bred Anglo-Americans, diplomats, royalty, and wealthy foreigners. ♦ 10 Place de la Concorde (between Rues Boissy-d'Anglas and Royale). Métro: Concorde. 44.71.15.00

Within the Hôtel Crillon:

Ambassadeurs Restaurant ★★$$$$ Innovative chef **Christian Constant's** restaurant features a savory *St. Pierre, agneau de Pauillac,* and a tasty chocolate mousse *à l'orange.* ♦ Lunch and dinner. Reservations required. 44.71.16.16

Obelisk ★$$ Serving delicious pastas and regional cheeses, this restaurant offers meals suitable for lighter appetites and slimmer purses. ♦ Lunch and dinner; lunch only on Saturday. Closed Sunday and in August. Reservations recommended. 44.71.15.15

Bar du Crillon International journalists and visiting diplomats often stop here for a glass of champagne before dinner. Its hot *feuilletés* (croissantlike pastries) are great snacks. ♦ Daily noon-1:30AM. 44.71.15.39

38 Maxim's ★★★$$$ Paris without Maxim's? *Pas possible.* Where would all those rich business executives lunch? And where would the bona fide blue bloods, glitzy jet-setters, and fashionably late diners find such a Belle Epoque setting? Maxim's has given the royal treatment to **Edward VIII** of England and **Leopold II** of Belgium, as well as to prominent Americans such as **John Paul Getty, Jackie Onassis,** and **Elizabeth Taylor.** Not everyone is admitted to the **Pierre Cardin** landmark that has since been cloned in New York, Mexico, Tokyo, Singapore, and Beijing. If you are allowed to pass through the doors, expect unsurpassed champagne and service, disappointing food, and a splendid and expensive Parisian evening. ♦ Lunch and dinner. Hours change July through August. 3 Rue Royale (between Rue St.-Honoré and Place de la Concorde). Reservations required. Métro: Concorde. 42.65.27.94

39 Au Bain Marie This elegant housewares shop sells silver asparagus tongs, crystal carafes, and other signatures of refinement. ♦ M-Sa 10AM-7PM. 10 Rue Boissy-d'Anglas (between Rues de Rivoli and du Faubourg St.-Honoré). Métro: Concorde. 42.66.59.74

Restaurants/Clubs: Red	Hotels: Blue
Shops/ 🌿Outdoors: Green	**Sights/Culture:** Black

The Restaurant: A Revolutionary Invention

During the French Revolution, food was so scarce that most people were far more concerned with sheer survival than they were with gastronomy. Never before had the humble potato, introduced to the Court of Versailles by Parmentier on 25 August 1785, been so revered. And Parisians were in no condition to appreciate the inadvertent humor of Marie Antoinette's legendary suggestion that they eat cake if they had no bread. Of course, "the baker, the baker's wife, and the baker's son" (a reference to the royal family) did not survive the Revolution.

Far from being a mere digression in culinary history, however, the Revolution did much to determine its course. It interrupted an unprecedented refinement in taste and decorative arts, and as soon as the initial turmoil subsided, frustrations that had been mounting amid deprivation gave way to an explosion of culinary creativity that would last throughout the 1800s. In a broad sense, the Revolutionary period was a crucial stage in the evolution of taste and in the creation of restaurants as we know them today.

The cuisine of the *Ancien Régime* (see "Revolutionary Expressions" on page 135) was legendary for its heaviness. Rousseau, who apparently wished only for a simple chervil omelet, complained in his *Confessions* of the overly elaborate dishes his patrons lavished upon him. Diderot, completely exhausted by the Baron d'Holbach's dinner parties, used to tell about taking walks to aid digestion, "if such a thing was possible." Twenty-odd courses of rich foods could weaken even the heartiest resolve.

Under the circumstances, the time was ripe to impose what was then referred to as *la cuisine moderne*. The luminaries of the day felt that cooking, like the other arts, should contribute to the march of progress. Food became less rich, and those who could afford it hired a cook.

Then everything grew complicated. The cookbook appeared, later to evolve into a particularly prolific literary genre. The chef's métier became so specialized that besides the *cuisiner* himself, there was also the *pâtissièr* and the *rôtisscur*. A major turning point came when the art of cooking emerged from the kitchens of private mansions to reach the general public in the form of a restaurant.

Under the *Ancien Régime,* post houses, taverns, inns, and cafés throughout France offered hazardous fare, often in conditions of dubious cleanliness. The first true restaurant was the illustrious Beauvilliers, established in 1782. It boasted elegant dining rooms, a large wine cellar, and excellent cuisine. For more than 20 years, high-society diners would consider his address *sans pareil.* Even today, the restaurant on Butte Montmartre puts on grandiose airs.

Another major event of the time was the appearance of the first literary cafés. As author Gérard-Georges Lemaire wrote, these cafés revolutionized the spread of ideas. Paris had 2,000 cafés before the Revolution began; that number doubled by the early 1800s.

Coffee had just been introduced from the French West Indies, and cafés quickly came into vogue, animated by enlightened thinkers from dawn till dark. Lampoons and other rags made the rounds and were posted on the ceramic stove of the most famous café of all, Le Procope, which is still in business on Rue de l'Ancienne Comédie in Paris. The Café Anglais on Quai de Conti relayed political sparks originating in England, and activities at the cafés tucked under the arches of the Palais Royal created a veritable political powder keg. Speakers stood on tabletops, and journalists drifted from one place to another.

These cafés took on distinct personalities. Le Procope was the haunt of Danton and Marat; the Café de Foy was frequented first by the aristocrats and then by the Jacobins; and the terrifying *tricoteuses,* the radical women who took their knitting to the Convention deliberations, gathered at the Café des Feuillants. As for Robespierre, he enjoyed playing chess at the Café de la Régence.

Meanwhile, the provinces were braving drought and food shortages. The masses were convinced that the Duc d'Orléans and hoarders hoping to make big profits wanted to starve them, and there was talk of a "famine pact." Fortunately, the Revolutionaries had no objection to importing foreign wheat, and the return to more normal harvests in 1790 and 1791 tided them over until 1793. In these times of domestic insurrection and foreign wars, the Convention passed rationing measures, legislated price ceilings on basic foods (illicit price hikes were punishable by death), and instituted a bread card. Even the idea of a "civic fast" was considered, and the Revolutionaries planted vegetables in the Tuileries and Luxembourg gardens—more a symbolic statement than an effective solution to the hunger problem.

As supplies of the most basic ingredients dwindled, the idea of the civic banquet was born—ancestor of both the republican banquet and the soup kitchen. A certain Monsieur de Saint-Ange believed that all the bourgeois of Paris should serve an open-house meal in front of their residences as a grand community gesture in observance of the fall of the Bastille. This would give them the opportunity to feed the poor while demonstrating their Republican zeal. These civic banquets were held in 1794, but an atmosphere of suspicion prevailed. People worried about how their neighbors would judge them: too much generosity could be suspect, and too little could be interpreted as a lack of Revolutionary enthusiasm.

During Thermidor, the Revolutionary period marking the end of the Reign of Terror, signs of the good life reappeared in Paris. The Viscount Paul de Barras, who had a hand in the coup ousting Robespierre, resumed hosting his legendary feasts, and chefs unemployed since the *Ancien Régime* went back to work. But the Revolution continued to influence cuisine. For example, a well-known lobster dish was named after Sardou's play *Thermidor,* which apparently opened and closed on the same night, 24 January 1894. "But lobster thermidor," says chef Craig Claiborne, "is still a running hit."

Alexandre Lazareff
Reprinted with permission from *France Magazine*

40 Pont de la Concorde This five-arched bridge designed in 1791 by civil engineer **Jean Rodolphe Perronet** is constructed in part with stone souvenirs from the 1789 storming and demolition of the Bastille, allegedly so that people could forever trample the ruins of the old fortress. ♦ Métro: Concorde

41 Palais-Bourbon The French home of the **National Assembly** was constructed in 1728 by the **Duchess of Bourbon**, one of **Louis XIV's** daughters. In 1807 **Povet** designed the mansion's facade for Napoléon in the Greek-Revival style, to mirror the **Madeleine** across the river; it now houses the **Chamber of Deputies** (the lower house of the French Parliament). Nearly 500 deputies convene in a chamber decorated in crimson and gold and adorned with a large Napoleonic eagle (however, republicanism has since whittled that symbol down to a cock). Even the president of France is denied entrance into this exclusive club's assemblies. Ordinary people, however, can watch sessions from a public gallery (provided they are among the first in line, tag along with a journalist, or have a pass signed by a deputy). If you tour the building (which also requires written permission), don't miss **Delacroix's** allegorical *History of Civilization* on the library ceiling. To attend an assembly debate, write (while it's in session) to: Assemblée Nationale, 33 Quai d'Orsay, 75007 Paris. To tour the building, write to: Administrative Office, 126 Rue de l'Université, 75007 Paris. ♦ Entrance on Quai d'Orsay. Métro: Chambre-des-Députés. 40.63.64.08

42 Horses of Marly These rearing marble horses (titled *Africans Mastering the Numidian Horses*) were sculpted by **Nicolas** and **Guillaume Coustou.** They guard the entrance to the **Champs-Elysées** and were taken from the **Château de Marly** (the **Louis XIV** château that was destroyed in the Revolution) and brought to Paris in 1795. Sixteen live horses dragged the stone effigies

to Paris in five hours, a transportation feat considered so marvelous that the vehicle in which they were carried is on exhibition in the **Conservatoire des Arts et Métiers.** ♦ Métro: Concorde

42 Champs-Elysées The world's most famous boulevard was formerly a forsaken marshland, unsafe after dark until 1616, when **Marie de Médici,** the wife of **Henri IV,** decided to turn it into a fashionable carriage-drive, the **Cours-la-Reine** (Queen's Way). A half-century later, master landscaper **André Le Nôtre** planted double rows of chestnut trees along this wide avenue and renamed it the **Elysian Fields.** In 1724 the boulevard was extended to the top of the **Butte de Chaillot.** During the Second Empire, architect **Jacques Soufflot** leveled it by 16 feet to ease the climb for carriage-towing horses.

Since its creation, the Champs-Elysées has always been the place to promenade. Processions marking the liberation of Paris (26 August 1944), the student-worker demonstrations (30 May 1968), and the silent march after the death of **Charles de Gaulle** (12 November 1970) all made their way down the Champs-Elysées. If you fancy pomp and pageantry, show up here on Bastille Day (14 July), when the jets of the French Air Force streak over the Champs-Elysées at low altitude; Armistice Day (11 November), when the president lays a wreath on the **Tomb of the Unknown Soldier;** the finish of the grueling three-week Tour de France bicycle race in July; and at Christmas-time, when the avenue's trees twinkle with tiny white lights. The eastern half of the Champs-Elysées, from **Place de la Concorde** to **Rond Point,** is bordered by lush gardens of azaleas and mature chestnut trees where **Marcel Proust** played as a child. Within the garden today are a number of theaters (the **Théâtre de Marigny** and **Théâtre Renauld Barrault**) and exclusive restaurants with pretty garden terraces, such as **Laurent, L'Espace,** and **Elysée Lenôtre.**

Horses of Marly

Champs-Elysées

The western half of the avenue, between **Rond Point** and **Place de l'Etoile,** has lost its aristocratic sheen; today it is a crowded commercial strip of banks, airline offices, cinemas, outdoor cafés, fast-food parlors, and emporia selling perfume and Ray Ban sunglasses. A recent face-lift gave the avenue new granite paving and the city's fanciest underground parking garage. ♦ Métros: Concorde, Champs-Elysées-Clemenceau, Franklin-D.-Roosevelt, George-V, Charles-de-Gaulle-Etoile

43 American Embassy Designed in 1933 by the New York firm **Delano and Aldrich** and flanked by two bald eagles in stone, the embassy and nearby consulate are staffed by about 500 Americans working for an alphabet soup of agencies including the IRS, CIA, FBI, and, of course, departments of defense, state, agriculture, and commerce. ♦ Rue de Boissy-d'Anglas (at Ave Gabriel). Métro: Concorde. 42.96.12.02

44 L'Espace Restaurant ★★$$ This **Pierre Cardin**-designed restaurant with neo-1950s Miami Beach decor (floral beach parasols and plastic chairs) serves a dandy buffet of 110 entrées and 40 desserts. It is a favorite with international TV and film glitterati, whose autographed photos festoon the walls. **Liza Minnelli, Richard Gere, Brigitte Bardot,** and **Arletty** have all passed through at one time or another. There's dining on the garden terrace in summer and a Sunday brunch. ♦ Lunch and dinner; dinner only on Saturday; Sunday brunch. 1 Ave Gabriel (between Ave de Marigny and Place de la Concorde). Reservations recommended. Métro: Concorde. 42.66.11.70

45 Ledoyen ★★$$$$ During the reign of **Louis XVI** (1774-92), this restaurant (pictured below) was a country inn and dairy bar serving fresh milk to travelers. Dinner here on the south side of the Champs-Elysées can still seem pleasantly bucolic. **Régine,** the reigning

Ledoyen

queen of Paris nightlife, recently bought and redecorated the historic restaurant. The menu is Mediterranean-influenced: zucchini flowers with truffles, shellfish ratatouille, and *mille-feuille* of polenta and lobster. Within months of its 1988 opening, Ledoyen had earned its first Michelin star. ♦ Lunch and dinner. Closed Saturday and Sunday. Carré des Champs-Elysées (between Place de la Concorde and Ave Dutuit). Jacket and tie required. Reservations required. Métro: Champs-Elysées-Clemenceau. 47.42.23.23

46 Elysée Lenôtre ★★$$$$ In a **Louis XVI** pavilion that has served dinners to a range of notables from **Edward VII** to **Toulouse-Lautrec,** the celebrated pastry chef **Gaston Lenôtre** offers delectable meals topped off with his pièces de résistance: marvelous desserts. On the ground floor is the less expensive **Les Jardines de Lenôtre** (★★$$$), which opens onto a garden terrace where lunch and dinner are served in the summer. ♦ Le Pavillon: Dinner. Closed Sunday. Les Jardines: Lunch; dinner also in July and August. Closed Saturday and Sunday. 10 Ave des Champs-Elysées (in the Carré Marigny at Ave de Marigny). Métro: Champs-Elysées-Clemenceau. 42.65.85.10

47 Statue of Clemenceau Georges Clemenceau (1841-1929) was the outspoken French politician who at the end of World War I helped form a coalition government to rally French morale and fight the Germans. Sculptor **François Cogne** has captured Clemenceau's trademarks in bronze: the walrus mustache, high leather boots, walking stick, and wool scarf flapping in the wind. ♦ Place Clemenceau. Métro: Champs-Elysées-Clemenceau

48 Petit Palais This little turn-of-the-century palace houses the city's **Fine Arts Museum,** with a collection specializing in 19th-century French painters such as **Delacroix, Courbet, Monet, Cézanne,** and **Bonnard.** The architect, **Charles Girault,** crowned the building with a graceful cupola and decorated its two wings with Ionic columns and rococo embellishments. ♦ Admission. Tu-Su 10AM-5:40PM. Ave Winston-Churchill (at Place Clemenceau). Métro: Champs-Elysées-Clemenceau. 42.65.12.73

49 Pont Alexandre III Between the **Invalides** and the **Grand Palais** is an elegant Belle Epoque bridge embodying the architectural giddiness that celebrated the French spirit of ingenuity and optimism at the turn of the century. The Pont Alexandre III is encrusted with every Greco-Roman frippery in the book: human-size cupids, lavish garlands, huge golden statues of Pegasus and Renown, prides of lions, and reams of trumpets, tridents, shells, and shields. Built to commemorate the 1892 French-Russian alliance, the bridge bears the Russian and French coats of arms side by side and teams a

sculptural allegory of the Seine with one of the Neva. ♦ Métro: Champs-Elysées-Clemenceau

50 Grand Palais Along with the **Pont Alexandre III** and the **Petit Palais,** this exuberant stone, steel, and glass structure is an Art Nouveau creation at its excessive zenith. The Grand Palais and Petit Palais were built for the Universal Exhibition of 1900, the first world's fair in Paris. Famous for its domed and vaulted glass roof and superb staircase, the Grand Palais was designed by three architects: **Henri Deglane** built the principal facade; **Albert Thomas** the rear facade; and **Louis-Albert Louvet** the rest. With 54,000 square feet of floor space (equivalent to nearly 14 basketball courts), the Grand Palais is used for book fairs, car shows, and blockbuster art exhibitions. It has hosted major retrospectives of **Picasso, Léger, Chagall, Cézanne,** and **Manet.** ♦ Admission. Open only for special exhibitions and events. Check hours in *Pariscope.* Ave Winston-Churchill (at Place Clemenceau). Métro: Champs-Elysées-Clemenceau. 44.13.17.17

51 1 Avenue de Marigny In 1954, when American novelist **John Steinbeck** and his family moved into this house, he described it in a letter to **Richard Rodgers** and **Oscar Hammerstein:** "It is next to the Rothschilds and across the street from the president of France. How's that for an address for a Salinas kid?" ♦ Corner of Ave Gabriel. Métro: Champs-Elysées-Clemenceau

52 Résidence Maxim's $$$$ Near the intersection of the Champs-Elysées and the Place de la Concorde, **Pierre Cardin** has created an Art Nouveau architectural confection that accommodates visiting executives and sheiks for anywhere from $345 to $6,900 per night, depending on whether you prefer, say, the **Sarah Bernhardt** bed or the **Toulouse-Lautrec** painting in your room. Decisions, decisions. ♦ 42 Ave Gabriel (between Ave Matignon and Rue du Cirque). Métro: Franklin-D.-Roosevelt. 45.61.96.33

53 Restaurant Laurent ★★$$$ Just down the street from the official residence of the French president, this restaurant's parking lot is always crowded with chauffeured limousines bearing diplomatic license plates. Laurent is known for its lovely garden terrace, impeccable service, and nouvelle bourgeois cuisine, which includes salmon carpaccio with caviar, lobster salad, and New York sirloin steak. The wine list is overseen by the aptly named **Philippe Bourguignon.** ♦ Lunch and dinner; dinner only on Saturday. Closed Sunday. 41 Ave Gabriel (between Aves Matignon and de Marigny). Jacket and tie required. Reservations required. Métro: Champs-Elysées-Clemenceau. 47.23.79.18

Restaurants/Clubs: Red   **Hotels:** Blue
Shops/ ♦Outdoors: Green   **Sights/Culture:** Black

54 Théâtre Renaud Barrault After moving from the old Gare d'Orsay, the renowned theater company of **Jean-Louis Barrault** and **Madeleine Renaud** has taken up residence on the Champs-Elysées and performs everything from **Aristophanes** to **Pierre Corneille** and **Samuel Beckett**. Brief, often bravura programs take place every Sunday at 11AM from October through May. ♦ Box office: M-Sa 11AM-6PM. 2bis Ave Franklin-D.-Roosevelt (between Aves des Champs-Elysées and du Général-Eisenhower). Métros: Champs-Elysées-Clemenceau, Franklin-D.-Roosevelt. 44.95.98.00

Within the Théâtre Renaud Barrault:

Théâtre du Rond-Point Restaurant
★$$ On the lower level of the prestigious theater, this restaurant serves reasonably priced meals. Dine on the delightful terrace in summer. ♦ Lunch, afternoon tea, and dinner. Reservations recommended. 44.95.98.00

55 Palais de la Découverte The western part of the Grand Palais houses a sprawling science museum with Jacques Cousteau festivals, holography exhibitions, 9,000 stars twinkling on the ceiling of its celebrated planetarium, and daily demonstrations on everything from ants to astronomy. Kids love the Madagascar agates and, of course, metal replicas of dinosaurs. ♦ Admission. Tu-Sa 9:30AM-6PM; Su 10AM-7PM. Ave Franklin-D.-Roosevelt (at Ave du Général-Eisenhower). Métro: Franklin-D.-Roosevelt. 43.59.18.21

56 France Amérique If you want to give a party during your Paris stay and insist on nothing less than a Second-Empire town house for your setting, consider the France Amérique, which rents its three Louis XVI rooms (200 square meters) for festivities lasting just until midnight. Have your catering prepared by **Angélina** for the perfect lavish bash. ♦ 9 Ave Franklin-D.-Roosevelt (between Rues Jean-Goujon and François-1er). Métro: Franklin-D.-Roosevelt. 43.59.51.00, 42.25.98.27

56 Lasserre ★★★$$$$ In the same luxurious league (and price range) as the Tour d'Argent and the Grand Véfour, Lasserre is famous for its caviar, 1930s ocean liner decor, and service bordering on perfection. Owner **René Lasserre** got his start in the restaurant business washing dishes at the age of 13. Located in a small town house, Lasserre's main dining room is reached by a velvet-lined elevator. In warm weather, the ceiling, painted by **Touchagues,** rolls away to admit the stars and a little cool air. Menu masterpieces from a rather traditional repertoire include: Belon oysters, *canard à l'orange,* sea bass with sorrel, and crêpes Grand Marnier. The restaurant's wine cellar has 140,000 bottles. ♦ Lunch and dinner; dinner only on Monday. Closed Sunday and

in August. 17 Ave Franklin-D.-Roosevelt. Reservations required. Métro: Franklin-D.-Roosevelt (between Rues Jean-Goujon and François-1er). 43.59.53.43

57 7 Rue François-1er During World War II, this building, formerly the **Hôtel du Palais,** was the headquarters of the **American Red Cross.** It was here that American poet **e.e. cummings,** a volunteer ambulance driver, spent a glorious May in 1917 detached from his unit. This act of independence resulted, through a tragicomic series of events, in his spending six months in a French prison, an experience that provided cummings with ample material for *The Enormous Room,* published in 1922. ♦ Between Place François-1er and Cours Albert-1er. Métro: Franklin-D.-Roosevelt

The Guillotine

"The king heard his sentence with remarkable equanimity. They offered him a coat; he said: 'I don't need it.' He wore a brown jacket, black breeches, white stockings, and a white flannel waistcoat. He climbed into the carriage, a green one. He sat at the back with his confessor; two gendarmes sat in front. He read some psalms. . . . The steps of the scaffold were extremely steep. The king leaned on the priest. On the last step, he escaped, as it were, from his confessor and ran to the far end of the scaffold. He was very flushed; he gazed down at the square, waiting for the drums to cease beating for a moment. Voices called out to the executioners: 'Do your duty!' Four of them seized him: while they were binding him he let out a dreadful cry."

Michelet, on the execution of Louis XVI

58 San Régis $$$$ This sophisticated and discreet little Paris hotel has hosted **Gene Kelly, James Mason, Raquel Welch,** and **Lauren Bacall.** It's decorated with fine antiques and paintings and sits close (but not too close) to the Champs-Elysées. ♦ 12 Rue Jean-Goujon (between Place François-1er and Ave Franklin-D.-Roosevelt). Métro: Franklin-D.-Roosevelt. 43.59.41.90

59 25 Avenue Franklin-D.-Roosevelt From 1862 until the end of the Civil War, **John Slidell,** the Confederate commissioner to France, spent his time in a vain attempt to gain diplomatic recognition and financial support for the Southern cause. After the Confederacy's defeat, Slidell chose to remain in this house in Paris. ♦ Between Rue Jean-Goujon and Impasse d'Antin. Métro: Franklin-D.-Roosevelt

60 Avenue Matignon This is gallery alley for Right Bank art and antiques. Take note of the stamp-collectors' market along this street and the connecting **Avenue Gabriel.** ♦ Stamp market: Th, Sa-Su, holidays. Métro: Franklin-D.-Roosevelt

60 Le Berkeley ★$$ A classic oysters-and-champagne, steak-and-fries restaurant, Le Berkeley features the red decor of a first-class dining car. ♦ Breakfast, lunch, dinner, and late-night. 7 Ave Matignon (at Rue de Ponthieu). Reservations recommended. Métro: Franklin-D.-Roosevelt. 42.25.47.79, 42.25.72.25

61 Artcurial In the middle of this sprawling three-story complex of galleries is an extraordinary bookstore for art lovers. ♦ Tu-Sa 10:30AM-7:15PM. Closed three weeks in August. 9 Ave Matignon (between Rues de Ponthieu and Rabelais). Métro: Franklin-D.-Roosevelt. 42.99.16.16

62 La Place Boisterous Parisian university students dance to very loud music until the very wee hours at this popular nightclub (formerly Le Privé). ♦ Daily midnight-closing. 12 Rue de Ponthieu (between Ave Franklin-D.-Roosevelt and Rue Jean-Mermoz). Métro: Franklin-D.-Roosevelt. 42.25.51.70

63 Le Boeuf sur le Toit ★★★$$ This is the sixth and fanciest of **Jean-Paul Boucher's** marvelous group of old brasseries that includes Chez Flo, Julien, Terminus Nord, Vaudeville, and La Coupole. Note the superb Art Deco interior. ♦ Lunch, dinner, and late-night. 34 Rue du Colisée (at Ave Franklin-D.-Roosevelt). Reservations recommended. Métro: Franklin-D.-Roosevelt. 43.59.83.80

64 Jadis et Gourmande This is a chocolate-lover's sweetest dream. ♦ M 1-7PM; Tu-F 9:30AM-7PM; Sa 10AM-7PM. 49bis Ave Franklin-D.-Roosevelt (between Ave des Champs-Elysées and Rue de Ponthieu). Métro: Franklin-D.-Roosevelt. 42.25.06.04

65 Hôtel Colisée $$$ Quilted bedspreads and bamboo furniture embellish these rooms. The room numbers of the largest suites end in 8. ♦ 6 Rue du Colisée (between Ave des Champs-Elysées and Rue de Ponthieu). Métro: Franklin-D.-Roosevelt. 43.59.95.25

65 La Boutique à Sandwiches ★★$$ Stop here for the perfect late-night snack: all-you-can-eat Swiss raclette. This crowded two-story restaurant/snack bar also serves 40 kinds of sandwiches, as well as Welsh rabbit, ravioli, corned beef, *pickelfleisch,* and strudel. Better yet, it's a great value. ♦ Lunch, dinner, and late-night. 12 Rue du Colisée (between Ave des Champs-Elysées and Rue de Ponthieu). Reservations recommended. Métro: Franklin-D.-Roosevelt. 45.59.56.69

66 Franklin-D.-Roosevelt Métro Station This is the oldest métro station in Paris. On 4 October 1898 men with picks and shovels began digging a labyrinth beneath the city as directed by engineer **Fulgence Bienvenue.** Thus began the Parisian underground railway, or *métro* (short for *métropolitain*). Every day the métro trains travel the equivalent of three times around the world; since its opening in 1900, the métro has carried a number of passengers equivalent to more than 20 times the world's population. ♦ At Ave des Champs-Elysées and Rue de Marignan

67 L'Avenue ★★★$$ In this chic brasserie/restaurant, located on one of the most sumptuous avenues in the world, chef **Christian Hennin** prepares appropriate temptations: a classic Caesar salad, *gazpacho de tomates du soleil,* bouillabaisse, risotto with langoustines and thyme, chicken with an herbed vinaigrette, grilled duck with peaches and *carottes caramélisées,* and grilled beef filet in a béarnaise sauce. ♦ Breakfast, lunch, afternoon tea, and dinner. 41 Ave Montaigne (at Rues François-1er and de Marignan). Reservations recommended. Métros: Alma-Marceau, Franklin-D.-Roosevelt. 40.70.14.91

68 Avenue Montaigne This street is to haute couture what the Louvre is to art . The swank avenue is lined with high-fashion temples (**Christian Dior, Nina Ricci, Jean-Louis Scherrer, Valentino, Ungaro,** and **Laroche**). You will also find the **Canadian Embassy,** the luxurious **Plaza Athénée** hotel, and two smart theaters (the **Comédie des Champs-Elysées** and the **Théâtre des Champs-Elysées**). ♦ Between Place de l'Alma and Rond Point. Metros: Alma-Marceau, Franklin-D.-Roosevelt.

69 Chanel The dashing and successful Chanel collections are displayed here to their best advantage: in a setting of crisp white walls, gleaming mirrors, and spacious dressing rooms. ♦ M-F 9:30AM-6:30PM; Sa 10AM-6:30PM. 42 Ave Montaigne (between Rues Bayard and François-1er). Métros: Alma-Marceau, Franklin-D.-Roosevelt. 47.23.74.12

Revolutionary Expressions

Ancien Régime:
General term for the government and society of France before the French Revolution. Often rendered in English as "Old Regime."

Bastille:
Originally a fortress guarding eastern Paris, the Bastille was transformed into a royal prison by Cardinal Richelieu in the 17th century and acquired its sinister reputation under Louis XIV. In the 18th century several critics of the government—including Voltaire—were imprisoned there.

Commune of Paris:
The municipal government of Paris organized after the fall of the Bastille was largely composed of extremist revolutionaries who supported Robespierre. The Commune exerted great influence on the various national assemblies, but it was finally dissolved after Robespierre's fall.

Département:
The Constituent Assembly organized France into 83 approximately equal units called *départements*, which replaced the provinces of the *Ancien Régime*.

Empire:
The First French Empire was created in 1804 when Napoléon formally destroyed the Republic and had himself crowned emperor.

Guillotine:
A beheading device proposed by Dr. Joseph Guillotin in 1791 as an instantaneous and thus more humane instrument of death (see the illustration on page 133). It was adopted for all capital crimes in 1792. It is not true that Dr. Guillotin was the victim of the machine that bears his name; he died in his bed in 1814 at age 76.

Liberté, Egalité, Fraternité:
The slogan of the French Revolution. As the politics of the Revolution changed, different elements of the slogan were given more or less weight. Fraternity, for example, was especially stressed during the First Republic, when the Paris Commune played an important role.

Marianne:
The female allegorical figure of the First Republic, which was adopted in 1797. There is a complicated history of the transformations imposed on the image of Marianne; actress Catherine Deneuve served as the Marianne model for years. Marianne appears on numerous French postage stamps.

La Marseillaise:
Declared the national anthem in 1795 (and again in 1879), this martial song, whose words were written by Claude-Joseph Roget de Lisle, was first sung by the Army of the Rhine, but it was brought to Paris by volunteer troops from Marseilles.

Palais Royal:
This was once the palace of the Orléans branch of the royal family, first cousins to the Bourbons. The Duc d'Orléans rented out space under the elegant colonnade of his palace, and the place became a notorious haunt of gamblers, prostitutes, and, during the Revolution, political agitators.

Sans-Culottes:
Literally means "without culottes" (the knickers worn with silk stockings and pumps that were favored by the aristocracy). Originally the term designated the artisans and the working class, who wore trousers rather than culottes. As the Revolution became increasingly democratic, the term lost its pejorative sense and became an assertion of pride by those who espoused popular or radical politics.

Tricolore:
Taking its colors from the red, white, and blue *cocarde* (rosette), the tricolor flag with three vertical bands was adopted in 1790. With the exception of the Restoration (of the Bourbons, 1815–30), all French governments have used the *tricolore* as the nation's flag.

David P. Jordan

Reprinted with permission from *France Magazine*

70 Christian Dior In 1949 Dior signed the first designer licensing contract (for stockings), planning the day when women would be able to dress in his wares from top to toe. A stop in this three-floor, gray-and-white complex, which sells dresses, furs, jewelry, and gifts, makes that possible. ♦ M, Sa 10AM-6:30PM; Tu-F 9:30AM-6:30PM. 30 Ave Montaigne (at Rue François-1er). Métros: Franklin-D.-Roosevelt, Alma-Marceau. 40.73.54.40

70 26 Avenue Montaigne In 1857, when he was 14, **Henry James** moved here with his family. ♦ Between Place de l'Alma and Rue François-1er. Métro: Alma-Marceau

71 Nina Ricci Perhaps the most beautiful lingerie in the world is here, plus a stylish array of dresses, scarves, scents, and jewelry. The **Ricci Club,** an elegant menswear shop, is next door at 19 Rue François-1er. ♦ M-Sa 10AM-6:30PM. 39 Ave Montaigne (at Rue François-1er). Métros: Alma-Marceau, Franklin-D.-Roosevelt. 49.52.56.00

72 Isabel Canovas Looking for something special to consolidate your look? This shop is the last word in accessories. ♦ M-F 10:30AM-7PM. 16 Ave Montaigne (between Place de l'Alma and Rue François-1er). Métro: Alma-Marceau. 47.20.10.80

72 Bar des Théâtres ★★$$ This noisy bar/restaurant is patronized by theater critics before, bored ticket holders during, and bushed actors after the theater. The fare is simple: steak, Welsh rabbit, osso buco, and the like. It's a favorite lunch spot of film director **Roman Polanski.** ♦ Lunch, dinner, and late-night. 6 Ave Montaigne (between Place de l'Alma and Rue François-1er). Métro: Alma-Marceau. 47.23.34.63

73 Plaza Athénée $$$$ The Plaza Athénée has long enjoyed a reputation as the most fashionable palace hotel in Paris, largely because its **Relais Plaza** restaurant remains the favored lunchtime hangout of Paris couturiers. In fact, when the great designer **Pierre Balmain** died, the hotel management retired his table. The select out-of-town clientele includes the likes of **Rockefellers** and rich Brazilians. There's a profusion of flowers, and, indeed, the hotel staff boasts that the monthly florist's bill is higher than the electric bill. In 1918 West Point graduate **Captain George Patton** stayed here on his errand to France: learning to fence at the French Military Academy in Saumur. In this hotel, Patton discussed combat with the then 28-year-old **Charles de Gaulle.** ♦ 25 Ave Montaigne (between Rues Clement-Marot and du Boccador). Métro: Alma-Marceau. 47.23.78.33

Within the Plaza Athénée:

Relais Plaza ★$$ For a late-night, after-theater meal, try the filets of sole or braised beef in aspic, accompanied by a good house wine. ♦ Lunch, dinner, and late-night. 47.23.78.33

Bar Anglais After a performance at the **Théâtre des Champs-Elysées,** the concert crowd may come here and mix with the South American night owls staying at the hotel. ♦ Daily 11AM-1AM. Piano bar after 11PM. 47.23.78.33

Régence-Plaza ★★$$$$ The most expensive of the hotel's restaurants is peopled, as a rule, by the rich and famous. The *roulle de filet de veau rôti,* lobster filet, and *le petit Montaigne* with chocolate and spice cake are house specialties. **Patrick Jeanne,** the restaurant's manager, has mastered the art of mingling the stars and the not-yet-famous so that everyone can get a look at everyone else and see how the other half lives. ♦ Lunch and dinner. Reservations recommended. 47.23.78.33

74 2 Avenue Montaigne Back when this was the **Hôtel Elysée-Bellevue, Sinclair Lewis** passed the winter of 1924 here writing *Arrowsmith.* ♦ At Place Reine-Astrid. Métro: Alma-Marceau

75 Pont de l'Alma The Pont de l'Alma, built in 1855 to honor the first French victory in the **Crimean War** (1854), is decorated with a statue of a Zouave soldier that acts as a watermark. During the flood of 1910, the Seine reached his chin. ♦ Métro: Alma-Marceau

76 Avenue George-V Along this grand avenue named after the English king, you will find the spired 19th-century Gothic **American Episcopal Cathedral;** the salons of **Givenchy, Balenciaga,** and **Nina Ricci;** the **Chinese** and **Mexican** embassies; two swank hotels (**George V** and **Prince de Galles**); the **Crazy Horse Saloon,** with its sophisticated girlie shows; and the **Place de l'Alma** where the *Bateaux Mouches* and dinner cruises embark on their tour of the Seine. ♦ Between Ave des Champs-Elysées and Place de l'Alma. Métros: Alma-Marceau, George-V

76 Le Bistrot de Marius ★★$$$ Pagnol's Marius may have run away to sea, but this chef appears to have just returned. In a warm, provençal decor, the menu revolves around the freshest of seafood, from baby clams on a bed of spinach to *daurade grillé,* a sumptuous sea bream. ♦ Lunch and dinner. 6 Ave George-V (between Place de l'Alma and Rue de la Trémoille). Métro: Alma-Marceau. 40.70.11.76

76 Marius et Janette ★★$$$ For a taste of some of the finest provençal cuisine available in Paris, try this gracious seafood restaurant. Chef **Laurent Odiot** serves classic bouillabaisse, lobster salad, sea bass flambé, *loup grillé,* and a selection of dishes representative of the western maritime provinces. ♦ Lunch and dinner. 4 Ave George-V (between Place de l'Alma and Rue de la Trémoille). Reservations recommended. Métro: Alma-Marceau. 47.23.84.36

76 Chez Francis ★★$$ Formerly a *relais de poste* (stable for the post office's horses), this bistro boasts a three-star view of the Eiffel Tower and the largest outdoor terrace in Paris. A show-biz crowd assembles here for the fresh seafood platters, beef carpaccio with basil, *moules marinières,* grilled sole, and *confit de canard* with sautéed apples. ♦ Breakfast, lunch, dinner, and late-night. 7 Place de l'Alma (at Ave George-V). Reservations recommended. Métro: Alma-Marceau. 47.20.86.83

77 Valentino The Milan designer's Paris boutique, newly renovated in beige marble and glass, shows his sophisticated men's and women's fashions as well as his younger label, Oliver, composed of more casual, less expensive clothes. ♦ M-Sa 10AM-7PM. 17-19 Ave Montaigne (at Rue du Boccador). Métro: Alma-Marceau. 47.23.64.61

77 15 Montaigne, Maison Blanche ★★★$$$$ Fresh from the success of the trendy original Maison Blanche, **René Duran** has taken over an even trendier spot atop the Théâtre des Champs-Elysées and redecorated the space in fashionable monochromes. The culinary magic includes *croustillant d'anchois* (whole-grain toast infused with tomatoes and topped with anchovies and sea salt), oyster-stuffed cabbage, and braised veal with fresh pasta ♦ Lunch and dinner. 15 Ave Montaigne (between Place de l'Alma and Rue du Boccador). Métro: Alma-Marceau. 47.23.55.99

77 Théâtre des Champs-Elysées Here, on 29 May 1913, the **Ballet Russe** of **Sergei Diaghilev** first performed to the music of the **Stravinsky** piece *Le Sacré du Printemps.* Riots followed a performance shocking in its originality and modernity. Diaghilev, Stravinsky, **Nijinsky,** and **Cocteau** fled the mobs for the Bois de Boulogne and drove around while Diaghilev wept. This theater was one of the first buildings of reinforced concrete in Paris and the city's main concert hall. It was designed by **Auguste Perret,** who was later hired to reconstruct the entire port city of Le Havre after World War II.

American footnotes: On 2 October 1925, **John Dos Passos** painted the stage set, **Sidney Bechet** played clarinet, and **Josephine Baker** danced to "Yes, Sir, That's My Baby" for the opening here of *La Revue Nègre.* In May 1927 a **Charles Lindbergh** autograph sold for $1,500 at an auction held here (the name of his plane, *The Spirit of St. Louis,* pleased the French, who associated it not with Missouri, but with the saintliest of their line of kings); on 16 April 1928, the **Gershwins** attended the opening of a performance of *La Rhapsodie en Bleu* by the Ballet Russe. ♦ Box office: M-F 2-5PM. Closed holidays, in August, and the first week of September. 15 Ave Montaigne (between Place de l'Alma and Rue du Boccador). Métro: Alma-Marceau. 49.52.50.00

78 Crazy Horse Saloon The Saloon's upscale strip show is a knowing display of naughtiness featuring 16 mostly British, uniform (5 feet, 4 inches tall) lasses with silly stage names such as *Bianca Sundae, Ivy Speculation, Rita Cadillac,* and *Pompea Mackintosh.* The impresario of the Crazy Horse is former antique dealer **Alain Bernardin,** but the unseen star of the show is his lighting designer, who strobes, tints, patterns, and spotlights dancers with flair. ♦ Shows: M-F, Su 9PM, 11:35PM; Sa 8PM, 10:30PM, 12:50AM. 12 Ave George-V (between Place de l'Alma and Rue de la Trémoille). Métro: Alma-Marceau. 47.23.32.32

78 Hôtel de la Trémoille $$$$ This hotel is a bit of *Vieux France* in the heart of the high-fashion district. Do your shopping at Christian Dior or Nina Ricci in the afternoon, then dine here and charge your meal to your room at the nearby **Plaza Athénée,** which is under the same ownership. ♦ 14 Rue de la Trémoille (at Rue du Boccador). Métro: Alma-Marceau. 47.23.34.20

79 La Fermette Marbeuf 1900 ★★★$$ In 1978, when **Jean Laurent** purchased what had been a self-service restaurant since 1950, he had no idea of the treasure that lay behind the plastic and Formica. Renovations began, and as workers were tearing down the partition walls they discovered the tile, stained glass, and cast-iron pillars of a spectacular Art Nouveau room that had been hidden for 30 years. Laurent discovered that the room had been created in 1898 by two young, unknown designers named **Hutre** and **Wielharski.** Although the real star here is the interior, the cuisine runs a close second; some of the delectations are grilled lamb in a light béarnaise sauce, sliced duck breast with fresh rosemary and peaches, grilled sole with beurre blanc, nougat ice cream with apricot sauce, and bittersweet chocolate mousse. After dinner, a fine selection of eaux-de-vie, cognacs, and liqueurs await. ♦ Lunch and dinner. 5 Rue Marbeuf (at Rue du Boccador). Reservations required for the Art Nouveau dining room. Métro: Alma-Marceau. 47.23.31.31, 47.20.63.53

79 Ristorante Romano ★★$$ This pleasant restaurant features the charm of its smiling owner Romano, as well as a seasonally changing menu that might include *insalata caprese, spaghetti alle vongole, ravioli alla ricotta,* ravioli in a morel sauce, scampi, and saltimbocca with mozzarella. ♦ Lunch and dinner. 11 Rue Marbeuf (between Rues Clément-Marot and du Boccador). Reservations recommended. Métro: Alma-Marceau. 47.20.85.98

80 American Cathedral On 6 July 1905, one hundred years after his death, a service was held here for **John Paul Jones,** naval hero of the American Revolution, and more than 500 Americans attended. Afterward, his casket was taken to Annapolis, Maryland. ♦ Office hours M-F 9AM-12:30PM, 2-5PM; Sa 9AM-noon. Sunday services 9AM and 11AM. 23 Ave George-V (between Place de l'Alma and Ave Pierre-1er-de-Serbie). Métro: Alma-Marceau. 47.20.17.92

81 Chez Edgar ★$$ This noisy restaurant thronged with politicians, journalists, and actors serves meals to fit any pocketbook. Try the red *mullet au pistou,* salmon tartare, fresh pastas, pot-au-feu, or fresh shellfish. ♦ Lunch and dinner. 4 Rue Marbeuf (at Rue du Boccador). Reservations recommended. Métro: Alma-Marceau. 47.20.51.15

81 24 Rue du Boccador In the late 1940s this apartment building was rife with movie stars such as **Brigitte Bardot,** Ivy League CIA agents posing as novelists, and legitimate American writers, including **Theodore H. White, Art Buchwald,** and **Irwin Shaw.** This is where White, after working for six years as *Time* magazine's Beijing bureau chief, wrote his Pulitzer Prize-winning World War II novel, *The Mountain Road.* In a fifth-floor studio, Buchwald wrote his *Paris After Dark* column for the *Herald Tribune,* and Shaw, in much grander digs, completed his best-selling novel *The Young Lions,* which was published in 1948. ♦ Between Rue Marbeuf and Ave George-V. Métro: Alma-Marceau

To keep the newly refurbished Champs-Elysées in top condition, Paris has banned bicycles, motorbikes, and motorcycles from stopping or parking on the new granite pavements because of the oil stains they often leave behind.

Restaurants/Clubs: Red **Hotels:** Blue
Shops/ 🌳Outdoors: Green **Sights/Culture:** Black

82 Claridge-Bellman $$$ Redecorated with antiques, paintings, 17th-century tapestries, Chinese vases, and other costly objets d'art, this posh hotel is home to the Italian couturiers during the fashion collections. Reserve well in advance. ♦ 37 Rue François-1er (at Rue Marbeuf). Métro: Franklin-D.-Roosevelt. 47.23.54.42

Within the Claridge-Bellman hotel:

Relais Bellman ★$$ This restaurant and English bar is frequented by reporters from *Paris-Match* and the television station Europe 1. ♦ Lunch and dinner. Reservations required. 47.23.54.42

82 Chez André ★★$$ Unchanged since 1938, this bistro bustles at lunchtime with the dressed-for-success crowd from the Champs-Elysées and matronly waitresses loping through with hot plates of poached haddock and short ribs. Also recommended are roast leg of lamb with mashed potatoes, sponge cake with rum sauce, and the affordable house Muscadet and red Graves. ♦ Lunch, dinner, and late-night. 12 Rue Marbeuf (at Rue Clement-Marot). Reservations recommended. Métro: Franklin-D.-Roosevelt. 47.20.59.57

83 American Pershing Hall ★$ The restaurant of the American Legion's Paris Post #1 is patronized largely by over-the-hill legionnaires, sometimes dressed in tattered uniforms and apparently ready to reenlist. It's open to members and American citizens. ♦ Post: daily 11AM-midnight. Restaurant: Lunch and dinner. 49 Rue Pierre-Charron (between Ave George-V and Rue François-1er). Métro: George-V. 46.27.08.82

84 George V $$$$ **Art Buchwald** put it this way: "Paris without the George V would be Cleveland." Whether or not you agree, the George V hotel has something special to offer, and not just its red-leather elevator. **François Dupré,** who owned the hotel from its opening in 1928 until 1968, amassed a vast collection of antique furniture, baroque statues, Louis XIV tapestries (the value of these alone is estimated at $6 million), and paintings (among them, *Vase de Roses* by **Renoir**) that still decorates the public and private rooms. The George V has long attracted the greats of every field. **Duke Ellington** stayed here in 1933 while he was performing at the Salle Pleyel. He wrote in his memoirs that he spent a long time trying to get out of his suite: apparently, it was so enormous, with doors opening onto other rooms or closets, that it was difficult to locate the exit. ♦ 31 Ave George-V (between Ave Pierre-1er-de-Serbie and Rue Quentin-Bauchart). Métro: George-V. 47.23.54.00

Within the George V hotel:

Les Princes ★★$$$ The menu at this elegant restaurant runs from the delicate (filet of sole with spring truffles) to the hearty (veal kidneys in mustard cream sauce, flambéed in cognac). ♦ Breakfast, lunch, and dinner. Reservations required. 47.23.54.00

Bar du George V This bar has a glorious but too rarefied atmosphere. ♦ Daily 11AM-2AM. 47.23.54.00

Le Grill ★$ This is a fine place for snacking. ♦ Breakfast, lunch, dinner, and late-night. 47.23.54.00

84 37 Avenue George-V On their honeymoon in 1905, **Franklin** and **Eleanor Roosevelt** visited Franklin's aunt, **Deborah Delano,** who had an apartment at this address. She used to take the newlyweds driving; indeed it was in the **Bois de Boulogne** that FDR learned to drive. ♦ Between Ave Pierre-1er-de-Serbie and Rue Quentin-Bauchart. Métro: George-V

85 Hôtel François I $$$ This luxurious little hotel off the Champs-Elysées features a tasteful Art Deco interior. ♦ 7 Rue Magellan (between Rues de Bassano and Christophe-Colomb). Métro: George-V. 47.23.44.04

85 16 Rue Christophe-Colomb In 1898 **Henry Adams**, grandson of **John Quincy Adams** and professor of history at Harvard University, stayed in several rooms in this building while reading medieval manuscripts for his study, *Mont-Saint-Michel and Chartres*. ♦ Between Rues de Bassano and Magellan. Métro: George-V

86 L'Ecluse II ★★$$ The second of this chain of classy wine bars offers vintage Bordeaux and light meals of smoked salmon, carpaccio, and goat cheese. ♦ Lunch, dinner, and late-night. 64 Rue François-1er (between Rues Quentin-Bauchart and Lincoln). Métro: George-V. 47.20.77.09

87 Institut Geographique National The French counterpart of the **National Geographic Society** in Washington, DC, is a cartographer's heaven, selling maps of the entire universe (at least that which is recognized by the French) and more. You may purchase wall-size maps of the Paris métro, navigation charts for the Seine, infrared satellite photos of France, 1618 city maps of Paris, and four-by-four-foot color aerial photographs of 164 square-mile sectors of

downtown Paris so detailed you can make out pedestrians on the Champs-Elysées. ♦ M-F 8AM-6:50PM; Sa 10AM-12:30PM, 1:45-5:20PM. 107 Rue La Boétie (between Ave des Champs-Elysées and Rue de Ponthieu). Métro: Franklin-D.-Roosevelt. 43.98.85.00

87 Virgin Records' Megastore This majestic music shop looks like a **Cecil B. deMille** movie set, complete with a monumental marble staircase. Its various levels are replete with a mind-bending selection of records, CDs, tapes, and videos (in English and French), as well as books on music and stereo equipment. ♦ M-Th 10AM-midnight; F-Sa 10AM-1AM; Su noon-midnight. 52-60 Ave des Champs-Elysées (At Rue La Boétie). Métro: Franklin-D.-Roosevelt. 40.74.06.48

88 Régine's The notorious queen of Paris nightlife, Régine puts in only rare appearances at her enticing, dimly lit private club off the Champs-Elysées, but the Ritz/Tour d'Argent/Maxim's crowd keeps coming back anyway. ♦ Daily 11PM-dawn. 49 Rue de Ponthieu (between Rues de Berri and La Boétie). Métro: Franklin-D.-Roosevelt. 43.59.21.13

88 Gymnase Club The largest health club in Paris offers five floors of aerobics studios, body-building equipment, saunas, Jacuzzis, a solarium, and a juice bar. ♦ M-F 7:30AM-10PM; Sa 9AM-8PM. 55bis Rue de Ponthieu (between Rues de Berri and La Boétie). Métro: Franklin-D.-Roosevelt. 45.62.99.76

89 Guerlain Institut de Beauté You must reserve at least eight days in advance if you wish to visit this Regency-paneled beauty salon and undergo the royal treatment from the perfumed ladies in pink. ♦ M-Sa 9AM-6:45PM. 68 Ave des Champs-Elysées (between Rues La Boétie and de Berri). Métro: George-V. 47.89.71.84

89 Club Méditerranée Club Med, a chain of swinging summer camps, was started in the 1950s by a French tent salesman. Today it is the world's fifth-largest hotel group, and its owner, **Gilbert Trigano,** is one of France's most prominent businesspeople. ♦ M-Sa 9:30AM-7:30PM. 90 Ave des Champs-Elysées (between Rues La Boétie and de Berri). Métro: George-V. 42.96.10.00

90 1 Rue de Berri On 17 October 1785, 42-year-old **Thomas Jefferson** succeeded **Benjamin Franklin** as minister to France and moved into this mansion, the **Hôtel de Langeac,** designed by architect **Jean Chalgrin.** Jefferson resided here for the next four years. ♦ At Ave des Champs-Elysées. Métro: George-V

90 Lancaster $$$$ This first-class hotel has an atmosphere more like a rustic private house than a grand hostelery. **Helen Keller** stayed here in 1937, **John Steinbeck** in 1954, and a continuing parade of American luminaries since then. ♦ 7 Rue de Berri (between Ave des Champs-Elysées and Rue d'Artois). Métro: George-V. 43.59.90.43

91 The Chicago Pizza Pie Factory ★★$
Midwesterners pining for a taste of home should descend to the cavernous brick basement, bright with red-and-white checked tablecloths and reverberating with Chuck Berry, where they can order a deep-dish pizza with such traditional toppings as pepperoni and mushrooms. There's a happy hour with half-price cocktails Monday through Friday from noon to 3PM and every evening from 6-7:30PM. ♦ Lunch, dinner, and late-night. 5 Rue de Berri (between Ave des Champs-Elysées and Rue de Ponthieu). Métro: George-V. 45.62.50.23

Fouquet's

92 Fouquet's ★★★$$$ Irish writer **James Joyce** dined almost every night at this old high-priced café/restaurant that has become a watering hole for show-biz celebrities, glamour girls, and rubberneckers. American novelist **Ernest Hemingway** may have liberated the Ritz bar after World War II, but sexism still reigns here. For the last 80 years, a sign at Fouquet's seven-stool bar has read: *Les dames seules ne sont pas admises au bar,* which translates without much grace to "No single women allowed!" The maître d', one **Monsieur Casanova,** offers the spurious consolation that the house rule is for the ladies' own protection. ♦ Breakfast, lunch, dinner, and late-night. 99 Ave des Champs-Elysées (at Ave George-V). Reservations recommended. Métro: George-V. 47.23.70.60

93 Résidence Lord Byron $$$ This comfortably classy small hotel lacks the pretensions of the grander hotels in town. ♦ 5 Rue de Chateaubriand (between Rues de Balzac and Washington). Métros: Etoile, George-V. 43.59.89.98

94 Taillevent ★★★★$$$$ This is as close as a restaurant comes to perfection. **Jean-Claude Vrinat,** the owner and idea man, and chef **Philippe Legendre** have made this establishment (dare we say it?) the best restaurant in Paris. Named after **Guillaume Tirel** (a.k.a. Taillevent, the 14th-century royal cook who wrote the first treatise on French cooking), the restaurant, set in a town house with high ceilings, oak-paneled walls, and Louis XV furniture, has the feel of a grand bourgeois private club. Taillevent's innovative signature dishes include *fruits de mer* with truffles and pistachios, langoustines with fresh pasta, Barbary duck, veal kidneys, and almond ice cream. The wine list draws on a cellar of 130,000 bottles ranging from collector's items such as the Laffite-Rothschild 1806 to a less risky and far less expensive Château Haut Brion. Taillevent is the perfect restaurant for a first-class business lunch or that once-in-a-lifetime dining experience. ♦ Lunch and dinner. Closed Saturday, Sunday, one week in February, and four weeks beginning at the end of July. 15 Rue Lamennais (between Ave de Friedland and Rue Washington). Reservations required well in advance. Métro: Etoile. 45.63.39.94, 45.61.12.90

95 Hôtel de Vigny $$$$ This could be the best new little hotel in Paris. It features sumptuous wood paneling, a lobby resembling a private London club, and bright and airy rooms that are royally furnished with antiques, puffy down comforters, and private Jacuzzis. ♦ 9-11 Rue de Balzac (at Rue Lord Byron). Métros: George-V, Charles-de-Gaulle-Etoile. 40.75.04.39

96 Lido The largest cabaret in Paris, this lavish extravaganza outglitters Las Vegas with its $2.5-million stage set and famous **Bluebell Girls,** whose dance numbers are choreographed by computer. Dazzling special effects include a safari number (two elephants making a ponderous circuit of the stage), a sea battle, a dolphin-filled swimming pool, and a skating rink rising out of the floor. Throw in a few jugglers, acrobats, and bare-breasted dancers decorously lowered from the ceiling and you have your basic night at the Lido. It's always packed with Japanese tourists, car salesmen, and sailors on leave. ♦ Shows: daily 10PM, midnight. Doors open at 7:30PM. 116bis Ave des Champs-Elysées (between Rues Washington and de Balzac). Métro: George-V. 40.76.56.10

96 Burger King ★$ This bustling establishment (one of 12 in Paris) serves traditional American cuisine, called *le fast food,* to homesick Yankees and a young and foolish international clientele. *Spécialités de la maison* include *Le Whopper avec fromage, les frites, et le milk shake.* Note the bronze plaque marking the spot where on Bastille Day 1985 more Whoppers were sold than in any other Burger King in the world. ♦ Lunch, dinner, snacks, and late-night. 122 Ave des Champs-Elysées (between Rues Washington and de Balzac). No credit cards. Métro: George-V. 45.62.03.31

97 La Boutique Flora Danica ★★$$$ The enjoyments of Danish dining—pickled herring, eel, marinated salmon, shrimp salad, roast beef with onions, Tuborg on tap, and the flakiest pastries around—abound in this informal luncheonette with blond-wood tables and cheerful abstract art. In summer, meals are served in an umbrella-shaded courtyard. Takeout is available from 4PM through the evening ♦ Lunch and dinner. 142 Ave des Champs-Elysées (between Rues de Balzac and Arsène-Houssaye). Métro: Charles-de-Gaulle-Etoile. 43.59.20.41

97 Copenhague ★★$$$ Upstairs from **La Boutique Flora Danica,** this restaurant serves slightly higher-priced Danish cuisine. ♦ Lunch and dinner. Closed Sunday, in August, and first week in January. 142 Ave des Champs-Elysées (between Rues de Balzac and Arsène-Houssaye). Métro: Charles-de-Gaulle-Etoile. 43.59.20.41

98 Office du Tourisme de Paris Home of the city's official tourist bureau, here you can find free maps, sightseeing information, and for tourists stuck without a room for the night, same-day hotel reservations. ♦ Daily 9AM-8PM. 127 Ave des Champs-Elysées (between Rues de Presbourg and Galilée). Métros: Charles-de-Gaulle-Etoile, George-V. 49.52.53.54

98 Drugstore des Champs-Elysées This drugstore sells not only aspirin and Band-Aid bandages, but gourmet groceries, quick brasserie meals, wristwatches, banana splits; and Cuban cigars. ♦ Daily 9AM-2AM. 133 Ave des Champs-Elysées (at Rue de Presbourg). Métro: Charles-de-Gaulle-Etoile. 47.23.54.34

98 133 Avenue des Champs-Elysées After World War II, **General Dwight D. Eisenhower,** supreme commander of the Allied Forces in Europe, had his headquarters here in what was the old **Hôtel Astoria.** He asked for a room with a view of the **Arc de Triomphe,** his favorite structure in Paris. ♦ At Rue de Presbourg. Métro: Charles-de-Gaulle-Etoile

99 Raphael $$$$ This luxurious lodge with Oriental carpets, marble floors, and Louis XVI furniture attracts Italian and American movie stars. ♦ 17 Ave Kléber (between Rues de Presbourg and Paul-Valéry). Métros: Charles-de-Gaulle-Etoile, Kléber. 44.28.00.28

100 Les Salons de l'Arc de Triomphe ★★$$ The beautiful people who frequent this restaurant and nightclub come to see and be seen. If you don't want to stand outside under bright lights hoping you're cool enough to be allowed into the nightclub, make dinner reservations. You'll enjoy provençal food along with a stupendous view of the Arc de Triomphe, and afterwards you can go directly downstairs to the club, which boasts the best sound system in Paris. ♦ Lunch and dinner; dinner only on Saturday and Sunday. Nightclub: daily 11PM-4AM. 12 Rue de Presbourg (at Ave de la Grande-Armée). Reservations recommended for dinner. Métro: Charles-de-Gaulle-Etoile. 45.00.45.00

101 L'Arc de Triomphe If Emperor Napoléon hadn't changed his mind in the nick of time, Parisians would be staring not at this magnificent arch (pictured below), but at a 160-foot-high elephant squirting water from its trunk. The decision was so close that a model of the elephant was made and stood for a while at the Place de la Bastille. In the end, Napoléon chose the more tasteful triumphal arch to honor his army's victory at the **Battle of Austerlitz.** (And the story is that the sun sets exactly along this axis on 2 December, the anniversary of that victory.) This granddaddy of triumphal arches is 164 feet high and 148 feet wide.

Construction of the arch began in 1806, and the walls had scarcely risen above the ground by the time Napoléon divorced the childless **Empress Josephine** and wed **Princess**

L'Arc de Triomphe

Marie-Louise of Austria in 1810. As a result, the bridal procession passed through a fake arch of canvas, hastily constructed for the occasion by the architect **Chalgrin**. The arch was not completed until 1836, well after Napoléon's downfall, and only four years before the chariot bearing his body would pass beneath the arch on its way to the **Invalides**. On 14 July 1919, victorious French soldiers, led by their generals, marched through the arch. The following month, pilot **Sergeant Godefroy** flew a plane with a wingspan of nine meters (29 feet) through the 15-meter-wide (48 feet) arch. On 11 November 1920 the body of the **Unknown Soldier** was laid in state to commemorate the dead soldiers of World War I. The eternal flame at the tomb (first kindled in 1923) is lit each evening at 6:30PM. (A crudely irreverent Frenchman once cooked an omelet over the flame.) On 26 August 1944, after the Germans had been routed from the capital, **General Charles de Gaulle** led a jubilant crowd to the arch, then walked down the Champs-Elysées to Notre-Dame, where the famous **Te Deum Mass** was celebrated in thanksgiving. On state occasions, an enormous French flag hangs inside the arch.

It would be suicide to cross the **Place Charles-de-Gaulle** on foot (cars have a hard enough time). However, you can reach the arch by the underground passage. Then, an elevator, or 284 steps, will take you (during daylight hours only) to the platform at the top of the arch, which affords a magnificent panorama of Paris. ♦ Métro: Charles-de-Gaulle-Etoile

On the Arc de Triomphe:

La Marseillaise

Departure of the Volunteers Known as *La Marseillaise,* this sculpture (pictured above) by **Rude** is the arch's most inspired and noteworthy stonework. (It is on the right when your back is to the Champs-Elysées.) In 1916, on the day the **Battle of Verdun** started, the

sword brandished by the figure representing the Republic broke and fell off. The disarmed sculpture was immediately hidden to conceal the accident from the superstitious, who might have seen it as a bad omen.

101 Place Charles-de-Gaulle Baron **Haussmann** created this square in 1854 when he added another seven avenues to the existing five to create a 12-pointed star. The area is a snarl of traffic. Of the avenues beginning here, **Avenue Foch** is the widest (120 meters, or 390 feet) in Paris. It has always been the street where the rich and famous, such as **Aristotle Onassis**, the divine **Maria Callas**, composer **Claude Debussy**, the **Shah of Iran**, and **Prince Rainier** of Monaco, have had their mansions. Avenue Foch leads to the **Bois de Boulogne**, a 2,000-acre park. ♦ Métro: Charles-de-Gaulle-Etoile

102 Chiberta ★★$$$$ The most chic nouvelle-cuisine restaurant in Paris is made even more hip by its Art Deco decor. Chef **Philippe da Silva** offers seasonal specialties such as wild mushroom fricassee, truffle-and-parsley ravioli in autumn, and salmon with fresh artichokes and asparagus come spring. ♦ Lunch and dinner. Closed Saturday, Sunday, August, and from 25 December 1 to January. 3 Rue Arsène-Houssaye (between Aves des Champs-Elysées and de Friedland). Reservations recommended. Métro: Charles-de-Gaulle-Etoile. 45.63.77.90

103 Royal Monceau $$$$ The Italian Ciga hotel chain funneled $15 million into renovating these rooms, which apparently have something to please everyone from **Alexander Haig** to rock star **Sting.** The saunas, steam rooms, herbal massages, and low-cal restaurant at the adjoining **Thermes Health Spa** are open to hotel guests. ♦ 35-39 Ave Hoche (between Rue Beaujon and Ave Bertie-Albrecht). Métro: Ternes. 45.61.98.00

104 14 Rue de Tilsitt It was April of 1925: *The Great Gatsby* was selling briskly and American novelist **F. Scott Fitzgerald** was at the height of his fame. He and his wife, **Zelda,** took an apartment at this address. Fitzgerald's drunken binges began. There were times when he would stumble into the Paris bureau of the *Chicago Tribune* and **William L. Shirer** and **James Thurber** would have to pack him home in a taxi to greater ignominies ahead. ♦ Between Aves Hoche and de Wagram. Métro: Charles-de-Gaulle-Etoile

105 Guy Savoy ★★★$$$$ A shining star in the Parisian culinary firmament found this setting to match his enormous talent. Not so long ago chef Savoy took over the spacious quarters of **Maguy** and **Gilbert Le Coze** (who moved their famous fish restaurant Le Bernardin to Manhattan). Try the sardine and red mullet marinade, smoked eel with green beans in an onion sauce, and the *fondant au chocolat.* ♦ Lunch and dinner. Closed Saturday and

Sunday. 18 Rue Troyon (between Aves de Wagram and Mac-Mahon). Reservations recommended. Métro: Charles-de-Gaulle-Etoile. 43.80.40.61

105 L'Etoile Verte ★★$ This small, inexpensive neighborhood restaurant serves traditional French fare. The waitresses can be gruff, but, at these prices, politeness is perhaps too much to expect. Enjoy such fundamental cuisine as coq au vin, sautéed veal, and chateaubriand béarnaise. ◆ Lunch and dinner. 13 Rue Brey (between Ave de Wagram and Rue de Montenotte). Métro: Charles-de-Gaulle-Etoile. 43.80.69.34

Bests

Henry Pillsbury
Executive Director of the American Center

First of all, Paris is the best-run city of the 10 biggest cities in the world. It's as much a museum as Venice and as alive as L.A.

After 30 years here, I'd add the following to all the poetic musings on the city:

Jogging—All of the parks make this the best city for jogging.

Street cleaning and garbage collection—This is the only city where garbage is picked up every day of the year (except for Labor Day and during strikes).

Street Life—Unbeknownst to most Parisians, Paris is one of the most densely populated cities in the world, which explains all the shops, cafés, pedestrians, and effervescence. A model city for the 21st century.

Most telephone booths—The use of telephone cards instead of coins has greatly reduced the number of street phones smashed by thieves. This is emblematic of the enlightened way Paris and France use electronics, including Minitels (computerized phone books and information systems), and more efficient parking, banking, and ticketing.

Street and café toilets—Paris has provided pretty well for the most repetitive human need of all. By contrast, compare the availability of toilets in London, New York, or L.A.

Hon-Yin
Fashion Designer/Painter

I love to have a cup of tea at the **Hôtel Montalembert.** I buy tea from **Mariages Frère,** cakes from **Ladurée** (Rue Royale), and foie gras from **Dubernet** (1 Rue Augereau).

Walking by the **Canal St.-Martin,** near where I live. This is the real Paris of the 1930s and 1940s—it's quiet, artistic, but not snobbish.

Ile St.-Louis is great at night; there you'll find the best ice cream at **Berthillon.**

Porte de la Villette, with the **Cité des Sciences et de l'Industrie,** is great in the afternoon or on Sunday morning, when it's quieter. Bring something to drink with you.

Jack Lang
France's Former Minister of Culture

Passage des Panoramas

This old covered passage in the neighborhood around **La Bourse** begins at Boulevard Montmartre and opens onto Rue St.-Marc. During the brief regime called the Directoire (1795-99), people paraded here in eccentric but beautiful outfits. The free-spirited feeling of this place still remains, preserved by its very inexpensive restaurants and its Salons de Thé.

Marché d'Aligre (Aligre Market)

In this popular colorful market, a combination flea market and food market, you can find marvelous vegetables and specialty items sold by street vendors, as well as classic secondhand goods.

Rue Myrha

In the 18th arrondissement, Rue Myrha leads to **Boulevard Barbès,** a neighborhood that is a blend of the Orient and the West.

At the time of Ramadan, the sidewalks of **Rue Myrha** at night are filled with lots of small stands selling delicious Oriental pastries. This is also a place where you can buy a live chicken and the freshest eggs.

The lesser known works of Delacroix

I have discovered that many Parisians are not aware of the existence—even though it is easily accessible—of the magificent works of **Eugene Delacroix** that are located in two churches in the heart of Paris. One is "Déposition de Croix" (descent of the cross) in **Ste.-Denis-du-Ste.-Sacrament,** and three biblical frescoes, from the artist's later work, in **St.-Sulpice**.

Parisian restaurants

For the best cuisine, I believe that Joel Robuchon, Alain Senderens, Alain Dutournier, and Guy Savoy are forever at the peak of creativity. My favorite brasserie is probably **Louis XIV,** because of its remarkable choice of seafood and its chef, one of the last to roast duckling and game in season on a spit.

La Marée restaurant offers oysters from Colchester and New Zealand which, in my opinion, are the best in Europe. I also like **Le Duc** for its *poisson cru.*

Finally, like every lover of food, I have my favorite bistros, and, in particular, the amazing **Moissonier** across the street from the old **Halle aux Vins de Jussieu** that continues to serve great bowls of lyonnais salad. And naturally, I keep having the pleasure of rediscovering **Chez Benoît,** the academy of bistro cuisine; and **Ma Bourgogne,** the charm of its terrace under the archway of the Place des Vosges and its simple, but high quality, fare.

The pyramid designed by I.M. Pei isn't the first to grace the Cour Napoléon. After the murder of revolutionary Jean-Paul Marat, his corpse, along with his writing desk and the bathtub in which he met his demise, were placed in a wooden pyramid that stood near the Carrousel Arch.

Restaurants/Clubs: Red   Hotels: Blue
Shops/ 🌳 Outdoors: Green   **Sights/Culture:** Black

8 Rue de Miromesnil—in 1961 pop artist Robert Rauschenberg had his first solo show here

(M) **Miromesnil**

St.-Philippe-du-Roule— Jean-François Chalgrin, best known for designing the Arc de Triomphe, built this church

(M) **St.-Philippe-du-Roule**—

Dalloyau—perfecting its chocolate since 1802. Taste the "El Dorado"— cinnamon-and-praline-filled chocolates

Henri Picard et Fils— a bookstore founded in 1860 that sells 18th-century encyclopedias and a rare edition of Jules Verne for $40,000

Le Bristol Paris—in a class by itself with its sixth-floor penthouse swimming pool and marble bath-rooms, plus Paris' best hotel restaurant. Nearby at **Le Sphinx**, Bonaparte fans can gawk at one of Napoléon's trademark hats —or buy it for just $100,000

Palais de l'Elysée— France's elegant counterpart to the White House

Muriel—One of the few remaining boutiques that sells only gloves.

American Ambassador's Residence— upstairs is the bed where Charles Lindbergh slept after making the first non-stop solo transatlantic flight in 1927

British Embassy

St.-Honoré

Move over, Fifth Avenue and Rodeo Drive. The **Faubourg-St.-Honoré**, named after the patron saint of pastry chefs, takes the cake as the world's most glamorous shopping district. *La plus haute* of international haute couture is here en masse: Christian Dior, Yves Saint Laurent, Lanvin, Gucci, Hermès, Pierre Cardin, Guy Laroche, Ungaro, Courrèges, and Jean-Paul Gaultier, not to mention countless purveyors of such extravagances as diamonds, crystal, silver, mink, caviar, truffles, and champagne.

Lanvin—for women's scarves, perfumes, haute couture, and prêt-à-porter

Hermès—the most celebrated leather-goods emporium in the world

Chapelle Expiatoire—where victims of the Revolution (Marie Antoinette, Louis XVI, and Charlotte Corday) are interred

Place de la Madeleine—specialty food shops to spoil the spoiled; a lively flower market blossoms Tuesday through Sunday

Marquise de Sévigné—superlative macaroons and hot chocolate

American Express

Café de la Paix—a historical landmark once frequented by Salvador Dalí, Harry Truman, Maurice Chevalier, and Maria Callas

Charles Garnier's famous **Opéra**—don't miss the white marble Grand Staircase and Marc Chagall's 1964 ceiling masterpiece

Lucas-Carton—four-star nouvelle cuisine by superstar chef Alain Senderens

Cadolle—a lingerie shop run by a descendant of the woman who reportedly invented the brassiere

M Concorde

M Madeleine

Place Vendôme—home of the Hôtel Ritz and one of the world's greatest concentrations of jewelers, perfumeries, and banks

M Pyramides

M Opéra

Scribe—this deluxe hotel served as the Allied forces' press headquarters at the end of World War II

M Tuileries

Carita—a lavish hair salon whose clients include Catherine Deneuve, Paloma Picasso, and French rocker Johnny Hallyday

28 Rue Boissy-d'Anglas—site of the old **Le Bœuf sur le Toit**, a famous avant-garde nightclub

⬛ = Métro

Ⓜ 4-Septembre

Ⓜ Richelieu-Drouot

Chartier—a cavernous Belle Epoque soup kitchen with pinwheel fans, surly waiters, and reasonable prices

Bibliothèque Nationale—look through the glass doors of the Second Empire reading room at the breathtaking domed ceiling by Labrouste

Ⓜ Bourse

Willi's Wine Bar—one of Paris' most elegant watering holes bustles nonstop

Les Passages—on a rainy day chart a walk through these interconnecting turn-of-the-century tunnels

Le Grand Véfour—a favorite Parisian restaurant where Napoléon courted Joséphine, Victor Hugo romanticized, and Colette and Jean Cocteau, who lived nearby, enjoyed regular repasts

Robert Capia—Catherine Deneuve's favorite antique store

Chez Nous—Paris' best jock bar and restaurant is run by ex-rugby player Gilbert Ghiraldi

Palais Royal Garden—a six-acre enclave of flowering serenity perfect for picnics

Comédie Française—where Molière and the divine Sarah Bernhardt once performed

Ⓜ Palais-Royal

Manufacture Nationale de Sèvres—the famous Sèvres porcelain factory's showroom

Chez Pauline—a relaxed restaurant serving French classics

This district includes other dazzling sights as well. There is a small, remarkable art collection at the **Musée Jacquemart-André;** several architectural jewels, including **St.-Roch** (the city's finest baroque church), the splendid **Palais Royal** and its gardens, and the vaulted reading room of the **Bibliothèque Nationale;** the city's two most important theaters, the **Opéra Garnier** and the **Comédie Française;** and several grand hotels, such as **Le Bristol, St.-James et Albany**, and the **Hôtel Ritz**, whose name is synonymous with luxury. Rue du Faubourg-St.-Honoré is made for that favorite Parisian pastime, tasteful loitering.

Plan on visiting St.-Honoré on a weekday from Tuesday through Friday, since many shops and exhibits are closed on Monday, and the streets are crowded on weekends. Start with an early-bird pastry and coffee at one of the Right Bank's finest bakeries, **Boulangerie St.-Philippe** (open at 7:30AM), and continue down Rue du Faubourg-St.-Honoré to the street's most fashionable stretch, which lies between the presidential **Palais de l'Elysée** at Avenue Matignon and Rue Royale. Those getting a late jump on the day might consider visiting **Le Val d'Or,** a popular neighborhood wine bar, where an elite crowd stands *tuer le ver* (killing the worm) with a mid-morning Bordeaux. While lovers of the Italian Renaissance keep their date with **Donatello, Botticelli**, and **Titian** at the Musée Jacquemart-André, serious shoppers will head down embassy row (where the American, British, and Japanese ambassadors hang their hats) and make a mandatory stop at Hermès, the world-famous leather and accessories shop.

As you pass onto Rue Royale, which starts at legendary **Maxim's** and ends near **Fauchon** (the "millionaires' supermarket"), you will look upon the finest in antiques, tapestries, jewelry, and silver. By midday you will have reached **Place de la Madeleine.** Survey the plaza and whet your appetite with truffles at **La Maison de la Truffe,** chocolates at **Marquise de Sévigné,** and cheese at **La Ferme St.-Hubert.** When you're finished with those delicacies, why not splurge your life's savings on the four-star nouvelle cuisine at **Lucas-Carton** or on a feast of caviar and champagne at **Caviar Kaspia?** If, however, you're down to your last few francs, settle for a modest, though tasty, repast at **Ladurée** or **L'Ecluse.** Those feeling brash and regal by turns could knock back a shot of one of the 156 whiskeys sold at **Harry's Bar** and weave into **Charvet** to buy a cravat, as **Edward VII** was in the habit of doing not so long ago.

While your companion is changing money at **American Express,** line up for tickets inside the Opéra Garnier (also known as the Paris Opéra), **Charles Garnier's** architectural birthday cake. If you're an antique hound, **Le Louvre des Antiquaires** (240 dealers under one roof) will keep you occupied for hours. Otherwise, go admire the quiet splendor of the Bibliothèque Nationale's reading room or watch (as did everyone from **Louis XIV** to **Colette**) the sun set on the gardens of the Palais Royal.

Dinnertime already? Consider the best (and most expensive) sushi in Paris at **Issé** or an Alsatian specialty at **La Providence.** Or go for broke at **Le Grand Véfour** or the century-old **Restaurant Drouant.** Nightlife in the neighborhood might consist of polishing your French at the Comédie Française, catching a classical ballet or modern dance performance at the Opéra, taking in a movie on Boulevard Haussmann, or people-watching from the terrace of **Café de la Paix.** Or if you still have energy to spare, you can return to where you began the day's outing and spend the night dancing till dawn at **Keur Samba.**

1 St.-Philippe-du-Roule Before **Jean-François Chalgrin** (better known for his Arc de Triomphe) built this church (pictured above), its parishioners prayed in the chapel of a local leprosy asylum. The floor plan, three aisles divided by two rows of fluted Ionic columns, resembles that of the early Christian basilicas. ♦ 153 Rue du Faubourg-St.-Honoré (at Ave Myron-Timothy-Herrick). Métro: St.-Philippe-du-Roule

2 Le Val d'Or ★★★$ On the ground floor of St.-Honoré's most popular wine bar you'll find all the ingredients for a great quick lunch: quiche, charcuterie, perhaps the best sandwiches in Paris, and, of course, wines admirably selected by **Monsieur Rongier.** Downstairs, for those with leisure to dine, there's a hearty beef Bourguignon. Try the Côtes-du-Brouilly and Côtes-du-Rhône and, in November, the new Beaujolais, the best of which Rongier somehow always manages to snag. Under the exceedingly civil house rules, wine must be ordered by the bottle, but you pay only for what you drink. Lunchtime is the liveliest time. ♦ Breakfast, lunch, and snacks. Closed Sunday, Christmas Day, and New Year's Day. 28 Ave Franklin-D.-Roosevelt (between Rues du Colisée and du Faubourg-St.-Honoré). Métro: St.-Philippe-du-Roule. 43.59.95.81

3 Keur Samba This nightclub uncorks around 2AM when actors, models, musicians, and diplomats of every stripe and color push their way past **Kane** at the door. This black-upholstered, after-hours playpen is located near Régine's and Elysée Matignon. ♦ Cover. Daily midnight-7AM. 79 Rue La Boétie (between Rues du Faubourg-St.-Honoré and de Ponthieu). Métro: St.-Philippe-du-Roule. 43.59.03.10

4 Boulangerie St.-Philippe ★★$ This bakery's luncheonette (beside the crowded bread counter) features *foie de veau à la vapeur,* delicious house terrines, grilled meats, and wine by the glass. Order one of the éclairs, a slice of lime tart, or *tarte tatin* for dessert and find out why the bakery is always crowded. ♦ Breakfast, lunch, and snacks. Closed Saturday. 73 Ave Franklin-D.-Roosevelt (at Rues du Commandant-Rivière and du Faubourg-St.-Honoré). Métro: St.-Philippe-du-Roule. 43.59.78.76

5 Bradford $$ A surprising oasis of calm and friendliness is wedged between the harried Champs-Elysées and Rue du Faubourg-St.-Honoré. Rooms are spick-and-span and even big enough to dance in. ♦ 10 Rue St.-Philippe-du-Roule (between Rues d'Artois and du Faubourg-St.-Honoré). Métro: St.-Philippe-du-Roule. 43.59.24.20, 42.25.43.71

6 L'Artois ★★$$ Gray-suited business types come to this popular bistro for chef **Jean-Claude Poulnais'** escargots in a creamy butter and garlic sauce, steamed salmon, and crème brûlée with plum marmelade. ♦ Lunch and dinner; dinner only on Saturday. Closed Sunday, and one month in the summer. 13 Rue d'Artois (between Rues Frédéric-Bastiat and Paul-Baudry). Reservations recommended. Métros: Franklin-D.-Roosevelt, St.-Philippe-du-Roule. 42.25.01.10

7 C.T. Loo and Co. Located in a fantastic three-story pagoda equipped with a Chinese elevator, **Michael Bosc's** Asian art gallery traffics in Orientalia. Get a close look at lacquered hardwood furniture from the Ming Dynasty and 13th-century Nepalese sculpture. ♦ M-Sa 10:30AM-12:30PM, 2:30-6:30PM. Closed in August. 48 Rue de Courcelles (at Place du Pérou). Métro: Miromesnil. 45.62.53.15, 42.25.17.23

8 Musée Jacquemart-André Originally this neoclassical building was the private residence of banker **Edouard André** and artist **Nélie Jacquemart.** The couple poured considerable wealth into their exquisite art collection, which now belongs to the **Institut de France.** Among the Italian Renaissance and French 18th-century art still at home here are works by **Donatello, Botticelli, Tintoretto, Titian, Bernini, Watteau, Fragonard, Tiepolo, Rembrandt, Reynolds,** and **Murillo,** as well as four **Gobelins** tapestries. ♦ Free. M, Th-Su 11AM-6PM; Tu 1-6PM; W 11AM-10PM. 158 Blvd Haussmann (between Rues de Courcelles and de Téhéran). Métro: Miromesnil. 45.62.39.94

9 Ma Bourgogne ★$$ The owner of this reputable wine bar, **Louis Prin,** won the coveted *Meilleur Pot* award in 1962 and is known for his hot daily lunch specials. ♦ Breakfast, lunch, and snacks. Closed Saturday, Sunday, and in August. 133 Blvd Haussmann (between Rue de Courcelles and Ave Percier). Reservations recommended for lunch. Métro: Miromesnil. 45.63.50.61, 45.63.56.62. Also at: 19 Place des Vosges. 42.78.44.64

10 Le Marcande ★★$$$ Chef **Joël Veyron** prepares such dishes as pigeon with wild mushrooms, grilled sea bass, *salade de langoustines,* and a delicious *chausson de chocolat.* Ask for a table with a view of the charming courtyard. ♦ Lunch and dinner.

Closed Saturday, Sunday, and two weeks in August. 52 Rue de Miromesnil (between Rue La Boétie and Blvd Haussmann). Reservations recommended. Métro: Miromesnil. 42.65.19.14

10 René-Gérard Saint-Ouen Instead of clay, this artist shapes bread dough for any whim or occasion: elephants, chickens, half-moons, bicycles, even the Eiffel Tower. Your imagination sets the limit. If you can't bring yourself to eat these yeasty works of art, brush on some varnish and hang them in the kitchen. ◆ M-Sa 8AM-7PM. 111 Blvd Haussmann (at Rue d'Argenson). Métro: Miromesnil. 42.65.06.25

11 19 Rue La Boétie Thirteen-year-old **Henry James** developed an addiction to the croissants sold across the street when he lived here from 1856 to 1857. ◆ Between Rues de Miromesnil and Cambacérès. Métro: St.-Philippe-du-Roule

12 45 Rue La Boétie Here in the **Salle Gaveau,** in June 1921, Harvard's glee club became the first American glee club to sing in France. ◆ Between Rue du Faubourg-St.-Honoré and Ave Delcassé. Métro: St.-Philippe-du-Roule

13 Dalloyau This dessert shop has been perfecting its chocolate since 1802. Sample the El Dorado (cinnamon-and-praline-filled chocolates) or a *gâteau mogador* (a confection of chocolate cake and chocolate mousse with a racing stripe of raspberry jam) or the best-selling Opéra, with layer upon layer of differently textured chocolate. Sunday-morning lines bear witness to the best croissants in town. ◆ Daily 9AM-9PM. 101 Rue du Faubourg-St.-Honoré (between Rues du Colisée and La Boétie). Métro: St.-Philippe-du-Roule. 43.59.18.10

14 Cailleux This shop is full of works primarily by 18th-century artists: drawings and paintings by **Watteau, Boucher,** and **Fragonard.** ◆ M-F 9AM-noon, 2-6PM. Closed in August. 136 Rue du Faubourg-St.-Honoré (between Rues La Boétie and de Penthièvre). Métro: St.-Philippe-du-Roule. 43.59.25.24

14 Lord Sandwich ★★$ Umpteen varieties of sandwiches are served on pita bread or rye, as well as rich brownies and berry tarts. It's crowded, but pleasantly so. ◆ Breakfast, lunch, and afternoon tea. Closed Saturday and Sunday. 134 Rue du Faubourg-St.-Honoré (between Rues La Boétie and de Penthièvre). Métros: Miromesnil, St.-Philippe-du-Roule. 42.56.41.68

14 Henri Picard et Fils Founded in 1860, this exquisite bookstore deals in bound treasures such as **Diderot's** 35-volume, 18th-century encyclopedia and *Democracy in America* by **Alexis de Tocqueville.** ◆ M-Sa 10AM-12:30PM, 2-7PM. Closed in August. 126 Rue du Faubourg-St.-Honoré (at Rue de Penthièvre). Métro: St.-Philippe-du-Roule. 43.59.28.11

15 Chez Germain ★$ This inexpensive bistro serves quick lunches to the models, fashion designers, and art dealers who work in the neighborhood. Sample the coq au vin, *jarret aux lentilles,* or steak in Roquefort sauce. The delicious desserts come from Le Merisier, the restaurant's elegant cousin across the street. ◆ Lunch and dinner. Closed Saturday and Sunday. 19 Rue Jean-Mermoz (between Rues du Faubourg-St.-Honoré and de Ponthieu). Reservations recommended for lunch. Métro: Franklin-D.-Roosevelt. 43.59.29.24

Le Merisier

15 Le Merisier ★★★$$ The name means "wild cherry tree," and owners **Jean-Paul** and **Françoise Boyrie** have appropriately paneled the dining room in cherry wood. It's a warm and handsome setting for executives from the nearby embassies, who come here for the Continental breakfast and the exceptional lunch. Good choices are the *terrine a l'ancienne et sa confiture d'oignons* (duck pâté with Armagnac and onion preserves), the steak tartare, and the *pavé de rumsteack aux morilles.* For dessert, the *larme chocolat griottines* (a tear-shaped chocolate shell filled with chocolate mousse and kirsch-soaked cherries) is widely acclaimed. The friendly service is overseen by **Stéphanie Jitiaux,** the owner's nephew. ◆ Breakfast and lunch; dinner by appointment for 12 or more. Closed Saturday and Sunday. 28 Rue Jean-Mermoz (at Rue Rabelais). Reservations recommended. Métros: St.-Philippe-du-Roule, Franklin-D.-Roosevelt. 42.25.36.06

16 Au Petit Montmorency ★★★$$$ The culinary whimsy of chef **Daniel Bouché** lures chic customers back again and again. You'll find such offbeat specialties as baked hare with truffles, *foie gras de canard au caramel poivre,* warm potato and truffle salad, and, for dessert, hot chocolate soufflé. ◆ Lunch and dinner. Closed Saturday, Sunday, and in August. Reservations recommended. 5 Rue Rabelais (at Rue Jean-Mermoz). Métros: Franklin-D.-Roosevelt, St.-Philippe-du-Roule. 42.25.11.19

17 83 Rue du Faubourg-St.-Honoré Around 1840 **William Thackeray** took a small pied-à-terre here. ◆ Between Rue Jean-Mermoz and Ave Matignon. Métro: St.-Philippe-du-Roule

Restaurants/Clubs: Red   Hotels: Blue
Shops/ Outdoors: Green   Sights/Culture: Black

18 Jullien Cornic This prestigious shop is a Circe's Isle to connoisseurs and collectors of art books. Among its allures are beautifully bound catalogs of the oeuvres of artists as diverse as **Edouard Manet** and **Norman Rockwell,** and an eclectic assortment of books on interior design, architecture, and fashion (everything on the rag trade from Balmain to buttons). An annex around the corner specializes in rare art books. ♦ Tu-F 10AM-1PM, 2-7PM. 118 Rue du Faubourg-St.-Honoré; Annex: 29 Ave Matignon (at Rue du Faubourg-St.-Honoré and Ave Matignon). Métro: St.-Philippe-du-Roule. 42.68.10.10

19 Trompe-l'Oeil On the corner of Rue de Penthièvre and Avenue Delcassé, a man gazes from his balcony at a bronze nude as two doves flutter away, casting shadows on the walls. Painted by artist **Rieti** in 1985, this trompe l'oeil enlivens an otherwise unremarkable intersection. ♦ Métros: Miromesnil, St.-Philippe-du-Roule

20 Le Bristol Paris $$$$ One of the last and perhaps the most prestigious of Paris' grand hotels, the Bristol caters to the diplomats and dignitaries who conduct business down the street at the Elysée Palace. Features such as the sixth-floor penthouse swimming pool and marble bathrooms place the Bristol in a class by itself. This sumptuous hotel boasts of having had **Ulysses S. Grant** as a guest in the fall of 1887. **Sinclair Lewis** lived here in 1925, the year he won the Pulitzer Prize (which he declined to accept) for his novel *Arrowsmith*. And, in 1975, the celebration of **Josephine Baker's** 50th anniversary in show business was held in this hotel. ♦ 112 Rue du Faubourg-St.-Honoré (between Ave Matignon and Rue de Miromesnil). Métros: Champs-Elysées-Clemenceau, Miromesnil, St.-Philippe-du-Roule. 42.66.91.45

Within Le Bristol Paris:

Le Bristol ★★$$$$ Chef **Emile Tabourdiau** provides refined nouvelle cuisine that suits the elegance of the restaurant's Regency wood-paneled decor. Le Bristol is one of the very few

Paris hotel restaurants that has been awarded two Michelin stars. ♦ Lunch and dinner. Reservations recommended. 42.66.91.45

Bar du Bristol Don't order lemonade from this barkeep: **Michel** is vice president of the French Association of Bartenders. Try the *Nathaly* (a drink named after Michel's daughter, with Grand Marnier, white Martini vermouth, cognac, and raspberry brandy). ♦ Daily 10:30AM-1:30AM

20 Le Sphinx Together with its sister shop, L'Aigle Imperiale (around the corner at 3 Rue de Miromesnil, 42.65.27.33), Le Sphinx has one of the city's largest collections of antique weapons and Napoleonic memorabilia. Here you will find portraits of the emperor, a bottle of 1811 cognac he never got around to drinking, and one of Napoléon's trademark hats enshrined in a glass case. Le Sphinx's proprietor, **Pierre de Souzy,** will part with the latter item for a mere $100,000. ♦ M-Sa 10:30AM-1PM, 2-7PM. 104 Rue du Faubourg-St.-Honoré (between Ave Matignon and Rue de Miromesnil). Métros: St.-Philippe-du-Roule, Miromesnil. 42.65.90.96

21 Arts et Marine A veritable armada of handcrafted model wooden sailing vessels floats before your eyes. Among the replicas are the Navire Negrier (a 1780s slave ship) and the Navire Barlaresqué (a French copy of a Turkish pirate ship). Also for sale are old brass compasses, ivory-clad binoculars, and a great many frigates in bottles. Sufficient nauticalia, in short, to salt up any landlubber. ♦ M-F 11AM-7PM; Sa 2:30-6PM. Closed in August. 8 Rue de Miromesnil (between Rues de Faubourg-St.-Honoré and de Penthièvre). Métro: Miromesnil. 42.65.27.85

21 8 Rue de Miromesnil In May 1961, pop artist **Robert Rauschenberg's** first solo show was held here and received rave reviews. ♦ Between Rues de Faubourg-St.-Honoré and de Penthièvre. Métro: Miromesnil

22 Hôtel de Beauvau Le Camus de Mezières designed this mansion for **Prince Charles de Beauvau,** but the Revolution transferred its ownership to the state. The Ministry of the Interior has resided behind its ornate iron gates since 1861. ♦ 96 Rue du Faubourg-St.-Honoré (between Rues de Miromesnil and des Saussaies). Métro: St.-Philippe-du-Roule

23 Au Vieux Saussaies This shop trades in 18th- and 19th-century silver—from sugar bowls to samovars, evening bags to champagne ice buckets. You will find top-name *orfevrerie* here at lower prices than at some of the other dealers. ♦ Tu-Sa 11AM-7PM. 14 Rue des Saussaies (between Rues de Surène and Montalivet). Métro: St.-Philippe-du-Roule. 42.65.32.71

24 Muriel A remnant of Old Paris, this is one of the few remaining boutiques that sells only gloves. ♦ M-Sa 10AM-6:30PM Sept-June; M-F 10AM-6:30PM July-Aug. Closed one or two weeks in August. 4 Rue des Saussaies (between Rues Montalivet and Faubourg-St.-Honoré). Métro: St.-Philippe-du-Roule. 42.65.95.34

25 Palais de l'Elysée The most famous address on Rue du Faubourg-St.-Honoré, if not in all of France, is this country's counterpart of the White House. Built in 1718 to a design by **Molet,** the Elysée Palace has been the official residence of the French president since 1873. The public is not admitted, but you can glimpse the dignified facade through the gateway (see illustration below). The palace was purchased in 1753 by **Madame de Pompadour, Louis XV's** rich and spoiled mistress, who hired the architects **Lassurance, de Boucher,** and **de Van Lee** to expand the building and extend the gardens to the Champs-Elysées. Expropriated to serve as a government printing office (for the *Bulletin des Lois*) and dance hall during the Revolution, the mansion became a hideaway for the **Empress Joséphine** after she was divorced by **Napoléon.** At one time, the Elysée Palace was known as the **Hameau Chantilly** and was the site of a restaurant and fairgrounds run by an ice-cream maker named **Velloni.** On 22 June 1815 Napoléon signed his second abdication here. Subsequently, the **Duke of Wellington** and Russian **Czar Alexander I** stayed here. The history is rather confusing but worth a pause. ♦ 55 Rue du Faubourg-St.-Honoré (between Ave de Marigny and Rue de l'Elysée). Métro: St.-Philippe-du-Roule

26 American Ambassador's Residence In the 19th century the **Hôtel de Pontalba** was owned by financier and art collector **Baron Edmond de Rothschild.** (When the baron died in 1934 at the age of 89, he left 3,000 drawings and 43,000 postage stamps to the Louvre.) The U.S. government had the good taste to rent the *hôtel particulier* from **Baron Maurice de Rothschild** to serve as the residence of the American ambassador. The 40-room, 13-bathroom building is not open to the public, but if you are invited for dinner by the ambassador, you will see the original **Oudry** wood paneling and paintings by **John Singer Sargent, Cézanne,** and **van Gogh.** In one of the upstairs guest rooms is the bed where **Charles Lindbergh** slept after completing the first nonstop solo flight across the Atlantic on 21 May 1927. ♦ 41 Rue du Faubourg-St.-Honoré (between Rues de l'Elysée and Boissy d'Anglas). Métro: St.-Philippe-du-Roule

26 British Embassy The lovely **Hôtel de Charost,** built by **Mazarin** in 1720, was bought by **Napoléon's** sister, **Pauline,** who, after a tumultuous series of loves and marriages, became the **Princess Borghese.** In 1815, after Waterloo, the princess sold her **Palais Borghese** to **George III** of England, who turned it into his nation's embassy. Upstairs is Pauline's bed with gilded curtains descending from the talons of a Napoléonic eagle. The building is not open to the public. ♦ 39 Rue du Faubourg-St.-Honoré (between Rues de l'Elysée and Boissy d'Anglas). Métro: Concorde

26 33 Rue du Faubourg-St.-Honoré Built by the architect **Grandhomme** in 1714, this house was the home of **Duc Decres,** who was minister of the French Navy until 1820, when a bomb hidden beneath his bed dealt him a mortal wound. For seven subsequent years, it housed the Russian Embassy, until it was sold to **Nathaniel Rothschild.** In 1918, the house was born anew as **Cercle de l'Union Interalliée,** a swank international club for business people. ♦ Between Rues de l'Elysée and Boissy d'Anglas. Métro: Concorde

Palais de l'Elysée

26 Japanese Embassy In 1718 **Lassurance** built this *hôtel* for **Louis Blouin,** confidant and *premier valet de chambre* of **Louis XIV. Napoléon's** sister and brother lived here, as did the king of Bavaria. Currently, it's the Japanese ambassador's turn. ♦ 31 Rue du Faubourg-St.-Honoré (between Rues de l'Elysée and Boissy-d'Anglas). Métro: Concorde

27 Georges Bernard Antiquités Sate that craving to magnify, measure, and modify. Bernard, co-author of a book on corkscrews, specializes in old scientific instruments. ♦ M-Sa 10:30AM-1PM, 1:30-6:30PM. Closed two weeks in August. 1 Rue d'Anjou (at Rue Faubourg-St.-Honoré). Métro: Concorde. 42.65.23.83

28 Castiglione $$$ This hotel's high prices are in keeping with its choice location amid the splendorous boutiques. Unfortunately, a modern face-lift has left it a hostelry in search of character. ♦ 38-40 Rue du Faubourg-St.-Honoré (between Rues d'Anjou and Boissy-d'Anglas). Métro: Concorde. 44.94.25.25

28 Hermès Started in 1837 as a saddle store by **Thierry Hermès,** *artisan d'élite,* this is perhaps the most celebrated leather-goods emporium in the world. Having outlasted the age of the horse and carriage, Hermès now furnishes the leather fittings for Lear jets. Its bags are considered necessities, not accessories, while its gloves are unsurpassed in craftsmanship. Hermès signature scarves are huge and come in more than 200 styles, the most popular of which is the Brides de Gala; more than a half-million of these silken trifles are sold every year. ♦ M-Sa 10AM-1PM, 2:15-6:30PM July-Aug; M-Sa 10AM-6:30PM Sept-June. 24 Rue du Faubourg-St.-Honoré (at Rue Boissy-d'Anglas). Métro: Concorde. 40.17.47.17

Within Hermès:

Hermès Museum On the top floor is a private museum displaying old saddles, ornamented trunks, and even **Napoléon's** stirrups. ♦ For admission, write in advance to the store manager: Hermès, 24 Rue de Faubourg-St.-Honoré, Paris 75008

John Lobb On the second floor is the Paris branch of the reputable London shoe- and boot-maker. Join the ranks of other satisfied Lobb alumni: **Lyndon Johnson,** the **Shah of Iran, Gary Cooper,** and the **Duke of Edinburgh.** Stop in to be measured heel to toe, after which one of Lobb's cobblers will fashion two wooden lasts (one for each foot) on which to model your shoes. In the nearby studio, the skins are cut and stitched, and in one month (first-time customers must wait a year), this labor will have produced a noble pair of handmade shoes sure to last at least a decade—and all for a mere $2,000 per pair. ♦ M, Sa 10AM-1PM, 2:15-6:30PM; Tu-F 10AM-6:30PM. Closed in August. 42.65.24.45

29 28 Rue Boissy-d'Anglas **Le Boeuf sur le Toit,** the famous avant-garde nightclub, was located here. Its 10 January 1922 inaugural party was thrown by **Jean Cocteau** and attended by **Constantin Brancusi, Pablo Picasso,** and **Max Beerbohm,** among others. Leading the club's orchestra that night was **Vance Lowry,** a black American saxophonist who was partially responsible for introducing the French to jazz and the music of **George Gershwin.** ♦ Between Rues de Surène and du Faubourg-St.-Honoré. Métro: Concorde

LANVIN

30 Lanvin Shop here for women's scarves, perfumes, haute couture, and prêt-à-porter. ♦ M-Sa 9:30AM-6:30PM. 22 Rue du Faubourg-St.-Honoré (at Rue Boissy-d'Anglas). Métro: Concorde. 44.71.33.33

30 Gucci A four-floor marble palazzo is filled with the trademark Gucci red and green. ♦ M-Sa 9:30AM-6:30PM. 21 Rue Royale (at Rue du Faubourg-St.-Honoré). Métro: Concorde. 42.96.83.27

31 15 Rue du Faubourg-St.-Honoré In 1804, **Claude Rouget de Lisle,** composer of the *Marseillaise,* lived here, and after him, **Felix,** hairdresser to **Empress Eugénie.** (She was so superstitious she had the number 13 removed from the Faubourg address.) ♦ At Rue Boissy-d'Anglas. Métro: Concorde

November is France's official *Mois de la Photo,* when photography shows are held in dozens of museums and galleries throughout Paris.

Restaurants/Clubs: Red   **Hotels:** Blue
Shops/ 🌳 Outdoors: Green   **Sights/Culture:** Black

RUE DU CIRQUE
Pierre Cardin
men's clothing

AVENUE DE MARIGNY

RUE DE L'ELYSEE
Vissot
women's clothing
Alimia
women's clothing
Jean Lupu
antiques
Hiroko Koshino
women's clothing

British Embassy
Lancôme
cosmetics
Gucci
leather goods
Ted Lapidus
men's & women's clothing
Cartier
jewelry
Trussardi
men's & women's clothing
Revillon
women's clothing

RUE DU FAUBOURG-ST.-HONORÉ

Karl Lagerfeld
women's clothing

RUE D'ANJOU
Lanvin
men's clothing
Istante
women's clothing
La Baggagerie
leather goods
Jean de Bonnot
rare books
Poiray
jewelry
Hanae Mori
women's clothing
Jaeger
women's clothing
Igin
women's clothing

RUE BOISSY D'ANGLAS

RUE DE MIROMESNIL
Perrin
antiques
Armorial
engravers, leather goods
Espace Beauvau *art gallery, 18th c. to contemporary*

RUE DES SAUSSAIES
Jean Damien
women's clothing
Galerie de la Présidence
19th & 20th century art
Maud Frizan *women's shoes*
Lilane Romi
women's clothing
Louis Féraud
women's clothing
S.L. Dupont
men's clothing, fine gifts
Lecoanét Hemant
women's shoes & clothing
Maxim's *clothing*

RUE DE DURAS
Maxim's
tea salon
Remy S.
women's clothing
Burma
jewelry
Le Tanneur
leather goods
Sonia Rykiel
women's clothing
Arfan
jewelry
Etro
accessories
Pomellato
jewelry
Gianni Versace
women's clothing
Zilli
men's clothing

RUE D'AGUESSEAU
Chloé
women's clothing
Ungaro
women's clothing
Au Vieux Venise
antiques
Fratelli Rossetti
men's & women's shoes
Chloé
women's clothing
Rety
women's & children's clothing
Cour aux Antiquaires
antiques
Lefortier
antique rugs
Parfumerie Douglas
beauty products
Leonard
women's clothing
Courrèges
women's clothing

RUE D'ANJOU
Maxandre
women's clothing
Hôtel de Castiglione
Yves Saint Laurent
women's clothing
Jacques Fath
women's clothing
Brioni
men's clothing
Jun Ashida
women's clothing
Guy Laroche
women's clothing
Givenchy
women's clothing
Hermès
leather goods, scarves

RUE BOISSY D'ANGLAS
Maurice Segoura
art, antiques
André Chékière
men's clothing
Joan & David
men's & women's shoes
Christina Richard
jewelry

31 Carita This lavishly decorated hair salon (whose clients have included **Catherine Deneuve, Paloma Picasso,** and French rocker **Johnny Hallyday**) has a relaxed, down-to-earth staff that sets hairstyle trends. There are separate entrances for men and women. The salon is also noted for its skin-care treatments. ♦ Tu-Sa 9AM-7PM. 11 Rue du Faubourg-St.-Honoré (between Rues Boissy-d'Anglas and Royale). Métro: Concorde. 44.94.11.11 (women), 44.94.12.12 (men)

31 5 Rue du Faubourg-St.-Honoré The once-popular puffy pompadour burgeoned here in the salon of coiffeur **Henri de Bysterveld.** ♦ Between Rues Boissy-d'Anglas and Royale. Métro: Concorde

32 Christofle Want to make your little one's first baby tooth even more precious? How about encasing it in silver? Nothing is impossible for Christofle, the shop that has provided silver-plating services for more than a century. Christofle also features a fine selection of antique gold, as well as the stunning yellow and blue tableware **Claude Monet** designed for his house at Giverny. Peek into the museum at the same address. ♦ M 9:30AM-1PM, 2-6:30PM, Tu-Sa 9:30AM-6:30PM Oct-May; M 9:30AM-1PM, 2-7PM, Tu-Sa 9:30AM-7PM June-Sept. Closed 1-2PM in July and August. 9 Rue Royale (between Rue St.-Honoré and Place de la Concorde). Métro: Concorde. 49.33.43.00

33 Lachaume The city's oldest and most exquisite florist has catered to haute couturiers and other well-heeled clientele (who can afford long stemmed red roses in December) since 1845. Gaze into the shop window at the gorgeous bunches of tulips and orchids; it cures midwinter blues. ♦ M-F 9AM-7PM; Sa 9AM-6PM. Closed in August. 10 Rue Royale (between Rue St.-Honoré and Place de la Concorde). Métro: Concorde. 42.60.59.74, 42.60.57.26

34 Ladurée ★★★$ This turn-of-the-century *salon de thé* par excellence is posh and ultra-Parisian but not snobbish. The heavenly taste of the croissants is ample reason for taking breakfast here. Habitués recommend *financiers* (almond cakes), chocolate macaroons, *babas au rhum,* and *royals* (almond biscuits with a dash of chocolate or mocha). Don't miss the painting of the roly-poly, rosy-cheeked cherub-turned-pastry chef on the downstairs ceiling. ♦ Breakfast, lunch, and afternoon tea. Closed in August. 16 Rue Royale (between Rue St.-Honoré and Place de la Madeleine). Métro: Concorde. 42.60.21.79

Place de la Madeleine Shopping Map

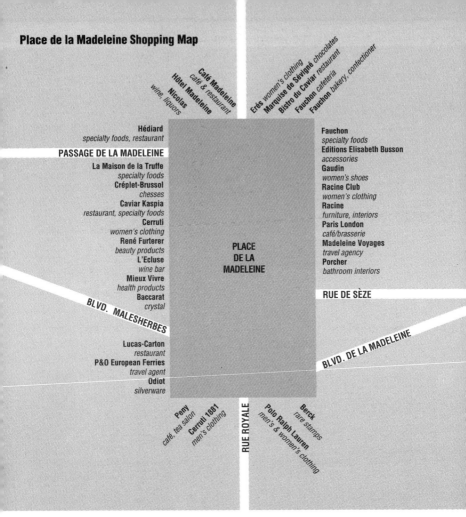

Café Madeleine
café & restaurant
Hôtel Madeleine
Nicolas
wine, liquors

Erés *women's clothing*
Marquise de Sévigné *chocolates*
Bistro du Caviar *restaurant*
Fauchon *cafeteria*
Fauchon *bakery, confectioner*

Hédiard
specialty foods, restaurant
PASSAGE DE LA MADELEINE
La Maison de la Truffe
specialty foods
Créplet-Brussol
cheeses
Caviar Kaspia
restaurant, specialty foods
Cerruti
women's clothing
René Furterer
beauty products
L'Ecluse
wine bar
Mieux Vivre
health products
Baccarat
crystal

PLACE DE LA MADELEINE

Fauchon
specialty foods
Editions Elisabeth Busson
accessories
Gaudin
women's shoes
Racine Club
women's clothing
Racine
furniture, interiors
Paris London
café/brasserie
Madeleine Voyages
travel agency
Porcher
bathroom interiors

RUE DE SÈZE

BLVD. MALESHERBES

Lucas-Carton
restaurant
P&O European Ferries
travel agent
Odiot
silverware

BLVD. DE LA MADELEINE

RUE ROYALE

Peny *café, tea salon*
Cerruti 1881 *men's clothing*

Polo Ralph Lauren *men's & women's clothing*
Berck *rare stamps*

34 La Maison du Valais ★★$$ An Alpine chalet, this restaurant serves *à volonté* (all you can eat) raclette (melted cheese served with potatoes, *cornichons,* and onions), delectable fondue, assortments of thinly sliced charcuterie, and cool Fendant wine. The cheerful waiters and Swiss food are heartening in winter when you fancy a ski weekend in the mountains but haven't time to escape the gray northern skies of Paris. ♦ Lunch, tea, and dinner. Closed Sunday. Reservations recommended, especially in winter. 20 Rue Royale (between Rue St.-Honoré and Place de la Madeleine). Métro: Madeleine. 42.60.23.75, 42.60.22.72

35 Cité Berryer The alley, formerly an open-air market, has been classified as a historic monument. ♦ Between Rues Royale and Boissy-d'Anglas. Métros: Concorde, Madeleine

35 Peny ★$ The coconut cake, *croque monsieur,* and yellow table umbrellas at this *salon de thé* are summertime favorites with Americans. ♦ Breakfast, lunch, afternoon tea, and dinner. 3 Place de la Madeleine (between Galerie de la Madeleine and Rue Royale). Métro: Madeleine. 42.65.06.75

35 Lucas-Carton ★★★★$$$$ The nouvelle cuisine of superstar chef **Alain Senderens,** who left the celebrated L'Archestrate to take over the Lucas-Carton kitchen, is better (and more expensive) than ever. Lucas-Carton, with its gorgeous Majorelle Belle Epoque maple and sycamore woodwork, is one of the Parisian capitals of nouvelle cuisine. Try the delicious foie gras in steamed cabbage, duck roasted with honey and spices, raviolis filled with clams, fig and cinnamon tarts, and a bittersweet chocolate soufflé. ♦ Lunch and dinner; dinner only on Saturday. Closed Sunday, three weeks in August, and two weeks over Christmas. 9 Place de la Madeleine (between Galerie de la Madeleine and Blvd Malesherbes). Reservations required. Métro: Madeleine. 42.65.22.90

36 Place de la Madeleine Around the edges of this square, the heart of luxury noshing in Paris, are specialty shops to spoil the spoiled (see the shopping map above). Amid the fumes of buses and a more-or-less perpetual rush hour, a lively flower market blossoms just east of the **Madeleine** church. Here, at her funeral in 1975, **Josephine Baker,** having already received the Legion d'Honneur and the

Medaille de la Résistance, became the first American woman ever to be honored with a 21-gun salute. ♦ Flower market: Tu-Su 6AM-3PM. Métro: Madeleine.

36 Kiosque-Théâtre In the Place de la Madeleine is a kiosk that sells half-price tickets to theater, dance, music hall, concert, café theater, and, occasionally, opera events on the day of performance. During the first two years of operation it sold 140,600 tickets. (Another kiosk is located inside the Châtelet-Les Halles métro station.) ♦ Tu-Sa 12:30-8PM; Su 12:30-4PM. Métro: Madeleine. No phone

36 Public Lavatory Even if nature isn't calling, look for a sign that reads: "Hommes et Dames W.C." It will lead you underground to an elegant 1905 facility with Art Nouveau wood paneling, stained glass, and tile built by **Etablissements Porcher,** now one of the largest plumbing suppliers in France. ♦ At Rue Royale and Place de la Madeleine. Métro: Madeleine

36 Eglise de la Madeleine The Madeleine's 28 monumental steps rise to meet 52 immense Corinthian columns, defining an edifice (pictured below) that dominates the hub of the financial district. However, the building has always been an architectural orphan. Begun as a church in 1764 under the reign of **Louis XV** and modeled after a Greek temple, the Madeleine has, at various times in its turbulent past, been slated to become a bank, parliament building, theater, stock exchange, banquet hall, and yet another temple to glorify **Napoléon's** army (as if the Arc de Triomphe and the Invalides were not enough). In 1837 the windowless structure, designed by **Pierre Vignon** and **Jean-Jacques Huvé,** was selected to be the capital's first railway station but was consecrated as a church dedicated to Saint Mary Magdalene five years later.

Not a single cross adorns the pediments of this church, and its rose marble and gilt interior is surprisingly sensual. The imposing bronze door portraying the *Ten Commandments* is by **Lemaire,** and his gigantic *Last Judgment* on the south pediment is the largest work of its kind in the world (and it contains one of the chubbiest Christs in Europe). On the north side of the church, the inscription beneath a headless statue of **Saint Luke** reads: "On 30 May 1918, a German shell struck the church of the Madeleine and decapitated this statue." The splendid organ was played by **Saint-Saëns,** and the *Funeral March* of **Chopin** debuted here as the composer himself was laid to rest. The grandest funeral ever accorded an American in Paris was that of **Josephine Baker,** held in the Madeleine on 15 April 1975. ♦ M-Sa 7AM-7PM; Su 8AM-1:30PM, 3:30-7PM. Place de la Madeleine. Métro: Madeleine

37 Edouard Berck Berck is the most renowned stamp dealer in the city. ♦ M-F 10AM-1PM, 2:30-6PM; Sa 10AM-1PM, 3-6PM. 6 Place de la Madeleine (between Rue Royale and Blvd de la Madeleine). Métro: Madeleine. 42.60.34.26

37 4 Place de la Madeleine Alas, this is no longer the home of **Durand's,** the famous music publisher, where, in 1831, **Liszt** first met **Chopin.** ♦ Between Rue Royale and Blvd de la Madeleine. Métro: Madeleine

38 Au Verger de la Madeleine Since 1936 this has remained one of Paris' finest family-operated *épiceries.* **Jean-Pierre Legras** will help you find an old Sauterne bottled in the year you were born, married, or made your first trip to Paris. ♦ M-F 10AM-1:30PM, 3-8PM; Sa 10AM-1:30PM, 3-7PM. 4 Blvd Malesherbes (between Place de la Madeleine and Rue de l'Arcade). Métro: Madeleine. 42.65.51.99

Eglise de la Madeleine

38 L'Ecluse ★★★$ One of a chain of six wine bars selling marvelous old Bordeaux by the glass, L'Ecluse is lively, fashionable, affordable, and ideal for people-watching. ◆ Lunch, snacks, and dinner. Closed Sunday. 15 Place de la Madeleine (between Passage de la Madeleine and Blvd Malesherbes). Métro: Madeleine. 42.65.34.69

38 Caviar Kaspia ★★★$$$ Besides purveying the finest in Russian and Iranian caviars, the chic little upstairs restaurant adorned in czarist turquoise and overlooking Place de la Madeleine offers vodka, aquavit, and blintzes languidly draped with smoked salmon. The shop downstairs sells all the makings for your own Russian dinner. ◆ Restaurant: Lunch, snacks, and dinner. Closed Sunday. Store: M-Sa 9AM-12:30AM. 17 Place de la Madeleine (between Passage de la Madeleine and Blvd Malesherbes). Métro: Madeleine. 42.65.33.52

38 La Maison de la Truffe ★★$$$ Brooklyn delicatessens never looked like this fancy place, which specializes in black gold (fresh truffles, in season from November through February) and any other delicacy your gourmand's heart could desire. ◆ Breakfast, lunch, snacks, and dinner. Closed Sunday. Shop: M-Sa 9AM-9PM. 19 Place de la Madeleine (at Passage de la Madeleine). Métro: Madeleine. 42.65.53.22

38 La Cave d'Hédiard Perhaps the grandest selection of Bordeaux wines in Paris is here, but taking an example home may cost you dearly. Armagnac, Calvados, and cognac are sold as well. ◆ M-Sa 9:30AM-9PM. 21 Place de la Madeleine (at Passage de la Madeleine). Métro: Madeleine. 42.66.04.84

38 Hédiard Recent renovations have diminished the Old-World charm of this specialty shop. **Marcel Proust** once lingered here, surveying Hédiard's exotic selection of Asian and African delicacies: spices, oils, vinegars, 30 blends of tea, freshly roasted coffee beans, baskets of rare jellies, and old rums. ◆ M-Sa 9:30AM-9PM. 21 Place de la Madeleine (at Passage de la Madeleine). Métro: Madeleine. 42.66.44.36

39 Roblin $$ The English who cross the channel for a weekend of opera and luxurious take-out food from the Place de la Madeleine find refuge in this hotel. ◆ 6 Rue Chauveau-Lagarde (between Rues Tronchet and de l'Arcade). Métro: Madeleine. 42.65.57.00

40 Chapelle Expiatoire This memorial chapel, commissioned by **Louis XVIII** and designed by **Pierre Fontaine,** has become a shrine for French royalists. It was erected in 1815 on the grounds of the cemetery where, among the thousands of other victims of the Revolution, **Marie Antoinette, Louis XVI,** and **Charlotte Corday** lie. In the chapel's right apse is a statue of Louis XVI being ushered into heaven by an angel resembling **Henry Essex Edgeworth,** the friend who accompanied the

king to the guillotine. Downstairs, an altar marks the spot where Louis XVI's body was found. ◆ No admission. Year-round W 10AM-12:45PM, 2-3:45PM. Groups by appointment only on Thursday. 29 Rue Pasquier (between Rue des Mathurins and Blvd Haussmann). Métro: Madeleine. 42.65.35.80

41 Trousselier Since 1885 this atelier has been creating gardens full of lovely silk flowers, all hand-painted, cut, and embossed. ◆ M-Sa 9:30AM-6:30PM. 73 Blvd Haussmann (between Rues Pasquier and de l'Arcade). Métro: St.-Augustin. 42.66.97.95

42 Aux Tortues Established in 1864 (long before politically correct consumerism), Aux Tortues sells hairbrushes for baby, chess sets, Japanese netsuke, picture frames, combs, and carved balls within balls made from tortoiseshells. ◆ M-Sa 9:30AM-6:30PM. 55 Blvd Haussmann (between Rues de l'Arcade and Tronchet). Métro: Havre-Caumartin. 42.65.56.74

43 Hôtel Opal $$ For the frugal traveler, here's a renovated hotel with doll-size chambers and modern bathrooms that's located behind the Madeleine church. It's a handy place to stay if you love going to the Opéra and shopping in the nearby stores. ◆ 19 Rue Tronchet (between Rues de Castellane and des Mathurins). Métro: Madeleine. 42.65.77.97

44 La Maison du Miel Run by the **Gallands** family since 1908, this shop is devoted entirely to honey and products containing honey, such as soap and oil. There are sample tastings and an array of honeys in miniature jars for the undecided. Don't pass up the *bruyère* (heather) honey. ◆ M 9:30AM-6PM; Tu-Sa 9:30AM-7PM. 24 Rue Vignon (between Rues de Sèze and des Mathurins). Métro: Madeleine. 47.42.26.70

44 Le Roi du Pot-au-Feu ★★$$ For some warm consolation on a frigid evening, visit this offbeat little bistro with its red-checked tablecloths and tableside jukeboxes. The specialty is its namesake: pot-au-feu, a marrow-rich beef broth served with the meat and vegetables that gave up their substance to the stew. ♦ Lunch and dinner. Closed Sunday. 34 Rue Vignon (between Rues de Sèze and des Mathurins). Métro: Madeleine. 47.42.37.10

45 La Ferme St.-Hubert A cheese-lover's heaven with 140 different cheeses, La Ferme is especially known for its excellent Roquefort and Beaufort. The **St.-Hubert** restaurant is next door. ♦ Shop: M-Sa 8:30AM-7:30PM. Restaurant: Lunch and dinner; lunch only on Monday. Closed Sunday. 21 Rue Vignon (between Rues de Sèze and Tronchet). Métro: Madeleine. 47.42.79.20

46 Marquise de Sévigné ★★$ The ambience in this combination tea salon/chocolate shop is as unctuous as the rich hot chocolate it serves. ♦ Breakfast, lunch, and afternoon tea. Closed Sunday. 32 Place de la Madeleine (between Rues Tronchet and Vignon). Métro: Madeleine. 42.65.19.47

46 Fauchon One look in the window tells the story. Inside is a supermarket for millionaires, with every exotic fruit and vegetable on earth artistically arrayed in gorgeous still life. Fauchon is the most famous food shop in town, stocked with more than 20,000 items, from Scottish salmon and chunky peanut butter to Tonganese mangoes. Customers are not allowed to handle any of the merchandise; they pay first and then are presented with their prize at the door. Everything's expensive.

On-the-spot overindulgence used to mean standing at the store's self-service cafeteria across the street, but to Fauchon fans' delight, a restaurant opened upstairs featuring a view of the illuminated Church of the Madeleine. Chef **Bruno Deligne's** menu includes delicacies such as hot oysters and leeks with truffle sauce, and, for lighter summer fare, melon and Sauternes soup. Fauchon will also cater your next cocktail party in Paris. ♦ Store: M-Sa 9:40AM-7PM. Restaurant: Lunch and dinner. Closed Sunday. 26 Place de la Madeleine (northeast corner). Métro: Madeleine. 47.42.60.11

47 Bar Romain ★$$ One of the Right Bank's most handsome bars, with a basement restaurant decorated like a Belle Epoque railroad car, Bar Romain offers steak tartare and lentils vinaigrette as well as 350 cocktails. ♦ Restaurant: Lunch and dinner. Closed Sunday. Bar: M-Sa noon-2AM. Closed in August. 6 Rue de Caumartin (between Blvd de la Madeleine and Place Edouard-VII). Métros: Madeleine, Opéra. 47.42.98.04

48 Olympia Music Hall Playing here is an obligatory engagement for top pop singers. **Edith Piaf** sang her heart out on this stage. Years later so did a group of Brits named the **Beatles,** who had just launched their first world tour. ♦ 28 Blvd des Capucines (at Rue Caumartin). Métro: Madeleine. 47.42.25.49

49 14 Boulevard des Capucines On 28 December 1895 the brothers **Auguste** and **Louis Lumière,** inventors of the cinematograph, projected their first public movie here in what was called the **Salon Indien.** ♦ Between Rues Edouard-VII and Scribe. Métro: Opéra

50 Scribe $$$ Completely renovated behind its Napoléon III facade, this luxurious hotel was the Allied forces' press headquarters at the end of World War II. Correspondent **John Dos Passos,** who stayed here, wrote home describing **Charles de Gaulle** after a press conference: "He has two voices, the Sorbonne voice and the *père de famille, Henri Quatre, bonne soupe* kind of voice. There's more to him than we had been led to believe." ♦ 1 Rue Scribe (at Blvd des Capucines). Métro: Opéra. 44.71.24.24
Within the Scribe:

Les Muses ★$$$ Chef **Pierre Miecaz** proposes entrées such as marinated crayfish, monkfish with saffron, and filet of lamb in pastry. ♦ Lunch and dinner. Closed Saturday and Sunday. Reservations recommended. 44.71.24.24

Le Bar St.-Laurent Business executives habitually gather around the elegant mahogany bar, sipping one of the different Canadian whiskey cocktails offered each day. ♦ Daily 9AM-2AM. 44.71.24.24

50 Grand Hôtel $$$$ Designed in 1860 by **Charles Garnier,** the 600-room Grand Hôtel is one of Europe's oldest luxury hotels. Although major renovations have stripped away some of its old-fashioned grandeur, the hotel offers such first-class perks as a sauna, tanning rooms, masseuses, and a gymnasium. Its proximity to the Opéra Garnier makes it a favorite of visiting prima ballerinas. ♦ 2 Rue Scribe (at Blvd des Capucines). Métro: Opéra. 40.07.32.32

50 Bar du Grand Hôtel Tucked under the arches of the hotel is this multilevel opera-goers' watering hole. ♦ Daily 11AM-2AM. 12 Blvd des Capucines (between Rues Scribe and Auber). Métro: Opéra. 42.68.12.13

51 Café de la Paix ★★$$ Looking like a scene painted by Renoir with green-and-white-striped umbrellas, a dance of light, and brightly clothed patrons, this lovely old café is classified as a historic landmark. **Salvador Dalí** enjoyed it, as did **Harry Truman, Maurice Chevalier, Maria Callas,**

Restaurants/Clubs: Red   Hotels: Blue
Shops/ Outdoors: Green   Sights/Culture: Black

Opéra Garnier

and **General Charles de Gaulle,** who ordered a take-out cold plate here on 25 August 1944—the first in liberated Paris. Tradition holds that if you sit on the terrace long enough, you will see someone you know walk by. ♦ Breakfast, lunch, dinner, snacks, and late-night. 3 Place de l'Opéra (at Blvd des Capucines and Rue Auber). Métro: Opéra. 40.07.30.20

51 Le Restaurant Opéra ★★$$$ Alas, its luscious setting inspires only uneven cuisine. ♦ Lunch and dinner. 3 Place de l'Opéra (at Blvd des Capucines and Rue Auber). Reservations recommended. Métro: Opéra. 40.07.30.10

51 Place de l'Opéra Six main thoroughfares, bank headquarters, a theater district, and luxury boutiques are the spokes in this imposing hub. Back when the Opéra was where one scaled the social heights, the *haut monde* and *demimonde* frequented nearby beaneries such as Café de la Paix, Café de Paris, and the Café Riche. ♦ Métro: Opéra

52 Musée Fragonard This museum is devoted entirely to perfume, its history, and its objets d'art. ♦ M-Sa 9AM-5:30PM. 9 Rue Scribe (between Rues Auber and des Mathurins). Métro: Opéra. 47.42.04.56

52 American Express If you did leave home without it, go no farther. Here you will find traveler's checks, a foreign exchange bank, and mail pickup. ♦ M-F 9AM-7PM; Sa 9AM-5PM (for changing money and sight-seeing tours only). 11 Rue Scribe (at Rue Auber). Métro: Opéra. 47.77.77.07

53 Opéra Garnier (Paris Opéra) An opera house fit for an emperor, the pièce de résistance of **Baron Haussmann's** revamped Paris, and a last hurrah of Second-Empire opulence, this grandiose culture palace was once the world's largest theater, with an area of nearly three acres and a stage vast enough to accommodate 450 performers. Designer **Charles Garnier,** a 35-year-old previously unknown architect, was selected from among a field of 171 other competitors (including the empress' favorite architect, **Viollet-le-Duc**).

Garnier's design gave the facade (pictured above) a unique look–with ornate friezes, winged horses, golden garlands, and busts of famous composers. He crowned this architectural exaggeration with a copper-green cupola topped by **Millet's** *Apollo* thrusting a lyre above his head. A golden bust of the author of all this effulgence stands on the Rue Scribe side of the theater. Garnier's orgiastic mishmash of styles (from classical to baroque) and materials (every possible hue of marble, from green to red and blue) was less than the hit he hoped it would be. The empress, wife of **Napoléon III,** is said to have barked in disgust at the design, "What is this style supposed to be? It is neither Greek nor Roman nor Louis XIV nor Louis XV!" Searching for a name, Garnier diplomatically replied: "It is Napoléon III, Your Majesty." Second-Empire advocates of family values were in an uproar over the sensual **Carrier-Belleuse** lamp-bearing statues and the famous sculpted group *La Danse* by **Carpeaux.**

Inside the opera house, however, the effect is eminently upright, even majestic. Though **Renoir** loathed the opera house, you may find a night here to be worth your while. The best of classical ballet and modern dance is performed here (all operas now take place at the Opéra Bastille); furthermore, the gold ornaments, allegories in marble, **Chagall** ceilings, and the parade of Parisian society are all good for a gape. Horror-movie fans will be interested to know that the underground grotto where **Leroux's** *Phantom of the Opéra* lurked actually exists. It lies beneath the Opéra's cellars, an artificial lake that provides water for the city's fire brigade. The less-than-inspired **Opéra Museum** in the **West Pavilion** displays opera and ballet memorabilia (such as the crown **Pavlova** wore when dancing in *Swan Lake* and the ballet slippers and tarot cards of **Nijinsky**). Tickets to performances at the nearby but lesser-known **Opéra Comique** are cheaper and easier to get, and the presentations there are often more amusing. ♦ Admission. Museum: M-Sa 10AM-4:30PM. Box office: M-Sa 11AM-6:30PM. Place de l'Opéra. Métro: Opéra. 40.17.35.35 (box office)

Within the Opéra Garnier:

Grand Foyer and Staircase Of this apotheosis of splendor (pictured above), **Henry James** wrote: "If the world were ever reduced to the domain of a single gorgeous potentate, the foyer would do very well for his throne room." The baroque white Carrara marble Grand Staircase with its Algerian onyx balustrade measures 32 feet wide at its center. At the first landing, it divides and sweeps upward in two flights of steps to the second-floor gallery. The Grand Foyer, 175 feet long and decorated with mirrors and allegorical paintings, is encrusted with gilt ornament, and its ceiling glows with Venetian mosaics

and colored marble from the island of Murano. The annual **Ecole Polytechnique Ball** and presidential galas are still held here every year. ♦ Daily 10AM-4:30PM

Auditorium The theater is famous for its six-ton chandelier and five tiers of loges dressed in red velvet and gold. It is adorned with **Marc Chagall's** 1964 masterpiece depicting Parisian scenes and images from operas ranging from *Giselle* to *The Magic Flute*. The ceiling is as colorful as the rest of Garnier's palace, yet oddly out of place. Backstage is the **Foyer de la Danse** so often painted by **Edgar Degas.** ♦ Daily 1-2PM

54 Boulevard Haussmann This drab expanse fronted with mammoth department stores becomes festive in December, when it's strung with Christmas lights. In 1784, two months after his arrival in Paris as American ambassador to France, **Thomas Jefferson** signed a nine-year lease on a new town house located on what is now the north side of Boulevard Haussmann. The meticulous Virginian filled it with furniture, then set about acquiring a collection of paintings, books, and engravings that would eventually adorn his beloved Monticello. History records that during his sojourn in Paris, Jefferson kept a black servant, **James Hemings,** whom he apprenticed to a local caterer, **Combeaux,** perhaps so he could take home some French culinary art along with his other acquisitions.

54 Au Printemps In the 1870s Paris introduced the world to *grands magasins* (department stores, such as La Samaritaine and Bon Marché), and the city's shopping giants have been drawing crowds ever since. Today, two outclass the rest: Les Galeries Lafayette and Au Printemps, right next to each other along the Boulevard Haussmann. These are great places to get a peek at the latest in Parisian fashion as well as some indication of what it costs. Rest your feet and have a cup of tea or a slice of tart in the sixth-floor tea salon beneath Au Printemps' Belle Epoque stained-glass rotunda. If possible, shop on weekday mornings, as afternoons and Saturdays in these stores can resemble a stampede at the Chicago stockyard. ♦ M-Sa 9:45AM-7PM. 64 Blvd Haussmann (between Rues du Havre and de Caumartin). Métros: Havre-Caumartin, Opéra. 42.82.50.00

55 Les Galeries Lafayette With its magnificent glass-and-steel dome and Art Nouveau staircase built by the architect

Cahnautin in 1912, this 10-story department store is classified as a historic monument. More than 10,000 customers visit its fashion department every day. Now there's an added attraction: **Galeries Lafayette Gourmet.** At sit-down counters throughout the food department, you can sample each section's specialty: grilled meats near the butcher, salads in the produce area, etc. And on the top floor there's incomparable browsing and a marvelous vista of the Right Bank's rooftops. ♦ M-Sa 9:30AM-6:45PM. 40 Blvd Haussmann (between Rues de Mogador and de la Chaussée-d'Antin). Métros: Chaussée-d'Antin, Opéra. 42.82.34.56

Place Vendome Shopping Map

RUE DES CAPUCINES

RUE DE LA PAIS

Emporio Armani *men's & women's clothing*

Alexandre Reza *jewelry*
Cartier *jewelry*
Ritz Hotel
Cartier *jewelry*
Chanel *jewelry*
Hôtel Vendôme
Morabito *jewelry, purses*

RUE DANIELLE-CASANOVA

Charvet *men's & women's clothing*
Comptoir sud Pacific *accessories*
Boucheron *jewelry*

Van Cleef & Arpels *jewelry, watches*
Mauboissin *jewelry*
Piaget *watches*
Pascal Morabito *bags, luggage*
Chaumet *jewelry*
Mikimoto *jewelry*
Repossi *jewelry*
Giorgio Armani *men's & women's clothing*
Gianmaria Buccellati *fine silver, jewelry*
Galerie Alexander Butman *Impressionist and Post-Impressionist paintings, prints, and lithographs*
Lhullier *florist*
Ebel *jewelry*
Guerlain *perfume, accessories*

RUE ST.-HONORE

chocolates **Godiva**
bar & restaurant **Le Lotti**
accessories **Ilonka**
Weedly
children's clothing, T-shirts
watches **Le Montres**
Hotel Lotti
Dominique France *men's ties, accessories*
costume jewelry **Anémone**
men's clothing **Namani**
optician **Meyrowitz**

RUE DE CATIGLIONE

Annick Goutal *oils & perfume*
Rhodes & Brousse *men's clothing*
Agry *engraving*
Carré des Feuillants *restaurant*
Kenneth Jay Lane *jewelry*
British Airways
Aquascutum *men's & women's clothing*
Luce Brett *antiques*
Payot *beauty products, salon*

RUE DU MONT-THABOR

Hotel Intercontinental
Casty *purses, jewelry*

Cristal Vendôme *crystal*

Les Arcades *books*
Parfumeria Catherine *perfume*
Hôtel Meurice *(back entrance)*
Swann Pharmacy
Jacqueline Perès *women's clothing*
Sulka *men's clothing*

56 Multistore Opéra Not quite your Main Street soda fountain, this slick and sprawling institution draws more than 20,000 customers a day through its entrances on Boulevard des Capucines and Rue Halévy. They apparently come for the junk shop, jewelry store, and tobacco and gift shops. All those drugstore things are here: newspapers, makeup, stuffed animals, medicine, and film. Last but not least, for those who have an aversion to French salesclerks, there is a battery of self-service machines: a compact-disc distributor, while-you-wait business cards, tarot readings, and horoscopes. ♦ Daily 10AM-midnight. 6 Blvd des Capucines (at Rue Halévy). Métro: Opéra. No phone

56 8 Boulevard des Capucines It was at this address in 1880, the year of his death, that 61-year-old **Jacques Offenbach** composed his masterpiece *The Tales of Hoffmann.* ♦ Between Place de l'Opéra and Rue de la Chaussée-d'Antin. Métro: Opéra. 47.42.19.00

56 Le Grand Café ★$ God bless it, one of the few Parisian bistros open 24 hours a day, Le Grand Café serves good seafood to boot. This haunt of **Oscar Wilde** is now a hangout for journalists, graveyard-shift laborers, and anyone else out walking the streets at the hour of the wolf. ♦ Daily 24 hrs. 4 Blvd des Capucines (between Place de l'Opéra and Rue de la Chaussée-d'Antin). Métro: Opéra. 47.42.19.00

57 Restaurant Drouant ★★$$$$ At the end of each November since 1903, 10 novelists have met here to award the **Prix Goncourt,** France's prestigious prize for the year's best fiction. (The prize isn't much money, but fame and fortune in the form of lucrative publishing contracts follow.) The selection made, the jury adjourns to the Louis XVI chairs in **Salon 15** (a private third-floor dining room) and addresses a sumptuous repast, which ends traditionally with Reblochon cheese from the Savoy mountains. The specialties of this century-old restaurant are roast pigeon in a potato shell with coral sauce, grilled salmon, and a fine house Muscadet. Drouant is popular with the elegant crowd from the Opéra. If you forget to make reservations, consider having a meal in the café. ♦ Lunch and dinner. Reservations required. 18 Rue Gaillon (at Rue St.-Augustin). Métro: 4-Septembre. 42.65.15.16

58 6 Rue Danou Dr. **Oliver Wendell Holmes** (father of the famous jurist) knew this as the Hotel d'Orient and stayed here when he made a brief trip to Paris in 1886 to meet **Louis Pasteur,** who had just developed the vaccine for rabies. ♦ Between Ave de l'Opéra and Rue de la Paix. Métro: Opéra

The French Revolution has been the subject of more than 200 feature films by directors such as Jean Renoir, Abel Gance, D.W. Griffith, Ettore Scola, and Andrzej Wajda.

Restaurants/Clubs: Red
Shops/ ♣Outdoors: Green
Hotels: Blue
Sights/Culture: Black

59 Harry's Bar Opened in 1911, "Sank-Roo-Doe-Noo" (the American pronunciation of the bar's address) really came into its own two years later, when it was purchased from an American jockey by a bartender named **Harry MacElhone**. Here **F. Scott Fitzgerald** stared at the bleary surfaces of successive Scotches and watched the plot lines of his novels take form. At Harry's Bar, **George Gershwin** dreamed up his great fantasy *An American in Paris;* **Ernest Hemingway** dodged swinging fists; **Gloria Swanson** glowed; **Noel Coward** quipped; and **Jean-Paul Sartre,** despite himself, discovered both bourbon and hot dogs. The night before each U.S. presidential election, the regulars around the bar are polled as to their guesses of the outcome; the legendary poll has an uncanny track record for predicting the winner. ♦ Daily 10:30AM-3AM. 5 Rue Danou (between Ave de l'Opéra and Rue de la Paix). Métro: Opéra. 42.61.71.14

60 Rue de la Paix Before 1815 this street was Rue Napoléon, but today for some reason no street, square, or public place in Paris is named after the emperor. ♦ Métro: Opéra

60 Ermenegildo Zegna The understated high fashions for men at this sophisticated shop are made with the richest of fabrics and have an appeal that's beyond snobbery. For more than a century the Zegna family has been known as the maker of the world's finest wools, providing the best European designers with their raw materials. ♦ M 11AM-7PM, Tu-Sa 10AM-7PM Sept-July; M 11AM-1PM, 2-7PM, Tu-F 10AM-1PM, 2PM-7PM Aug. 10 Rue de la Paix (between Rues Danou and Danielle-Casanova). Métro: Opéra. 42.61.67.61

61 Alfred Dunhill The Paris branch of a famous English company, this mahogany-paneled shop sells all manner of smoking paraphernalia. Dunhill pipes made from the best French brier, with ebony mouthpieces, are among the world's finest (and most costly). And where else will you find a thuja-wood cigar box? ♦ M-Sa 10AM-6:30PM. 15 Rue de la Paix (between Rues des Capucines and Danou). Métro: Opéra. 42.61.57.58

61 Hôtel Westminster $$$ In the 19th century, this hotel catered to Americans such as **Hamilton Fish,** who was Secretary of State under **Ulysses S. Grant,** and the family of **Henry James,** who stayed here when the future novelist was 12. ♦ 13 Rue de la Paix (between Rues des Capucines and Danou). Métro: Opéra. 42.61.57.46

Within the Hôtel Westminster:

Bar Les Chenets Frequented by a neighborhood business clientele, this bar specializes in Campari-based cocktails, which sounds misleadingly innocent. ♦ Daily 7:20AM-11:30PM. 42.61.57.46

61 Kitty O'Shea's The most Irish of pubs in Paris serves Guinness, the most Irish of brews, on tap. Businesspeople headquartered around the Opéra congregate here. ♦ M-Th, Su noon-1:30AM; F-Sa noon-2AM. 10 Rue des Capucines (at Rue Volney). Métros: Madeleine, Opéra. 40.15.00.30

62 Le Castille $$$ This comfortable new hotel is decorated in the Venetian style, with marble, colorful damasks, a faux patina on the walls, and a courtyard with a fountain. Some of the rooms have views of the Chanel ateliers, where **Coco Chanel** created her first haute couture designs. ♦ 35-37 Rue Cambon (between Blvd de la Madeleine and Rue St.-Honoré). Métros: Concorde, Madeleine. 44.58.44.58

Within Le Castille:

Il Cortile ★★$$ Chef **Alberto Porta** prepares genuine Italian dishes, including *crostino di mozzarella Napoletano, prosciutto di Parma con melone,* risotto with peas and herbs, swordfish filet with olives, and cassoulet of rabbit, mushrooms, and polenta. ♦ Lunch and dinner. Closed Sunday. 44.58.45.67

63 Charles Jourdan Forty years ago, celebrated Monsieur Jourdan became the first cobbler to use glue instead of nails to hold his shoes together; the result was the first truly delicate feminine footwear. ♦ M-Sa 10AM-7PM. 5 Blvd de la Madeleine (between Rues Cambon and Duphot). Métro: Madeleine. 42.61.50.07, 42.65.35.22

64 Hôtel Burgundy $$ The last pages of *Look Homeward, Angel* sprang from the fertile imagination of **Thomas Wolfe** while he was here in 1928. ♦ 8 Rue Duphot (between Rue St.-Honoré and Blvd de la Madeleine). Métro: Madeleine. 42.60.34.12

64 29 Rue Cambon Upon his return to Paris in November 1875, young *New York Tribune* correspondent **Henry James** took up residence on the third floor of what is now **Chanel** headquarters. This is where *The Americans,* his novel set in Paris, was written. ♦ Between Rue St.-Honoré and Blvd de la Madeleine. Métro: Concorde

65 Goumard Prunier ★★$$$ Fresh shellfish, ginger grilled Brittany lobster, sea bass, and frogs' legs are a few of the specialties served here. ◆ Lunch and dinner. Closed Sunday and Monday. 9 Rue Duphot (between Blvd de la Madeleine and Rue St.-Honoré). Reservations recommended. Métro: Madeleine. 42.60.36.07

65 Gaya ★★$$ Settle on one of the comfortable banquettes in this seafood bistro, owned by **Jean-Claude Goumard** of **Goumard Prunier** down the street, and order the delicious anchovies, marinated raw sardines *à l'escabèche,* or tuna *au piment d'Espelette.* ◆ Lunch and dinner. Closed Sunday. 17 Rue Duphot (between Blvd de la Madeleine and Rue St.-Honoré). Reservations recommended. Métro: Madeleine. 42.60.43.03

66 Au Nain Bleu The Paris equivalent of **F.A.O. Schwarz** sells toys luxurious enough to spoil any child. ◆ M-Sa 9:45AM-6:30PM. 406-410 Rue St.-Honoré (at Rue Richepance). Métro: Concorde. 42.60.39.01

67 Christian Tortu One of the hottest florists in town, Tortu creates opulent, original designs with flowers and vegetables here and at his Left Bank boutique (6 Carrefour de l'Odeon, 43.26.02.56). He also sells garden furniture. ◆ M-F 10AM-7PM; Sa 10AM-6PM. 13 Rue St.-Florentin (between Rues St.-Honoré and de Rivoli). Métro: Concorde. 42.86.94.69

68 Toraya ★★$$ In Japanese, *toraya* means "tiger"; for Parisians, it denotes this elegant black-and-gray Japanese tea salon and pastry shop. Dishes include sweet bean noodles, *kuzukiri* (noodles made from jellied arrowroot), and energizing pots of green *ocha* (tea). ◆ Lunch and afternoon tea.

Closed Sunday. 10 Rue St.-Florentin (between Rues St.-Honoré and de Rivoli). Métro: Concorde. 42.60.13.00

68 Notre-Dame-de-l'Assomption This church, built in 1676, was originally part of a convent where destitute widows and abandoned wives were given shelter; it has served a Polish parish since 1850. The massive cupola on top has been dubbed *le sot dôme* (the silly dome). ◆ 263bis Rue St.-Honoré (between Rues St.-Florentin and Cambon). Métro: Tuileries

69 Cadolle The lady who is credited with inventing the brassiere in 1900, **Hermine Cadolle,** was the great-grandmother of Cadolle's current proprietor, Alice Cadolle. All manner of deluxe lingerie, French beachwear and perfume is sold here. ◆ M-Sa 9:30AM-1PM, 2-6:30PM. 14 Rue Cambon (between Rues du Mont-Thabor and St.-Honoré). Métro: Concorde. 42.60.94.94

70 France et Choiseul $$$ **Franklin** and **Eleanor Roosevelt** stayed in this hotel on their honeymoon in 1905, during which time a clairvoyant told Roosevelt that he'd become president of either the U.S. or the Equitable Life Insurance Company (he wasn't sure which). In 1946, after *The Heart Is a Lonely Hunter* and *Reflections in a Golden Eye* had been published in French, **Carson McCullers** and her husband moved in here. Now the hotel is known for its old-fashioned charm, modern conveniences, small rooms, and courteous staff, which, unfortunately, in peak season seems also to be on holiday. ◆ 239 Rue St.-Honoré (between Rues Cambon and de Castiglione). Métros: Concorde, Tuileries. 42.61.54.60

70 Godiva The world-renowned chocolatier takes its name from the 11th-century English noblewoman who sacrificed her modesty and rode naked through the streets of Coventry to plead with her husband, the earl, to reduce taxes on the townsfolk. If these exquisite bonbons had been available then, they might have made a better bribe. ◆ M-Sa 9:30AM-7PM. 237 Rue St.-Honoré (between Rues Cambon and de Castiglione). Métros: Concorde, Tuileries. 42.96.44.64

70 Jolly Hôtel Lotti $$$$ This small luxury hotel is favored by British and Italian bluebloods who are drawn to the large, tastefully decorated rooms, period furniture, and impeccable service. ◆ 7 Rue de Castiglione (between Rues St.-Honoré and de Mont-Thabor). Métros: Concorde, Tuileries. 42.60.37.34

71 Carré des Feuillants ★★★$$$$ While **Nicole Dutournier** minds Au Trou Gascon, their marvelous family restaurant in the 12th arrondissement, her husband, chef **Alain Dutournier,** pioneers this second, fancier, 19th-century-style restaurant near Place Vendôme. His specialty is inventive southwestern-French cuisine such as lobster with white gazpacho, wild hare with truffles, and veal with eggplant in a casserole. Don't skip dessert or his marvelous old cognacs.
♦ Lunch and dinner; dinner only on Saturday. Closed Sunday. Closed Saturday and Sunday in July and August. 14 Rue de Castiglione (between Rues St.-Honoré and du Mont-Thabor). Reservations required. Métros: Concorde, Tuileries. 42.86.82.82

72 Place Vendôme Like the **Place de la Concorde, Place des Victoires,** and other magnificent squares, this was conceived as a setting for a royal equestrian statue. The subject was **Louis XIV,** and the sculptor was **François Girardon.** In 1685, to make way for his monument, Louis bought and demolished the **Duke of Vendôme's** town house and the nearby Capucines convent. **Jules Hardouin-Mansart** designed gracefully formal mauve limestone facades with Corinthian pilasters and sculpted masks that were added to the square's periphery in 1715. The Sun King, a budding real estate shark, encouraged speculators to buy the lots behind the facades, then hire their own architects to fill in the blanks. During the Revolution the heads of nine victims of the guillotine were displayed here on spikes, and for a while the Place Vendôme was known as the **Place des Piques** (Pike Square).

On 19 June 1792 a huge bonfire in the square incinerated bundles of genealogical documents concerning the French nobility's title deeds. Needless to say, the king's gilt statue didn't survive the mob's wrath, either; it was felled in August of the same year. Today the 440- by 420-foot octagon is characterized by an aloof opulence. It is the home of the Hôtel Ritz and of one of the world's greatest concentrations of banks, perfumeries, and jewelers, including Boucheron, Van Cleef & Arpels, Cartier, Chaumet, Schiaparelli, and Guerlain (see shopping map on page 160).
♦ Métros: Madeleine, Opéra, Tuileries

72 Vendôme Column In place of the toppled statue of **Louis XIV, Napoléon** raised a 144-foot-high bronze monument modeled on Trajan's column in Rome. Made to commemorate Napoléon's military victories in Germany, the Vendôme Column is faced with 378 spiraling sheets of bronze supplied by 1,200 cannons captured from the Austrian and Russian armies defeated at the Battle of Austerlitz in 1805. After the emperor's defeat at Waterloo, the Bourbons mounted their own symbol, the fleur-de-lis, atop the column, commandeering the monument. Along came

Louis Philippe, and the fleur-de-lis was replaced with a small statue of Napoléon. But on the afternoon of 1 May 1871, the column was toppled again, crashing down along Rue de la Paix and breaking into 30 pieces. This act of destruction was masterminded by the painter **Gustave Courbet** for aesthetic and political reasons. When the Third Republic took power, it ordered Courbet to restore the monument at his own expense. The column was thrust up yet again (this time with Napoléon dressed as Julius Caesar), and Courbet was plunged into bankruptcy.
♦ Métros: Madeleine, Opéra, Tuileries

73 Hôtel Vendôme $$$ Fred Astaire stayed here in 1936 during his time-out from kicking up his heels with Ginger Rogers in *Swing Time* and *Shall We Dance?* The hotel has old-fashioned charm, large rooms, and a chic clientele.
♦ 1 Place Vendôme (at Rue de Castiglione). Métros: Concorde, Madeleine, Tuileries. 42.60.32.84

73 3-5 Place Vendôme This was formerly the **Hôtel Bristol.** From 1890 to 1910, whenever financier and art collector **John Pierpont Morgan** came to Paris, he would stay in the same corner suite in the old hotel, which was run by one of his father's butlers. The building is now owned by **IBM Paris.** ♦ Southwest corner. Métro: Madeleine

73 Cartier Since 1847 Cartier has offered the best and the brightest in French bijous, with commensurately dazzling price tags. The tourist discount on gold, however, almost brings those pretty jewels within reach. ♦ M, Sa 10:30AM-7PM, Tu-F 10AM-7PM Apr-Sept; M, Sa 10:30AM-6:30PM, Tu-F 10AM-6:30PM Oct-Mar. 7 Place Vendôme (Southwest corner). Métro: Madeleine. 42.61.55.55

74 11-13 Place Vendôme This is the **Ministry of Justice,** where, in 1848, the official measure for the meter was set in the facade. ♦ West side. Métro: Madeleine

74 Hôtel Ritz $$$$ Got a pooch who's hard to please? Take him to the Ritz, where even dogs are treated like social lions. The Ritz has been, well, the ritziest hotel in Paris since 1898, when **Cesar Ritz** first took it over. During that time, millionaires, Arab princes, divas, and cinema stars have stayed here. **Marcel Proust** used to arrive sporting lavender gloves and a variety of clothes that never seemed to fit him. **Barbara Hutton** loved it; **Coco Chanel** liked it so much she took up residence here. There are 440 employees (a third of whom have been here more than a quarter century) catering to the occupants of the hotel's 210 rooms. Sixty of these stalwarts are available for duty as private servants if your vacation just isn't a vacation without Jeeves. The prices are astronomical but, by all accounts, justified. The suites on the second floor overlooking the Place Vendôme are actually registered with the Bureau of Fine Arts. ♦ 15 Place Vendôme (west side). Métros: Concorde, Tuileries. 42.60.38.30

Within the Hôtel Ritz:

Ritz Espadon ★★★$$$$ The culinary reputation of the hotel's lovely garden restaurant was made from the very start by the presence of that great turn-of-the-century chef, **Escoffier.** He first met **Cesar Ritz** when Ritz was manager of the Grand Hotel in Monte Carlo. Escoffier's celebrated recipe for foie gras in port is still used. Latter-day creations include *suprême de Saint-Pierre* studded with olives and served with a saffron sauce as well as lobster medaillons in a tarragon sauce. The wine list is nonpareil and the prices are unsurpassed. ♦ Lunch and dinner. Reservations recommended. 42.60.38.30

Ritz Bars Just off Rue Cambon is the more famous little bar, which **Hemingway** "liberated" at the end of World War II. Here the legendary barman **Georges** served drinks to **President Teddy Roosevelt,** just back from an African safari. Other big-time tipplers here were the **Prince of Wales, Greta Garbo, Noel Coward, Douglas Fairbanks, Winston Churchill, J.P. Morgan, Andrew Carnegie, F. Scott Fitzgerald,** and **Marlene Dietrich.** It's still an English-style pub, right down to its tweedy, rubicund patrons. The Vendôme bar has a terrace for drinks or tea in the summer. ♦ Both bars: daily 8AM-1AM. 42.60.38.30

75 Charvet Edward VII bought his neckties and cravats here, and so can you. ♦ M-Sa 10AM-6:30PM. Closed Monday in August. 28 Place Vendôme (at Rue Danielle-Casanova). Métro: Opéra. 42.60.30.70

76 16 Place Vendôme Here **Franz Anton Mesmer** (1734-1815), the Austrian charlatan physician who invented mesmerism (later called hypnosis), conducted animal magnetism seminars wrapped in robes decorated with astrological signs. And in the 1930s **Obelisk Press** had its office at this address. Headed by Englishman **Jack Kahane,** Obelisk published works that no one else would, such as **Henry Miller's** *Tropic of Cancer,* which appeared in 1934. ♦ East side. Métros: Concorde, Tuileries

76 12 Place Vendôme In 1849 **Frederic Chopin,** Polish composer and pianist, died here at the age of 39. ♦ East side. Métros: Concorde, Tuileries

76 6 Place Vendôme The Hôtel du Rhin became the temporary residence of **Napoléon III** during his 1848 presidential campaign. ♦ East side. Métros: Concorde, Tuileries

77 Rue St.-Honoré This ranks as one of the oldest and most historic thoroughfares in Paris. In 1622 **Molière** was born on this street at the corner of Rue Sauval, near Les Halles. On 6 October 1793, a tumbril traveled down Rue St.-Honoré, carrying a woman whose prison-shorn hair was hidden under a frumpy bonnet. Nearby, **Jacques-Louis David** sketched her as she passed, bequeathing to history a poignant image of **Marie Antoinette,** her hands tied behind her back, en route to the guillotine. ♦ Métro: Tuileries

77 Chichen-Itza Fine hand-worked leather bags, briefcases, and wallets fashioned from ostrich, Madagascar crocodile, and the like are sold here. More nonessentials are made from the skins of rare creatures. ♦ M-F 1-7PM. Closed in August. 231 Rue St.-Honoré (between Rues de Castiglione and d'Alger). Métro: Tuileries. 42.60.80.16, 42.60.61.35

77 Royal Saint-Honoré $$ This hotel next door to the Tuileries Gardens has quiet rooms and a refined air. ♦ 221 Rue St.-Honoré (between Rues de Castiglione and d'Alger). Métro: Tuileries. 42.60.32.79

77 4 Rue du Mont-Thabor In the summer of 1820, still enjoying the afterglow of the triumphant reception of *Rip Van Winkle* and *The Legend of Sleepy Hollow,* 39-year-old **Washington Irving** moved into an apartment here. Mitigating his pleasure was Irving's powerful fear of growing old, the same problem that obsessed old Rip. ♦ Between Rues de Castiglione and d'Alger. Métro: Tuileries

78 Tuileries $$ Down a quiet side street, this renovated hotel retains much of its 18th-century charm, having added 20th-century accoutrements: color TVs, minibars, and direct-dial phones. These modern conveniences come at old-fashioned prices. ♦ 10 Rue St.-Hyacinthe (between Rues du Marché-St.-Honoré and de la Sourdière). Métros: Pyramides, Tuileries. 42.61.04.17, 42.61.06.94

79 Dave ★★★$$$ A hideout for celebrities such as **George Michael** and **Yves Saint Laurent,** this excellent Sino-Vietnamese restaurant is named after its star-struck *maître d'* who keeps a Polaroid collection of his most famous customers. ♦ Lunch and dinner; dinner only on Saturday. Closed Sunday and three weeks in August. 39 St.-Roch (between Rues St.-Honoré and Gomboust). Métro: Pyramides. 42.61.49.48

Restaurants/Clubs: Red	Hotels: Blue
Shops/ 🍽 Outdoors: Green	Sights/Culture: Black

French Feats: Two Hundred Years of Discoveries in Science and Technology

1791: Jean-Baptiste Delambre and Pierre Méchain develop the decimal system.

1795: Gaspard Monge creates descriptive geometry.

1800-30: Georges Cuvier and Jean-Baptiste Lamarack develop paleontology.

1811: Bernard Courtois isolates iodine and discovers morphine.

1815: René Laennec invents the stethoscope. Louis-Sebastien Lenormand invents the revolver.

1818: Louis Thenard discovers boron and hydrogen peroxide.

1820: Pierre Pelletier and Joseph Caventou discover quinine.

1829: Louis Braille develops the braille alphabet.

1830: Barthélemy Thimonnier invents the sewing machine.

1834: Jacques Daguerre invents the daguerreotype process for photography.

1852: Léon Foucault invents the gyroscope.

1853: Charles Gerhardt invents aspirin.

1857: Ferdinand Carré invents the mechanical compression refrigerator, capable of producing ice.

1859: Gaston Planté invents the electric storage-cell battery.

1862: Louis Pasteur discovers anaerobic germs and founds the science of microbiology.

1865: Louis Pasteur invents pasteurization.

1867: Aristide Bergès develops the concept of hydroelectric power.

1876: Eugène Woillez invents the iron lung.

1884: Hilaire Chardonnet de Grange invents rayon.

1885: Louis Pasteur develops the rabies vaccine.

1889: André Chantemesse and Fernand Widal develop the typhoid vaccine.

1890: Edouard Branly invents the radio conductor, making wireless telegraph reception possible.

1896: Henri Becquerel discovers radioactivity.

1898: Pierre and Marie Curie discover radium.

1900: Victor Grignard discovers the compounds used for organic synthesis.

1906-23: Albert Calmette and Camille Guérin develop the BCG vaccine (Bacillus Calmette-Guérin) against tuberculosis.

1910: Georges Claude invents the neon lamp.

1920: Jean Perrin outlines the concept of nuclear transmutation.

1924-27: Louis de Broglie discovers the wave nature of the electron and develops wave mechanics.

1934: Frédéric and Irène Joliot-Curie discover artificial radioactivity.

1950: Alfred Kastler discovers optical pumping, permitting the development of lasers and masers.

1952: Félix Trombe invents the solar oven.

1957: Jean Berlin invents the hovercraft.

1961: François Jacob, André Lwoff, and Jacques Monod discover the role of RNA in the transmission of genetic information.

1983: A research team discovers the AIDS virus.

1985: Researchers at the Pasteur Institute and the American Department of Health and Human Services invent the AIDS blood-screening test.

1987: Scientists develop RU 486 (the "week-after" birth-control pill).

1989: Astronomers discover a luminous arc in the Abell 370 galaxy cluster. It is a gravitational mirage, the first ever observed in a galaxy cluster.

Researched by **Beth Levin**
Reprinted with permission from
France Magazine

79 Yakitori ★$ Try the morsels of cheese-stuffed pork, teriyaki chicken, and marinated shrimp skewered and grilled *à la Japonaise*. This restaurant is perpetually crowded, but it's worth the effort to grab a seat at the counter and watch the chefs perform. ♦ Lunch and dinner. Closed Sunday. 34 Place du Marché-St.-Honoré (east side, between Rues Gomboust and St.-Hyacinthe). Métro: Pyramides. 42.61.03.54

79 L'Absinthe ★$$ Monsieur Malabard's sophisticated 1900s-style bistro has withstood the test of time, maintaining high quality at moderate prices. *Magret de canard,* chicken cooked in champagne, fresh salads, and homemade ice creams and sorbets come highly recommended. In summer, request an outdoor table on the square. ♦ Lunch and dinner; dinner only on Saturday. Closed Sunday. 24 Place du Marché-St.-Honoré (east side, between Rues Gomboust and St.-Hyacinthe). Reservations recommended. Métro: Pyramides. 42.61.03.32, 42.60.02.45

79 Louise Delpuech A rare, immaculate self-service laundry is run by two redoubtable women inexplicably dubbed *Romeo* and *Juliet* by the neighborhood. Behind their stern scowls lurk hearts of gold. Read the hand-scrawled instructions (in English for Americans) and don't cram your machine too full. Overload and you're in big trouble with this imposing pair, and police headquarters is just across the street. ◆ Daily 8AM-9PM. 24 Place Marché-St.-Honoré (east side, between Rues Gomboust and St.-Hyacinthe). Métro: Pyramides. 42.61.04.49

79 Flo Prestige For those who enjoy dining *sur l'herbe* and can afford not to bother with preparing the meal, this take-out gourmet deli offers a delectable selection of cheeses, charcuterie, salmon, salads, wines, and pastries of a quality that merits a limo for the tailgate picnic. For a setting, the nearby Tuileries or Palais Royal gardens should do just fine. ◆ Daily 8AM-11PM. 42 Place du Marché-St.-Honoré (east side, between Rues Gomboust and St.-Hyacinthe). Métro: Pyramides. 42.61.45.46

Brentano's

80 Brentano's For the greatest hits in English literature, try this, one of the best and oldest English-language bookstores in Paris. ◆ M-Sa 10AM-7PM. 37 Ave de l'Opéra (between Rues d'Antin and Danielle-Casanova). Métros: Opéra, Pyramides. 42.61.52.50

81 Auberge des Trois Bonheurs ★★$$ Despite the oh-so-French name, classic, elegant Chinese cuisine is what you'll find here. The chef is from Hong Kong and specializes in steamed trout, Peking duck, and jumbo shrimp *à la Cantonaise*. ◆ Lunch and dinner. 280 Rue St.-Honoré (between Rues des Pyramides and de l'Echelle). Reservations recommended. Métro: Pyramides. 42.60.43.24

81 Le Ruban Bleu ★★$$$ The maritime decor and blue-ribbon name of this World War II-style restaurant commemorate the record transatlantic crossing by a French vessel called the *Normandie*. The menu is trim and shipshape: grilled chèvre on toast, monkfish in sorrel, and saddle of hare with fresh pasta. ◆ Lunch. Closed Saturday, Sunday, and in August. 29 Rue d'Argenteuil (between Rues des Pyramides and de l'Echelle). Métro: Pyramides. 42.61.47.53

81 Gargantua ★★$$$ King Kong could leave here with a full tummy (and an empty pocketbook). The portions are so grand, the food so delicious, the prices, alas, so outrageous! In the rear is a marble lunch counter. Pastries, charcuterie, wines, and salads are packed to go. ◆ Breakfast, lunch,

and dinner. 284 Rue St.-Honoré (between Rues des Pyramides and de l'Echelle). Métro: Tuileries. 42.60.52.54

82 St.-Roch The bullet holes in this church's facade chronicle one of the most significant military debuts in French history. This is the site of a fierce Revolutionary skirmish that occurred on 5 October 1795, when Royalist troops took a stand on the steps of St.-Roch and were boldly scattered by a then-unknown 27-year-old soldier named **Napoléon Bonaparte.** Ten days later Napoléon was appointed commander-in-chief of the home forces. St.-Roch, an architectural mix-and-match, is the city's finest baroque church and is best known today for its splendid 1752 rococo organ and weekly evening concerts. Built to handle the overflow from St.-Germain-l'Auxerrois, St.-Roch was originally designed by **Jacques Lemercier,** and no less a personage than **Louis XIV** laid its cornerstone in 1653. But it took another century to complete.

Jules Hardouin-Mansart was responsible for the oval **Lady Chapel,** and sculptor **René Charpentier** decorated the edifice in carved imagery. The church is dedicated to an Italian holy man who, accompanied by his dog, ministered to plague victims in the 14th century. Inside are memorials to the playwright **Corneille,** the philosopher **Diderot,** and Louis XIV's beloved gardener, **Le Nôtre,** whose bust by **Coysevox** is left of the chancel. ◆ M-Sa 8AM-7:15PM; Su 8AM-1PM, 5-7:15PM. 296 Rue St.-Honoré (between Rues St.-Roch and des Pyramides). Métros: Pyramides, Tuileries. 42.60.81.69

83 La Providence ★★$$ Country cuisine with an Alsatian accent is featured at this wonderful little restaurant. Among the daily specialties on its changing menu: *baeckkeefa* (marinated lamb, beef, and pork on a bed of onions and potatoes), lamb chops, broiled goat cheese salad, fresh pear tart, and a light chocolate mousse. A respectable list of Alsatian wines is offered. Try a Pinot Noir or Gewürztraminer in the Alsatian *winstub* downstairs. ◆ Lunch and dinner. Closed Saturday and Sunday. 6 Rue de la Sourdière (between Rues St.-Honoré and Gomboust). Reservations recommended. Métro: Tuileries. 42.60.46.13

83 Tartanous ★★$ For a tasty lunch on the run, try this juice bar/quiche parlor. The quiches are filled with imaginative combinations of tastes, such as chicken and carrot with mustard, fennel, and mushroom, and *oiseille* and Chavignol cheese. For dessert, try the red and green rhubarb pie or the coconut cream. A horde of well-heeled St.-Honoré office workers and the occasional Birkenstock-shod Californian stopping by for a freshly squeezed carrot-cucumber juice keep this place busy at lunchtime. ♦ Lunch and snacks. Closed Saturday and Sunday. 21 Rue St.-Roch (between Rues St.-Honoré and Gomboust). Métro: Tuileries. 42.97.50.40

84 St.-James et Albany $$$ Portions of this residential hotel date back to the reign of Louis XIV, which is appropriate, since for years its clientele was strictly old European aristocracy. It now offers home-away-from-home suites, duplexes, and studios equipped with kitchenettes, so that after stocking up at the garden-floor delicatessen, guests can entertain their friends with crêpes suzette and a view of the Tuileries. The nicest rooms are nestled in the attic beneath low-beamed ceilings. The hotel incorporates parts of the old **Noailles Mansion,** where **General Lafayette** married one of the Noailles daughters in 1774. ♦ 202 Rue de Rivoli (between Rues du 29-Juillet and St.-Roch). Métro: Tuileries. 44.58.43.21

Within St.-James et Albany:

Les Noailles ★$$$ Love will blossom when you stroll through the Tuileries with that special someone and then dine tête-à-tête in the courtyard of the elegant Les Noailles. ♦ Lunch and dinner. Closed Saturday and Sunday. 44.58.43.21

Bar St.-James ★$$ This is one of the classiest snack bars around. Try the club sandwich or cabbage salad with breast of duck. ♦ Lunch, dinner, and late-night. 44.58.43.21

85 Montana Tuileries $$ Conveniently located near the Tuileries and St.-Roch church (which has marvelous evening concerts), this small hotel is an isle of economy in an archipelago of extravagance. ♦ 12 Rue St.-Roch (between Rues de Rivoli and St.-Honoré). Métro: Tuileries. 42.60.35.10

86 Hôtel Regina $$$ Offering a splendid view of the Tuileries Gardens, this quiet hotel is furnished with antiques, crystal chandeliers, and a Louis XV-style elevator cage that has been retired from service and put on display in the lobby. ♦ 2 Place des Pyramides (at Rue de Rivoli). Métros: Tuileries, Pyramides. 42.60.31.10

86 Le Canard Enchaîné France's famous leftist satirical weekly, celebrated for its irreverent cartoons and editorials, is based here. The paper specializes in covering scandals and is usually first to the scene of the crime. ♦ 173 Rue St.-Honoré (between Rues des Pyramides and de l'Echelle). Métro: Palais-Royal. 42.60.31.36

86 7 Rue de l'Echelle The loveliest of cities can be capricious, as **Mark Twain** found Paris to be when he stayed here at the **Hôtel Normandy** between April and July 1879. Paris scowled, its gray sky poured, and its legendary springtime never happened. So Twain spent his bleak vacation rereading the doleful *History of the French Revolution* by **Thomas Carlyle** and scribbled what he could. ♦ Between Rues de Rivoli and St.-Honoré. Métro: Palais-Royal

87 Rue des Italiens The prestigious Parisian daily *Le Monde* is headquartered here. ♦ Métros: 4-Septembre, Richelieu-Drouot

88 Au Petit Riche ★★$ A favorite of journalists, this warm century-old restaurant offers a tasty marinated octopus salad, roast rabbit, hot apple tarts, and carafes of Bourgueil. ♦ Lunch and dinner. Closed Sunday. 25 Rue Le Peletier (at Blvd Haussmann). Reservations recommended. Métro: Le Peletier. 47.70.68.68

89 Hôtel Drouot The closest thing to a Sotheby's in Paris, the Drouot specializes in estate sales and auctions of everything from Cartier jewels, Louis XIV furniture, and African sculpture to baskets of kitchenware and collections of rare illustrated manuscripts. On the top floor, the most valuable objects d'art are overseen by renowned auctioneer **Ader Picard Tajan.** Auctions take place in the afternoons, but it's best to arrive early to scan the merchandise—a great experience in itself. ♦ M-Sa 11AM-6PM. 9 Rue Drouot (between Rues Rossini and de la Grange-Batclière). Métro: Richelieu-Drouot. 48.00.20.20

90 Chopin $$ At the end of the peaceful Passage Jouffroy (which is classified as a French historic monument), this modest hotel offers small rooms at small rates. ♦ 46 Passage Jouffroy (between Blvd Montmartre and Rue de la Grange-Batelière). Métro: Rue Montmartre. 47.70.58.10

90 Chartier ★$ This cavernous turn-of-the-century soup kitchen with pinwheel fans and surly waiters serves better theater than cuisine but is worth a visit nevertheless. The place is always mobbed with tourists, so get here when the doors open. ♦ Lunch and early dinner. 7 Rue du Faubourg-Montmartre (between Blvd Montmartre and Rue de la Grange-Batelière). No credit cards. Métro: Rue Montmartre. 47.70.86.29

91 Musée Grevin The city's largest wax museum is populated with distinguished paraffin personalities, including **Charles de Gaulle,**

Catherine Deneuve, Woody Allen, and Yehudi Menuhin. Children love it. ◆ Daily 1-7PM. 10 Blvd Montmartre (between Passage Jouffroy and Rue du Faubourg-Montmartre). Métro: Rue Montmartre. 47.70.85.05

92 Passage des Panoramas Nineteenth-century American inventor **Robert Fulton** painted and displayed 18 panoramas, including a portrayal of the burning of Moscow, in two large cylindrical towers on the Boulevard Montmartre. The French flocked to see the sagas, and, with his profits, Fulton bankrolled his steamboat and submarine schemes. ◆ Between Rue St.-Marc and Blvd Montmartre. Métros: Bourse, Rue Montmartre

92 Aux Lyonnais ★★$$ Long patronized by Bourse des Valeurs traders in the neighborhood, this bistro's reputation is founded on classic, unadventurous cuisine. ◆ Lunch and dinner. Closed Sunday. 32 Rue St.-Marc (between Rues Vivienne and Montmartre). Reservations recommended. Métro: Bourse. 42.96.65.04

92 Claude Brissemoret ★★★$$This slightly decrepit hole-in-the-wall is a place to enjoy excellent unpretentious cuisine. Either the homemade foie gras or the fresh artichoke hearts will begin the meal nicely. The carefully prepared entrées include marinated baby lamb chops in red wine sauce, guinea hen stewed with apricots and carrots, and curried veal kidneys. As for dessert, the rich dark chocolate cake in a creamy custard sauce needs no further description. Reserve well in advance. ◆ Lunch and dinner. Closed Saturday and Sunday. 5 Rue St.-Marc (between Rues Notre-Dame-des-Victoires and Vivienne). Reservations required. Métros: Bourse, Montmartre. 42.36.91.72

93 49 Rue Vivienne On this site stood the Salle Musard, an old concert hall where **Tom Thumb,** headliner for **P.T. Barnum's** traveling show, performed in 1844. ◆ Between Rue St.-Marc and Blvd Montmartre. Métros: Bourse, Richelieu-Drouot

94 La Tour de Jade ★★$ This restaurant was founded by a former minister to Indochina's **Emperor Bao-Dai.** Stuffed duck, lemon chicken, broiled mullet with anchovies, duck with lotus seeds, and pork balls in soy sauce are the highlights. ◆ Lunch and dinner; dinner only on Sunday. 20 Rue de la Michodière (between Blvd des Italiens and Rue de Hanovre). Reservations recommended. Métro: 4-Septembre. 47.42.07.56

95 Le Vaudeville ★★$$ This vintage 1925 brasserie was rescued from decline and obscurity by brasserie king **Jean-Paul Bucher** and is now packed at lunchtime with execs from the Bourse des Valeurs and Club Med headquarters, and at night by theater patrons. Specialties include andouillette, foie gras, grilled lobster, shellfish (year-round),

homemade *saumon rillette,* and a chilled house Reisling. Summer dining is pleasant on the sidewalk. ◆ Lunch and dinner. 29 Rue Vivienne (between Rues du 4-Septembre and de la Bourse). Reservations recommended. Métro: Bourse. 40.20.04.62

96 Bourse des Valeurs Napoléon II commissioned this "Temple of Money" in 1826, and architect **Alexandre Brogniart** was inspired to adorn it with 64 Corinthian columns. The Stock Exchange's design is epic, and so is the chaos of brokers on the floor. You are welcome to head for the spectators gallery and watch French capitalism at work. On a day of stiff trading, the excitement rivals that of European Cup soccer, and admission is free. Be sure to bring I.D. ◆ M-F 11AM-2PM. Two organized tours every afternoon; call for hours. 4 Place de la Bourse. Métro: Bourse. 42.33.99.83 (tours), 42.33.99.83 (information)

97 Pile ou Face ★★★$$$ A coin's throw from the Stock Exchange, this intimate restaurant, whose name means "heads or tails," serves exquisite nouvelle cuisine without any of the pretentions that normally garnish such food. The owners, **Alain Dumberque** and **Claude Udron,** raise chickens and rabbits on their farm outside Paris, and their refined tastes are exemplified in the delicious *magret de canard, poulet en croûte,* rabbit in rosemary, and chocolate cake. The Cahors, Gamay de Touraine, and Moulin de Bellegrave are among the highlights of the wine list. This is a perfect setting for a romantic dinner. ◆ Lunch and dinner. Closed Saturday, Sunday, and in August. 52bis Rue Notre-Dame-des-Victoires (between Rues 4-Septembre and Paul-Lelong). Reservations required. Métro: Bourse. 42.33.64.33

98 Hollywood Savoy ★★$$ This restaurant becomes a nightclub when the Ivy League waiters and waitresses take to the stage and belt out creditable renditions of "Stormy Monday" and other Yankee classics. ◆ Lunch and dinner. Closed Sunday. 44 Rue Notre-Dame-des-Victoires (between Rues Paul-Lelong and du Mail). Reservations recommended. Métro: Bourse. 42.36.16.73

98 Aux Petits Pères ★★★$$$ Chef **Marcel Boutard** prepares traditional French cuisine with fatherly care in this small, appealing restaurant. A memorable meal may start with the red mullet and crab pâté or the velvety homemade foie gras. *Confit de canard aux cèpes* and *coquilles St.-Jacques* are splendid entrées, though if it's hunting season the wild boar in a red wine sauce shouldn't be missed. ◆ Lunch and dinner. Closed Saturday, Sunday, and in August. 8 Rue Notre-Dames-des-Victoires (between Place des Petits-Pères and Rue Paul-Lelong). Métro: Bourse. 42.60.91.73

99 Galerie Vivienne From its mosaic floors to the arching glass canopy, the gussied up Galerie Vivienne, established in 1923, is a most fashionable arcade. A myriad of boutiques sells everything from high-tech jewelry and rare books to children's masks and the best brownies in Paris. ♦ Daily 8AM-8PM. 6 Rue Vivienne (off Rue des Petits-Champs). Métro: Bourse

Within Galerie Vivienne:

Si Tu Veux Babar, the universally loved French elephant, comes in plush, plastic, or posters at this old-fashioned toy store. And enough paper hats and masks are available to regale any party of six-year-olds. ♦ M-Sa 11AM-7PM. 68 Galerie Vivienne. 42.60.59.97

Jean-Paul Gaultier Your eyes will be drawn to this boutique of the young fashion eclectic who brought miniskirts to men and ice-cream-cone bras to women. Check out the video screens—on the floor! ♦ M-F 10AM-7PM; Sa 11AM-7PM. 6 Rue Vivienne. 42.86.05.05

Legrand Filles et Fils From the back of this Rue de la Banque épicerie, **Francine Legrand** sells French red wines by the case (see page 110 in the Marais & Les Halles chapter). ♦ Tu-F 8:30AM-7:30PM; Sa 8:30AM-1PM, 3-7PM. 12 Galerie Vivienne. 42.60.07.1

A Priori Thé ★★$ Three expatriate American women started this tearoom/restaurant. Wicker chairs and tables and fresh-cut flowers spill into the charming Galerie Vivienne. A creative selection of quiches and salads is served, followed by divine apple crumble and brownies for dessert. The wine list is chosen by **Francine Legrand,** whose wine shop (see entry above) is in the same arcade. ♦ Lunch and afternoon tea. 35-37 Galerie Vivienne. 42.97.48.75

99 Galerie Colbert Like the adjoining Galerie Vivienne, the Galerie Colbert has recently enjoyed a stylish renaissance. The **Bibliothèque Nationale,** which owns the passage, has spent millions to restore the walkways, glass-roofed rotunda, faux marble pillars, and 19th-century bronze fixtures. The library has also installed two museums to house part of its huge collection: a museum of the theater and a museum of sounds and recordings (where you can find the voices of **Sarah Bernhardt** and **Captain Dreyfus** among 800,000 other records). There are two exhibition halls for prints and photos. ♦ Daily 8AM-8PM. Entrance on Rue des Petits-Champs (between Rues Vivienne and de la Banque). Métros: Bourse, Pyramides

100 Bibliothèque Nationale In 1537 a copyright act was passed to ensure that a copy of every book published in France would be housed in a royal library. The result of four and a half centuries of book and document assembly is now kept in one of the world's greatest national libraries, in a building whose architectural design is as impressive as its collection.

Bibliothèque Nationale

The library came to occupy its present site in the 17th century, when **Cardinal Mazarin** merged two of his mansions, the **Hôtel Tubeuf** and the **Hôtel Chivry.** The collection initially included 500 pictures and art objects owned by the cardinal himself. When **Colbert,** finance minister to **Louis XIV,** moved the library to his own mansion on Rue Vivienne in 1666, the collection numbered 200,000 volumes. In 1720, the library was combined again with the original Mazarin collection. Today the library's 68 miles of shelves bend under the weight of more than nine million books, including two **Gutenberg** bibles, first editions of **Rabelais,** and manuscripts of **Proust** and **Hugo.**

The library received its most dramatic space in 1854, when the architect **Henri Labrouste** was commissioned to design a reading room within the old courtyard of the Palais Mazarin. The result is the magnificent top-lit **Salle des Imprimés** (illustrated on page 169), which consists of nine square vaulted bays supported by 16 cast-iron columns and a network of perforated semicircular iron arches. The room reveals a further development of ideas Labrouste first explored in the design of his Bibliothèque Ste.-Geneviève, a landmark building that was the first monumental public edifice to freely employ iron as both a structural and a decorative element. Peek through the glass doors of the reading room at the Bibliothèque Nationale (admittance is for members only, although proof that you're an architect often works) and admire the beautifully attenuated columns, the gleaming lens-like skylights in the ceiling, and the graceful curves of the iron latticework. Also be sure to see the **Houdon** statue of **Voltaire** in the **Salle d'Honneur** (State Room) on the ground floor. The writer's heart is ensconced in the pedestal.

The library is divided into 11 departments: printed books; periodicals and newspapers; manuscripts; prints and engravings; maps and plans; medals, coins, and antiques; technical; audiovisual; arms and weapons; performing arts; and music. One weekend every year in October, the entire library is open to the public with guided tours; call for exact day.
♦ Galleries Mazarin and Mansart: open for temporary exhibitions. Musée des Médailles et Antiques: M-Sa 9AM-4PM. Photo Gallery (4 Rue Louvois): M-Sa noon-6:30PM. 58 Rue de Richelieu (between Rues Colbert and des-Petits-Champs). Métros: Bourse, Palais-Royal. 47.03.81.26

101 Café San José The **Cahen** family, owners of this tiny stand-up coffee bar, roast their own beans and serve the best cappuccino in town. At midday, neighborhood workers seeking a caffeine fix swarm here. ♦ M-F 7AM-7PM. 30 Rue des Petits-Champs (between Rues de Richelieu and Ste.-Anne). Métros: Pyramides, Bourse. 42.96.69.09

101 Issé ★★★$$$ The city's best (and most expensive) sushi bar also serves impeccable sashimi, grilled salmon, steaming miso soup, red caviar, delectably light tempura, and *chirashi,* the house specialty. ♦ Lunch and dinner; dinner only on Monday and Saturday. Closed Sunday. 56 Rue Ste.-Anne (at Rue Rameau). Reservations recommended. No credit cards. Métro: Pyramides. 42.96.67.76

102 Pandora ★★$ Behind the chocolate-brown facade is a comfy little tearoom that in summer offers light lunches of cucumbers in yogurt and mint, Baltic herring, lemon tarts, and mincemeat pies. Warm winter dishes include chili con carne and chicken *tajine* (stew). ♦ Lunch and afternoon tea. Closed Saturday, Sunday, and in August. 24 Passage Choiseul (off Rue des-Petits-Champs, between Rues Ste.-Anne and Méhul). Métro: 4-Septembre. 42.97.56.01

103 Coup de Coeur ★★$$ House specialties in this small, friendly restaurant with modern decor include salmon tartare with chives, *magret de canard,* roasted red mullet filets, and a sinfully delicious chocolate dessert. ♦ Lunch and dinner; dinner only on Saturday. Closed Sunday. 19 Rue St.-Augustin (between Rues Ste.-Anne and Monsigny). Reservations recommended. Métros: 4-Septembre, Pyramides. 47.03.45.70

104 Juveniles ★★$$ This lively *bistrot à vin* just down the street from the Bibliothèque Nationale is the brainchild of wine-lovers **Mark Williamson** (of Willi's Wine Bar) and his partner, **Tim Johnston.** It's a comfortable spot for noshing on tapas, rabbit pâté, chicken wings, ample sandwiches (chicken salad, beef, and watercress), and afterwards enjoying a slice of the dense, flourless chocolate cake. Wash it all down with an excellent, reasonably priced Rioja. ♦ Lunch and dinner. Closed Sunday. 47 Rue de Richelieu (between Rues des Petits-Champs and Villedo). Métro: Pyramides. 42.97.46.49

105 Mercure Galant ★★$$$ Attractive decor, first-rate service, and specialties such as homemade duck foie gras, shellfish in puff pastry, lobster gratin, and lamb marinated in spicy oil make this a perfect choice for business lunches. ♦ Lunch and dinner; dinner only on Saturday. Closed Sunday. 15 Rue des Petits-Champs (between Rues Vivienne and Richelieu). Reservations recommended. Métros: Bourse, Pyramides. 42.97.53.85, 42.96.98.89

Restaurants/Clubs: Red		**Hotels:** Blue
Shops/ ♥ Outdoors: Green		**Sights/Culture:** Black

05 Willi's Wine Bar ★★$$ The city's most elegant wine bar bustles nonstop with journalists, lawyers, fashion designers, and the PR crowd who come to partake of 99 French wines and daily specials such as grilled salmon steak, braised oxtail, leg of lamb, pork with fennel, and spinach tarts. The place is run by Willi, the affable Englishman **Mark Williamson,** who knows his Côtes-du-Rhônes. ◆ Lunch and dinner. Wine bar: daily 11AM-11PM. 13 Rue des Petits-Champs (between Rues Vivienne and Richelieu). Reservations recommended. Métros: Bourse, Pyramides. 42.61.05.09

05 Chantal Thomass Everything in this boutique is magically appealing, from the billowing curtains of the dressing rooms to the star-studded ceiling and the curvaceous furniture (not to mention the outfits, shoes, lingerie, and accessories for women). Thomass worked closely with interior designer **Jean-Louis Ricardi** to create a shop that reflects her sensuous style. ◆ M 11AM-7PM; Tu-Sa 10AM-7PM. 1 Rue Vivenne (at Rue des Petits-Champs). Métros: Pyramides, Bourse. 40.15.02.36, 40.15.02.40

05 Herboristerie du Palais-Royal Herbs, oils, and lotions for needs both medicinal and pleasurable are crammed floor to ceiling in this small shop. Every potion is designed to stimulate the senses. **Michel Pierre,** who has co-authored a book on salutary plants, can select just the herb to remedy your ailment. *Passiflore* from South America promotes relaxation, *eleuterocoque* from Siberia increases energy, and *harpagophytum* from Namibia helps ease arthritis and rheumatism. ◆ M-F 8:30AM-7PM; Sa 10:30AM-6:30PM. 11 Rue des Petits-Champs (between Rues Vivienne and de Richelieu). Métros: Pyramides, Bourse. 42.97.54.68

06 Le Grand Véfour ★★★$$$$ A favorite Parisian haunt since the 1760s, this fine restaurant is named after **Jean Véfour,** chef to **Philippe,** the **Duke of Orléans** (who voted to send his relative **Louis XVI** to the guillotine and later wound up there himself). Seductively and appropriately timeworn, Le Grand Véfour's Louis XVI-Directoire interior is classified as a historic monument. Here **Napoléon** courted **Joséphine, Victor Hugo** romanticized, and **Colette** and **Jean Cocteau,** who lived nearby, enjoyed regular repasts. ◆ Lunch and dinner. Closed Saturday, Sunday, and in August. 17 Rue de Beaujolais (in the Palais Royal). Reservations required. Métros: Bourse, Palais-Royal. 42.96.56.27

107 Bar de l'Entracte ★★$ Tucked in a corner behind the Palais Royal, this amusing restaurant and bar is festooned with old costumes from the theater across the street. Paper currency from all around the world flutters on the ceiling. On a warm summer day, enjoy a glass of cool St. Joseph on the outdoor terrace. ◆ Lunch, dinner, and late-night. Closed Sunday. 47 Rue de Montpensier (at Rue de Beaujolais). No credit cards. Métros: Palais-Royal, Pyramides. 42.97.57.76

107 Matsuri Sushi ★$$ Customers hunker around a circular bar to snag plates of raw salmon and tuna sailing by on a conveyor belt. To tally the check, waiters simply count the dishes in front of each diner. At lunch, every fifth item is free. So is home delivery throughout the day within Paris city limits. ◆ Lunch and dinner; dinner only on Monday. Closed Friday, Saturday, Sunday, and in August. 36 Rue de Richelieu (between Rue des Petits-Champs and Passage Hulot). Métro: Palais-Royal. 42.61.05.73 (reservations), 40.26.12.13 (delivery)

108 Chez Pauline ★★$$$ When tradition works this well, why change? This relaxed restaurant serves French classics such as beef Bourguignon, *poularde de Bresse*, creamed wild mushrooms with chives, warm foie gras salad, fricassee of sole and crayfish, game in season, and a variety of *plats du jour* such as stuffed cabbage, cassoulet with preserved goose, bacon with lentils, and calf's liver. ◆ Lunch and dinner. Closed Saturday and Sunday. 5 Rue Villedo (between Rues Ste.-Anne and de Richelieu). Reservations recommended. Métro: Pyramides. 42.96.20.70, 42.61.79.01

109 Molière Fountain The fountain was dedicated in 1773, the centennial of the playwright's death. The monument was designed by **Visconti** and the statue by **Seurre.** Molière's statue is seated atop, pen in hand, flanked on either side by marble statues representing both light and serious comedy. ◆ At Rues Molière and de Richelieu. Métro: Pyramides

109 Barrière Poquelin ★★$$$ The original nouvelle cuisine comprises steamed fish with mushrooms, salmon *unilatérale,* spicy chicken, roast game, and, to top it off, a hot apple tart. ◆ Lunch and dinner; dinner only on Saturday. Closed Sunday, and the first three weeks of August. 17 Rue Molière (between Ave de l'Opéra and Rue Thérèse). Reservations recommended. Métro: Pyramides. 42.96.22.19

Palais Royal

110 Les Boucholeurs ★★$$ *Boucholeurs* are the farmers who cultivate the small, finer tasting variety of mussels featured in many of the dishes served here. These particular mussels come from a *parc à huitres* (shellfish farm) near Rochelle on the west coast, while the bankers and stockbrokers who eat them come from the nearby Bourse. Try the superb *mouclade Rochelaise*, in a velvety saffron and cognac sauce, with a bottle of Fiefs Vendeen de Pissotte. Other specialties include *moules sauce au gingembre* (mussels in a ginger sauce), *moules au curry*, and *haddock poché.* ♦ Lunch and dinner; dinner only on Saturday. Closed Sunday, from mid-April to mid-May (or whenever the mussel season has run its course), and one week in August. 34 Rue de Richelieu (at Passage Hulot). Reservations recommended. Métros: Pyramides, Palais-Royal. 42.96.06.86

110 La Boutique du Bridgeur The only store in Paris catering strictly to bridge players, this boutique sells bridge tables, score pads, playing cards, and instruction manuals. If you write in advance, its affiliated bridge club might help find you a partner. ♦ M-F 10AM-6:30PM; Sa 10AM-6PM. 28 Rue de Richelieu (between Passages Hulot and Potier). Métro: Palais-Royal. 42.96.25.50

110 L'Incroyable Restaurant ★★$ What's incredible about this seven-table restaurant hidden on a cobbled passage are the generous portions and bargain prices. ♦ Lunch and dinner; lunch only on Saturday. Closed Monday. 26 Rue de Richelieu or 23 Rue Montpensier (between Passages Hulot and Potier). No credit cards. Métro: Palais-Royal. 42.96.24.64

Each January Parisians celebrate the Epiphany (*La Fête des Rois*) with *galette des rois*, a holiday puff-pastry pancake filled with almond paste and a hidden trinket. The person whose portion of cake contains the charm is king or queen for the day. The best galettes des rois come from Dalloyau, a dessert shop which has been making kings and queens of the Parisian elite since 1949.

---

111 Palais Royal This six-acre enclave of flowering serenity is surrounded by, yet separate from, the urban bustle. Commissioned by **Cardinal Richelieu** and designed by his architect **Lemercier** in 1642, the palace (pictured above) was christened Palais Royal when **Anne of Austria** temporarily lived here with her son, young **Louis XIV.** In 1780 the property fell into the hands of the shrewd **Philippe, Duke of Orléans,** who embarked on a lucrative and fancy bit of real estate speculation. He hired the architect **Victor Louis** (who built the nearby Théâtre Français) to design a square like Venice's Piazza San Marco, but containing a garden (700 feet by 300 feet), to be faced on three sides with elegant apartments incorporating arcades that had space for 180 shops, which the duke then sold for immense profit. (He also named the bordering streets after his three sons: Valois, Beaujolais, and Montpensier.)

Strolling through the lime-tree groves here became the fashion for French aristocrats as well as for American visitors such as **Thomas Jefferson** and **Washington Irving.** The garden's elegance soon frayed, however, when the profligate Philippe became chronically broke and began renting the galleries to magicians, wax museums, circuses, and brothels. Under his dissolute management, the Palais Royal attracted the Parisian rabble, questionable dandies, and women of easy virtue; it became a raffish, depraved enclave. (As late as 1804, historians listed the presence of 11 loan sharks, 18 gambling houses, and 17 billiard halls in the palace arcades.) **Marat** referred to the garden as the "nucleus of the Revolution." Ironically, it was here that **Charlotte Corday** bought the dagger she used to kill Marat. It was also here on 13 July 1789 that **Camille Desmoulins** incited his fellow Parisians to take up arms. Like the Tuileries Palace, the Palais Royal was ransacked during the revolt of 1848; a giant bonfire was kindled in the courtyard with gilt chairs, paintings, and canopies thrown from the windows by the mob. Among the furnitur destroyed was the throne on which **Louis Philippe** first sat as king of France.

By the 20th century the luxurious apartments overlooking the gardens housed a number of famous residents. Poet and dramatist **Jean Cocteau** lived here, as did **Colette.** She resided at 9 Rue de Beaujolais and was often seen writing at her window overlooking the courtyard. Colette died as stylishly as she'd lived: suddenly and painlessly after drinking a glass of champagne. Today the Palais Royal arcades are occupied by curiosity shops selling antiques, old books, jewelry, lead soldiers, medals, and rare stamps. The garden is embellished by the fountain where the infant Louis XIV once sailed his toy boats and by two quite modern fountains resembling giant ball bearings. The larger court of the Palais Royal has been the focus of an aesthetic debate reminiscent of the one surrounding the Louvre transformation. Minister of Culture **Jack Lang** initiated a project (conceived by sculptor **Daniel Buren**) that involved the planting of 252 black-and-white striped columns, deep pools, and airport lights in the courtyard floor. In the winter of 1986 residents of the palace who objected to the scheme won a court order to halt construction on the site temporarily. The project, however, was completed the following summer. ◆ Métro: Palais-Royal

12 Restaurant Pierre ★★★$$$ In the shadow of the Comédie Française, this restaurant offers a warm immersion in the mood of France's Massif Central region. Try veal kidneys, *St. Pierre à la rhubarbe,* roast rabbit with mustard sauce, *gratin dauphinois,* a more refined pike with chives, or *estofinade rouergate,* in which the simple codfish achieves transcendence. ◆ Lunch and dinner. Closed Saturday, Sunday, and in August. 10 Rue de Richelieu (between Rue Molière and Place du Théâtre Française). Reservations recommended. Métro: Palais-Royal. 42.96.09.17

12 Montpensier $$ The fact that this hotel was once the residence of a baroness who was a favorite of **Louis XV** explains why it has rooms of varying dimensions and prices. ◆ 12 Rue de Richelieu (between Rue Molière and Place du Théâtre Française). Métro: Palais-Royal. 42.96.28.50

12 Dynasty ★★$ This reasonably priced Chinese restaurant with pink tablecloths features a menu that's enlivened by several incendiary Vietnamese and Thai specialties. ◆ Lunch and dinner. Closed Sunday. 12 Rue de Richelieu (between Rue Molière and Place du Théâtre Française). Métro: Palais-Royal. 42.86.06.58

On the Right and Left banks, addresses on streets perpendicular to the Seine begin at the river with the number 1 and increase as they move away from the river.

Voltaire

112 Comédie Française In 1673, while performing in his own *Le Malade Imaginaire,* the 51-year-old dramatist **Molière** collapsed onstage and died as the curtain came down. (Legend has it that there were several doctors in the audience who were so enraged by the play's criticism of medicine that they would not treat its dying author.) Seven years later **Louis XIV** founded the Comédie Française with the remaining members of the playwright's troupe. Today it is France's most prestigious theatrical group, residing since the end of the 18th century in this rather small Doric-style theater designed by **Victor Louis.** The company has survived the Bourbon monarchy, the Revolution, two empires, and four republics, and still plays to packed houses. After Molière, the theater's most celebrated thespian was the spirited tragic actress **Sarah Bernhardt** (the "Divine Sarah," born **Rosine Bernard** in Paris), who played roles ranging from Cleopatra to Hamlet, thereby reviving Shakespeare in France. Bernhardt was a dynamic character who was fond of saying, even in old age, "Rest? With all eternity before me?"

Today the Comédie Française sticks to serious classical French drama, though not too long ago it conceded the existence of foreign playwrights. A foyer-bar opens onto a gallery displaying busts of famous playwrights. The upstairs foyer is graced with a notable stone statue of **Voltaire** by **Houdon** (illustrated above) and the leather armchair into which Molière collapsed during his last act on stage. ◆ Tours for individuals: third Sunday of each month at 10:15AM starting at the administration entrance on the Place Colette. Tours for groups: second and fourth Sunday of each month (must be reserved three to four months in advance). Box office: daily 11AM-6PM. A special window around the side of the building opens 45 minutes before the curtain to sell reduced-price tickets for the night's performance. 2 Rue de Richelieu (at Place du Théâtre Française). Métro: Palais-Royal. 40.15.00.15 (box office), 42.96.10.24 (administration)

113 Place du Théâtre Française/Place Andṛé-Malraux In 1874, these two squares were graced by a duo of elegant but simple **Davioud** fountains decorated with bronze nymphs by **Carrier-Belleuse** and **Math Moreau.** ♦ Métros: Palais-Royal, Pyramides

113 Manufacture Nationale de Sèvres This showroom lies adjacent to the famous and venerable (circa 1738) Sèvres porcelain factory. An exhibition of designs ranges from Louis XVI dinner plates to an abstract lamp designed in 1984 by Japanese artist **Asuka Tsu-Boi.** All items sold here are tax-free. ♦ Tu-Sa 11AM-6PM. 4 Place André-Malraux (between Rues de l'Echelle and de Rohan). Métro: Palais-Royal. 47.03.40.20

113 Osaka ★★$ An authentic, inexpensive Japanese soup kitchen, Osaka serves the hundreds of Tokyo tourists who frequent the Opéra-Palais Royal neighborhood. Miso soup, thick with noodles, and pot stickers are the best bets. Next door is a pricey sushi bar and restaurant under the same management. ♦ Lunch and dinner. Closed Sunday. 1 Place André-Malraux (between Rues de l'Echelle and de Rohan). Reservations recommended. Métro: Palais-Royal. 42.60.65.35

113 161 Rue St.-Honoré On this site of the Moroccan Tourist Office once stood the old **St.-Honoré Gate,** where **Jeanne d'Arc** was wounded in the thigh by an English archer in 1429. She was hit while measuring the depth of the moat with her lance in preparation for an assault on the city. ♦ Between Rues de l'Echelle and de Rohan. Métro: Palais-Royal

114 Hôtel du Louvre $$$ This modern hotel is situated beside the Palais Royal, Tuileries, and Comédie Française, and within walking distance of the Opéra and the Louvre. What more could you ask for? ♦ Place André-Malraux (at Rues de Rohan and St.-Honoré). Métro: Palais-Royal. 42.61.56.01, 42.61.52.52

114 A la Civette For more than two centuries this store has been in the forefront of tobacconists. It was the first shop in Paris to import the fine Montecristo cigar from Cuba. Shelves are cluttered with chewing tobacco, pipes, cigarillos, and stogies to delight the wheeziest connoisseur. ♦ M-Sa 8:30AM-7PM. 157 Rue St.-Honoré (between Rue de Rohan and Place du Palais-Royal). Métro: Palais-Royal. 42.96.04.99

114 Delamain The window of this wonderful old bookshop displays museum-worthy items, from 18th-century hand-bound volumes on **King Clovis** to modern editions of **Samuel Beckett.** ♦ M-Sa 10AM-7PM. Closed Saturday in August. 155 Rue St.-Honoré (between Rue

de Rohan and Place du Palais-Royal). Métro: Palais-Royal. 42.61.48.78

115 Le Louvre des Antiquaires An association of more than 240 antique shops encompasses three floors. You'll find Art Deco prints, period perfume bottles, miniature 16th-century manuscripts, rare Japanese woodcuts, fin de siècle dolls and children's clothes, African tribal masks, and Thai Buddhas. One can find any old thing here except a bargain. Be advised that many of these dealers have their main antique shops (generally larger and less expensive) on the Left Bank, so take a card and pay them a visit when you're on the other side of the river. Also, before making a purchase, be sure you understand the complicated regulations concerning the removal of antiques from the country.

This building was formerly the **Grand Hôtel du Louvre,** where **Mark Twain** stayed in 1867. It was here that Twain met the tour guide **Ferguson** who figures in *The Innocents Abroad* (1869). ♦ Tu-Su 11AM-7PM. 2 Place du Palais-Royal (between Rues St.-Honoré and de Rivoli). Métro: Palais-Royal. 42.97.27.00

116 Galerie Véro-Dodat Named after two pork butchers who were here from the start, this covered passageway was the city's first public thoroughfare to be illuminated by gas lighting ♦ Off Rue Jean-Jacques-Rousseau, between Rues St.-Honoré and Coquillère. Métros: Louvre, Palais-Royal

116 Robert Capia This antique doll store is a favorite of **Catherine Deneuve.** ♦ M-Sa 10AM-7PM. 24-26 Galerie Véro-Dodat (between Rues Jean-Jacques-Rousseau and Croix-des-Petits-Champs). Métros: Louvre, Palais-Royal. 42.36.25.94

116 Christian Louboutin The specialty of this women's shoe designer is hand-sculpted heels. Many of them are covered in gold leaf to give you a dazzling walk. ♦ M-Sa 10AM-6PM Sept-July. 19 Rue Jean-Jacques-Rousseau (at Galerie Véro-Dodat). Métros: Palais-Royal, Louvre. 42.36.05.31

117 Maison Micro A Greek bazaar of produce from Hellas: vats of olives and hot peppers, burlap sacks of whole grains and flour, crates of dried fruits, and barrels of *tarama*. Step inside and take an Aegean whiff. ♦ M 2-6:45PM; Tu-Sa 8:30AM-12:30PM, 1:30-6:45PM. 142-144 Rue St.-Honoré (between Rues Jean-Jacques-Rousseau and du Louvre). Métros: Louvre, Palais-Royal. 42.60.53.02, 42.60.65.17

117 Chez Nous ★$$ The city's best jock bar and restaurant is run by **Gilbert Ghiraldi,** an ex-rugby player. If you manage to outmaneuver the French national rugby team that huddles here, grab a table and order one of chef **Véronique's** Basque specialties. ♦ Lunch and dinner. 150 Rue St.-Honoré (between Rues Jean-Jacques-Rousseau and du Louvre). No credit cards. Métros: Louvre, Palais-Royal. 42.60.29.75

118 **115 Rue St.-Honoré** Here, two centuries ago, **Count Fersen** bought the invisible ink with which he penned his famous letters to **Marie Antoinette.** ♦ At Rue de l'Arbre-Sec. Métro: Louvre

Bests

Bill Murray
Actor/Former Sorbonne Student

The hors d'oeuvres at **A l'Impasse.** We used to live just up the street and it was my favorite restaurant, though I never tried the tripe. It doesn't seem fair to ask one stomach to digest another.

Afternoon tea dancing downstairs at **La Coupole; Le Select Latin** for the best *croque monsieur* served on *pain Poilâne,* the **Passages** (the farther north the better, because the stores get cheaper); the **Parc des Buttes-Chaumont;** the 20th arrondissement, where it gets the most African; the Tunisian temple in the **Parc de Montsouris;** the **Place des Vosges,** where my son always played; the Chinese restaurants in **Belleville;** and the beekeepers in the **Luxembourg Gardens.**

The **statue of Beaumarchais** near the Bastille. The neighborhood is always dressing him up with funny underwear, painting his lips, and adorning him with a blind-man's cane.

The way the *bateaux mouches* pivot around the Statue of Liberty on the **Seine,** with the **Eiffel Tower** in the background. It's like a panning movie camera.

Richard Reeves
American Author/Columnist

The women. The magic of Paris is that each Parisienne is a work of art, spending, it seems, hours and years making themselves the best they can be.

The movies. There are hundreds of movie screens operating day and night, all chronicled and described weekly in *Pariscope* for just a few francs.

The **Gare de Lyon**—and everything that comes in and goes out of it.

Hôtel Drouot, where every day anything from old Mixmasters to Old Masters is sold on the spot to the highest bidder.

The **St.-Ouen Flea Market** at Porte de Clignancourt. The place where most of Drouot's stuff ends up— at half the price that Americans pay at home.

The bridges, the florists, the **Rodin Museum,** the Sunday market on Rue de Buci near St.-Germain-des-Prés, and the **Luxembourg Gardens.**

Les soldes. The sales in Paris in January and June are the most extraordinary in the world. Advertised even in *Le Monde,* they attract everyone from Saudi princesses to shop girls looking for 50 to 80 percent off everything.

Small hotels. Why don't America's largest cities have even one good small hotel, when every block in Paris has two?

The **Bazaar de l'Hôtel-de-Ville (BHV)** is my favorite department store in the world. The hardware department alone takes a morning to understand.

Reservations. The French actually honor reservations. Your reserved table is yours and not a commodity to be turned over as many times as possible each night.

Vietnamese restaurants. Perfect (and cheap) relief from the riches of French cuisine. If there is a bad Vietnamese restaurant in Paris, I have yet to find it.

Anne Willan
President of La Varenne Ecole de Cuisine

The triangle in the seventh arrondissement bounded by the Eiffel Tower, Les Invalides, and the air terminal is my home ground. To wander the little back alleys is a constant pleasure, for they shelter traditional artisans—shoemakers, bookbinders, basket-weavers—who have been forced off the high-rent main streets.

Rue Augereau and **Rue de l'Exposition** (renamed at the time of the Great Paris Exhibition of 1867) are particularly rich in little restaurants and shops such as **l'Oiseau Bleu** on Rue Augereau, a picture-frame store where you can always find a few attractive bargain items for sale.

In need of refreshment? Pastry chef **Denis Ruffel** at **Millet,** on Rue St.-Dominique, is renowned beyond the arrondissement for his honey madeleines, flaky croissants, and *pain au chocolat,* stuffed with not one but two sticks of chocolate. Or pick up a box of his chocolates to take away—they are made on the premises, of course.

For a true bistro meal (my favorite kind), I suggest three possibilities. The **Fontaine de Mars** on Rue St.-Dominique is modest, full of chattering locals, and known for its hot dandelion salad with bacon and its quail with cabbage. Spots farther along the street such as **Thoumieux** are harder and harder to find. Here *confit de canard* and steak *frites* are best-sellers. Waiters in their shirtsleeves open bottles of house red wine with a conjurer's dexterity, and the noise level reaches a maximum around 11PM. For the very best bistro food I go to **De Chez Eux** on Avenue de Lowendal. It has everything—baskets of dried mountain sausages, homemade terrines, and hors d'oeuvres so copious the dishes must be stacked in towers on the table.

In 1858, a would-be assassin known as Orsini the Carbonaro threw a homemade bomb at a carriage carrying Napoléon III to an opera house. Though the emperor was unharmed, 156 bystanders were killed or injured. With this incident in mind, architect Charles Garnier added a special entrance to his design for another opera house on Rue Auber; it allowed Napoléon III's coach to be driven directly to the level of the dress circle via a curved double ramp into the royal box. Rumor has it that this thoughtful touch helped Garnier's opera design win out over 171 other competing architects.

Montmartre

Crowned with that alabaster wedding-cake church known as **Sacré-Coeur**, Montmartre is the balcony of Paris—half dream, half nightmare. It is a tangle of contradictions: meandering country roads, seedy strip joints, early Christian sites, tourist clichés, sublime vistas, and hidden passages. The butte (which is what Parisians call this storied sandstone height) is geographically the highest point in town (427 feet) and the traditional home of poets, singers, painters, and bohemians of all kinds.

Moulin de la Galette—the last old windmill in Paris was painted by Renoir

Cartoon children frolic on the frieze of illustrator Poulbot's former house

An antique-car rallye is held on Rue Lepic the first or second Sunday of October

Terrass Hôtel—Montmartre's only four-star hotel. Ask for a cemetery-side room and take in the panoramic view of Paris from the Eiffel Tower to l'Opéra

Vincent van Gogh lived at **No. 54 Rue Lepic**

Stendhal, Berlioz, Degas, Fragonard, and Offenbach are buried at the **Cimetière de Montmartre**, also the home of some 300 cats

Great oysters are served from September through April at **Charlot**

(M) **Place-de-Clichy**

A turn-of-the-century billiards parlor

Guyot, one of Paris' last pipe artisans, works in a dance hall here

Bizarre bazaar at **Ophir Paris** on **Cité Véron**

Cancan dancers in ostrich plumes at **Moulin Rouge**

(M) **Blanche**

Rue Lepic open-air market (closed Mondays)

Androuet—a cheese restaurant offering more than a hundred varieties

(M) **St.-Georges**

(M) **Notre-Dame-de-Lorette**

(M) = Métro

aris' most exclusive movie theater—*Ciné 13*

Old-timers' bowling tournaments are held daily at **Square Suzanne-Buisson**, beneath the statue of a headless Saint Denis

Ⓜ **Lamarck-Caulaincourt**

On a clear day you can see north to the St.-Denis Basilica from the **St.-Vincent Cemetery**

Montmartre Vineyards, one of two remaining vineyards in Paris: don't miss the Harvest Festival on one of the first Sundays in October

Madame Delbey sells 50 kinds of goat cheese at **No. 9 Rue du Poteau**

Rue du Poteau, one of Paris' prettiest street markets

Ⓜ **Jules-Joffrin**

City Hall—see the collection of Utrillo paintings here. And wine from Montmartre Vineyards is sold in the basement

Beauvilliers—Montmartre's best restaurant

Toulouse-Lautrec posters and drawings are displayed in the **Montmartre Museum**

Best views of Paris at dawn and dusk are from the **Sacré-Cœur** steps and dome

St.-Pierre-de-Montmartre—the oldest church in Paris

Looking for sari silk or Toulouse-Lautrec dish towels? Try **Marché St.-Pierre**, in the heart of Paris' garment district

For the price of a métro ticket, you can take the funicular here and save yourself the 266 steps to Sacré-Cœur

Best view of Sacré-Cœur

A l'Angélus—hot cocoa that's as thick as chocolate mousse

Ⓜ **Anvers**

Le Tire Bouchon—the place for crêpes and jazz piano

If nagging street artists bother you, avoid **Place du Tertre**

Guimard's Art Nouveau métro station (its 285 steps makes this Paris' deepest)

Ⓜ **Abbesses**

St.-Jean-L'Evangéliste—the first reinforced-concrete church in Paris

Ⓜ **Pigalle**

an abandoned piano factory at **Place Emile-Goudeau**, painters asso, Braque, Gris, and Modigliani hered the modern art movement

The best day to visit Montmartre is on Tuesday, when the museums in other parts of Paris are closed, or when you feel like fleeing the center of the city for a few hours. Emerging from **Hector Guimard's** Art Nouveau **Abbesses Métro Station,** start the day with café au lait and brioches in one of the cafés along **Rue des Abbesses,** which is crowded with butchers, bakers, and fishmongers from the Rue Lepic market. Then begin the ascent to **Place du Tertre,** a 14th-century square that in summer is a free-for-all among street artists, outdoor restaurant waiters, and tourists. The best bets for lunch are crêpes at **Le Tire Bouchon,** fish at **La Crémaillère 1900** on Place du Tertre, or the sublime *foies de volaille* at **L'Assommoir.** After the obligatory pilgrimage to Sacré-Coeur, wind down Rue Lepic past the **Moulin de la Galette** until you see the red neon signs of that other temple of folklore, the **Moulin Rouge.** Stay for the cancan show or return to the butte for the evening cabaret at the legendary **Au Lapin Agile.** The métro closes at 12:45AM, but you will find a taxi just down the hill on **Rue Caulaincourt,** the same street taken by revelers in the wine-festival parade held in October.

The name Montmartre has two possible origins: the "Mount of Mercury," to whom a Roman temple on the butte was once dedicated, or the "Mount of Martyrs," commemorating **Saint Denis,** the first bishop of Paris, who, along with the priest **Rusticus** (his own sort of Sancho Panza) and the deacon **Eleutherius,** was tortured and decapitated by the Romans in AD 250. According to the legend, Saint Denis picked up his severed head and carried it 12 miles over the hill. One thousand years later, the Basilica of St.-Denis was built on that hill, where for centuries the kings and queens of France have been buried. (The priest and deacon did not make the headless trek, and as consolation had streets in Montmartre named after them.)

A lesser-known local martyr was **Pierre-Charles Debray,** the mill owner who during the **Franco-Prussian War** was crucified on the blades of his Moulin de la Galette, a windmill with a garden tavern and dance hall that a half-century later would ironically symbolize *Gay Paree* on a **Renoir** canvas. Artists such as Renoir, **van Gogh, Dufy,** and **Utrillo;** poets **Apollinaire, Max Jacob,** and **Jacques Prévert;** and novelist **Boris Vian,** songwriter **Aristide Bruant,** and illustrator **André Gill** all worked in Montmartre. In the late 19th century, **Toulouse-Lautrec** sketched the cancan dancers at the Moulin Rouge, and in the early 1900s, **Picasso, Braque,** and **Gris,** working out of an abandoned piano factory nearby, gave birth to cubism. Cabarets such as Au Lapin Agile further encouraged *la vie bohème,* and the life was much romanticized by Americans in Paris. Writer **John Roderigo Dos Passos,** for instance, rhapsodized in 1918 that he wanted his heart "to be preserved in a pitcher of *vin de Beaujolais* in the restaurant in Place du Tertre on the summit of Montmartre."

After World War I, the artistic center moved to another of the city's seven hills, **Montparnasse,** on the Left Bank. The nightlife, however, remained in Montmartre and grew in notoriety. Though Montmartre reputedly contains the oldest church sanctuary in Paris (**St.-Pierre**) and was dominated in the 12th century by an abbey run by women, today the area is best known for women (and men disguised as women) plying an older, less pious profession. Painters may have once scouted out portrait models among the seamstresses and dancers in **Place Pigalle,** but the seamier live sex shows, porn films, and peep shops took over at the end of World War II. Avoid the crowded butte on weekends. The notable exceptions to this rule are the first Saturday and second Sunday of October, the dates of the local annual wine-harvest festival and the vintage-car rally, respectively. Both events are worth attending.

1 Abbesses Métro Station Named after *les abbesses,* the nuns who ran the abbey here in the Middle Ages, this métro station (shown above) is 300 feet below grade, the deepest in Paris. The reason lies in Montmartre's old gypsum mines. Gypsum, a soft stone, was burned to make the internationally famous plaster of paris used, among other things, to mold busts of George Washington and Thomas Jefferson in the U.S. capitol. Over the years, the growing network of quarry tunnels beneath Montmartre turned the hill, geologically speaking, to Swiss cheese. In the 1840s the mines were closed, but not before 27 houses and several Parisians had disappeared into the void.

The City of Paris is still filling Montmartre's cavities with high-pressure concrete. The métro platform was built at bedrock, precisely 285 steps below **Place des Abbesses.** Take the elevator and save your breath for the Montmartre summit.

The turn-of-the-century exterior of the Abbesses métro station, with its green, vinelike, wrought-iron arches and amber lights, is one of the most picturesque in Paris and typifies the early Art Nouveau designs of architect **Hector Guimard.** At first, nationalistic Parisians criticized Guimard's choice of German green and suggested he paint his métro stations *bleu, blanc, et rouge*. His concession to chauvinism was a ship shield (the symbol of the City of Paris) in the middle of the roof, but he stubbornly held his ground on garden green. *Et voilà!* (The only other Guimard station that still has its original glass roof is Porte-Dauphine near the Bois de Boulogne.) However, the Abbesses métro entrance is not original to the butte. For decades it stood in front of Hôtel de Ville (city hall), but when **Mayor Jacques Chirac** gussied up the plaza, he moved Guimard's masterpiece to Montmartre. New York's Museum of Modern Art has an old *Métropolitain* sign and one of these early Guimard arches. ♦ At Place des Abbesses

---

staurants/Clubs Red   Hotels: Blue

ops/ Outdoors: Green   **Sights/Culture: Black**

2 St.-Jean-L'Évangéliste Soon after its construction, this Moorish grab bag of architectural tricks (trimmed with what looks like turquoise Art Nouveau jewelry) was rechristened by the neighborhood "Brick St.-John." Looking amazingly contemporary for a nonagenarian, the 1904 church distinguishes itself as the first erected in Paris with reinforced concrete. ♦ M-Sa 8:30AM-noon, 3-7:30PM; Su 8:30AM-noon, 4-7PM. 19-21 Rue des Abbesses (at Rue André-Antoine). Métro: Abbesses

3 Hôtel Régyn's Montmartre $$ This hotel is in the heart of Montmartre, but otherwise it's nothing fancy. ♦ 18 Place des Abbesses (NW corner). Métro: Abbesses. 42.54.45.21

4 Tim Hôtel $$ Had this two-star hotel been here 70 years ago, you might have asked your neighbors **Pablo Picasso** or **Georges Braque** over for coffee and croissants. ♦ 11 Rue Ravignan (off Place Emile-Goudeau). Métro: Abbesses. 42.55.74.79

4 Four Graces Fountain Layered in green paint, this drinking fountain (and 99 other identical ones around Paris) was the gift of **Richard Wallace,** an Englishman who collected 18th-century French art and frequently lamented that it was impossible in his beloved Paris to enjoy a glass of water in a café without paying for it. The metal drinking cup originally attached to it in the 1870s disappeared in the 1950s when the city gave way to sanitation standards. ♦ Rue Ravignan (off Place Emile-Goudeau). Métro: Abbesses

4 Relais de la Butte $ Run by a cheerful former barge captain, this restaurant is heavy on the "little old Montmartre" ambience (reminiscent of when Montmartre was a small village) but offers a pot-au-feu, homemade *rillettes*, foie gras, filet of sole with salmon soufflé, and chocolate mousse at bargain prices. ♦ Lunch and dinner; dinner only on Tuesday. Closed Monday. 12 Rue Ravignan (off Place Emile-Goudeau). Métro: Abbesses. 42.23.94.64

5 Rue de la Mire Getting lost in the twisting streets of Montmartre can be done with the greatest of ease, except on this short pedestrian street. An 18th-century trail marker (*mire*, hence the street name) points due north. ♦ Between Rues Ravignon and Lepic. Métro: Abbesses

6 Gilbert Peyre's Studio This talented metal sculptor with a riotous mustache constructs fantastic contraptions that come to life with the pull of a string or the flick of a switch. Using bicycle chains, coffee cans, camera bellows, and other found objects, Peyre creates whimsical flying machines, trapeze artists, sword swallowers, and other characters to make you giggle. Good luck getting the sword swallower into your suitcase, but stop by anyway to watch Peyre at work. ♦ M-Sa 2-8PM. Closed whenever he chooses (best to call for an appointment). 24 Rue Durantin (between Rues Burq and Ravignan). Métro: Abbesses. 42.64.06.55

6 Place Emile-Goudeau On the former site of a renowned *guinguette* (garden tavern) where Parisians came to eat and drink was the famous old piano factory at 13 Place Emile-Goudeau that art historians call the Villa Médici of Modern Art. By the turn of the century this place had attracted poets **Apollinaire** and **Max Jacob,** and modern painters **Picasso, Braque, Gris,** and **Modigliani.** Picasso worked here for eight years, painting works such as *Les Demoiselles d'Avignon* (which is now in the collection of New York's Museum of Modern Art and is often cited as the first example of cubism). This ramshackle building, which had but one water spigot to serve the 40 artists housed here, was sarcastically dubbed *Bateau Lavoir* after those Renaissance laundry barges inundated with water from the Seine. The original structure burned in 1970, and the City of Paris now rents rebuilt studios (and provides plenty of water) to the far more prosperous, though certainly not more talented, artists of today. ♦ Métro: Abbesses

7 Le Restaurant ★★$$ Modern, minimalist decor complements the array of original and revived cuisine served here: oyster and sorrel omelet, beef marrow tart with red wine sauce, persillade of stuffed squid, and an exquisite crème brûlée. ♦ Lunch and dinner. Closed Sunday, Monday, and the second half of August. 32 Rue Véron (between Rues Aristide-Bruant and Audran). Reservations recommended. Métro: Abbesses. 42.23.06.22

8 Bruno Maître Tattooist Would you like a goldfish on your ankle? Perhaps a mermaid on your chest? Bruno, one of the more popular body artists in Paris and an officer of the artisanal Order of Artistic Merit, practices safe tattooing, using only fresh needles and disposable ink cartridges. Even if you're not ready to commit to a permanent bodily souvenir of your trip, it's fun to look in the window and imagine. ♦ M-Tu, Th-Sa 10AM-7PM. 4 Rue Germain-Pilon (between Blvd de Clichy and Rue Véron). Métro: Pigalle. 42.64.35.59

9 Place Pigalle Nineteenth-century sculptor **Jean-Baptiste Pigalle's** celebrated rendering of the Virgin Mary is displayed in **St.-Sulpice,** but his name became synonymous with porn films, sex shops, and prostitutes by being associated with this square. Known as **Pig Alley** to World War II GIs who came stalking the professional wildlife, Place Pigalle has lost many of its hookers to Rue St.-Denis and Bois de Boulogne; these days transvestites predominate. ♦ Métro: Pigalle

10 Caravelle $$ This comfortable hotel has 33 air-conditioned rooms. Ask for one in back and avoid the noise of traffic and the electric-guitar store across the street. ♦ 68 Rue des Martyrs (between Blvd Rochechouart and Rue Lallier). Métro: Pigalle. 48.78.43.31

11 Carlton's $$ Surprise, surprise—there's a three-star hotel amid the strip joints and kun fu cinemas of Pigalle. ♦ 55 Blvd Rochechouar (between Rue des Martyrs and Rue Bochart-de-Saron). Métro: Anvers. 42.81.91.00

12 Résidence Charles-Dullin $$ These kitchen-equipped flats, located on a tranquil square, are rented by the night or by the week ♦ 10 Place Charles-Dullin (SE corner). Métro Anvers. 42.57.14.55

12 Théâtre de l'Atelier When this charming theater was first built in 1822 on the cobblestoned square (named in 1957 after actor **Charles Dullin**), it was known for the **Stefan Zweig** adaptation of **Ben Jonson's** *Volpone* and for **L'Opéra Bouffe,** which critic called the best stage performances outside Paris. Today, under the direction of **Pierre Franck,** the theater is truly Parisian, and there isn't a bad red-velvet seat in the house. ♦ Box office: M-Sa 11AM-7PM. 1 Place Charles-Dull (at Rue d'Orsel). Métro: Anvers. 46.06.49.24

13 Le Gastelier ★$ The tea salon at the foot of Sacré-Coeur is a perfect luncheon stop before making the final ascent up the white stairs. Try a Milanese tart (spinach, tomato, and cheese) and a dish of fresh mandarin sorbet. Better yet, indulge in a few scoops of nougat i cream or a plate of macaroons, and then waddle over to the funicular and ride up. ♦ Breakfast, lunch, afternoon tea, and dinner. Closed Monday. 1bis Rue Tardieu (across fro Funicular). Métro: Anvers. 46.06.22.06

13 A l'Angélus The path to this nonsmoking neighborhood candy store/tea shop is well worn by schoolchildren and Sacré-Coeur pilgrims alike. The *fait maison* (homemade) bonbons and *Angélus* (almond paste and chocolate mousse) are rich enough to sate any sweet tooth. Try the *Alesien* coffee pralines and the *orangettes*, strips of orange rind dipped into a velvety mixture of melted chocolate and almond chips. And on a drizzling winter afternoon, nothing beats the hot cocoa made from melted chocolate bars. ◆ M-Tu, Th-Su 7:45AM-7:30PM. 1 Rue Tardieu (across from Funicular). Métro: Anvers. 46.06.03.75

14 Le Progrès ★$ This authentic, economical neighborhood café and bar is patronized by Parisians rather than tourists. The food isn't gourmet but simple and tasty, while decent wines are poured by the pitcher. There is always a daily prix-fixe lunch such as roast beef and potatoes or *rognons provençaux*. Charcuterie and cheese are served all day. ◆ Lunch, snacks, and late-night. Closed Sunday. 1 Rue Yvonne-Le-Tac (at Rue Chappe). Métro: Abbesses. 42.51.33.33

15 Martyrium Just off the Street of Martyrs, where **Saint Denis** was thought to have been decapitated, is the **Chapel of the Auxiliatrices Order.** In the crypt of an earlier medieval sanctuary on this site, Spaniards **Ignatius Loyola** and **Francis Xavier** founded the mighty Jesuit order on 15 August 1534. ◆ M-W, F-Su 10AM-noon, 3-5PM. 11 Rue Yvonne-Le-Tac (between Rues des Martyrs and Chappe). Métro: Pigalle

16 L'Abat-Jour Patrick Rossingol and Chantal Juan want people of all ages, professions, and lifestyles to feel comfortable in their cozy hair salon. No photographs of pouty models with trendy hairdos are displayed. The stylists will cut, shape, color, or perm your hair to suit you, using many products with natural ingredients. The salon's name means "the lamp shade," which refers not to any coiffure but to the business formerly located at this address, a lamp shade manufacturer. ◆ Tu-W, F-Sa 10AM-7:30PM; Th 11:30AM-8:30PM. 19 Rue Yvonne-Le-Tac (between Rue des Martyrs and Place des Abbesses). Métro: Abbesses. 42.64.39.32

17 Wanouchka ★$$ Eastern European immigrants swarm here for classic Polish cuisine (pirogi, blintzes, Baltic herring, and borscht) prepared by chef **Roman Rybicki,** a veteran of the Russian Tea Room in New York. Forget the wine list (when in Warsaw, do as the Poles) and order the plum-and-lemon vodka. ◆ Dinner. Closed Wednesday. 28 Rue la Vieuville (between Place des Abbesses and Rue des Martyrs). Reservations recommended. No credit cards. Métro: Abbesses. 42.57.36.15

18 Funicular The shortest, steepest métro line in Paris runs every few minutes between **Place Suzanne-Valadon** and the base of **Sacré-Coeur.** While the fitness freaks take the stairs, the rest ride up in comfort and enjoy the view, all for the price of a normal métro ticket. ◆ Métro: Anvers

18 Rue Foyatier The most photographed steps in Montmartre, all 266 of them, run from **Rue Azais** down to **Place Suzanne-Valadon** (named after **Maurice Utrillo's** mother, a talented painter in her own right). All hell breaks loose here at 4:30PM each day when an elementary school lets out and scores of screaming children with miniature leather briefcases on their backs dart across the square in search of their mothers and fathers—the local butchers, bakers, and souvenir-makers—who have come to walk them home. ◆ Métro: Anvers

MARCHÉ St-PIERRE

19 Marché St.-Pierre Paris' most celebrated discount fabric warehouse is the hub of the city's garment district. In this four-story bazaar, pandemonium reigns over acres of tweed, bolts of polyester, and bins of last year's argyle socks. Everyone comes here: students searching for cheap curtains, Punjabi women rummaging for sari silk, and New Wave couturiers stalking ersatz panther pelts. The costumes of the surly salesclerks range from three-piece suits to studded leather jackets and turquoise tights. The method in this madness? Take it from the top: fifth floor, linens and sheets; fourth floor, lace curtains and duvet covers; third floor, silks, velours, and *incroyables* (exotic odds and ends); second floor, wools and polyesters; ground floor, a bit of everything. ◆ M 1:30-6:30PM; Tu-Sa 9:30AM-6:30PM. 2 Rue Charles-Nodier (at Rue Pierre Picard). Métro: Anvers. 46.06.92.25

20 L'Été en Pente Douce ★★$ This café and *salon de thé,* whose name means "summer on a soft slope," is hidden on a little square at the base of Sacré-Coeur's sloping grassy park. Its outdoor terrace is a peaceful haven in this lively neighborhood. Daily specialties like rabbit in mustard sauce are served along with your typical *salade niçoise* and your-not-so-typical *filet mignon Sylvestre aux champignons* (wild boar steak with mushrooms). ♦ Lunch, afternoon tea, and dinner. 23 Rue Muller (at Rue Charles-Nodier). Métros: Abbesses, Anvers. 42.64.02.67

21 Sacré-Coeur Diocesan architect **Paul Abadie's** Roman-Byzantine marble tribute, universally panned by his peers, has nevertheless become enshrined in the Tourists' Top Ten. For most people, the highlight of the church (pictured below) is not its design, but the view from its steps—or even better, from the dome (access through the north aisle) at dusk or dawn. The church is devoted to atonement for the massacre of some 58,000 citizens during the **Franco-Prussian War,** and within its mosaic-encrusted interior you can see priests praying for forgiveness for those war crimes 24 hours a day, a tradition that has been carried on since the church was consecrated more than half a century ago. Begun in 1876, Sacré-Coeur took decades to complete; for the first 15 years of construction, pylons were sunk below grade to stabilize the foundation over the old quarry mines. The towering campanile was added in 1904 by **Lucien Magne;** one of the world's heaviest bells, the 19-ton **Savoyarde,** hangs in the belfry.

From the north side of the dome you can see in the distance the green roof of the basilica built on the site where Saint Denis finally put down his head. A trip to the St.-Denis Basilica is worthwhile (one métro ticket will get you there), if only to see the extraordinary collection of tombs where France buried its kings until the time of the Revolution. Most macabre are the tombs of **Marie de Médici** and **Henri IV,** who lie twice in effigy. On the top they are adorned in their finest Renaissance collars and jewels; below, in marble, are their skeletons eaten away by worms. ♦ Admission for dome. Basilica: daily 6:30AM-11PM. Dome: daily 9AM-7PM in summer, 9AM-6PM in winter. Parvis du Sacré-Coeur. Métros: Abbesses, Anvers

22 St.-Pierre-de-Montmartre An important example of early Gothic architecture, this modest, three-aisled structure was begun 16 years before Notre-Dame and claims to be the oldest sanctuary in Paris (two other churches, St.-Germain-des-Prés and St.-Julien-le-Pauvre, make similar claims). What appears to be a tiny provincial church is all that remains of the original abbey, which was founded in 1134 by **King Louis VI** (the Fat) and his wife, **Queen Adélaide,** who is buried here. The church was dedicated and consecrated by **Pope Eugene III** in 1147. Both **Dante** and **Loyola** worshiped here.

Architecturally, the church is a composite. The vaulted choir assuredly dates from the 12th century (notice the walls buckling beneath the weight of more than 800 years), but archaeologists remain divided over whether

Sacré-Coeur

the four capitaled columns incorporated in the church came from a Roman temple to Mercury or a Merovingian (AD 500-751) church on the site. The original church windows were shattered at the end of World War II by a bomb intended for a nearby bridge. The new windows, added in 1953 by **Max Ingrand,** closely resemble in style the original Gothic stained glass; the three bronze west doors and the cemetery door depicting the Resurrection are by a contemporary Italian sculptor.

Each Good Friday, the archbishop of Paris carries a crucifix up this Mount of Martyrs to St.-Pierre to perform a stations-of-the-cross ceremony. This church's tiny cemetery is the smallest in Paris, with only 85 occupants, among whom are the sculptor **Pigalle,** the navigator **Bougainville** (after whom the purple flowering creeper is named), and Montmartre's first mayor, **Felix Desportes,** as well as the **Debray** family, the original owners of the **Moulin de la Galette** (the family grave is easy to find: look for the miniature windmill on top). ◆ Church: M-Th, Sa-Su 8:30AM-7:30PM; F 8:45AM-5PM. Cemetery: open only on All Saints' Day (1 Nov) 8AM-7PM. 2 Rue du Mont-Cenis. Métro: Abbesses. 46.06.57.63

23 Place du Tertre Part village carnival, part operetta set, this 14th-century square (*tertre* means hillock or mound) is the hub of Montmartre, where busloads of tourists descend to pay homage to the Unknown Artist's awful landscapes and pathetic paintings of melancholy wide-eyed children. In summer (when the square sprouts parasoled restaurant tables), white-aproned waiters and hustling artists jealously guard their territories; the daily border wars make for great theater. During the Middle Ages the abbey had a scaffold here to hang anyone who disobeyed its rules, including any vineyard owner on the butte who refused to donate a quarter of the wine he pressed to the ladies of the cloth, *les abbesses.*

The tradition of exhibiting paintings in Place du Tertre comes from the 19th century, but unfortunately the quality of art has changed. Located in front of St.-Pierre-de-Montmartre, the square is hard to miss, though you may leave wishing you had. ◆ Métro: Abbesses

23 Le Clairon des Chasseurs $ In this bustling artists' café, where all the patrons seem to have sketchbooks under their arms and charcoal pencils behind their ears, painters gather by the window to case prospective clients in the square. The kitchen performs such improbable feats as ruining a *croque-monsieur* (grilled ham-and-cheese sandwich), and the coffee is as muddy as the canvas of Notre-Dame adorning the rear wall. Nevertheless, this café scores big points as a refuge. Ironically, the only way to escape the nagging street artists of Place du Tertre is by

entering their midst; ... strictly to take a break and ... ◆ Breakfast, lunch, dinner, and ... Place du Tertre (east side). Métro: Ab... 42.62.40.08

23 La Bohème $$ No-frills traditional French cuisine here means beef Bourguignon, au gratin potatoes, and apple tarts. The dining room straddles a harshly lit cabaret stage where bored accordion and piano players boom out *chansons de Montmartre.* On weekend afternoons, this is the only music on the square. ◆ Breakfast, lunch, dinner, and late-night; late lunch only on Sunday. Closed in January. 2 Place du Tertre (at Rue du Mont-Cenis). Métro: Abbesses. 46.06.51.69

23 La Mère Catherine ★$$ Founded in 1793 and, as house legend has it, commandeered in 1814 by the Russians who conquered the Montmartre villagers, this is still the oldest brasserie on Place du Tertre, and the waiters swagger as if to show it. You'll find Belle Epoque reproduction mirrors, red-velvet benches, escargots, rack of lamb, tournedos Mère Catherine (filet of beef cooked in port and foie gras sauce), piano and violin music from the 1920s, and outdoor dining on the terrace. ◆ Lunch and dinner. 6 Place du Tertre (north side). Métro: Abbesses. 46.06.32.69, 42.58.07.42

23 La Crémaillère 1900 ★★$$ This brasserie, with an arbored garden, fin-de-siècle decor, and Edith Piaf's greatest hits played nightly on the piano, has a healthy neighborhood following. Seafood (fresh oysters, mussels, and sole stuffed with shrimp mousse) is the strong suit. ◆ Breakfast, lunch, and dinner. 15 Place du Tertre (west side). Métro: Abbesses. 46.06.58.59

Restaurants/Clubs Red	Hotels: Blue
Shops/ 🌴Outdoors: Green	**Sights/Culture:** Black

...in the mood
...er *bouché*
...eaf Rag," go no
...zz pianist upstairs
...Waller and Scott
...niscent of an early-
...dive, with the vintage
...iti-scarred beams, and
... posters and photos of
str... ...usicians. ♦ Afternoon snacks,
dinner, ...-night. 9 Rue Norvins (between
Rues des Saules and du Mont-Cenis). No
credit cards. Métro: Abbesses. 42.55.12.35

24 Au Clair de la Lune ★★$$ **Alain Kerfant,**
a talented chef, admirably overcomes the
restaurant's loud decor with his excellent wine
list and in-season specialties. Try the wild
boar and chanterelle mushrooms with a 1988
Remoissenet Meursault or, if you hit the
jackpot last weekend in Deauville, splurge on a
rare bottle of the 1975 Château d'Yquem
Sauterne to complement your *coquilles St.-
Jacques* in lime sauce. ♦ Lunch and dinner;
dinner only on Monday. Closed Sunday. 9 Rue
Poulbot (off Rue Norvins). Métro: Abbesses.
42.58.97.03

25 L'Auberge de la Bonne Franquette ★$$
This former **van Gogh** studio is now an
intentionally rustic restaurant/cabaret serving
escargots, *confit de canard*, and *pâté en
croute* to Japanese, Dutch, and German bus
tours. Guitarist **Jack Jacquemin** and
accordion player **Jacques Vassart** lead the
equivalent of a nightly French hootenanny and
hawk their cassettes and records at
intermission. ♦ Lunch and dinner. 18 Rue St.-
Rustique (between Rues des Saules and du
Mont-Cenis). Reservations recommended.
Métro: Abbesses. 42.52.02.42

26 Montmartre Museum Located just behind
12 Rue Cortot (whose roll call of former
tenants includes **Jean Renoir, Maurice
Utrillo,** and **Raoul Dufy**), this pleasant little
museum is housed in a delightful 17th-
century town house called **Le Manoir de Rose
de Rosimond,** which is surrounded by two
charming gardens. The house was the country
residence of **Rosimond,** a 17th-century actor
who appeared frequently in the plays of
Molière and who, like Molière, died while
performing *Le Malade Imaginaire.*

The museum's eclectic collection includes
caricatures by **Honoré Daumier** and **André
Gill,** posters and drawings by **Toulouse-
Lautrec,** stunning **Clignancourt** porcelain,
and the piano on which **Gustave Charpentier**
wrote his opera *Louise* in 1900.

Though it seems outlandish in Paris to visit
a museum in order to look at a bistro, the
Montmartre Museum displays an entire 19th-
century bistro complete with a scalloped zinc
bar. The exhibition relates the apocryphal
story that the term bistro originated on the
butte, where impatient Russian soldiers used
to shout at Montmartre's waiters: *"Bistraou,

bistraou!"* (Russian for "Get a move on").
On Wednesday evenings, the **Art et Humour
Montmartrois** meets in the museum for
poetry readings and art exhibitions; lectures
on local culture sponsored by the **Société
du Vieux Montmartre** are held Saturday
evenings. ♦ Admission. Tu-Su 11AM-6PM. 12
Rue Cortot (between Rues des Saules and du
Mont-Cenis). Métro: Lamarck-Caulaincourt.
46.06.61.11

27 Montmartre Vineyards This is one of the
last two remaining vineyards in Paris. Each
year's harvest yields enough grapes for about
500 bottles of red Clos Montmartre wine.
The labels are designed by Montmartre artists,
and half-bottles are sold each year in the
18th arrondissement's City Hall basement
(1 Rue Jules-Joffrin; Métro: Jules-Joffrin;
42.52.42.00). The wine is nothing special, but
the harvest fête, on the first or second
Saturday of October, is not to be missed.
Crowds line Rue Lamarck for a celebration
that feels like a combination of an academic
procession, the Rose Bowl Parade, and
Halloween. Participants might include baton
twirlers, Auvergnat farmers in wooden clogs,
or the mayor's wife picking the first grape.
Note the plaque dedicated to **Poulbot,** the
popular cartoonist who prevented the vineyard
from being sold to high-rise developers in the
1930s. ♦ Rue des Saules (at Rue St.-Vincent).
Métro: Lamarck-Caulaincourt

28 La Maison Rose ★$$ **Utrillo** once painted
a picture of this pink restaurant, and pink it
has stayed—even the cutlery. In the summer
the tables spill onto Rue de l'Abreuvoir, and if
the view doesn't make you dizzy, order
escargots or foie gras with a bottle of
champagne to ensure your head spins.
♦ Lunch and dinner. 2 Rue de l'Abreuvoir
(between Rues Girardon and des Saules).
Métro: Lamarck-Caulaincourt. 42.57.66.75

29 Au Lapin Agile ★$$ The original **Cabaret
des Assassins** was rechristened in 1880 when
André Gill painted a rabbit, complete with a
red bow tie, bounding from a copper kettle.
Lapin à Gill (The Rabbit by Gill) became *Lapin
Agile* (The Nimble Rabbit), and this famous
cabaret turned into a stomping ground for
intellectuals and artists who came for poetry
readings and folk songs. (In 1985 the French
government issued a five-franc stamp of
Utrillo's oil canvas of the cabaret.) A century
later you can still grab a wooden stool, order a
Kir, and sing along to those same old songs,
as updated by pianist **Eric Robrecht.** Don't
miss the 19th-century whimsy in front: a
concrete fence made to look like knotty pine.
♦ Dinner and late-night. Closed Monday. 22
Rue des Saules (at Rue St.-Vincent). No credit
cards. Métro: Lamarck-Caulaincourt.
46.06.85.87

30 St.-Vincent Cemetery Musician **Honegger**
and painters **Steinlen** and **Utrillo** are buried
in Paris' most intellectual cemetery. Enjoy the

ivy-covered walls, a tranquil view of **Sacré-Coeur,** and (if you need to get off your feet) south-facing benches that catch the afternoon sun. The old caretaker is generally helpful but becomes cantankerous between noon and 2PM, when he is emphatically out to lunch. ◆ Daily 8:30AM-6PM, 15 Mar-5 Nov; daily 8:30AM-5:30PM, 6 Nov-14 Mar. At Rue St.-Vincent. Métro: Lamarck-Caulaincourt

31 Au Poulbot Gourmet ★★$$ Innovative **Jean-Paul Langevin** runs a simple, cozy restaurant decorated with early Montmartre photos and original **Poulbot** illustrations. His specialties are *foie gras de canard,* escargots with garlic cream and fresh artichokes, and a two-chocolate charlotte with pistachio sauce. ◆ Lunch and dinner. Closed Sunday. 39 Rue Lamarck (between Rues l'Abbé-Patureau and du Mont-Cenis). Métro: Lamarck-Caulaincourt. 46.06.86.00

32 Musée d'Art Juif If your schedule can coincide with the **Jewish Art Museum's** brief weekly visiting hours, you'll be rewarded by its exhibitions of traditional drawings, crafts, and engravings, and its collection of scale-model synagogues. ◆ Admission. M-Th, Su 3-6PM. Closed Jewish holidays and in August. 42 Rue des Saules (between Rues Caulaincourt and Francoeur). Métro: Lamarck-Caulaincourt. 42.57.84.15

33 24 Rue du Mont-Cenis Composer **Hector Berlioz** lived with his English wife, **Constance Smithson,** in a house on this site from 1834 to 1837. ◆ Between Rues Lamarck and St.-Vincent. Métro: Lamarck-Caulaincourt

34 L'Ermitage Hôtel $$ Those who prefer an elegant yet soothing atmosphere will delight in this small hotel, housed in a three-story 1860 residence. Indeed, being greeted by the warm and smiling **Maggie Canipel** feels like coming home. The 12 breezy rooms contrast with the more somber corridors, and each has been lovingly decorated by Maggie and her husband. Rooms 11 and 12 open onto a bewitching terraced garden full of chirping birds, while other rooms have splendid views of the city. Breakfast, served in each guest's room, is included in the already reasonable price. ◆ 24 Rue Lamarck (between Rues Becquerel and Chevalier-de-la-Barre). Métro: Lamarck-Caulaincourt. No credit cards. 42.64.79.22

35 Beauvilliers ★★★$$$ The restaurant's name is borrowed from **Antoine Beauvilliers,** who was *officier de bouche* to gluttonous **Louis XVIII** and founder of the first restaurant in Paris in 1784, but the restaurant itself has a style all its own. **Edouard Carlier** has created one of the most elegant *salons à manger* in Paris. What was once an old bakery is now three intimate Louis-Philippe-style dining rooms. In one of these hang 18th- and 19th-century engravings of the Montmartre windmills and, in another, a portrait gallery of Beauvilliers' contemporaries painted by **Louis-Léopold Boilly** and the like. The dining rooms are adorned with a profusion of bouquets that are masterpieces themselves. Chef **Michel Deygat** changes the menu weekly. Try the grilled red mullet with pimiento, lamb terrine with thyme, Brittany lobster salad, or duck with passion fruit, and sample the lemon pie in white rum for dessert. Pair the meal with a white St.-Joseph wine and watch the bill climb like Rue Lepic. ◆ Lunch and dinner; dinner only on Monday. Closed Sunday. 52 Rue Lamarck (at Rue l'Abbé-Patureau). Dinner reservations required. Métro: Lamarck-Caulaincourt. 42.54.54.42

36 Le Château des Seigneurs de Clignancourt Along with the **St.-Pierre-de-Montmartre,** this is one of the oldest relics of this district's past. In the original manor house was a famous porcelain manufacturer (founded in 1767) that provided **Louis XVIII** with plates and saucers. Regrettably, the early 16th-century house was demolished in 1861, and all that remains is its renovated turret decorating the corner of a modern restaurant. ◆ Rue du Mont-Cenis (at Rue Marcadet). Métro: Jules-Joffrin

37 City Hall When artist **Maurice Utrillo** died in 1955, he left two paintings to the local *mairie* (town hall), not as Pablo Picasso did in payment of estate taxes, but simply as a gift. You can still see his collection here; ask the *secrétariat générale* on the second floor. (Half-bottles from the **Montmartre Vineyards** are for sale in the basement.) ◆ M-F 9AM-6PM. 1 Place Jules-Joffrin (at Rue du Mont-Cenis). Métro: Jules-Joffrin. 42.52.42.00

38 Rue du Poteau Along this street (where **Utrillo** was born in 1883) lies a charming and lively neighborhood market. From behind a fog of simmering *choucroute,* ruddy-faced women chant *"Chaud, chaud, Mesdames!*

...! Blood
...nds peddle
...eeses. Follow
...row Rue
...erly through the
...cker-basket-toting
...op with the finesse and
...ican football players.
...AM-12:30PM, 4-7:30PM;
Su... ...M. Métro: Jules-Joffrin

38 Pâtisse... ...e Montmartre Try to choose between heavenly cherry tarts and divine *Rose-Maries* (brioches filled with almond cream). ♦ M-Sa 9AM-7:30PM; Su 8AM-7:30PM. 81 Rue du Mont-Cenis (between Place Jules-Joffrin and Rue Lavy). Métro: Jules-Joffrin. 46.06.39.28

39 Fromagerie de Montmartre **Madame Delbey** offers nearly 50 varieties of goat cheese. ♦ Tu-Sa 8:45AM-12:30PM, 4-7:30PM. 9 Rue du Poteau (between Rue Duhesme and Place Jules-Joffrin). Métro: Jules-Joffrin. 46.06.26.03

40 Central Hotel $ Hardly what its name suggests, this clean, often noisy hotel is a 15-minute walk from **Sacré-Coeur.** But the prices border on philanthropic. ♦ 110 Rue Damrémont (between Rues Ordener and Championnet). Métros: Lamarck-Caulaincourt, Jules-Joffrin. 42.64.25.75

41 Le Maquis ★★$$ This little bistro at the base of Avenue Junot offers light prix-fixe lunches of such dishes as pumpkin soup, leek quiche, and *coquilles St.-Jacques.* ♦ Lunch and dinner. Closed Sunday. 69 Rue Caulaincourt (at Square Caulaincourt). Métro: Lamarck-Caulaincourt. 42.59.76.07

42 Clodenis ★★$$ Seasonal produce inspires this charming bistro's menu. Only the freshest ingredients are used for the crab salad *en chiffonnade,* codfish soufflé with garlic, veal sweetbreads, and homemade pasta. Clodenis is less chic than its main competition, Beauvilliers, and that's reflected in the prices (fortunately). ♦ Lunch and dinner; lunch only on Sunday. Closed Monday. 57 Rue Caulaincourt (between Square Caulaincourt and Rue Constance-Pecqueur). Métro: Lamarck-Caulaincourt. 46.06.20.26

CINÉ 13

43 Ciné 13 This is the best little projection room in Paris. In 1983 French filmmaker **Claude Lelouch** built this elegant 130-person screening room beside his Montmartre town house. Ciné 13 now draws cinema glitterati such as French film's tough guy **Jean-Paul Belmondo** and American director **Robert Altman,** who comes to screen the rough cuts of his new movies. While you may never get to see Altman's rushes, for a reasonable $150 an hour ($300 after 7PM), you can rent Ciné 13, which is now run by **Martine Lelouch,**

Claude's sister, and show home movies if you like. No popcorn is permitted, but the theater can arrange catering. ♦ Call ahead for hours and for screening and catering reservations. 1 Ave Junot (at Rue Girardon). Métro: Lamarck-Caulaincourt. 42.54.15.12

L'ASSOMMOIR

44 L'Assommoir ★★★$$ Montmartre's best bistro takes its name from the **Emile Zola** novel. Proprietor **Philipe Larue,** gourmand and art buff, serves his faithful clientele a flaky *feuilleté de Roquefort, tripes à la mode de Caen, terrine de foies de volailles* (which he makes himself), and *fondant au chocolat* (chocolate cake), the recipe of which he will never divulge. An avid and eclectic art collector, Larue enjoys showing off his latest acquisition, be it an African mask in the dining room or a precious 12th-century Buddha he has hidden away. ♦ Lunch and dinner; lunch only on Sunday. Closed Monday, mid-July through mid-August, and two weeks at Christmas. 12 Rue Girardon (between Ave Junot and Rue de l'Abreuvoir). Reservations recommended. Métro: Lamarck-Caulaincourt. 42.64.55.01

45 Square Suzanne-Buisson This unexpected little square (named after a World War II Resistance fighter) was once the backyard of the adjoining **Château des Brouillards** (Castle of Fog), an 18th-century mansion turned dance hall. According to religious lore, **Saint Denis** paused here to rinse his severed head. Today a statue of the forlorn-looking bishop surveys neighborhood elders playing an afternoon game of *pétanque,* Lyonnais-style. The sand bowling alley has stone benches for spectators, and there's no better way to learn about the old Montmartre than eavesdrop on the conversations of these tweed-capped codgers. Admission is free (as is the gossip), and the games gather steam around mid-afternoon. ♦ Ave Junot and Rue Girardon. Daily dawn to dusk. Métro: Lamarck-Caulaincourt

The *International Herald Tribune,* the century-old English-language daily newspaper based in Paris, has a paid circulation of 178,000 and is distributed in about 164 countries. Today, less than half of its readership is American. The paper was founded by James Gordon Bennett, Jr., who ran the *New York Herald* until a scandal sent him fleeing to Paris in 1877 (legend holds that he urinated in his fiancée's fireplace in front of shocked guests at a New Year's Eve party). He controlled the New York paper from France and, in 1887, decided to start a European edition.

Restaurants/Clubs: Red	**Hotels:** Blue
Shops/ ♣Outdoors: Green	**Sights/Culture:** Blac...

Second Floor · Third Floor · Ground Floor · First Floor

46 Maison Tristan Tzara In the 1920s Viennese architect **Adolf Loos,** a pioneer of the Modern movement, was the only designer whose work reflected Dadaism. It is not surprising, then, that his "architecture without qualities" should have appealed to the Romanian Dadaist poet **Tristan Tzara,** who brought Loos to Paris with a commission to build this house. Set into a rising embankment, the five-story building has a rigorously symmetrical facade that is punctured by a huge double-height square terrace. The arrangement is a superb example of the Loos predilection for tensely juxtaposed, unadorned cubic forms. The interior (see diagram above) is just as eccentrically organized. A patchwork of intersecting split-level spaces, typical of Loos' *raumplan* (room plan), provided Tzara with the sort of ironic, theatrical, and vaguely aggressive setting that befitted a Dadaist artist. ♦ 15 Ave Junot (between Villa Leandre and Rue Girardon). Métro: Lamarck-Caulaincourt

Moulin de la Galette

46 Poulbot's House This residence (1879-1946) of Poulbot, the Montmartre illustrator chubby little children with cowlicks. For his cartoon characters frolic across the tile frieze of the house. In homage to the artist, Montmartre residents still call their children *petits poulbots.* (Near Place du Tertre, you will find a sign at the corner of Norvins and Impasse du Tertre that reads: "Drivers go slow. Watch out for the little poulbots.") This local folk hero is also credited with saving **Montmartre Vineyards** and with founding the **Fraternal Association of Wooden Billiard Players,** a faddish Montmartre bar game in which winning is considered immoral (the winner always pays for the drinks). ♦ 13 Ave Junot (between Villa Leandre and Rue Girardon). Métro: Lamarck-Caulaincourt

46 Hameau des Artistes Behind the gate marked *Interdit* (No Trespassing) are footpaths leading to opulent artists' studios ranging from a gray cement castle to a Tuscan villa. The gate to the **Artists' Hamlet** is open during the day; be adventurous but tactful. ♦ 11 Ave Junot (between Villa Leandre and Rue Girardon). Métro: Lamarck-Caulaincourt

47 Rue Lepic Montmartre's meandering old quarry road is the site of an antique-car rally held on the first or second Sunday in October. ♦ Métro: Blanche

47 Moulin de la Galette Painted by **Renoir** and many others, this windmill (and its former dance hall) is the best known of the scores of mills that once crowned Montmartre (see illustration below). In the 19th century the Parisian hoi polloi journeyed

...eir
..e, and eat
..r from the
...te has a grisly
...n the Franco-
...ntmartre was overrun
..diers, they crucified the
..erre-Charles Debray, on
...lin. ♦ 79 Rue Lepic
(b... ..irardon and Caulaincourt).
Métro: ... ..-Caulaincourt

47 Da Graziano ★$$ Federighi Graziano's Tuscan restaurant, crowned with an old windmill, is frequented by the celebrities who visit the Ciné 13 screening room next door. The carpaccio, San Daniele crêpes, homemade pastas, and light chocolate cake come highly recommended. ♦ Lunch and dinner. 83 Rue Lepic (between Rues Girardon and Caulaincourt). Reservations recommended. Métro: Lamarck-Caulaincourt. 46.06.84.77

47 La Petite Galette $ Right across the street from Montmartre's last old windmill, this bistro provides an inexpensive post-theater stop for a steak and *tarte tatin* (apple pie). Other specialties are foie gras, escargots, and nougat glacé with red berry sauce. ♦ Dinner. 86bis Rue Lepic (at Rue Tholozé). Métro: Lamarck-Caulaincourt. 42.52.99.72

47 Villa Léandre Down this unexpected country lane leading off Avenue Junot is a hidden village where the eccentric little houses mirror the idiosyncrasies of the artists who have inhabited them (a ballerina, two successful painters, and a few genuine hermits). It's worth a quick detour. ♦ 25 Ave Junot. Métro: Lamarck-Caulaincourt

48 Résidence Montmartre $$ This recently remodeled hotel is convenient to the Rue Lepic open-air market. ♦ 10 Rue Burq (at Rue Durantin). Métro: Abbesses. 46.06.51.91

49 54 Rue Lepic Vincent van Gogh and his brother **Theo** lived here. ♦ Between Rues Durantin and Joseph-de-Maistre. Métro: Blanche

49 Marché Quatre Saisons Tucked away in this alley of artisans are a woodworker, a marionette maker, and **Goudji,** a Russian jewelry artist who fashions his own tools for the hammer-hollowing technique that is his trademark. Goudji's primeval designs in gold and silver are exhibited in museums around the world. For a small fortune, you can acquire a piece of his jewelry at **Jansen** on Rue Royal or take a less expensive look at his work on display in the **Musée des Arts Décoratifs** on Rue de Rivoli. ♦ 45 Rue Lepic. Métro: Blanche

50 Toulouse-Lautrec's Studio The innovative graphic artist spent his most productive years (1886-1897) at this studio, just a stroll away from his favorite nocturnal haunts. ♦ 21 Rue Caulaincourt (at Rue Tourlaque). Métro: Blanche

51 Terrass Hôtel $$$ Built in 1912, this is the only four-star hotel in Montmartre, with a stellar panorama that takes in the **Opéra, Arc de Triomphe,** and **Eiffel Tower.** Ask to stay on the cemetery side, which in local parlance means a room with a view, unobstructed because you're overlooking the low-rise Montmartre Cemetery. There are plaid carpets, Napoléon III-style wallpaper, and a fireplace in the lobby. ♦ 12-14 Rue Joseph-de-Maistre (at Rue Caulaincourt). Métro: Blanche. 46.06.72.85

52 Cimetière de Montmartre The **Montmartre Cemetery** is a veritable academy of writers, composers, and painters. Among those at eternal rest here are **Zola, Stendhal, Dumas, Offenbach, Degas,** and **Fragonard,** as is **Greuze,** whose eloquent headstone lauds him for having painted "virtue, friendship, beauty, and innocence, thereby breathing soul into his paintings." Another striking memorial is the **Rude** bronze of a reclining **Cavaignac.** And **Hector Berlioz** lies between his first wife, an English actress, and his second wife, an opera singer. ♦ M-F 8AM-5:30PM, 16 Mar-5 Nov; M-F 8AM-5PM, 6 Nov-15 Mar. 20 Ave Rachel. Métro: Blanche. 43.87.64.24

53 Charlot 1er Merveilles des Mers ★$$ Some of the freshest oysters and other wonders of the sea are available at this traditional restaurant near the Moulin Rouge. ♦ Lunch and dinner. Closed Monday. 128bis Blvd de Clichy (at Rue de Dovai). Métro: Place-de-Clichy. 45.22.47.08

54 Grandgousier ★$$ Diners get an inspired menu and a warm reception amidst the muted pastoral decor of this elegant restaurant. Don't miss the terrine of leg of lamb with foie gras, quail and foie gras salad, the *panaché* of meats, or any of the luscious desserts, such as nougat ice cream. ♦ Lunch and dinner; dinner only on Saturday. Closed Sunday and two weeks in August. 17 Ave Rachel (between Blvd de Clichy and Rue Caulaincourt). Métro: Blanche. 43.87.66.12

55 Moulin Rouge Founded in 1889 (the year the Eiffel Tower was built) and still kicking after all these years, this legendary temple of the risqué proffers all the bare-breasted women, ostrich plumes, rhinestones, and multicolored lights the stage can support. The show recalls the days of the famous cancan dancers: **Jane Avril, Yvette Guilbert, Valentin le Désossé,** and **La Goulue,** who were limned by **Toulouse-Lautrec.** Not long ago, animal-welfare representatives stopped a Moulin number in which a performing dolphin was stealing the show. Dinner is rather expensive and nothing to write home about. ♦ Dinner: daily 8PM. Show: daily 10PM, midnight. 82 Blvd de Clichy (between Rue Lepic and Cité Véron). Métro: Blanche. 46.06.00.19

55 Cité Véron To the left of the Moulin Rouge is this intriguing passageway where the widows of French writers **Jacques Prévert** and **Boris**

Vian have made their homes. Along the alley you will also find a voodoo club; the highbrow **Théâtre Ouvert;** the **Boris Vian Foundation,** which is housed in an old hunting lodge and offers exhibitions, dance, and theater classes; and a cluttered warehouse called **Ophir Paris.** This boutique camouflages a back-room treasure trove with racks of cheap Indian imports. Unfortunately, much of the best stuff (19th-century wooden carousel figures, Moulin Rouge stage props, and Balinese shadow puppets) collected by the owners **Jacqueline** and **André Marcovici** is not for sale. ♦ Ophir Paris: M-Th 9AM-noon, 3-5:30PM; F 9AM-noon, 3-4:30PM. Cité Véron (off Blvd de Clichy). Métro: Blanche. 42.64.58.40, 42.64.42.96

56 **La Poste** ★★$$ Once the residence of illustrator **Gustave Doré** and **Georges Bizet,** composer of *Carmen,* this cavernous *hôtel particulier* (mansion) was turned into a post office after World War II. Restored to its former artistic splendor, La Poste boasts frescoes, colonnades, and caryatids to rival the old Opéra Garnier. **Georges Vernotte,** formerly the chef at **Beauvilliers,** offers seafood specialties such as scallops with lime, New England clam chowder *à la française,* and salmon stuffed with roe. This is gracious, trendy dining at its best, and there's even a piano bar downstairs. ♦ Dinner. 34 Rue Duperré (at Rues Fontaine and Fromentin). Reservations recommended. Métro: Pigalle. 42.80.66.16

57 **A l'Annexe** ★$$ This lively bistro is only a quick stroll from the glitter of Pigalle. Try the hearty *raie* (skate) *au beurre noir.* ♦ Lunch and dinner. Closed Saturday, Sunday, and in August. 15 Rue Chaptal (at Rue Henner). Métro: St.-Georges. 48.74.65.52

58 **Place-de-Clichy** Stop by the *académie de billiard* (pool hall), a converted 1900 stable, and then wander down Rue d'Amsterdam, past carpet shops, used-furniture stores, and homeopathic pharmacies. ♦ At Ave de Clichy. Métro: Place-de-Clichy

59 **Charlot, Le Roi des Coquillages** ★$$$ If you happen to be in Montmartre during an "R" month (the months spelled with the letter R—September through April—denote prime shellfish season), stop here for a no-nonsense lunch of mussels, clams, oysters, and baby shrimp. ♦ Lunch, dinner, and late-night. 12 Place-de-Clichy (at Rue de Dova). Métro: Place-de-Clichy. 48.74.49.64

59 **Guyot** One of Paris' last pipe artisans, **Monsieur Guyot** works out of the old dance hall where **Mistinguett** made her debut. Selling meticulously crafted brier pipes, he also restores meerschaums. Flatter him by asking about his extraordinary personal pipe collection. ♦ Tu-Sa 10AM-7PM. Closed in August and for 10 days at Easter. 7 Ave de Clichy (off Place-de-Clichy). Métro: Place-de-Clichy. 43.87.70.88

60 **Androuet** This salon has been in business since 1909 and sells 30,000 pounds of cheese every month. The original rustic decor was recently refreshed. Connoisseurs of ripened curds should settle in the accompanying restaurant and order the *dégustation du fromage* (samples of 120 cheeses), accompanied by a salad and a hearty Bordeaux. ♦ Tu-Sa 10AM-7PM. Closed holidays. 41 Rue d'Amsterdam (between Rues de Liège and de Londres). Métro: Place-de-Clichy. 48.74.26.90 (store), 48.74.26.93 (restaurant)

Bests

V. Pimentel
Painter/Artist

I like to walk along the **Pont Alexandre III** at night, to watch the fog on the **Pont Marie** in winter, and to stroll on the **Ile St.-Louis,** just along the edge of the Seine. I like **Montmartre** and all its history, the **Butte aux Cailles** in the 13th arrondissement, the charm of the **Marais,** the shouting heard at the **Aligre Market,** the **Louvre** and the **Musée de l'Homme.** I like breathing amidst the nature of the **Bois de Vincennes** and to collect my thoughts in the church of **St.-Julien-le-Pauvre.**

Veronique Lopez
Owner, Agence Veronique Lopez

Galerie Vivienne—enter by 4 Rue des Petits-Champs. I fell in love with this place and chose it for my office more than 10 years ago. I relaunched the arcade by introducing new shops and a tearoom.

Palais Royal—the new **Mark Rudkin English garden,** the shops under the arcades.

Le Grand Colbert—restaurant at the Galerie Vivienne arcade.

Mariane Robic—wonderful flowers.

Brentano's—all English books and travel guides.

Ever wonder what happened to the guillotined bodies during the Reign of Terror? In some cases, their skin was used to bind books. One poor soul's flesh ended up as the cover of a two-by-three-inch Christian prayer book that's part of the rare book collection at the University of California at Berkeley. Inside the book's cover is the following inscription: "During the French Revolution, there were tanneries devoted to curing the skins of the victims of the guillotine. The fine grain made these skins particularly suitable for binding books. Although the centuries have removed the macabre or even horrible implications, it remains a curious evidence of gross insensitivity that human skin should have been employed on a religious book. Or was it, perhaps, a grim jest of the overwhelming anticlerical movement of the period?"

Additional Highlights

There are some wonderful spots in Paris that are off the beaten path of the itineraries in this book. This section features Paris' other major highlights, which include something for everyone: the majestic **Eiffel Tower**, eerie catacombs, famous parks such as **Monceau** and the **Bois de Vincennes**, as well as the high-tech **La Villette** science museum and the fascinating **Musée de la Contrefaçon** (Museum of Forgeries).

Blvd. Périphérique

Porte de
Clignancourt · Blvd. Ney · Porte de
la Chapelle

Blvd. Ornano

e Ordener

Rue Custine

Place
du Terte
Sacré-
Coeur

Blvd. de Clichy

Blvd. Barbès

Blvd. de la Chapelle

Rue Marx
Dormoy

Rue de la Chapelle

Rue Riquet

Gare du
Nord

Rue du Faubourg St.-Denis

Rue du Faubourg St.-Martin

Rue de Flandre

Porte de
la Chapelle

Blvd. Macdonald
Porte
d'Aubervilliers

Ave. Jean Jaurès

15

Porte de
la Villette

Blvd. Macdonald

Rue de Crimée

Ave. Jean Lolive

Porte de
Pantin

Rue du Général
Brunet

Blvd. Sérurier

Rue Châteaudun

e de
Châteaudun

Rue La Fayette

Gare de
l'Est

Rue d'Hauteville

Rue de Strasbourg

Blvd. de Magenta

16

Blvd. de Strasbourg

Blvd. St.-Martin

vd. Montmartre

Ave. Claude
Vellefaux

Blvd. de la Villette

Rue Marin

14
Parc des
Buttes-
Chaumont

Ave. Simon Bolivar

Rue de Belleville

Rue des Pyrénées

Porte
des Lilas

Ave. Gambetta

Blvd. Mortier

Bibliothèque
Nationale

Rue Réaumur

Rue du Faubourg du Temple

Blvd. de Belleville

Ave. Parmentier

13

Ave. Gambetta

Rue Belgrand

e des Petits Champs
Palais
Royal

Rue de Turbigo

Blvd. du Temple

Ave. de la République

Blvd. de Ménilmontant

12
Cimetière
Père-Lachaise

Rue du Louvre

Les Halles
Garden

Blvd. de Sébastopol

Rue Beaubourg

Archives
Nationales

Rue Rambuteau

Rue du Temple

Blvd. Beaumarchais

Blvd. Richard Lenoir

Rue du Chemin Vert

Blvd. Voltaire

Blvd. Davout

Pont
Neuf

Tour
St.-Jacques

Rue St.-Antoine

Picasso
Museum

Place des
Vosges

Palais de
Justice

Ste.-
Chapelle

Notre-
Dame

Place de
la Bastille

Rue St.-Antoine

Ave. Philippe
Auguste

Rue d'Avron

Rue des Pyrénées

Blvd. Périphérique

vd. St.-Germain
La
Sorbonne

Rue Monge

Rue Henri IV

Blvd. Bourdon

Blvd. de la Bastille

Ave. Ledru Rollin

Place de
la Nation

Cours de
Vincennes

Blvd. Soult

ais du
xembourg

Panthéon

Ave. Daumesnil

Blvd. Diderot

Rue de Charenton

Ave. de
St.-Mandé

Rue de Picpus

Ave. du Dr. A. Netter

St.-J.-
Lussac

Rue Gay-

Rue Mouffetard

Jardin
de Paris

Quai St.-Bernard

Quai de la Rapée

Gare de
Lyon

Ave. de
St.-Mandé

Ave. M. Bizot

Rue Claude
Bernard

Ave. des Gobelins

Blvd. St.-Marcel

Gare
d'Austerlitz

Blvd. de Bercy

Blvd. de Reuilly

Blvd. Soult

de Port Royal

Observatoire
e Paris
vd. Arago

Blvd. de l'Hôpital

Quai de la Gare

11
Velodrome
D'Hiver

Ave. du
Gen. M. Bizot

Porte
Dorée

d. St.-Jacques

Place
d'Italie

Rue Bobillot

Blvd. Vincent Auriol

Seine

Blvd. Poniatowski

Bois de
Vincennes

10

ntre
spitalier
-Anne

e d'Alésia

Rue de Tolbiac

Rue de Paris

rc
ntsouris

Blvd.
Kellermann

Ave. d'Italie

Ave. de Choisy

Ave. d'Ivry

Blvd. Masséna

Porte
d'Ivry

Blvd. Périphérique

Quai des Carrières

9

Porte
d'Italie

é
iversitaire

1 Tour Eiffel In 1889, the world was drunk on science. The decade had produced one technological marvel after another: the automobile, the telephone, the electric light, and the **Eiffel Tower.** First dubbed a monstrosity, then considered the definitive symbol of Paris, the tower was built to commemorate the centennial of the storming of the Bastille and to stand as the centerpiece of the 1889 International Exhibition of Paris. The now-classic design by **Gustave Eiffel** beat 700 other entries in the design competition. (Among the losers, for obvious reasons, were a giant guillotine and a mammoth lighthouse.) The tower was the tallest structure in the world until 1930, when the title was usurped by the Chrysler Building in New York. Eiffel, who also engineered the iron bones of the Statue of Liberty (undergirding the **Frédéric Bartholdi** copper structure), was himself a diminutive man, only five feet tall.

Spanning 2.5 acres at its base, the tower is made of 15,000 metal parts held together with 2.5 million rivets and covered with 40 tons of paint. A thousand feet high (more than three times the height of the Statue of Liberty), it weighs 7,000 tons and sways no more than 4.5 inches in strong winds. The weight is distributed so elegantly that it exerts no more pressure on the ground per centimeter than does a person seated in a four-legged chair.

When the Eiffel Tower was first completed, much of Paris was unimpressed. Its stark, geometric structure offended the prevailing beaux-arts sensibility. Prominent critics, including luminaries such as **Paul Verlaine, Guy de Maupassant,** the younger **Dumas,** and **Emile Zola,** denounced it as the Tower of Babel and a dishonor to Paris. Maupassant used to say he liked to have lunch here because it was the only place in Paris where he didn't have to look at it.

In later years it was discovered the tower could function as the world's largest antenna, and during World War I it became one of France's most vital weapons. Since then, it has served as a radio and meteorological post, and

in 1985, was fitted with broadcasting equipment for France's fifth television channel.

Despite these eminently utilitarian applications, the Eiffel Tower's primary effect is to incite the imagination. One man tried to fly from it and was killed when his wings failed him. In 1923 a bicycle-riding journalist careened down the steps to the ground from the top floor. A mountaineer scaled it in 1954, and in 1984 two Englishmen parachuted from it.

In 1980, a nine-year renovation program began, which brought great changes to the tower. About 1,500 tons of extraneous concrete (mostly in the form of concession areas) were removed from the first platform; four new electronic glass elevators and new visitors facilities were installed; and the pavilion housing the tower's restaurant, the **Jules Verne** (★★★$$$), was remodeled. Most dramatic of all, however, is the 292,000-watt interior lighting system inaugurated on New Year's Eve 1986, replacing the old floodlights. The new lights illuminate the entire structure from within, creating a golden tracery against the sky at night. The renovation program was completed in time for the tower's hundredth birthday on the bicentennial of the French Revolution in 1989. ♦ Admission varies for each level. Daily 9:30AM–11PM. Jules Verne restaurant: lunch and dinner. Ave Gustave Eiffel. Métros: Bir-Hakeim, Champ-de-Mars. 45.55.91.11, 45.55.61.44

1 Parc du Champ-de-Mars Named for the god of war, this large rectangular park stretching from the Ecole Militaire to the Eiffel Tower has long been a site of battles, both actual and prospective. Here, in 52 BC, Roman legions defeated the Parisii; in 886 the Parisians beat back the invading Vikings; and, in the early 18th century, when the Champ-de-Mars served as the parade ground for the Ecole Militaire, **Napoléon** drilled with his fellow cadets here.

Now the flowering trees, shrubs, and miniature cascades adorn the site of pony rides, marionette theaters, organ-grinders, occasional parades for children, and fairs and reindeer at Christmastime. You can do most anything in the Champ-de-Mars except have a picnic on the lawns. French grass is sacred grass, and a bluecoat (guard) will appear and order you off before you've even had time to unwrap your salami and uncork the Bordeaux. ♦ Between Aves de Suffren and de la Bourdonnais. Métros: Bir-Hakeim, Champ-de-Mars, Ecole-Militaire

A special Eiffel Tower five-franc coin was designed and issued for the centennial. On one side of the coin is artist Frédéric Joubert's rendering of the Eiffel Tower; on the opposite side is designer Joaquim Jiminez's bird's-eye view of the tower.

2 Ecole Militaire In an attempt to rival the Hôtel des Invalides of **Louis XIV, Louis XV** and his mistress, **Madame de Pompadour,** hired **Jacques-Anges Gabriel,** the architect who created Place de la Concorde in the 1770s, to design a military school (pictured above). Unfortunately, money was a problem. It was the inspiration of **Beaumarchais,** who wrote *The Marriage of Figaro* and gave harp lessons to Louis XV's daughters, to pay for the building by authorizing a lottery and a tax on playing cards.

Standing at the culmination of the Champ-de-Mars, the Ecole Militaire, with its Corinthian columns, statues, dome, double colonnade, and elegant wrought-iron fence, is considered to be one of Gabriel's masterpieces. Its most famous cadet was **Napoléon Bonaparte.** ♦ Open by appointment only. For more information, write to: Général Direction, Ecole Militaire, 1 Place Joffre, 75007 Paris. Ave de la Motte-Piquet (between Aves de Suffren and Duquesne). Métro: Ecole-Militaire. No phone

3 UNESCO Secretariat This building was designed by architects from three member countries: **Bernard Zehrfuss** of France, **Luigi Nervi** of Italy, and **Marcel Breuer** of the U.S. When it was built in the late 1950s, the headquarters of the United Nations Educational, Scientific, and Cultural Organization was a hopeful symbol of a new era of international cooperation.

The complex, however, is better known for the works of art it contains than for its architecture or politics. UNESCO headquarters possesses a black metal **Calder** mobile; **Henry Moore's** *Reclining Figure;* two ceramic walls executed by **Artigas** after designs by **Miró;** sculpture by **Giacometti;** and a mural by **Picasso,** appropriately titled *The Victory of the Forces of Light and Peace over the Powers of Evil and Death.*

Casually visiting UNESCO is somewhat difficult. The security is tight; you'd do best to organize or join a group tour, and, even then, bring your passport. ♦ M-F 9AM-6PM. 7 Place de Fontenoy (between Aves de Lowendal and de Saxe). Métro: Ségur. 45.68.10.00, 45.68.03.71 (group tours by appointment)

4 Sewers The *égouts* (sewers) of Paris are always a popular underground attraction. This 1,305-mile network of tunnels was constructed during the reign of **Napoléon III** and is considered one of **Baron Haussmann's** finest achievements. If laid end to end, the tunnels would reach from Paris to Istanbul. The sewers house freshwater pipes, telephone wires, traffic-light cables, and the city's pneumatic postal network, which was shut down in 1984. The hour-long sewer tour includes a film, a photograph exhibition, and a walk through the 18-foot-high by 14-foot-wide tunnels. Ever since a notorious bank heist in which the robbers made their getaway via the sewers, underground boat cruises have not been permitted. ♦ Admission. W-Sa 11AM-5PM May-Sept; W-Sa 11AM-4PM Oct-Apr. Quai d'Orsay (at Pont de l'Alma). Métro: Pont-de-l'Alma. 47.05.10.29

5 Petrossian Parisians have flocked here since 1924 for caviar, smoked salmon, and foie gras. Sit down to savor a light meal and a glass of champagne in an elegant atmosphere. ♦ Tu-Sa 10AM-7PM. 18 Blvd de La Tour-Maubourg (between Quai d'Orsay and Rue de l'Université). Métro: La Tour-Maubourg. 45.51.59.73

5 Michel Chaudun Once chief *chocolatier* at Maison du Chocolat, Chaudun now turns out his own bonbons; particularly dangerous is the diamond-shaped mint truffle. ♦ Tu-Sa 9:30AM-7:30PM. 149 Rue de l'Université (at Rue Malar). Métro: La Tour-Maubourg. 47.53.74.40

6 Hôtel des Invalides This monumental group of buildings was erected by **Libéral Bruant** on the orders of **Louis XIV** to house the king's old soldiers, many of them invalids who had been reduced to begging or seeking shelter in monasteries. When the *hôtel* (pictured above) was completed in 1676, 6,000 aging pensioners moved in. It is still used as a home for old soldiers, though only a dozen or so still live here. The year after completion, the "Sun King" (Louis XIV's nickname derived from his brilliance and his fondness for gold) commissioned a second church for the complex, which was built by

Restaurants/Clubs: Red   Hotels: Blue
Shops/ 🌳 Outdoors: Green   **Sights/Culture:** Black

Jules Hardouin-Mansart. Attached Siamese-twin-style to Bruant's original church (**St.-Louis-des-Invalides**), the **Dome Church** is one of the most magnificent baroque churches of the *grand siècle*. Its dome is decorated with garlands and crowned with a 351-foot-tall spire.

France's bravest soldiers and greatest warriors are entombed in the Dome Church: **Turenne, Vauban, Duroc, Foch,** and, of course, **Napoléon.** "I do not think that there is a more impressive sepulchre on earth than that tomb; it is grandly simple," wrote **Theodore Roosevelt** of Napoléon's resting place. "I am not easily awestruck, but it certainly gave me a solemn feeling to look at the plain, red stone bier which contained what had once been the mightiest conqueror the world ever saw.*"*

Concealed by the outward simplicity of red porphyry, Napoléon's remains are contained in seven coffins, one inside the other, made of iron, mahogany, lead, ebony, oak, and marble. Napoléon was originally interred on the island of St. Helena, where he died in 1821. The British finally agreed to repatriate his remains in 1840, thus fulfilling the emperor's wish to be buried "on the banks of the Seine among the people of France whom I have loved so much."

The tomb of Napoléon's son, the emperor of Rome, who died in Vienna at age 21, sounds a morbid footnote to history. In 1940 his remains were given to Paris in a grandiose gesture by a heady **Hitler.**

Bruant's church, St.-Louis-des-Invalides, where the occupants of the *hôtel* worshiped, is separated by a glass barrier from the domed edifice. You enter from **Cour d'Honneur.** The church's most impressive feature, perhaps, is the collection of captured banners hanging from the upper galleries. Among these tattered mementos of French military victories there is even the flag with the rising sun of Japan, a relic of World War II. In 1837 **Berlioz'** *Requiem* was performed here for the first time.

Cour d'Honneur, an impressive courtyard also designed by Bruant, is where French army officer **Alfred Dreyfus** was publicly disgraced and where **de Gaulle** kissed **Churchill.** The statue of **Napoléon** by **Seurre,** which used to be on the top of a column in Place Vendôme, now stands in this courtyard. Among the other Napoléonic memorabilia exhibited in Les Invalides: the emperor's death mask, his dinner jacket, and the dog that was his companion during his years on the island of Elba, stuffed for posterity. ♦ Admission. Daily 10AM-5PM (6PM in summer). Place des Invalides (between Blvds de La Tour-Maubourg and des Invalides). Métros: La Tour-Maubourg, Varenne. 44.42.37.38, 44.42.30.11

6 Musée de l'Armée At the north end of the Invalides complex, the **Army Museum** houses one of the largest collections of military paraphernalia in the world. Swords, guns, armor, flags, and other articles are on display, along with innumerable models, maps, and images that trace the evolution of warfare from prehistoric times until World War II. Understandably, Napoléonic souvenirs are most conspicuous, but there are also intriguing exhibitions of medieval, Renaissance, and Oriental militaria. ♦ Admission. Daily 10AM-6PM Apr-Sept; daily 10AM-5PM Oct-Mar. Métros: La Tour-Maubourg, Varenne. 44.42.37.70, 44.42.37.72

7 Catacombs The catacombs began as a network of quarries extending for miles beneath Paris. In 1785, several million skeletons were transported from the overcrowded **Innocents Cemetery** near Les Halles to the catacombs. Here the skulls, femurs, and tibias were stacked in a neat but rather macabre fashion. Carved near the entrance is an ominous medieval sign: "Stop. Beyond Here Is the Empire of Death." Apparently the warning deterred the occupying Nazis, because they never did discover that the secret headquarters of the French Resistance was literally under their feet. The dark reaches of the catacombs then housed radios capable of reaching London, as well as a telephone switching system handling Resistance communications for hundreds of miles around.

If you tour the catacombs, take along a flashlight and a sweater, and be sure to stay close to the group. In 1793 a Parisian took a wrong turn from his own wine cellar, wandered into the catacomb tunnels, got lost and was not discovered until nine years later, by which time the poor fellow was quite mummified. ♦ Admission. Tu-F 2-4PM; Sa-S 9-11AM, 2-4PM. 1 Place Denfert-Rochereau (at Ave du Général-Leclerc). Métro: Denfert-Rochereau. 43.22.47.63

8 Parc Montsouris Prior to the 19th century **Montsouris Park** was an abandoned granite quarry stubbled with windmills. At the turn of the century the 50-acre Montsouris was a refuge for the artists and literati of nearby Montparnasse; when **Hemingway** fled the bustling Latin Quarter, he often came here. Today, joggers run the park's half-mile perimeter, matrons feed the swans, and military brass bands play **Sousa** marches in the band shell. Not to be missed are the *puré de guacamole* and *soupe de fruits rouge* at **Le Jardin de la Paresse** (Garden of Idleness ★★$$), a Belle Epoque glass-and-iron restaurant whose outdoor terrace has accommodated a great many customers, including **Leon Trotsky** and **Jean-Paul Sartre.** ♦ Daily dawn to dusk. Le Jardin de la Paresse: Lunch, afternoon tea, and dinner. 20 Rue Gazan (between Ave Reille and Blvd Jourdan). Métro: Cité Universitaire. 45.88.38.52

9 Musée de Pain The eccentric little **Bread Museum** on the edge of Paris is certain to delight the inveterate traveler who does not hear the call of the Louvre or feel the pull of the Pompidou Center. The museum was founded by **Jacques Lorch**, who, like his father before him, has spent his life as a miller in the service of the Parisian bakeries. In a small building that was once a dairy, Lorch has used his personal fortune to amass a collection on the art of baking as eclectic as it is passionate. You will find bread from every corner of the world; bread excavated from Egyptian tombs (2,400 BC); a display of erotic postcards whose theme is the seduction of the baker's wife; a letter from **Marie Antoinette** to her personal baker, **le Paneterie;** an exhibition of the origins of the croissant (evidence from the Byzantine Empire, seventh century); and, perhaps the most moving historical document in the collection, a Revolutionary order from the infamous minister of police **Joseph Fouché** decreeing that henceforth bakers must bake the same bread for the rich as for the poor: the French must eat the "bread of equality." ♦ Tu, Th 2-4PM. Closed July-Aug. 25bis Rue Victor-de-Hugo (between Rue de Paris and Quai des Carrières) in Charenton-le-Pont. Métro: Charenton-Ecoles. 43.68.43.60

10 Bois de Vincennes Only slightly smaller than the Bois de Boulogne to the west, the Bois de Vincennes acts as the second principal recreation area for the City of Paris. Like the Bois de Boulogne, Vincennes was a former royal hunting ground and was given to the city by **Napoléon III** in 1860. The major attraction of the park is its **Château de Vincennes**, a stern medieval fortress that has served variously as a royal residence, prison, porcelain factory, and arsenal. The *bois* (woods) that extends to the south of the château contains the **Floral Garden; Daumesnil Lake;** the **Buddhist Center,** which houses the largest Buddha sculpture in Europe; and the **Zoological Park.** ♦ Floral Garden: daily 9:30AM-5PM. Château: daily 10AM-7PM. Zoological Park: daily 10AM-5:15PM. Métros: Château-de-Vincennes, Vincennes (RER). 43.73.60.49

A recent survey revealed that more than half of the residents of Paris, given the opportunity, would live elsewhere. Reasons cited: property prices, cost of living, pollution, noise, and traffic jams. And when asked to describe the principal personality traits of Parisians, 91 percent said stressed and nervous.

11 American Center Founded by the American community in Paris in the 1930s, this unique institution was housed in a building on the Boulevard Raspail until recently, when the City of Paris invited the center to build a new headquarters at **Bercy Park** as part of the east side development that includes the **Bastille Opèra,** the **Palais Omnisports,** the **Ministère des Finances,** and the **Bibliothèque de France** across the river. The largest American cultural institution on foreign soil, it exists to foster understanding between Americans and Europeans in Paris through art and education.

The building is a prize-winning design by bad-boy American architect **Frank Gehry,** who conceived it as a relaxed, welcoming, accessible meeting place that would express the spirit of the United States and at the same time respect the center's European context. These goals are spatially achieved through innumerable conversation points throughout the building, gently curved surfaces, and natural lighting at dramatic angles. Respect for the Parisian surroundings is expressed in the stone-clad facade, an atypical material for Gehry, who further acknowledges the urban condition by having the center face the street and follow existing building lines. On the park side he allows the structure to display more exuberance, giving free rein to his characteristic fragmentation and juxtaposition of shapes.

The American Center's many facilities showcase artistic work in virtually all fields, including dance, theater, music, visual arts, electronic art, cinema, and literature. There are classes in languages and arts, as well as a student advisory service for temporary housing and jobs. The complex houses a travel agency, a restaurant, and a bookstore selling English and French titles. ♦ Call for hours and activities. 51 Rue de Bercy (between Blvd de Bercy and Rue de Dijon). Métro: Bercy. 44.73.77.77

12 Cimetière Père-Lachaise This famous graveyard named after **Louis XIV's** confessor, **Father La Chaise,** and designed by **Brongniart,** is the largest and most elite cemetery in Paris. Here lie the remains of France's most famous lovers, **Abélard** and **Héloïse,** in company with **Molière, Balzac,** and the painters **Corot, Daumier, Pissarro, David, Seurat,** and **Modigliani.** Also buried here are the 19th-century photographer **Nadar;** the city-shaping **Baron Haussmann; Jane Avril** and **Yvette Guilbert,** two cancan dancers who modeled for **Toulouse-Lautrec; Fulgence Bienvenue,** who built the Paris métro; and **Ferdinand de Lesseps,** who designed the Suez Canal.

In remembrance of things past, a single red rose may grace the black marble slab marking **Marcel Proust's** grave, and singer

Edith Piaf's unremarkable resting place is always surrounded with flowers. Music lovers might also search out **Callas, Bizet,** or **Poulenc. Chopin's** body is buried here (his heart is interred in Warsaw), as are the remains of **Eugène Delacroix, Prosper Mérimée,** and **Alfred de Musset,** who, like Chopin, loved **George Sand,** a great luminary of women's literature. Literati flock to **Oscar Wilde's** tomb, a stylish sphinx sculpted by **Sir Jacob Epstein** in 1909, and leftists make the pilgrimage to the grave of **Laura Marx,** daughter of **Karl. Sarah Bernhardt, Gertrude Stein,** and **Alice B. Toklas** lie here, as well as **Jim Morrison,** the Doors' singer who died of a drug overdose in 1971.

This lush 108-acre sanctuary in eastern Paris is a museum of French history, but it's also as much a park as a cemetery. Not only do some 400 cats live here, but Parisians by the hundreds come to Père-Lachaise to picnic, harvest escargots off the tombs, or neck on the benches. Chopin's tomb is used for posting love letters, and legend holds that women who kiss or rub the statue of **Victor Noir** will marry within a year. If you're lucky you may encounter **Vincent de Langlade,** a bearded elf of a man who has spent his life studying and explaining the elegies and enigmas of Père-Lachaise. Langlade is the author of a dozen books on the necropolis. If you can't find him, make do with a detailed map available at the cemetery's entrance and begin the celebrity search. ♦ M-F 7:30AM-6PM, Sa-Su 9AM-6PM, 16 Mar-5 Nov; M-F 8AM-5:30PM, Sa-Su 9AM-5:30PM, 6 Nov-15 Mar. Blvd de Ménilmontant (at Ave Gambetta). Métro: Père-Lachaise.

13 Musée Edith Piaf In a tiny museum filling two rooms of a private apartment near her grave in the Père-Lachaise Cemetery, the most renowned French chanteuse lives on through the adoration of her fans, who come to look at her dressing gown, shoes, the portraits of her star-crossed lovers, autographed letters, birth certificate, and photographs. Recordings of the "little sparrow" of Paris play softly in the background and the museum's devoted curator is ever present to recount the final days of the great entertainer's life. ♦ M-Th 1-6PM by appointment only. 5 Rue Crespin-du-Gast (between Rues de Ménilmontant and Oberkampf). Métro: Ménilmontant. 43.55.52.72

14 Parc des Buttes-Chaumont If you're tired of the crowds in the Luxembourg Gardens (the Central Park of Paris) and need a break from the deadly symmetry of the Tuileries, do as the French do. Buy a baguette, some ripe Brie, and a hearty Bordeaux, and head for a taste of urban wilderness in this unusual park in the northern end of Paris.

The park was built in 1867 by **Baron Haussmann,** who also laid out the sewers and the city's grand boulevards for **Napoléon III.**

Before Haussmann, Buttes-Chaumont was a city dump. In what must count as the most inspired use of landfill in French history, a then-new material—concrete—was used to form cliffs, ravines, rivers, and an artificial lake. The grotto and waterfall were restored and reopened several years ago after having been closed since World War II because of deterioration.

Buttes-Chaumont's island is capped with a classical colonnaded temple and commands one of the city's most striking views of Montmartre and Sacré-Coeur. Travelers not inclined to mountaineering may prefer sipping a *citron pressé* on the terrace of the **Pavillon du Lac,** which serves tea and light lunches and is located on the park's west side. ♦ Daily 9AM-5PM in winter, 9AM-9:30PM in summer. Rue Botzaris (bound by Rues de Crimée and Manin and Ave Simon-Bolivar). Métro: Buttes-Chaumont

15 Porte de la Villette The old slaughterhouse district, a 75-acre site in northeastern Paris that had been the last undeveloped space in the city, was transformed into a huge complex of buildings and parks devoted to science and technology. The design is united by a series of bright-red *Follies,* whimsical structures designed by architect **Bernard Tschumi** that are uniformly plotted on a grid and serve a variety of functions.

La Villette's centerpiece is the **Cité des Sciences et de l'Industrie,** an 880-foot-long $600 million research and exhibition building designed by French architect **Adrien Fainsilber.** The gray granite, glass, and dark steel Cité des Sciences (pictured above) was built around the shell of an enormous 19th-century slaughterhouse, whose lack of central pillars created the 1.5 million square feet of usable space. The exhibitions are organized around general themes such as the earth and space, matter and physics, language and communication, and life on earth. Many of these shows are multilingual and invite public participation. The most popular attraction is **La Géode,** a polished-steel sphere 117 feet in diameter that houses a movie theater where films are projected 180 degrees above and around the audience. **La Mediathèque** houses a thousand videodiscs, 150,000 books, and a conference center for a thousand people.

◆ Hours and admission for exhibitions vary. Cité des Sciences: Tu-Su 10AM-6PM. 211 Ave Jean-Jaurès. District bounded by Ave Jean-Jaurès, Blvds Sérurier and Macdonald, and Canal St.-Denis. Métro: Porte-de-Pantin. 40.03.75.00

16 Rue de Paradis This shabby little street is the domain of the finest French and European tableware outlets. Nearly 50 shops selling porcelain, silver, earthenware, crystal, and glass are crowded along its three blocks. All the most elegant brands of tableware may be found here (Limoges, Lalique, Christofle, Têtard, Meissen, Rosenthal, Baccarat, and Villeroy and Boch) and often at prices 30 to 50 percent lower than in the U.S. The **Musée du Cristal** of Baccarat displays decanters and glasses of its famous crystal. Some of the pieces on display here were used by heads of state ranging from the **Queen of Siam** to **King Louis Philippe.** Also on view are the Baccarat glasses commissioned for **Henry Ford II's** yacht and **Franklin Roosevelt's** White House in 1936. The most dazzling exhibitions, perhaps, are the two one-ton 79-light candelabras ordered by Russian czar **Nicholas II** for his St. Petersburg palace. ◆ Musée du Cristal: M-F 9AM-5:30PM; Sa 10AM-noon, 2-5PM. 30bis Rue de Paradis (between Rues d'Hauteville and du Faubourg-St.-Denis). Métro: Château-d'Eau. 47.70.64.30

16 Musée de l'Affiche et da la Publicité The **Poster and Advertising Museum** displays more than 40,000 posters from the 18th century to the present in a building that provides a superb vision of Paris during La Belle Epoque. This glass-roof building was the headquarters of the ceramic-tile company that at the turn of the century provided 100,000 square meters of decoration for the first métro stations. The walls are covered with large ceramic murals whose diverse styles served as advertisements to prospective customers. The museum, open since 1978, offers beautiful temporary exhibitions and has a large, reasonably priced selection of posters. ◆ Admission. M, W-Su noon-6PM. Closed mid-July to mid-Sept. 18 Rue de Paradis (between Rues d'Hauteville and du Faubourg-St.-Denis). Métro: Château-d'Eau. 42.60.26.60

17 Parc Monceau The eccentric character of this small park dates back to 1778, when **Philippe-Egalité,** the Duke of Orléans, commissioned the painter **Carmontel** to design a private garden on the Monceau Plain, then outside the city limits. Carmontel indulged the duke by creating a whimsical landscape full of architectural follies: a pyramid, a pagoda, a Roman temple, windmills, and artfully placed ruins. The park changed hands a few times after the Revolution, but its picturesque qualities (after the English tradition) were completed as we see them today in 1862 by **Alphand, Baron** Haussmann's engineer. Of particular interest are the **Naumachie,** an oval basin with a colonnade said to have come from the unfinished mausoleum of **Henri II** at St.-Denis, and the round **Pavillon de Chartres,** one of four extant *barrières* (tollhouses) built by **Claude-Nicholas Ledoux** along the old city wall in 1784. ◆ Along Blvd de Courcelles. Métro: Monceau

17 Musée Cernuschi Near the east gate of the Parc de Monceau are two small but exceptional museums. The Cernuschi, once the mansion of a wealthy financier, contains a fine collection of Chinese art. ◆ Tu-Su 10AM-5:40PM. 7 Ave Vélasquez (at Blvd Malesherbes). Métro: Villiers. 45.63.50.75

17 Musée Nissim de Camondo Around the corner from the Cernuschi, this museum exhibits the furniture and decorative art (including several Gobelins tapestries) of the **Count de Camondo,** who once owned this house. ◆ W-Su 10AM-noon, 2-5PM. 63 Rue de Monceau (between Blvd Malesherbes and Place de Rio de Janeiro). Métro: Villiers. 45.63.26.32

18 Grande Arche de La Défense The axis that starts with the Carousel Arch in front of the Louvre and runs westward through the Tuileries Gardens to the Obelisk of Luxor, then down the Champs-Elysées to the Arc de Triomphe, has been extended westward with a 300,000-ton white Carrara marble monument in the La Défense district. Designed by **Johan Otto von Spreckelsen,** who won an international competition for the commission, the arch is actually a hollow cube built on 12 pillars set 30 meters into the ground. The building houses the **Ministry of Planning and Development,** private offices as well as several cultural foundations, and the **Foundation for the Rights of Man.** Inaugurated in July 1989 as part of the 200th anniversary of the French Revolution, the building brings monumental dazzle to a sterile high-rise jungle that has become the business district of Paris. ◆ Place de La Défense. Métro: La Défense

19 Musée de la Contrefaçon The one-room **Museum of Forgeries** in the elegant 16th arrondissement might be of particular interest to the tourist who is tempted to take advantage of a fluctuating currency and do some serious shopping. It is not unusual to see the great ladies of Parisian society stopping by the museum to compare a new handbag or a Cartier watch to the near-perfect forgeries on exhibit. The museum is a veritable capitalist's cabinet of curiosities, where the *authentique* products are on display surrounded by their imitations. Ingenious copies of Louis Vuitton luggage wear counterfeit tags guaranteeing they are genuine Vuitton. Japan, Korea, Italy, Morocco, and Taiwan are said to be among the most frequent sources of fakes and forgeries. A short visit to this fascinating museum is enough to cast doubt forever on that little shop near the hotel that has a good buy on Dior key chains, Omega watches, bottles of Benedictine, flacons of Chanel No. 5, and magnums of Cordon Rouge champagne. ♦ M, W 2-4:30PM; F 9AM-noon. 16 Rue de la Faisanderie (between Place du Paraguay and Rue Benouville). Métro: Porte-Dauphine. 45.01.51.11

20 Musée Guimet The finest collection of Asian art in Paris is on view at the **Guimet Museum.** Founded by industrialist **Emile Guimet** in 1879 to house his own collection of Oriental antiquities, the museum was later nationalized as the **Département des Arts Asiatiques des Musées Nationaux.** As such, the Musée Guimet exhibits most of the Louvre's Far East collection and has steadily built up its holdings to include more than 50,000 works from China, Japan, India, Indochina, Afghanistan, and Tibet. Of particular interest are the **Rousset Collection** and the **Michel Calmann Room,** which contain Buddhist sculpture and Chinese porcelain. The museum has expanded to include a library, a research center, and an auditorium. ♦ Admission. M, W-Su 9:45AM-6PM. 6 Place d'Iéna (between Ave d'Iéna and Rue Boissière). Métros: Boissière, Iéna. 47.23.61.65

21 Palais de Chaillot Perched on its hill across the Seine from the Eiffel Tower, the Palais de Chaillot serves as the Right Bank's termination for the monumental axis that sweeps up across the **Champ-de-Mars** from the **Ecole Militaire.** The white sandstone twin pavilions of the palace were built for the Paris Exhibition of 1937, replacing the earlier **Palais du Trocadéro,** a massive barrel-shaped building erected for the 1878 exhibition. Although its stark forms and groups of heroic statuary uncomfortably recall the type of Fascist architecture emerging during the period in Germany and Italy, the Palais de Chaillot succeeds both as a monument and a cultural complex. Within its two curving wings (which cradle a series of descending gardens and pools) are four museums, two theaters, a library, and a restaurant. The **Théâtre National de Chaillot,** located beneath the **Palais Terrace,** was renovated and seats 1,800 people. The smaller **Théâtre Gémier** was added in 1966 as an experimental playhouse. ♦ Admission. Musée de la Marine: M, W-Su 10AM-6PM; 45.53.31.70. Musée de l'Homme: M, W-Su 9:45AM-5PM; 44.05.72.72. Musée des Monuments Français: M, W-Su 10:30AM-5PM; 44.05.39.10. Musée du Cinéma: guided tours reserved in advance; 45.53.74.39. Cinémathèque (Film library): Tu-Su 10AM-5PM; 45.53.21.86. Entrance on Ave Albert-de-Mun (between Aves du Président-Wilson and des Nations-Unies). 47.04.24.24. Métro: Trocadéro

22 Bois de Boulogne Stretching along the western flank of Paris and occupying more than 2,200 acres, this is the ultimate playground and escape for the city's population. It began as a forest (*bois*) in which the Merovingians hunted wild boar and wolves. It was enclosed by **Henri II** in 1556, and in the 17th century **Jean-Baptiste Colbert** transformed the park into a royal hunting domain. After **Napoléon III** gave the forest to the City of Paris, **Baron Haussmann** remodeled the landscape after London's Hyde Park and built many of the lakes, restaurants, racetracks, and paths. Haussmann designed the park so it would be entered from his own **Avenue Foch,** which leads grandly down to the **Porte Dauphine.** Once in the park, you can choose from an infinite variety of attractions. The most notable include the **Bagatelle,** a magical park with an 18th-century villa built by the then-future **King Charles X;** the **Jardin d'Acclimatation,** an amusement park and miniature zoo; the **Auteuil** and **Longchamp** racecourses; and the **Pré Catelan,** another flower and tree garden that shelters the luxurious café/restaurant (★★$$) of the same name. There are numerous facilities for sport, including the nearby **Roland Garros Stadium,** where the French Open tennis tournament is held. ♦ Métros: Porte-d'Auteuil, Porte-Dauphine, Porte-Maillot. Pré Catelan restaurant: Lunch and dinner. Closed Sunday dinner and Monday. Route de Suresnes. Métro: Porte-Dauphine. 45.24.55.58

23 Musée Marmottan The 16th arrondissement in Paris, which stretches from the Arc de Triomphe down between the Bois de Boulogne and the Seine, is a haven for the Proustian bourgeoisie. Out-of-town shoppers know this quarter as a place to buy old table linens, fine chocolates, and designer silk dresses, and as the location of **Omar Sharif's** private gambling club. The best-kept secret of the select 16th, however, is the 19th-century Passy town house that contains the **Marmottan Museum.** More than a hundred original paintings, pastels, and drawings by **Claude Monet** are displayed here. While tour-bus loads of noisy London schoolchildren and itinerant backpackers elbow past each other in the Musée d'Orsay to glimpse Monet's *Wild Poppies,* the Marmottan, a treasure trove of the artist's work from Giverny, is relatively deserted.

A word of advice: in touring the Marmottan, take a good look at the 300 illuminated medieval manuscripts on the ground floor, skip the two floors devoted to the cold First-Empire furniture and Flemish tapestries, and head for the basement. Here you may see the essential spirit of Monet's Giverny work: the joyous splash and swirl of poppies, tulips, irises, and apple blossoms. The exhibition culminates in a circular gallery with the artist's notebooks and palette in the center and 16 of his water-lily canvases on the walls. Stand in the middle of the room and pivot around to behold the sun's daily round as it illuminated Monet's magical pond. (In summer you can visit the actual pond and gardens at Monet's Normandy home in Giverny. For more information, see "Day Trips" on page 205.) ♦ Admission. Tu-Su 10AM-5:30PM. 2 Rue Louis-Boilly (between Blvd Suchet and Ave Raphaël). Métro: La Muette. 42.24.07.02

23 Ranelagh Gardens Directly across Avenue Raphaël from the Marmottan are the sumptuous English-style Ranelagh Gardens, home to one of the last hand-cranked merry-go-rounds in Europe. It is powered by a middle-aged woman with forearms rivaling those of Arnold Schwarzenegger. Children in ruffled pink dresses or seersucker suits and buckled shoes use one hand to hold on for dear life to the carved wooden ponies and the other to jab red sticks in the air, trying to hook the brass rings dispensed on the merry-go-round's periphery. ♦ Ave Raphaël (at Rue Louis-Boilly). Métro: La Muette

24 Castel Béranger French architect **Hector Guimard** established his reputation in 1898 as the country's premier art nouveau designer with this seven-story apartment building, which sits along a quiet residential street in the 16th arrondissement. Guimard's quasi-organic expressionism is seen here in full glory, particularly in the curvilinear details of his ironwork, faience, and carved-wood elements, which prefigure the architect's more purely sculptural métro entrances of 1900. An inspired blend of rational planning and whimsical effusion, the private building contains 36 apartments, none alike. ♦ 14-16 Rue La Fontaine (at Hameau Béranger). Métro: Jasmin. No phone

25 Foundation Le Corbusier Charles-Edouard Jeannerct, better known as **Le Corbusier** (1887-1965), was the Swiss architect who helped revolutionize today's urban environment with his passion for cubist forms. Within Paris and its suburbs stand 15 of his modular buildings, including the apartment house where he lived in 1933; a **Salvation Army** headquarters built in 1933 of glass, brick, and exposed concrete; and the famous **Swiss Dormitory** and **Brazilian Pavilion** (constructed in 1932 and 1959, respectively) at Cité Universitaire. The headquarters and research library of the **Le Corbusier Foundation** are housed in **Villa Jeanneret;** the adjoining **Villa La Roche,** also designed by the architect in 1923, contains a sparse collection of Le Corbusier's own painting, sculpture, and furniture design and is open to the public. ♦ Le Corbusier Foundation, Villa La Roche, and Villa Jeanneret: M-Th 10AM-12:30PM, 1-6PM; F 10AM-12:30PM, 1-5PM. 8-10 Square du Docteur-Blanche (off Rue du Docteur-Blanche, between Rues Henri-Heine and Raffet). Métro: Jasmin. 42.88.41.53

26 Parc André Citroën When the offices of automobile manufacturer **André Citroën** moved outside the city in the 1980s, an expanse of land the size of 50 football fields was left free in the quiet 15th arrondissement. The city transformed half this area into public grounds, now the only park in Paris where it isn't forbidden to sit on the grass. Water appears in many places: shallow pools border the park and waterfalls tumble from small stone structures. The park's north side has six small gardens, each with a different theme and dominant color. The red garden, for example, contains cherry and apple trees. ♦ M-F 7:30AM-10PM; Sa-Su 9AM-10PM. Entrance at 25 Rue Leblanc (park bounded by Rue Leblanc and Quai André Citroën). Métro: Boulevard Victor

27 Jardins Albert Kahn At the turn of the century, **Albert Kahn,** an idealist as well as a banker, envisioned a society in which there would be a crossbreeding of cultures; these enchanting gardens are the transposition in plant form of his humanitarian ideals. Kahn was determined that the more than 360 species in his horticultural collection would acclimatize from their native lands and cohabit, serving as a symbol of what he hoped was possible on earth. The result is a skillfully ordered mosaic of green: there is the friendly disorder of an English garden, French flower beds, a rose garden, and a meticulous Japanese garden with streams, footbridges, water lilies, and a wooden teahouse where genuine Japanese tea ceremonies are conducted. This Eden has been a sanctuary of meditation for such notables as **Colette, Albert Einstein, Ferdinand Foch, Edouard Herriot,** and **Arthur Honegger.** When your stomach's needs transcend those of your mind, go to the **Palmarium** (★★$), a glass-and-iron rotunda where sandwiches and pastries are served.

In addition to his enthusiasm for cultural integration, Kahn had an interest in photography that was furthered by his friendship with cinematography inventor **Louis Lumière.** Between 1910 and 1920, Kahn sent documentary photographers all over the world to compose his Archives de la Planète. Over 72,000 photographs and over half a million feet of film are housed in the **Musée Albert Kahn,** on the grounds of his gardens. ♦ Admission. Park, Palmarium, and Museum: Tu-Su 11AM-6PM winter; Tu-Su 11AM-7PM summer. Japanese tea ceremony: two Tuesdays a month Sept and May-June; reserve in advance through museum. 14 Rue du Port (at Rue des Abondances), Boulogne-Billancourt. Métro: Boulogne-Pont de St.-Cloud. Museum: 46.04.52.80. Palmarium 46.05.25.10

Index

Restaurants

Only restaurants with star ratings are listed below. All restaurants are listed alphabetically in the main (preceding) index. Always call in advance to ensure a restaurant has not closed, changed its hours, or booked its tables for a private party. The restaurant price ratings are based on the average cost of an entrée for one person, excluding tax and tip.

★★★★ An Extraordinary Experience
★★★ Excellent
★★ Very Good
★ Good
$$$$ Big Bucks ($40 and up)
$$$ Expensive ($25-$40)
$$ Reasonable ($10-$25)
$ The Price Is Right (less than $10)

Hotels

The hotels listed below and at right are grouped according to their price ratings; they are also listed in the main index. The hotel price ratings reflect the base price of a standard room for two people for one night during the peak season.

$$$$ Big Bucks ($225 and up)
$$$ Expensive ($150-$225)
$$ Reasonable ($75-$150)
$ The Price Is Right
    (less than $75)

Features

Bests

Maps

Credits

Writer/Researcher	Researchers	Research and Writing
Lisa Victor	**Ling Li**	*(Previous Editions)*
	Joanne Shin	**Stewart McBride**
	Hélène Prevost	

ACCESS®PRESS

Managing Editor
Linda Weber

Project Editor
Charlotte Knabel

Staff Editors
Karin Mullen
Lisa Zuniga

Assistant Editor
Erika Lenkert

Editorial Assistant
Karen Decker

Contributing Editor
Antonia Moore

Editorial Consultant
Rebecca Forée

Proofreaders
Susan Charles
Elizabeth Ferguson
Denise Lawson
Bennett N. Miller

Word Processor
Jerry Stanton

Design/Production Manager
Cherylonda Fitzgerald

Designer
Claudia Goulette

Maps
Michael Blum
Teresa Cunniff
Kitti Homme
Patricia Keelin
Jesse Kline
Teresa Romero

Special Thanks
Jim Andrews
Barbara Bahning Chin
Carré Furukawa

Cover Photograph ©
Doug Armand/
Tony Stone Images

Printing and Otabind
Webcom Limited

The maps introducing each **PARIS-ACCESS**® itinerary are excerpts of a remarkable map called the *Plan du Paris à Vol D'Oiseau (A Bird's-Eye View of Paris),* created by Georges Peltier. Inspired by the famous *Turgot Map of Paris* (completed in 1739), Peltier, an artist and cartographer, began his axonometric rendering of Paris in 1920. He spent 20 years and 30,000 hours creating the map. Since he completed it in 1940, numerous revisions have been made to keep the map up to date. Permission to use excerpts of the *Plan du Paris* was granted by the publishers, **Blondel La Rougery.** A copy of the Paris map may be purchased by writing to: Blondel La Rougery, 268 Rue de Brémont, 93112, Rosny-Sous-Bois, France; or call 48.94.94.52.

Place du Palais-Royal

Printed in Canada

ACCESS® Guides

Order by phone, toll-free: 1-800-331-3761

Name _____ Phone _____

Address _____

City _____ State _____ Zip _____

Please send me the following **ACCESS**® Guides:

☐ **BARCELONA**ACCESS® $17.00
0-06-277000-4

☐ **BOSTON**ACCESS® $18.00
0-06-277049-7

☐ **CARIBBEAN**ACCESS® $17.00
0-06-277042-X

☐ **CHICAGO**ACCESS® $18.00
0-06-277048-9

☐ **FLORENCE/VENICE/
MILAN**ACCESS® $17.00
0-06-277001-2

☐ **HAWAII**ACCESS® $18.00
0-06-277068-3

☐ **LAS VEGAS**ACCESS®
$18.00 (available 12/93)
0-06-277055-1

☐ **LONDON**ACCESS® $18.00
0-06-277051-9

☐ **LOS ANGELES**ACCESS®
$18.00
0-06-277047-0

☐ **MEXICO**ACCESS® $17.00
0-06-277041-1

☐ **MIAMI & SOUTH
FLORIDA**ACCESS® $18.00
0-06-277070-5

☐ **NEW YORK CITY**ACCESS®
$18.00
0-06-277052-7

☐ **ORLANDO & CENTRAL
FLORIDA**ACCESS® $18.00
0-06-277069-1

☐ **PARIS**ACCESS® $18.00
0-06-277038-1

☐ **ROME**ACCESS® $18.00
0-06-277053-5

☐ **SAN DIEGO**ACCESS® $18.00
0-06-277004-7

☐ **SAN FRANCISCO**ACCESS®
$18.00
0-06-277046-2

☐ **SANTA FE/TAOS/
ALBUQUERQUE**ACCESS®
$18.00
0-06-277054-3

☐ **SEATTLE**ACCESS® $18.00
0-06-277050-0

☐ **SKI COUNTRY**ACCESS®
Western United States
$18.00
0-06-277066-7

☐ **SOCCER**ACCESS® $12.00
0-06-277107-8

☐ **THE WALL STREET
JOURNAL** Guide to
Understanding Money
& Markets $13.95
0-06-772516-3

☐ **WASHINGTON
DC**ACCESS® $18.00
0-06-277039-X

☐ **WINE COUNTRY**ACCESS®
Northern California $18.00
0-06-277006-3

Prices subject to change without notice.

Total for **ACCESS**® Guides:	$
Please add applicable sales tax:	
Add $4.00 for first book S&H, $1.00 per additional book:	
Total payment:	$

☐ Check or Money Order enclosed. Offer valid in the United States only.
Please make payable to HarperCollins*Publishers*.

☐ Charge my credit card ☐ American Express ☐ Visa ☐ MasterCard

Card no. _____ Exp. date _____

Signature _____

Send orders to:
HarperCollins*Publishers*
P.O. Box 588
Dunmore, PA 18512-0588

Send correspondence to:
ACCESS®PRESS
10 East 53rd Street, 7th Floor
New York, NY 10022